Snapshots of Great Leadership

Snapshots of Great Leadership offers a thorough look into leaders who have either accomplished amazing feats or brought destruction. Now in its third edition, this key volume explores what it means to be a great leader, and clearly explains the lives, triumphs, and challenges of a range of diverse leaders across history and into the modern day.

Packed into easily digestible chapters, the authors demonstrate how, although the goals of these individuals were often quite different, the leadership processes they used were frequently similar. The opening chapter explains the latest theories of leadership and this new edition features one new leadership theory, Authentic Leadership, as well as recent research findings on the most popular theories. The authors have replaced nine leaders from earlier editions with new leaders including Elon Musk, Maria Montessori, and Virginia Hall. These new leaders exemplify unique leadership attributes and outstanding leadership effectiveness. Each leader snapshot adds an important "reality check" to the theories and models described in most introductory leadership textbooks, making this a key text for students taking leadership courses.

Scholars and students of leadership and management will benefit from this accessible and comprehensive volume, as will leadership practitioners looking to reflect on and develop their own leadership skills. Offering valuable insights into the lives of historical and corporate leaders, the book is a compelling read for casual readers as well.

Jon P. Howell was Professor Emeritus of Management in the College of Business at New Mexico State University (NMSU), USA.

Isaac Wanasika is Chair and Professor of Management at the University of Northern Colorado (UNCO), USA.

Maria J. Mendez is Associate Professor of Management at California State University, Chico (CSUC), USA.

Leadership: Research and Practice Series

In Memoriam Georgia Sorenson (1947 – 2020), Founding Editor

Series Editor

Ronald E. Riggio, Henry R. Kravis Professor of Leadership and Organizational Psychology and former Director of the Kravis Leadership Institute at Claremont McKenna College.

Donald Trump in Historical Perspective
Dead Precedents
Edited by Michael Harvey

Intentional Leadership
Becoming a Trustworthy Leader
Karen E. Mishra and Aneil K. Mishra

Leadership and Virtues
Understanding and Practicing Good Leadership
Edited by Toby P. Newstead and Ronald E. Riggio

Leadership Mindsets for Adaptive Change
The Flux 5
Sharon Ravitch and Liza Herzog

Leadership on a Blockchain
What Asia Can Teach Us About Networked Leadership
Frederique Covington Corbett

Navigating Leadership
Evidence-Based Strategies for Leadership Development
Susanne Braun, Tiffany Keller Hansbrough, Gregory A. Ruark, Rosalie J. Hall, Robert G. Lord, and Olga Epitropaki

Snapshots of Great Leadership, Third Edition
Jon P. Howell, Isaac Wanasika and Maria J. Mendez

For more information about this series, please visit: www.routledge.com/Leadership-Research-and-Practice/book-series/leadership

Snapshots of Great Leadership

Third edition

Jon P. Howell, Isaac Wanasika and Maria
J. Mendez

NEW YORK AND LONDON

Cover Image: © zhengshun tang/Getty Images

Third edition published 2025
by Routledge
605 Third Avenue, New York, NY 10158

and by Routledge
4 Park Square, Milton Park, Abingdon, Oxon OX14 4RN

Routledge is an imprint of the Taylor & Francis Group, an informa business

© 2025 Jon P. Howell, Isaac Wanasika and Maria J. Mendez

The right of Jon P. Howell, Isaac Wanasika and Maria J. Mendez to be identified as authors of this work has been asserted in accordance with sections 77 and 78 of the Copyright, Designs and Patents Act 1988.

First edition published by Routledge 2012

Second edition published by Routledge 2018

ISBN: 978-1-032-36820-7 (hbk)
ISBN: 978-1-032-36700-2 (pbk)
ISBN: 978-1-003-33393-7 (ebk)

DOI: 10.4324/9781003333937

Typeset in Sabon
by Taylor & Francis Books

To Jon, dear husband and true friend.

We are never ready to say goodbye to those who have held a monumental place in our lives and hearts. We can only cherish the time we had together and recognize that we are better people for having known you.

Julie Howell

Contents

Series Foreword

I am so pleased to introduce this third edition of the very successful *Snapshots of Great Leadership*, for so many reasons. First, it provides profiles of a very wide variety of leaders, and looks at their leadership through the lens of scholarship—providing an integration of leadership theory and research into the real-life stories of noted leaders. Second, the range of leaders profiled is vast. There are well-known leaders of nations and social movements, but also leaders of businesses, nonprofits, and religious organizations. Third, the book isn't just a recitation of leader successes, but it deals with the very complex issue of what distinguishes "good" and "bad" leaders and leadership. Moreover, the book concludes with profiles of some current leaders, and challenges the reader to decide whether these leaders and their work is positive and productive, or negative and destructive. Finally, this book is a tribute to an outstanding leadership scholar, Jon P. Howell, whose work in leadership—teaching and scholarship—impacted so many, including me. Professor Howell was always on the cutting edge of our ongoing inquiry of leadership, and his many contributions, including *Snapshots of Great Leadership*, will continue to inspire us for generations to come.

Ronald E. Riggio, Ph.D.
Kravis Leadership Institute
Claremont McKenna College

Preface

Our first author, Jon P. Howell, passed on during the writing of this book. We met Jon during our doctoral programs, and he chaired both of our dissertation committees. Jon was a highly respected and exceptional scholar, deeply committed to his students, and remarkably personable and kind-hearted. He was more than a mentor; he was a friend who was always curious about our perspectives and enjoyed rich conversation. Over the years, he remained close, collaborating with us on several academic projects, and reaching out regularly to check on us and our families, share pictures of his beautiful grandchildren, and ask about our views regarding world events. This book gave us a final and beautiful opportunity to spend time with Jon, enjoying fun conversations and working together before his tragic accident and passing. We miss our friend dearly and dedicate this work to his memory.

In this edition of *Snapshots of Great Leadership*, we have continued our tradition of stories (Snapshots) about actual leaders. Each Snapshot includes descriptions of the leaders' background, major life experiences, and environmental context that help explain their behavior and accomplishments. Each one also contains a paragraph briefly describing how the leaders' characteristics and behavior are described in specific leadership theories.

We believe most leadership scholars view leaders' biographies as excellent learning techniques. Based on our combined experience in teaching university leadership courses for over 40 years, we believe that future leaders will benefit from *both* knowledge of leadership theory and research as well as descriptions of how real leaders enact these theories. This helps students operationalize their learning and helps them remember important leadership issues and behaviors that are effective. Our belief is supported by classroom observations that stories of real leaders are recalled most often in classroom discussions and student responses on essay exams.

We have maintained the structure of earlier editions with brief summaries of popular leadership theories in the first chapter, followed by the leadership Snapshots beginning in Chapter 2. Chapter 1 has been updated to include one new leadership theory, Authentic Leadership, as well as recent research findings on the most popular theories. We also replaced nine leaders from earlier editions. This decision was based on our belief that the learning to be obtained from these leaders was available in other leader Snapshots, and we were restricted to a specific page count for the book to prevent it from becoming too long. We consider seven of the new leaders to be great in the sense that they produced results that are truly outstanding. One example is Dr. Maria Montessori, who was an independent, assertive, and charismatic woman whose scientific innovations revolutionized early childhood education and can be found in most preschools today.

We also added one bad leader to this edition for unethical, fraudulent, greedy behavior that severely damaged people and their organizations. One such leader was Elizabeth Holmes, who started and led an organization claiming to make medical testing easier and more efficient based on fraudulent behavior and lies.

One important point regarding the bad leaders was missed by some readers of earlier editions—not all bad leaders are the same. Two of the bad leaders described in this book are generally viewed as immoral or evil—Adolf Hitler and Idi Amin. They inflicted horrible torture and murder on thousands of people. Other bad leaders described here (such as Sep Blatter and Bernie Ebbers) inflicted serious harm on the financial security, reputation, and careers of many people, but these leaders may have simply been greedy or incompetent by not recognizing the numerous valid stakeholders in their organization. One bad leader (David Koresh) may fall somewhere in between evil and incompetent leaders.

For this third edition, we have continued and expanded the section titled *You Decide*. This section now includes Snapshots of five leaders whose accomplishments transformed their country or industry but also generated serious ethical concerns. A new Snapshot has been written especially for this section about Elon Musk, who generates in equal measure cult-like admiration for his drive to resolve the world's complex problems and condemnation for his business decisions and social and political opinions. Two additional Snapshots have been moved to this category, Jeff Bezos and Mark Zuckerberg, as both have faced ethical and legal challenges to their business practices since the last edition of our book in 2018. Because they are still important leaders of today, their story is not yet complete and the evaluation of these leaders will likely change over time. The leaders in this section demonstrate that all leaders are human and possess weaknesses and faults that we wish were not present. In this section, students are asked to evaluate each leader and decide for themselves whether the leader is great or bad. The first edition of this book was initially conceived as a supplement to any major leadership textbook. The Snapshots were designed for classroom discussion and student analysis to demonstrate how the leadership theories are applied. This would likely be done with the instructor's guidance and clarification of the leader's behavior and the theory that describes it. Over time, it is expected that students will develop their own insight into the theories and how they can be applied. We found, however, that numerous instructors began using earlier editions as stand-alone textbooks for their leadership course, apparently supplementing it with their own experience and materials.

For leadership students, using another textbook along with this book, the theory descriptions will hopefully provide brief synopses to refresh them regarding key points of each theory. Some readers may have little or no interest in leadership theories and may decide to skip Chapter 1, preferring real-life examples as their learning source. We hope these readers realize, however, that well over 100 years of scholarly leadership research has led to the development of these theories. Much of this research has been developed by excellent scholars, and their insights are reflected in these theories. We believe there is much useful knowledge to be gained from both leadership theory and stories of leaders.

Jon P. Howell
New Mexico State University
Isaac Wanasika
University of Northern Colorado
Maria J. Mendez
California State University, Chico

About the Authors

Jon P. Howell was Professor Emeritus of Management in the College of Business at New Mexico State University (NMSU). He received his MBA from the University of Chicago and his Ph.D. from the University of California at Irvine. He taught and conducted research on leadership for 31 years and was previously the Bank of America Distinguished Professor of Management. He received awards for excellence in teaching and research at NMSU. Professor Howell published a leadership textbook titled *Understanding Behaviors for Effective Leadership* (2nd edition, 2006, Pearson Prentice Hall) and the 1st edition of *Snapshots of Great Leadership* (2013, Taylor & Francis). He also published numerous book chapters and articles in the *Academy of Management Journal, Academy of Management Review, Leadership Quarterly, Organizational Dynamics, Journal of Management, Journal of International Business Studies, Journal of World Business*, and other journals. He received awards for his research from the Society of Industrial and Organizational Psychology, Academy of Management, the Center for Creative Leadership, and the Global Leadership Advancement Center. He served on the editorial board for *Leadership Quarterly* and *Journal of World Business*. He was a country co-investigator on the Global Leadership and Organizational Behavior Effectiveness (GLOBE) Project which was led by the late Robert House of the Wharton School, University of Pennsylvania. His primary research interests were leadership and followership, substitutes for leadership, and leadership across cultures.

Isaac Wanasika is Chair and Professor of Management at the University of Northern Colorado (UNCO). He holds a Ph.D. in Strategic Management from New Mexico State University (NMSU) and serves as a consultant, and various corporate boards. His research, focused on leadership, corporate innovation and efficiency, new institutional theory, and base-of-the-pyramid strategies, has been published in prestigious journals such as the *Journal of World Business* and the *Journal of Managerial Issues*, as well as in numerous book chapters. He is co-author of the second edition of *Snapshots of Great Leadership* (2019, Taylor & Francis). He is a frequent presenter at national and international conferences, including the Academy of Management (AOM), where he also serves as Representative-at-Large for the Management Consultancy Division. Dr. Wanasika's commitment to excellence in both teaching and research has been recognized with awards at both NMSU and UNCO.

Maria J. Mendez is Associate Professor of Management at California State University, Chico (CSUC). She received a Ph.D. in Business Administration with a concentration on leadership from New Mexico State University. Her research centers on shared leadership, although she has also published in the areas of followership, global leadership, and management education. Her work has been published in *Business Ethics Quarterly, Leadership and Organization Development Journal, Journal of World Business*, and the book *The Art of Followership*.

Part I

Theoretical Basis of Leadership

1 Theories of Leadership

Like the earlier editions, this is primarily a book of stories. Most of the stories describe great leaders who accomplished amazing feats such as creating, preserving, or changing a nation or industry, or saving a group of people from exploitation or annihilation. Some of the stories demonstrate both good and bad leadership. A few of the stories describe bad leaders who brought destruction or death to scores of people. In retrospect, the disastrous effects of these bad leaders are no less astounding than the incredible accomplishments of the great leaders. Although the goals of these individuals were often quite different, the leadership processes they used were frequently similar. Stories of these leaders describe who they were, what they accomplished, and how they did it. We have referred to existing leadership theories to help explain their leadership tactics and behavior as well as their effects on others. The use of these leadership theories will hopefully make the leaders' effects more understandable and will clarify how the theories relate to leadership in action.

Scholars have developed theories of leadership to help understand and explain how leaders influence the organizations and people they lead. Organizations are simply groups of people working together in a cooperative and coordinated effort to achieve some goals. Based on research, leadership theories generally focus on specific leader characteristics and/or behavior patterns that are important in shaping societies and organizations over time.

Different scholars have focused on separate leader characteristics and behaviors, resulting in numerous distinct leadership theories being proposed and researched. The most popular theories are described in well-accepted leadership textbooks, and these theories are briefly summarized in this chapter. For students of leadership, this chapter may repeat information they previously studied. For readers without this background, this chapter provides a framework to help them understand how the great and bad leaders described in this book shaped and changed the societies and organizations they led.

A definition of leadership seems appropriate at this point to give readers an idea of what is described in this book. Leadership is an influence process, usually (but not always) carried out by one person. The leader influences a

DOI: 10.4324/9781003333937-2

group, who view the influence as legitimate, toward the achievement of some goal or goals. The leader may utilize many different strategies to influence followers' efforts toward goal achievement. She might describe a desirable vision of the future that includes a mission with inspirational goals to be achieved, she might offer rewards to followers when they achieve the goals, or she might encourage followers to participate with her in setting desirable goals and strategies as a means of gaining followers' ownership of the goals and their commitment to achieve them. These are all examples of leaders influencing followers to achieve goals, which is the essence of leadership. *Snapshots of Great Leadership* describes how different leaders used these and other strategies to lead their followers in achieving outstanding results.

Trait Theories

Through much of the 20th century, most people believed that great leaders were born, not made. We now know that leadership is complex and not simply the result of one or more personal characteristics of an individual. Over 100 years of research on personal characteristics of leaders (often called *leadership traits*) failed to demonstrate that any single trait or set of traits make a person a great leader. Leadership traits are characteristics of an individual that do not change from situation to situation, such as intelligence, assertiveness, or physical attractiveness. Literally hundreds of studies were carried out on scores of different traits and many traits were identified that *may help* an individual become an effective leader in *specific situations*. However, the key traits for one situation may be different for another situation. The following set of categories summarizes the mass of trait research and encompasses the most important leadership traits found in research: *determination and drive, cognitive capacity, self-confidence, integrity*, and *sociability*.

Determination and drive encompass traits such as initiative, energy, assertiveness, perseverance, masculinity, and occasionally dominance. Individuals with these traits work long hours, pursue goals with a high degree of energy and perseverance, are often ambitious and competitive, and may dominate others. *Cognitive capacity* includes intelligence, analytical and verbal ability, behavioral flexibility, and good judgment. Individuals with strong cognitive capacity are able to integrate large amounts of information, formulate strategic plans, create solutions to complex problems, and adapt to changing situations. Great leaders such as Steve Jobs and Abraham Lincoln clearly exhibited the determination and drive as well as the cognitive capacity to persevere and deal effectively with their complex changing environments.

Self-confidence includes the traits of high self-esteem, assertiveness, emotional stability, and self-assurance. Self-confident individuals believe in their own capabilities and judgments, they do not hesitate to act on their beliefs, and they project their self-confidence onto others to build trust, respect, and commitment among followers. *Integrity* describes individuals who are truthful, trustworthy, principled, consistent, dependable, loyal, and not deceptive. Leaders with integrity are honest and open, they keep their word, adhere to generally accepted principles of behavior, and share common values with followers. Winston Churchill and Nelson Mandela demonstrated self-confidence, integrity, and determination to persist with assertive and principled behavior in achieving their goals.

Sociability describes individuals who are friendly, extroverted, tactful, flexible, and interpersonally competent. Sociable leaders like to interact with followers and others, they adapt their behavior effectively in social situations, and they are diplomatic when solving problems and relating to other people. Leymah Gbowee was highly sociable, determined, and showed amazing integrity in her diplomatic dealings with influential individuals outside her organization.

Despite problems with the early trait research, these categories of leadership traits appear to be helpful for effectiveness in many situations. Few great leaders possessed all the important leader traits, but these leaders all demonstrated characteristics that were essential to succeed in their situation. Leadership traits themselves do not cause an individual to emerge as a leader or to become a great leader. The key traits for a specific leadership position make it more likely that a leader will take effective action by demonstrating needed leadership behaviors in the situation. A leader who is sociable and controls her emotions will likely be effective at providing needed encouragement and interpersonal support for followers during stressful, threatening episodes that sometimes occur in organizations. Leaders who are intelligent, original, and assertive are more likely to create and instill an inspiring vision and mission for the organization. Leaders who are self-confident, assertive, and energetic will be comfortable in providing directive leadership for followers in solving difficult job or organizational problems. Specific leadership traits can clearly be important preconditions for effective leadership behavior, especially when they are aligned with other variables such as relevant skill for a position or social identity of followers. When a leader possesses the traits needed for a specific position and reflects those traits in her behavior, she is more likely to obtain the trust, respect, and cooperation needed from others for effective group or organizational performance. Recent studies have started to examine the "dark side" of personality that might lead to destructive/toxic leadership.

Early Behavioral and Contingency Theories

In the 1950s, several university-based research programs began to focus on identifying the most effective behavior patterns of leaders. At first, these programs sought to identify one or two behavior patterns that characterized all effective leaders. This was later described as the "one best way" approach to leadership effectiveness. After numerous investigations, they identified two behavior patterns that seemed especially important. The different researchers used several labels for these two behaviors. One behavior pattern was called *consideration, relationship orientation, concern for people,* or *supportive leader behavior* and included showing a concerned and caring attitude toward followers, being friendly, encouraging followers' feelings of personal worth, and supporting efforts to develop their capabilities. The second leader behavior pattern was called *initiating structure, task orientation, concern for production,* or *directive leader behavior* and emphasized a focus on task accomplishment by clarifying followers' roles and the leader's expectations of followers. This often included goal setting or setting performance standards, assigning tasks, scheduling, and explaining rules and procedures. These two leadership behavior patterns became the basis of several leadership theories developed over the next 25 years.

The Leadership Grid

One such theory that became popular with consultants was the Managerial Grid, later renamed the Leadership Grid, which was developed by Robert Blake and Jane Mouton. This model includes the two leader behavior patterns described above in a two-dimensional coordinate system that provides a grid-like representation of different levels of *concern for people* and *concern for production.* Concern for production is represented on the horizontal axis and concern for people is on the vertical axis. Five distinct leadership styles were described by Grid developers, depending on the amount of each leader behavior a leader demonstrates in her/his behavior.

Consultants who emphasize the Grid use questionnaires to obtain scores for each leader on the two behavior patterns, allowing leaders to plot their own position on the Grid. Working with the consultants, leaders presumably determine how they can adapt their style to improve their leadership effectiveness. Grid developers maintain that *Team Leadership,* which describes leaders who are high on both concern for people and concern for production, is the most effective style. Despite its popularity with consultants, research shows no single leadership style is best for all situations. Grid developers recently acknowledged this and describe some leaders as shifting styles over time, but maintain that most leaders have a single dominant style. The Grid developers do not describe different situations as requiring different leadership styles.

The Contingency Theory of Leadership

Another leadership theory that was developed about the same time emphasized the same two leader behavior patterns. The Contingency Theory of Leadership, developed by Fred Fiedler, labeled these two behaviors *task-oriented* and *relationship-oriented* leadership and included a unique questionnaire for measuring these behavior patterns. It was more complex and realistic than the Grid theory. The theory specified that the most effective combination of the two leader behavior patterns must fit the situation to be most effective. No single level of task and/or relationship-oriented leadership was effective for all situations.

Fiedler described three important situational characteristics that determined which combination of the two behavior patterns was optimal. These situational characteristics were the *leader's power* to control rewards and punishments for followers, the *quality of the relationship* between the leader and her followers (that is, are followers friendly and cooperative with the leader), and the clarity of *task structure* for followers (that is, are the task goals, procedures, and measures of their performance clearly specified). Fiedler rated situations as high or low on each of these three factors. The three were then combined to classify a situation as favorable or unfavorable for the leader. If the situation reflected high leader power, good leader-member relations, and high task structure, then the situation was considered highly favorable to the leader. A moderately favorable situation might include a poor leader-member relationship, high position power, and high task structure or some other combination of high and low scores on the situational factors. A very unfavorable situation had a poor leader-member relationship, low leader power, and low task structure.

The Contingency Theory predicted that a leader's style was either task oriented or relationship oriented. A leader could not be both task and relationship oriented, although Fiedler later added a *socio-independent* leadership style that was apparently medium on both leader behaviors. Task-oriented leaders were predicted to be most effective in highly favorable or highly unfavorable situations. Relationship-oriented leaders were most effective in moderately favorable situations. Socio-independent leaders were predicted to be effective in very favorable situations.

Fiedler and his associates believe that leaders have a predominant style and attempts to change this style are unrealistic. They suggest that if a leader is ineffective, his style does not match the situation and he should be moved to another situation that is more appropriate. If this is not possible, the leader's situation could be modified to fit the leader's style. A training program was developed to teach leaders how to assess their own style and the situation, and to modify the situation to improve their effectiveness. The Contingency Theory has been researched extensively with conflicting results, but it has many advocates among practicing leaders.

The Situational Leadership Theory

The Situational Leadership Theory, developed by Paul Hersey and Ken Blanchard, also emphasized the same two leadership patterns which they later renamed *directive* and *supportive* leadership. Their model is presented in a two-dimensional coordinate system similar to the Leadership Grid. However, the Situational Leadership Theory asserts that the most effective leadership style must match the situation. In this sense, it is similar to the Contingency Theory, but Hersey and Blanchard describe a very different situational factor as important for the leader to consider. They point to the *followers' maturity and readiness to perform* as the key factor the leader must evaluate as he adjusts his leadership style.

Followers with a low level of maturity and readiness are described as unable and unwilling to work on their own, requiring a *telling* leadership style that is highly directive with little supportiveness. Followers who are high in maturity and readiness are both willing and able to work on their own and require a *delegating* leadership style, with little direction or support by the leader. Followers who are in between low and high on maturity and readiness, require different combinations of directive and supportive leadership. Although the Situational Leadership Theory has been popular with consultants, perhaps because it is easy to understand, it has not received strong empirical support from researchers.

Directive and supportive leadership are basic behaviors for leadership and most great leaders reflect one or both of these behaviors in some form. When the United Farm Workers Union members were threatened and exploited by growers, the great labor leader, César Chávez, became highly directive with union members to organize a quick response. He also developed a credit union for union members, participated in picket lines and marches, and provided strike funding and other activities that reflected his supportive leadership. Steve Jobs was extremely directive with his employees as he demanded they produce ever smaller computers with additional features within unreasonable time constraints.

Fiedler's Contingency Theory and the Situational Leadership Theory are both considered contingency theories because they assert that the most effective style must fit (is contingent on) the situation. Fiedler's model is unique in assuming leaders cannot adapt their style to the situation. Although the three models described above all focus on leaders' behavior, today they are generally considered overly simplistic because they fail to consider other important leadership behaviors needed for effective group and organizational performance.

Advanced Behavioral/Contingency Theories

The Path-Goal Theory

The Path-Goal Theory was first developed by Bob House and his colleagues in the early 1970s as a contingency approach that included a more inclusive set of important leadership behaviors than earlier approaches. In addition to the traditional *directive* and *supportive* leadership behaviors, it included *participative* and *achievement-oriented* leadership.

Participative leader behavior involves encouraging followers' input for decision making with the leader concerning operations of the group, and consulting with followers by asking their opinions, and building consensus. Achievement-oriented leader behavior involves encouraging followers to strive for excellence by setting high performance goals, continually seeking improvement, and showing confidence in followers. This behavior pattern formed a basis for later charismatic theories. Numerous situational factors were proposed in this theory to modify the effectiveness of specific leader behaviors. When followers' work tasks are not clear and the methods for successful performance are uncertain, then directive leadership is said to be especially effective. When organizational members are faced with deadlines, their organizations are threatened with intense competition or their tasks are dangerous then they generally appreciate and respond well to a supportive leader who sympathizes with their situation and shows a friendly caring attitude. When organizational members are highly competent and their work tasks require creativity and cooperation, then a participative approach by the leader encourages input from all members to develop the best solution to their demanding tasks. And when constant improvement and excellence in performance is critical to success, achievement-oriented leadership behavior may be needed.

Path-Goal Theory is based on two major assumptions that may limit its effectiveness in some situations. It assumes that people are motivated to perform well because they expect some type of favorable reward. The outcome may be money, a promotion, an award, or a positive feeling of accomplishment, but the favorable outcome is personal to the follower who experiences it. This theory also assumes that people are rational in their deliberations regarding how much effort they expend on a specific task. They will only perform well if the effort seems reasonable for the expected outcome. These assumptions of rationality and exclusive self-interest are limitations because people are sometimes motivated by emotional appeals, symbolic behaviors (such as self-sacrifice by the leader), or improving their own self-image.

In the 1990s, Bob House developed a Reformulated Path-Goal Theory that added several other leader behavior patterns to the model. The new leader behaviors included *work facilitation* (providing resources, developmental experiences, and mentoring), *interaction facilitation* (resolving conflicts, encouraging collaboration and teamwork, and facilitating communication), *representation* (advocating for the group, obtaining resources, and defending the group from criticism), *charismatic leader behavior* (inspiring followers, engaging their identities in the group effort, and increasing follower self-image through identification with an outstanding group), and *shared leadership* (developing followers' abilities to assume leadership roles within the group). Several of these leader behaviors address *group* performance, which was not specifically included in the original theory.

Path-Goal Theory has been researched with mixed results. For example, supportive leadership is often found to be effective under stressful conditions as predicted, but is also found effective under most other conditions. Directive leadership improves performance in many studies, but not always in the situations predicted by the theory. Research on participative and achievement-oriented leadership in this model is very limited and inconclusive. The complexity of the *Reformulated Theory* makes it difficult to test its predictions but the new leadership behavior patterns it identifies are clearly important for individual and group performance.

The Multiple Linkage Model

The Multiple Linkage Model is another sophisticated contingency theory developed in the 1980s by Gary Yukl. This model describes how several leader behaviors affect intervening variables which are essential for group or organizational performance. Examples of these intervening variables include the degree of followers' understanding and commitment to their work tasks, their training and ability to complete those tasks, the organization of the work, the adequacy of cooperation and team effort to complete the groups' tasks, availability of resources needed for the task, and degree of coordination with other groups needed for successful organizational performance.

The essential leader behavior patterns in the Multiple Linkage Model have been modified over the years, but an unusually complete list was provided in Yukl's excellent textbook. Leaders are described as *supporting and helping* with follower development, *consulting and delegating* tasks to followers, *recognizing and rewarding* followers, *clarifying and monitoring* task performance, *motivating and inspiring* followers, *planning and organizing* the work tasks, *problem solving and informing* followers of needed information, and *representing and networking* for the group with higher ups and other groups. This latter behavior is currently referred to as a type of *boundary spanning*.

This model also describes situational and follower characteristics that influence the leadership process. Some characteristics may *neutralize* a specific leadership behavior by making it ineffective. This can occur when a large spatial distance between leaders and followers can make leaders' efforts at clarifying and monitoring task performance ineffective. Other characteristics may *substitute* for particular leader behaviors, making that leadership pattern unnecessary. This occurs when a professional, trained, and committed work force requires little or no clarification or motivational efforts by the leader. These employees are already motivated and capable of completing their tasks effectively without input from their leader. This aspect of the Multiple Linkage Model was adapted from Substitutes for Leadership Theory which is described later in this chapter.

The Multiple Linkage Model suggests that the leader's primary role in the short run is to fill in for deficiencies in the intervening variables, and in the long run to modify situations to improve the intervening variables. Like other contingency models, the Multiple Linkage Model describes effective leadership as requiring a pattern of leader behaviors that fit the group or situation. Yukl has recently emphasized how leaders must be flexible to correctly adapt to the environmental situation, especially during times of changes in technology, political or economic turbulence, or major competition. In addition to the leader behavior patterns described earlier, effective adaptation may require changes in products or services, as well as marketing and supply procedures. Research findings on this model are sparse, but existing studies of individual elements in the model show that all the leader behavior patterns are important for individual and group performance.

The Reformulated Path-Goal Theory and the Multiple Linkage Model present a more realistic picture of the activities of effective leaders than the theories described earlier in this chapter. While their complexity makes them difficult to test with empirical research, many great leaders have utilized numerous behaviors specified in these theories. Bill Wilson avoided making any major organizational decisions in leading Alcoholics Anonymous, without thorough participation and approval by his group of alcoholic members. And Pat Summitt inspired the Lady Vols basketball team of the University of Tennessee to achieve unprecedented success in women's college sports while supporting and clarifying to her players that hard work and dedication can produce amazing results in all aspects of life. Summitt's numerous boundary spanning activities on behalf of her university are unmatched.

Charismatic Theories

In the 1980s and 1990s the study of charismatic leaders became popular. Previously charisma had been viewed as a mysterious quality some people possessed and was not easily studied by behavioral scientists. Interest in charisma eventually led to new leadership theories being proposed with various labels including charismatic leadership, visionary leadership, value-based leadership, and transformational leadership. The most common versions today are charismatic and transformational leadership, which are very similar and are based on work by Bob House, James McGregor Burns, Bernard Bass, and Bruce Avolio. Charismatic leaders have exceptionally strong effects on followers by appealing to their individual emotions, aspirations, needs, and values. Followers attribute charisma (literally meaning "divine gift") to a leader because s/he seems extraordinary and followers become convinced the leader will help them achieve a noble goal or vision of the future that is more important and desirable than they had previously thought was possible.

Early leadership theories focused on directive and supportive leadership, sometimes supplemented with other task related leadership behaviors and the use of recognition and rewards for good performance. These theories were very rational and were labeled "transactional" by advocates of charismatic leadership. The transaction involves the leader providing guidance, support, and rewards in exchange for followers' efforts and good performance. This simplified description of transactional leadership is often presented in contrast to charismatic leadership. But charismatic leadership also involves a transaction that is more intense and emotional than transactional models. The leader is said to offer an inspiring *vision* or *mission* that transcends typical organizational and individual goals. Through *carefully crafted communications* the leader describes the vision and mission to achieve goals and the *critical roles followers must play* to achieve them. The vision *appeals to followers' higher order needs and ideological values*, it "feels right." Followers respond by *identifying with the vision and the leader, believing that together they can achieve the vision, putting forth extra effort*, and the *collective goals take precedence* over their own wants, needs and goals.

Charismatic leaders also act as *role models* for followers and thus embody the principles and ideals that are consistent with their vision and commitment to the vision. Examples are leading protest marches or soldiers into battle, or accepting a salary of one dollar a year to save an organization in financial trouble. These leaders convey an *inspirational message* that arouses strong emotions and motivation in followers and increases their identification with the leader and the mission. Examples are Martin Luther King's "I Have a Dream" speech or John Kennedy's famous inaugural address. They *encourage innovative and creative behavior* that includes "thinking outside the box" to create novel solutions to problems. Examples are Steve Jobs of Apple Inc. challenging engineers to make "killer products" that change the world or Mohandas Gandhi advocating peaceful resistance against the British to attain Indian independence. They also exhibit *symbolic behaviors* that demonstrate dedication to the vision and mission and the ideological values they reflect. Examples are self-sacrifices by Mohandas Gandhi who lived under extremely ascetic conditions as he led the Indian movement for independence or César Chávez who turned down well-paying jobs to earn $6,000 per year as leader of the struggling Farm Workers Union.

Charismatic leaders also possess certain personal traits such as a *high need for power* which is the desire to influence and control their environment, often including other people. Need for power may be expressed in two ways. Leaders may dominate others, allow followers little autonomy, and make all the decisions themselves—often called *personalized need for power*. Alternatively, they may build up and support followers to make them more capable and give them autonomy of action to create an organization that influences and controls its environment—often called *socialized need for power*. Although the socialized version of need for power is normally the best leadership strategy in the long run, charismatic leaders emerge with both types of need for power. These leaders also have a *strong belief in the correctness of their own values and motives* and are highly *self-confident*. These theories predict that the leader's vision and mission as well as their behaviors and traits build followers' self-confidence and infuse their tasks with a higher purpose, making their work tasks meaningful and personally satisfying rather than simply asking followers to perform for a specific material reward.

Transformational leadership has become very popular in recent years and includes three charismatic leader behavior patterns described earlier and one behavior pattern from earlier leadership theories. These patterns are labeled *charisma* or *idealized influence* which is displaying self-confidence and ideological arguments with dramatic emotional rhetoric; *inspirational motivation* which involves communicating a noble vision and mission and exhibiting symbolic behaviors to model the leader's commitment to the vision; *intellectual stimulation* where leaders encourage followers to challenge the status quo and attack problems using creative and innovative approaches and perspectives; and *individualized consideration* which includes showing concern and support for individual followers as needed and fostering their future development. Transformational leadership places a stronger emphasis on intellectual stimulation than other charismatic theories and its emphasis on individualized consideration is unique among charismatic theories. Transformational leaders appear to reflect the socialized need for power described earlier. The overall results predicted by this model are similar to other charismatic theories.

Charismatic and transformational theories have removed the mystique from charismatic leadership and identified specific behaviors and traits used by these leaders. Research on these theories often shows the strong effects that some leaders have on their followers. Followers usually like these leaders and identify with them. They generally have positive effects on followers' job satisfaction, organizational commitment, organizational citizenship behaviors, and follower performance. Effects on organizational performance are sometimes positive, although these effects can be complicated by other factors such as the surrounding culture. Elements of transformational leadership may have different effects on employee creativity and organizational innovation

These theories ignore other important leadership behavior patterns such as participative, directive, and boundary spanning leadership. They often ignore important risks such as the abuse of power by some charismatic leaders, and possible violations of societal expectations and environmental factors. These issues are shown later in this book in the descriptions of bad leaders such as David Koresh and Adolf Hitler. The emphasis in transformational leadership on individualized consideration and socialized need for power may prevent the abuse of power that occurs with some charismatic leaders. Advocates of these theories seem to believe charismatic/transformational leadership is appropriate for all situations—similar to the "one best way" approach of early leadership theorists. Others maintain it is most effective in crises or during times of environmental uncertainty or turbulence. There have been efforts to separate transformational leadership from pure charismatic leadership. Other studies have started exploring reciprocal effects of followers on transformational leaders. More research is needed to identify conditions under which charismatic/transformational leadership is most effective.

Other Behavioral Theories

Other leadership theories have been developed that focus on specific aspects of the leadership process. Most are not intended to describe all aspects of effective leadership, but they often identify and clarify elements of leadership not addressed or emphasized by the more comprehensive contingency theories.

The Normative Decision Theory of Participation

The Normative Decision Theory of Participation was developed by Victor Vroom, Phillip Yetton, and Art Jago. This theory deals with the degree of involvement of followers in a leader's decision-making process—often termed participative leadership. Numerous great leaders used participative leadership including Abraham Lincoln, Bill Wilson, and Nelson Mandela. The Normative Decision Theory addresses the issue of *what process a leader should use to make a specific decision*. Should he make the decision on his own, relying on his own knowledge and expertise without input from followers? Should he gather information from individual followers about the decision before deciding himself? Should he hold a meeting with followers to get their help as a group in making a decision? This model identifies multiple ways a leader can involve followers in decision making and tries to identify which approach is best for a given decision situation.

Consistent with other contingency theories, Vroom pointed out that different decision situations facing a leader often require different degrees of follower involvement. This model has evolved over the years, and the following five categories—called *decision styles*—now represent these different degrees of involvement. *Decide*—The leader makes the decision himself, relying on his own expertise and any information he collects on his own. *Consult Individually*—The leader discusses the decision problem with individual followers to obtain their suggestions and makes the decision himself. *Consult Group*—The leader discusses the decision problem with followers as a group to obtain their suggestions, he then makes the decision himself. *Facilitate*—The leader presents the decision situation to the group and acts as a facilitator to obtain group consensus on a solution. He helps the group develop and analyze possible decision alternatives and may specify constraints on the alternative chosen. *Delegate*—The leader describes the decision situation to followers as a group and allows them to generate solutions and to make a decision. The leader provides encouragement, resources and information if requested, but the group makes the decision.

This theory identifies several *situational characteristics* that are used to determine which decision style is best for a given decision problem. These situational characteristics are described in a series of questions to be answered by the leader, using a computer program that allows for identification of the best decision style very quickly. The major situational questions are described here. *Decision Significance*—Is the decision of critical importance to the success of the group's project or organization? *Importance of Commitment*—Is group member commitment to the decision alternative chosen essential for successful implementation? *Leader's Expertise*—Does the leader possess the necessary knowledge and expertise to make a good decision without follower input? *Likelihood of Commitment*—Is the group likely to commit itself to successful implementation of a decision alternative if it is chosen by the leader without their input? *Group Support for Objectives*—How well does the group support the organization's objectives that may be affected by the decision? *Group Expertise*—How much expertise do group members possess that can be useful in resolving the decision problem? *Team Competence*—How skilled are group members at working together to solve problems? With this model, the leader must have the authority to make the decision and implement a solution, and there must be an identifiable group of followers who are available to participate in the decision process. The theory specifies four *criteria* for measuring the success of the decision process used. *Quality of the Decision*—Does the decision alternative chosen advance the achievement of group or organizational goals? This criterion is especially important when a decision is significant, and there are a large number of alternative solutions. *Acceptance of the Decision*—Do followers accept the alternative solution chosen and are they willing to commit themselves to implement the decision successfully? Participation usually increases follower commitment for implementation. *Costs of the Decision*—For a given decision problem, are the costs of a specific decision style greater than the benefits? Considerable time is required for group decision making, and this can be costly. *Development of Followers*—Is follower and/or team learning and development an important issue in this decision situation? Participation can build follower competence and improve team skills.

Research on the Normative Decision Theory generally supports its usefulness for leaders and it is popular with managers. When leaders use the decision styles recommended by this theory, they usually make more successful decisions. This model is a contingency theory because its recommendations depend on the decision situation, even though it deals exclusively with the degree of participative leadership used by a leader. It is important to remember that this theory tells a leader which decision style to use in making a specific decision; it does not specify which decision alternative is optimal.

The Leader-Member Exchange Theory

Another theory that addresses a specific aspect of the leadership process is the Leader-Member Exchange (LMX) Theory, which evolved from an earlier theory called the Vertical Dyad Linkage (VDL) Model. Both of these models focus on the interaction between leaders and individual followers. Similar to the transactional approach described earlier, this interaction is viewed as a fair exchange whereby the leader provides certain benefits such as task guidance, advice, support, and/or significant rewards and the followers reciprocate by giving the leader respect, cooperation, commitment to the task, and good performance. However, LMX recognizes that leaders and individual followers will vary in the type of exchange that develops between them.

Over time, some exchanges between a leader and specific followers become very close, whereas other exchanges may be somewhat distant. This can create *in-groups* and *out-groups* of followers who vary significantly in their effort, commitment, and active cooperation. In-group members are said to have *high quality exchanges* with the leader who perceives these followers as being more experienced, competent, and willing to assume responsibility than other followers. The leader begins to rely on these individuals to help with especially challenging tasks. If the follower responds well, the leader rewards her with extra coaching, favorable job assignments, and developmental experiences. If the follower shows high commitment and effort followed by additional rewards, both parties develop mutual trust, influence, and support of one another. Research shows that in-group members usually receive higher performance evaluations from the leader, higher satisfaction, and faster promotions than out-group members. Great leaders like Ernest Shackleton and Abraham Lincoln developed high quality exchanges with followers, and these close relationships were invaluable in their success.

Time constraints and personal characteristics often result in the leader spending less time with some followers and entering in less intense and more distant exchanges than with in-group members. This can create out-groups whose members have *low quality exchanges* with the leader. In theory, low quality exchanges are considered fair since the leader expects no more than adequate job performance, good attendance, reasonable respect, and adherence to the job description in exchange for a fair wage and standard benefits. But the leader spends less time with out-group members, they have fewer developmental experiences, and the leader tends to emphasize her formal authority to obtain compliance to leader requests.

Research shows that out-group members are less satisfied with their job and organization, receive lower performance evaluations from the leader, see their leader as less fair, and are more likely to file grievances. They may also exhibit counterproductive behavior or leave the organization.

Similarity of attitudes or socio-economic background and personal liking between the leader and follower help determine a follower's exchange. Research indicates that effects of gender and race have complicated and uncertain effects on the quality of the exchange. Additional research shows quality of an exchange between leaders and their followers may be influenced by the leader's communication style or degree of knowledge sharing, or follower's locus of control, work engagement, or organizational justice perceptions. The exchange quality is usually established early in their relationship and is resistant to change, making it difficult for out-group members to achieve in-group status. When leaders are trained to develop high quality exchanges, performance of all followers increases but the largest increases are for out-group members. This may indicate that the capabilities and willingness of some out-group members were overlooked by the leader. These individuals may be ready and willing to contribute more and simply need to spend more time with the leader.

Research shows that high performance ratings for in-group members may occur regardless of their actual performance. This may indicate a halo effect where the leader has already decided the in-group follower is competent and deserving of a high rating. The reverse may occur for out-group members resulting in low performance ratings and resentment by these followers. This theory does not consider the effects of individual exchanges on the overall group's performance or the effects of one exchange on other exchanges in the group. Although high quality exchanges can result in positive attitudes by followers and possibly high performance and retention, leaders should be open to the possibility of high quality exchanges for all followers.

The Implicit Leadership Theory

Most people have an image in their heads of the characteristics of an ideal political leader, military leader, or business leader. These images are often called *prototypes* and they dictate who a person perceives as a leader or not a leader. This process is described by the Implicit Leadership Theory (ILT) which was first developed by Robert Lord and his colleagues. The great Apache war leader Geronimo embodied the characteristics of a fearless warrior who refused to surrender, yet was loyal and generous to his own people. The great football coach Vince Lombardi demonstrated the characteristics of toughness, hard work, and fierce competitiveness that epitomize the game of professional football. Followers of these leaders expected their leaders to have these characteristics since they were required for success. They demonstrate how ILTs can influence leader–follower relationships.

The ILT describes the perceptual processes used by followers and others to classify individuals as leaders or non-leaders, effective or ineffective leaders, or business or sports leaders. Lord and his colleagues argued that individuals' beliefs about the attributes and behaviors of leaders are clustered together in their memory in categories (also called schemas). The prototype is the individual's best example of the leadership category. When an observer or follower meets a person who holds a leadership position or a potential future leader, the person's attributes are compared against the observer's prototype. The better the match, the more likely the person is seen as a leader. This increases the person's social power and the observer likely assumes this individual has the ability to motivate and direct others. This can be an important factor in followers' decision to cooperate and actively carry out a leader's requests.

An individual's ILT likely develops over time, from early experiences with parents, coaches, siblings, friendship groups, and teachers as well as movies and books. These experiences cause us to encode specific attributes and behaviors as characteristic of leaders, effective leaders, or ineffective leaders. If we see a leader being kind to a follower, we may decide the leader is humane and encode this characteristic as an attribute of effective leaders. If we notice a leader effectively organizing a project and clarifying work assignments and expectations for followers, we may decide that good leaders are directive. As we mature and add experience, our learning process continues resulting in rich prototypes for different types of leaders. These prototypes are called "fuzzy sets" because they may overlap with one another so sports leaders may have some of the same characteristics as business leaders. Attributes such as dynamic, organized, and supportive may characterize many types of leaders in varying degrees.

Research shows that ILTs are affected by contextual factors such as cultural characteristics and identification with a group, as well as the leader's ethnicity. ILTs influence followers' expectations of leaders and affect the leader/follower relationship. If a group of followers expects a leader to be autocratic, a participative leader will likely be viewed as weak and have difficulty obtaining active cooperation from those followers. This is true in countries that accept major power differences among individuals as normal and proper, such as Russia and Iran. In countries that do not accept power differences as normal and necessary, such as the Netherlands and Denmark, family and organizational leaders are expected to make decisions through extensive discussion and participation. A leader's evaluations by her supervisor may be affected by the supervisor's internal categories, who may rely on these categories more than the leader's actual behavior or performance. These perceptions may therefore increase or limit resources for the leader or her team and are therefore important for an individual's career progression, team cohesion, and organizational performance. Recent ILT research has been extended to Implicit Followership Theories (IFTs). Early research shows the better the fit between a leader's IFTs and follower characteristics is associated with higher ratings and performance by the follower. Understanding followers' ILTs and leaders IFTs can be important in establishing productive relationships between leaders and followers.

Substitutes for Leadership

Another leadership theory that is related to contingency theories is Substitutes for Leadership, which was developed in the late 1970s by Steve Kerr and John Jermier. These scholars noted that all leadership theories assumed some type of hierarchical leadership was important in all situations, although one leadership style might be effective in one situation and a different style in another situation. They proposed that there are characteristics of followers, their work task, or the organization that reduce the importance of hierarchical leadership. These characteristics essentially *neutralize* the effects of specific leader behaviors. Other characteristics were proposed to *substitute* for certain leader behaviors by having an important effect of their own on followers' performance and attitudes independent of the leader. Their model reflected the realization that numerous factors in organizations can provide guidance, motivation, and good feelings that followers need to complete their tasks effectively. Although Kerr and Jermier described the effects of neutralizers and substitutes on directive and supportive leadership, they noted that these characteristics also likely affect other leadership behavior patterns. A recent development in the Substitutes for Leadership Theory includes adding leadership *enhancers*, which are situational and follower characteristics that increase a leader's influence on followers.

One example of a possible leadership neutralizer is *spatial distance* between a leader and follower that makes it difficult for the leader to effectively monitor the follower's performance and to provide useful guidance for the follower in carrying out his work tasks. Another neutralizer is a strong *need for independence* by the follower that can make the follower less willing to accept a leader's efforts to provide task guidance. An example of a leadership substitute occurs when followers have a high degree of *ability, experience, training, and knowledge*, and a *professional orientation* that provides them with the capabilities they need to do their job well and the desire to work independently of their hierarchical leader. They may resist a leader's efforts to provide task guidance and be perfectly satisfied to work on their own. Another substitute occurs when followers belong to a *closely knit cohesive work group with high performance norms* they may receive all the task guidance, encouragement, and interpersonal support they need from other group members. In this situation, followers may prefer to interact with their group of peers and tacitly ignore task guidance and relationship-oriented efforts by their hierarchical leader.

Some type of task guidance, encouragement and/or support is important for most organizational members, but the leader is not the only source of these factors. If the needed guidance, motivation, and support are available from non-leader sources such as leadership substitutes, then the leader may not need to provide them, and he can concentrate on other important activities. In recent years, management programs that emphasize non-leader sources of influence involving several types of leadership substitutes have become popular. Programs for *self-leadership, shared leadership*, and *self-managed work teams* incorporate substitutes such as increased followers' ability, experience, training and knowledge, self-administered performance feedback, and closely knit work groups. *Total Quality Management* involves continuous training to increase workers' ability and job knowledge and continuous feedback from customers and work tasks rather than from a formal leader. *Computerized workplaces* and *telecommuting* rely on networked computer systems and groupware that provide job guidance and information on demand without reliance on hierarchical managers.

The popularity of programs like those described above and a recent upsurge in research has provided considerable support for the existence of substitutes for leadership. Researchers have found substitutes, neutralizers, or enhancers for other leader behaviors including charismatic/transformational leadership, leader reward and punishment, and servant/ethical leadership behaviors. The recent findings have occurred in numerous organizational contexts, such as consulting, health care, universities, small business, and student groups. Writers emphasize that organizational trends reflect a rapidly changing economy and workplace where informational technology is prevalent that alleviates many traditional leadership behaviors. However, research also shows that substitutes and neutralizers do *not* make all leadership unnecessary or irrelevant.

Ethical Theories

Ethical theories have a common focus on the leader's moral priorities and altruistic behaviors. There are two main categories—Servant Leadership Theory and Principle-Centered Leadership. These theories yielded little research until recently, especially Servant Leadership which has become popular with researchers and practicing leaders. They are not contingency theories, but describe personal characteristics and behaviors that their developers believe all leaders should demonstrate. They emphasize issues of personal values, ethics and morality, integrity, personal character, trust, service to others, openness, humility, and self-knowledge/self-awareness. They may include some form of spiritual leadership. As such, nearly all the great leaders contained in this book can be described by one or both of these theories. The bad leaders demonstrate a conspicuous absence of the elements described in these models.

The Servant Leadership Theory

The Servant Leadership Theory was first developed by Robert Greenleaf in the 1970s and has slowly gained popularity. It specifies a *caring* and *ethical* approach toward others with a strong element of *supportive leadership behavior*. With this theory, the leader's primary responsibility is to serve the needs of followers and other organizational constituents with a special concern for the least privileged individuals. Assessing followers' needs requires *careful and active listening* and being viewed as *trustworthy*. Leaders are viewed as trustworthy when they are *open* and *honest* and *role model the values of empathy, fairness, altruism, humility*, and *trust*. Servant leaders are also said to inspire followers' trust by *demonstrating optimism, a firm belief in the importance of the group mission or goal, showing confidence, competence, openness to change*, and *granting autonomy* to followers in controlling their own actions.

The Servant Leadership Theory also emphasizes the importance of the *leader's self-knowledge* or *self-awareness* which emerges over time as the leader becomes aware of his strengths, core values, beliefs, and desires.

Self-knowledge is discussed by other writers as resulting from *self-reflection* and *connection*. Self-reflection may occur with meditation, religious practices, or other techniques. Connection may be with the inner self, a higher deity or (in the case of servant leaders) with followers. Missions and goals reflect the leader's self-knowledge and connection with followers, and servant leaders always place others above themselves. Greenleaf predicted that servant leaders would have followers who are healthier, freer, wiser, more empowered and autonomous, and would likely become servant leaders themselves.

Recent reviews of research indicate that Servant Leadership may meet the challenges of today's workplace. By engaging followers ethically, emotionally, and spiritually they may improve followers' self-worth and sense of belonging. Corporate stewardship is also a focus of effective Servant Leadership by considering all stakeholders. Research in many contexts and countries shows that Servant Leadership improves followers' organizational citizenship behaviors, job satisfaction, engagement, psychological well-being, as well as follower, team, and organizational performance. Knowledge sharing, service quality and trust in the leader is also improved. Several studies showed that Servant Leadership predicted follower performance, organizational commitment, team and firm performance above and beyond Transformational Leadership, although these two leadership styles are positively correlated.

Companies who use Servant Leadership include Intel, Marriott, Ritz Carlton, Starbucks, Southwest Airlines, and TDIndustries. Ernest Shackleton was a great leader who exemplified the Servant Leadership Theory, as he gave himself completely to the service of his followers and constituents.

Principle-Centered Leadership

Principle-Centered Leadership was developed by Stephen R. Covey based on his earlier book, *The Seven Habits of Highly Effective People*. Principle-Centered Leadership describes overall principles that all leaders can use to guide their decision making and interactions with followers and others. Covey maintains these principles apply in all situations and, when they are followed, they result in fair and kind leaders who develop trust and commitment among followers, as well as efficient and effective organizations.

Principle-Centered Leadership emphasizes the *leader's character and competence* as essential for effective leadership. Covey describes character as composed of: (1) *integrity*, which is knowing one's values and behaving consistently with these values; (2) *maturity*, which is expressing one's true feelings and beliefs with courage and consideration in one's behavior and communications; and (3) *abundance mentality*, which involves believing that life is not a zero-sum game and sharing recognition, responsibility, and profits. Competence is developed by prolonged effort and practice through useful experience.

Covey also emphasizes the importance of *personal and organizational values* in this theory. He defines *values* as our own personal convictions about what we believe are most important and desirable in our lives, our most basic priorities. Values are often classified as terminal or instrumental. Terminal values are desired end states we wish to achieve in life such as happiness, freedom, salvation, or a comfortable life. Instrumental values are desirable characteristics of people that help them achieve terminal values, such as honesty, ambition, courage, or politeness. Most of the values Covey describes are instrumental and he asserts that focusing on one's values will help leaders to be more self-aware and ethical in their behavior, to prioritize tasks, and to be seen by others as trustworthy and credible.

This theory emphasizes the principle of creating *trust* and *trustworthiness* which result from character and competence. The principle of follower *empowerment* results from the leader as helper, performance contracts with jointly set goals, follower participation in performance appraisals, and self-management. Covey asserts many other principles such as maintaining a *service orientation* by viewing life as a mission to serve others; *continuous learning* through reading, taking courses, listening, observing, and asking questions; *radiating positive energy* by being cheerful, optimistic, enthusiastic, and happy; *believing in others* by showing faith in their character and competence; *seeing life as an adventure* by taking risks and trying new methods and techniques; *showing humility* in all dealings with others; *listening and obeying one's conscience* in all actions; *refraining from speaking unkindly* to others to build relationships; and *keeping all promises and commitments* to build trust. He continually emphasizes that people must be treated as economic, psychological, social, and spiritual beings who want *meaning* in the work activities. Involving people in developing a mission statement that includes a vision and purpose for the organization can help provide this meaning.

Principle-Centered Leadership is popular with many managers who have participated in seminars conducted by the Covey Leadership Center. The model is appealing because it is based on Covey's best-selling book on personal development and it specifies guidelines that are easy to understand. It includes many elements that are similar to Servant Leadership. The theory has not been carefully researched by other scholars so its overall validity is difficult to judge. However, great leaders such as Nelson Mandela and Ernest Shackleton appeared to embody many of the principles of this theory.

Emergent Leadership Perspectives

New perspectives on leadership have emerged in the recent past. These include complexity leadership theory, collective leadership theory, cross-cultural leadership, and toxic leadership. These new approaches are increasingly relevant in a changing environmental landscape.

Complexity Leadership Theory

Complexity Leadership Theory (CLT) has been articulated by scholars in recent years, notably Mary Uhl-Bien, Russ Marion, and Bill McKelvey. CLT has its foundations in complexity theory. Organizational scholars are increasingly using complexity theory from the natural sciences as a means of understanding and explicating organizational response to environmental changes over time. While there are many formulations of complexity theory, CLT is largely based on complex adaptive systems (CAS). This approach describes a system in which a complete understanding of the individual parts does not automatically convey a complete understanding of the whole system's behavior. In complex adaptive systems, organizations exist in increasingly complex, non-linear, and dynamic environments. Chaos is perceived as a necessary condition for the growth of these non-linear dynamic systems, while outcomes of organizational actions are deemed unpredictable. Adaptation and survival of the system depends on developing rules that are capable of keeping organizations on the "edge of chaos," since too much stability leads to organizational mortality while instability leads to chaos. These simple order-generating rules govern organizational outcomes.

In CLT, leadership is conceived as a complex interactive dynamic out of which adaptive outcomes such as learning, innovation, and adaptability emerge. The fundamental assumption is that traditional top-down leadership theories are simplistic, static, based on extinct organizational technologies and processes, and unsuitable for the fast-changing knowledge economy. The knowledge era has created a new set of challenges for organizations and their leaders. In the knowledge economy, the main challenge is to create an environment where knowledge is created and shared rapidly and in an efficient manner. The goal is to cultivate and protect knowledge assets that are often the core value and competence of the organization. In order to survive and thrive, organizations must increase their complexity to match with the complexity of the environment rather than simplify and rationalize their structures. In CLT cause is hardly proportional to effect. Cause often has more than one effect, resulting in a non-linear complex relationship between inputs and outputs. In addition, there is a recognition of the dominance of decentralized organizing structures and co-evolutionary ecologies of firms, institutions, and markets.

CLT questions the assumption that leadership rests within the character or behavior of leaders and their symbolic, motivational, or charismatic actions. CLT also casts doubt on the leader's capacity to act on organizations in order to achieve the leader's objectives, given insights that organizations are highly complex and non-linear. Consequently, the focus is on inter-connected behaviors among agents which may be individuals or collective entities such as groups or organizations. Directional influence such as hierarchical power is minimized while co-generation and mutuality is amplified. This notion of leadership and the capacity to influence others is based on individual interactions, collective interactions, and synergistic effects from these interactions. This leads to a state of emergence. Individuals adjust their behavior in response to changes in behavior from other entities and how they interpret those changes. This process of emergence leads to a change in the system itself as the organization constantly evolves from one state of behavior to another state.

Borrowing from complexity theory, CLT applies the concept of complex adaptive systems (CAS) to describe and operationalize the leadership process. CAS are a basic unit of analysis in complexity science. CAS are neural-like networks of interacting, interdependent agents that are bonded in a cooperative dynamic by common goal, outlook, and/or need. They are changeable structures with multiple, overlapping hierarchies, and like the individuals that comprise them, CAS are linked with one another in a dynamic, interactive network. Applying this concept, leadership is not only a position, skill, or authority but an emergent, interactive dynamic; a complex interplay from which a collective impetus for action and change emerges when heterogeneous agents interact in networks in ways that produce new patterns of behavior or new modes of operating.

In order for CLT to be effectively operationalized, organizations need to be self-organizing. Self-organizing is dependent on certain principles such as delegation of authority, empowerment of individuals with information at various levels within the organization, a balanced distribution of power and continuous learning. These conditions will facilitate appropriate responsiveness to environmental changes through creativity and continuous innovation.

A complex systems perspective introduces a new leadership "logic" to leadership theory and research by understanding leadership in terms of an emergent event rather than a person. A complexity view suggests a form of shared leadership that does not lie in a person but rather in an interactive dynamic, within which any particular person will participate as leader or follower at different times and for different purposes.

CLT is not a theory that has been validated by research. However, Travis Kalanick and Mark Zuckerberg exemplify Complexity Leadership Theory by creating and continuing to encourage an internal environment where new knowledge is sought out, created and shared efficiently, resulting in core organizational competencies that form the basis of their companies' success.

Collective Leadership Theory

Collective leadership is an emerging perspective that aims to go beyond traditional romanticized notions of attributing leadership to a single individual. This is in recognition of the limits of individual leaders, complexity of organizations, a need to make informed decisions in dynamic environments, and the increased dominance of the knowledge economy. Several efforts have been made to understand the dynamics of leadership characteristics among members of a collective, separate from the leader. Consequently different theoretical formulations have emerged that focus on collective leadership. Collective leadership can be described as the enactment of leadership among multiple individuals who may not be in formal leadership roles. While the focus on collective leadership is recent, a cursory examination of individual leaders points to the popularity of some form of pluralistic leadership.

There are different conceptual approaches for describing and researching collective leadership. One approach focuses on collective leadership from a *multiplex perspective*. Leaders often serve many functions and roles. Rather than one individual leader managing different functions, a collection of individuals can enact multiple leadership roles. For instance, within a team, a task-oriented leader and a relationship-oriented leader can both emerge in leadership roles to complement each other while interdependently influencing the whole team. Collective leadership can also be conceived from a *temporal perspective* where, based on the situation, individuals emerge on occasion to provide a leadership role and then retreat to let others lead when there is a situational change. The rotation of leadership roles may be based on a need for different skills at different times or as a means of engendering shared governance and collective responsibility for success. There is also a rich tradition of using the context of *network theory* to evaluate collective leadership. Network analysis enables the possibility of multiple leaders, multidirectional leadership influences and leadership emergence. Borrowing from network theory, leadership resides in interactions between members of a network rather than an individual. Through social behaviors, individuals may influence each other's actions. Leadership focus is removed from the individual and located in the interaction, while the process is enacted through communication. These joint actions, in turn, lead to other actions in a constant state of emergence. The collective leadership in this case is not a result of an individual's influence or action, but the joint behaviors that are distributed in a dynamic way within the group. The three perspectives, while not exhaustive, are representative of the main foundations and, to a large extent, complement each other.

As in other theories, collective leadership has been defined and explained in a variety of ways and with numerous names. Looking across varied conceptualizations, most models of collective leadership reflect three fundamental characteristics:

1   Lateral influence among peers, as opposed to the vertical leadership of an appointed or emergent leader.
2   Leadership is shared and distributed among various individuals, who take on leadership simultaneously and also consecutively.
3   Leadership is a dynamic and emergent group property that produces a continual and collective assignment and reassignment of the leadership role.

Empirical studies provide robust evidence to support the effectiveness of collective leadership on group behavior processes, team members' attitudes, team decision making, and team performance. Most notably, collective leadership is more effective than singular hierarchical leadership when members of a collective are engaged in complex tasks, working in teams, and face high task interdependence.

It should be noted that collective leadership is not a substitute for formal leadership. The formal leader can also play a significant role in facilitating or inhibiting collective leadership. The leader can act as a catalyst to nurture the collective's greater capacity for leadership. Beyond the formal leader, the organization has to be amenable to distribution of leadership by removing systemic and behavioral barriers. The future applications of collective leadership appear to be positive. Collective leadership minimizes deleterious effects of power influences and organizational politics. However, there are limits to this appeal. Organizations are assumed to be highly functional with well-aligned goals. It is also assumed that organizational members have enthusiasm for collective leadership and the capacity to move swiftly from leadership to followership roles. Wilma Mankiller in her facilitation of the Gadugi Cherokee development projects and José María Arizmendiarrieta in his inspiration of the Mondragón Cooperatives made collective leadership the foundation of their leadership styles. Both skillfully brought together communities and purposefully avoided assuming leadership roles, inspiring them to share the leadership of these projects. By relinquishing the leadership role to their communities, they helped instill a sense of collective pride and empowered rural Cherokee communities.

Cross-Cultural Leadership

In the 1980s and 1990s, policy changes in numerous Eastern European and Asian countries facilitated a large increase in international joint ventures and outsourcing by business organizations from highly developed countries. Organizational leaders began focusing efforts outside their own borders on global supply chains, global finance systems, global markets, global competitors, and global careers. Working across multiple borders with employees from multiple cultures quickly became necessary and competence at these activities became essential for success. The terms cross-cultural or global leader evolved for those who could direct and support multicultural activities, convey a collective vision, and span political and financial boundaries effectively.

Culture is a complex phenomenon. One major contributor to the understanding of culture is Geert Hofstede, who defined culture as the shared mental programming of members of a collective such as a group, tribe, society, or nation. This mental programming includes factors such as beliefs, values, traditions, and interpretations of key events in a group's background that are shared by the group members. One scholar often summed up his description of culture by saying, "If it isn't shared, it isn't culture."

Examples of shared cultural characteristics are individualism/collectivism (the extent that group members are expected to take care of themselves first or to place the group first in their behavior), paternalism (the extent that group members expect to be taken care of by someone in authority), power distance (the extent to which people accept unequal distributions of power in organizations and institutions), uncertainty avoidance (the extent to which individuals resist risk and unexpected events by emphasizing the importance of rules and norms), and masculinity/femininity (the degree to which masculine values such as assertiveness, advancement, earnings, and acquisition of objects is valued or feminine values such as a friendly atmosphere, position security, physical conditions, and cooperation are valued). Most of these cultural dimensions were defined and clarified by Hofstede in his study of the IBM Corporation in over 50 different countries and regions. His cultural dimensions (developed over 40 years ago) have been used in hundreds of cross-cultural research projects and by many international business organizations.

It is widely recognized that culture influences leadership processes. In individualistic societies (e.g., United States, Canada, Great Britain) leaders are often seen as highly visible and take charge while asserting a clear and favorable vision of the future that the leader can guide group members to achieve. Conversely, Asian societies (e.g., Japan, Laos, Malaysia) are often paternalistic where leaders are expected to work behind the scenes, to develop healthy relationships with individual followers, and to be seen as part of the group. However, assessing how strongly and in what ways culture affects leadership processes is difficult. It does appear that national cultures show considerable variation in what people believe to be effective and ineffective leadership behavior patterns such as charismatic or participative leadership. These and other similar findings have led most leadership scholars to adopt a contingency or cultural congruence approach to cross-cultural leadership. This approach assumes that to be effective, a leader must match her/his behavior to the cultural expectations of the society where it occurs.

Another large-scale study of cross-cultural leadership began in the early 1990s by Robert House and was labeled the Global Leadership and Organizational Behavioral Effectiveness Project (GLOBE). This project addressed whether there were leadership characteristics and/or behaviors that were universally effective in all cultures. It also sought to explore the degree that societal culture dimensions affected culturally contingent leadership characteristics and/or behaviors. The GLOBE study included 17,000 respondents in over 1,000 organizations in 62 countries. GLOBE researchers developed nine cultural dimensions that were labeled Assertiveness, Future Orientation, Gender Egalitarianism, Humane Orientation, In-group Collectivism, Institutional Collectivism, Performance Orientation, Power Distance, and Uncertainty Avoidance. Many of their dimensions were based heavily on Hofstede's earlier work. These same researchers also developed six global leadership characteristics/behaviors including Charismatic, Humane Oriented, Participative, Team Oriented, Autonomous, and Self Oriented.

Most of the GLOBE leadership dimensions were culturally contingent in terms of their desirability in different cultures. That is, some cultures desired somewhat different leader characteristics/behaviors than other cultures. For example, Charismatic Leadership was most desired in Gender Egalitarian, Performance-Oriented, Collective, Future-Oriented, and Humane-Oriented cultures. Charismatic Leadership is not viewed as effective in high Power Distance cultures. Autonomous Leadership was desirable in Performance-Oriented societies but not in Collectivist or Humane-Oriented societies. The most popular leadership dimensions across cultures were Charismatic, Team Oriented and Humane Oriented. Overall, GLOBE researchers found that the most important effect of culture was on the leadership characteristics/behavior desired by most people in a society. The desired leadership characteristics/behavior in a society importantly affected the actual behavior and effectiveness of a leader. GLOBE data showed that leaders were more effective in increasing team morale and organizational competitiveness when the leader's style matched the style desired in his/her culture.

When a leader's followers come from several diverse cultures, expecting the leader to be a chameleon and match her style to each follower may be extremely difficult. Recent research on the "global mindset" and "cultural intelligence" focuses on enduring personal competencies of leaders who direct these diverse groups. Global leaders are said to be interpersonally competent, non-judgmental, self-confident, tolerant of ambiguity, optimistic, and emotionally resilient. These competencies should help leaders manage conflicts, and deal with communication problems and tensions occurring in culturally diverse groups. Global mindsets are mental processes that guide how a person interprets and behaves in culturally diverse situations. The global mindset helps the leader to integrate across diverse cultural expectations of followers and overall organizational requirements. This can be especially difficult when followers are in diverse locations. The above competencies, a cosmopolitan outlook and cognitive complexity (that is, the ability to understand and work with multiple perspectives on a given issue) are said to help the global leader to understand and address local expectations and switch between local and organizational necessities as needed. Research is at an early stage on this approach and its validity and usefulness has yet to be demonstrated.

Another recent study of 18 countries describes a "license to lead" which specifies key interpersonal skills needed for cross-cultural leaders. Zander described these skills including empowering, coaching, directing, communicating and making people proud of their work through interpersonal interaction. Employee's preferences for these interpersonal skills varied significantly across cultures and there was much agreement with overall GLOBE's findings.

In summary, the literature on cross-cultural leadership clearly demonstrates that a society's culture influences the leadership behavior that is expected and effective when followers are relatively homogenous culturally. These findings agree with much of the earlier leadership research and theoretical work that emphasized the situation as a key determinant of effective leadership behavior. Mother Teresa successfully crossed multiple cultural boundaries in bringing the services of the Sisters of Charity to thousands of needy people around the world.

Toxic Leadership

The purpose of leadership is to bring together a group of people, to focus their efforts and to facilitate their cooperation in working toward their group or organizational goals. Toxic Leadership (also known as Destructive or Bad Leadership) is leadership that results in undesirable (sometimes disastrous) outcomes for a leader's followers, their group or organization and sometimes others outside the organization. Toxic Leadership frequently involves dominance and coercion instead of persuasion and commitment and a selfish orientation where the leader focuses on his/her own goals rather than the group or organization goals. It can also undermine the quality of life of followers and other stakeholders and detract from the organization's purpose.

Idi Amin and Joseph Stalin are generally viewed as bad leaders but Elizabeth Holmes and Bernie Ebbers were also destructive in many ways. These leaders are not viewed as equivalent but they represent the degrees and types of consequences of Toxic Leadership. Toxic Leadership can be viewed as a sequence or progression ranging from ineffective or incompetent to unethical or evil. The degree of undesirable outcomes varies among toxic leaders but they all have deleterious outcomes on followers, their organization, and sometimes others.

Researchers have documented examples of Toxic Leadership behaviors and the list is quite inclusive. Examples are described below:

1   undermining and demeaning followers and sometimes (in the case of political leaders) actually torturing or killing followers and other constituents;
2   violating basic human rights of followers and others;
3   misleading followers with lies and grand illusions (unrealistic goals) and claiming to have the power to achieve these goals with followers' full compliance;
4   suppressing criticism and dominating or threatening followers into compliance with the leader's decisions;
5   encouraging destructive competition among followers, creating scapegoats, and tolerating corruption and cronyism;
6   failing to develop or support new leaders and treating people at low organizational levels poorly;

7   squelching or eliminating structures and processes designed to generate truth and fairness and to curb the leader's power;

8   subverting legal requirements and processes and engaging in morally questionable behavior (Lipman-Blumen, 2011).

Leadership scholars have also identified several basic personal characteristics of toxic leaders that underlie their use of the Toxic Leadership behaviors such as:

1   Charisma. Not all charismatic leaders are toxic or destructive to people and organizations. As described earlier, there are many impressive charismatic leaders who have achieved valuable and constructive outcomes with supportive and committed followers. But, perhaps surprisingly, most toxic leaders are charismatic. Researchers have noted that charismatic leaders are dangerous because of their ability to inspire and excite followers to actively pursue a mission that seems noble but may be reckless, ill advised, and designed to bolster the leader's ego, reputation, power, or wealth. Because of their communication skills, persuasiveness, and a projected image that is almost "bigger than life," charismatic leaders can convince followers to pursue the leader's goals for a supposedly "better world."

2   All charismatic leaders have a high need for power—the desire to influence and or control others and their environment. When that need is oriented toward building their influence through working with others to build an effective team or organization that benefits all parties (termed socialized need for power), the results are usually very positive. However, when a leader's charisma is combined with a personalized need for power (oriented toward the leader's personal gain and self-promotion), the results are often destructive. These "negative charismatics" are typically extremely ambitious, arrogant, and have huge egos. They frequently dominate and coerce others, demean those who voice disagreement, and scapegoat dissidents and rivals in order to obtain their desires. This type of charismatic leader often describes lofty noble goals that seem constructive, but the leader's real goals are personal aggrandizement.

3   Another personality characteristic of toxic leaders is narcissism—a grandiose view of their own talents and a craving for admiration. Psychologists have described a relationship between narcissism, charisma, and personalized need for power. Narcissistic leaders often believe they have special knowledge that others don't possess, they demand obedience and believe they deserve privileges denied to others. They are preoccupied with their own interests and feelings and are not sensitive to the feelings of others. They are self-serving, ignore other viewpoints, are reckless, and may lack integrity or morality. When a narcissistic leader has charisma and a personalized need for power, the results can be destructive or disastrous for followers and other parties.

4   A few scholars have noted that toxic leaders often had very difficult early life experiences such as an abusive or criminal parent, violent parental discord, low socio-economic status, and powerlessness. This may create a destructive image of the world in a child and cause him/her to exploit others because they believe it necessary to survive. These experiences may also create a manner of thinking that reflects anger, resentment, and hatred of others who are unlike the individual or who disagree. Charismatic leaders with this background often espouse a vision of destroying rivals and eliminating or severely punishing those seen as opposing them. Toxic leaders such as Joseph Stalin, Benito Mussolini, and Raúl Castro all had a very difficult childhood. A top-level leader at Enron kept a conspicuous desktop symbol that said, "When Enron says it's going to 'rip your face off' ... it means it will rip your face off!" (Raghavan, 2002; Padilla, Hogan and Kaiser, 2007).

Several scholars have described follower characteristics and environmental factors that may make them most susceptible to toxic leaders. When people are deprived of basic needs (food and shelter, safety and security) they may be willing to tolerate an abusive leader who can provide for them. Individuals who have a low self-image or who lack a firm self-concept may welcome an apparently strong leader who paints an illusory picture of a great future for them if they comply with his/her directions and follow along. In times of extreme uncertainty and especially in the presence of a threatening environment (such as a possible bankruptcy or perceived threat of terrorism), quick action may be required and an authoritarian dominant leader who advocates a radical change to eliminate the uncertainty or mount a response may be preferred. Toxic leaders may maintain the perception of threat in order to stay in power. Certain cultures that are characterized by avoiding uncertainty and/or high power distance (accepting that there are power differences between individuals of different status) may facilitate the emergence of toxic leaders. And an absence of effective institutional checks and balances (such as different powers held by different branches of government or a board of directors that keeps watch on a company CEO) can also make toxic leadership possible.

Scholars are quick to point out that it is usually a collection of these leader characteristics and behaviors as well as follower and environmental characteristics that result in toxic leaders gaining control. They also note that highly ambitious people who share the toxic leader's beliefs and values will often collude with the leader to increase their own status and power. Once in charge, these individuals may act to weaken or eliminate institutional checks and balances or work to maintain the perception of eminent threat to help them stay in power.

One writer advised people to beware of leaders who describe grand illusions of the future if people follow their directives. Develop the habit of looking realistically at a leader's vision and assess if it is truly achievable, is it oriented toward a worthwhile goal and is it designed to help people. Adolf Hitler, Idi Amin, and David Koresh all demonstrated many of these characteristics of toxic leadership.

Authentic Leadership

This relatively new leadership theory emerged from a widespread concern about unethical conduct of many of today's leaders. Leadership failures in public and private organizations have resulted in distrust of leaders and the desire for honest leaders with integrity who seek to serve others and the common good. Popular writers began describing a leadership theory based on the leader's personal values, a strong moral compass, and the desire to serve others.

Early roots of Authentic Leadership also involved researchers on Charismatic/Transformational Leadership who sought to assure that leaders following their theory were genuine, humane, and ethical with a genuine desire to uplift followers to achieve goals beyond expectations. Elements of Servant Leadership, Principle-Centered Leadership, and Positive Psychology also played a large part in the development of Authentic Leadership. Servant and Principle-Centered Leadership are described earlier in this chapter. Positive Psychology is described as the study of what makes up a pleasant and meaningful life and includes positive emotions, engagement, relation-ships, meaning, and accomplishment. These appear to be goals of Authentic Leadership for both leaders and their followers.

Much has been published under the rubric of Authentic Leadership, and different definitions have been used to describe this approach. This divergence in definition and findings from some empirical research have prevented a defi-nitive theory from emerging. However, one finding has been common to much of the research and theorizing. When and if a well-accepted theory of Authentic Leadership is developed, it seems likely to contain the following four elements.

1 *Self-Awareness.* Leaders understand their own motives, goals, and values and how these may affect followers.
2 *Relational Transparency.* Leaders encourage an open and honest exchange of ideas with their followers, clarifying one's values, and appreciating of one another's ideas and values in a non-defensive manner.
3 *Balanced Processing.* Both leaders and followers actively listen to one another in an open manner; leaders evaluate information and opinions without favoritism before making decisions.
4 *Internalized Moral Perspective.* Leaders adhere to basic values and moral standards such as respect for others and justice, making it likely they will make ethical decisions and not simply impose their will on followers.

These leader processes of Authentic Leadership imply other leader beha-viors such as keeping their word, showing empathy, fairness, self-regulation/

self-control, and placing followers' needs above their own. Supportiveness and positive emotions such as optimism and satisfying exchanges with colleagues are also described with this theory. The leader's character and consistency in aligning one's behavior with their values are described as part of Authentic Leadership by some writers. Nelson Mandela is described as an authentic moral leader who inspired trust in followers, and his life is described in this book.

These Authentic Leadership behaviors are believed to inspire followers' trust in the leader. They are also believed to inspire authentic behaviors and trust among followers. Some researchers report increased follower job satisfaction, work engagement, organizational commitment, and job performance (although the empirical findings for performance do not exceed some other leadership theories). Many writers indicate that Authentic Leadership must be developed over time as a leader gains confidence and competence. Although numerous studies show some positive effects of Authentic Leadership, different definitions of the theory and many different measures have been used. These measures sometimes combine Authentic Leadership with outcomes/results of this theory, making the results difficult to interpret. Others describe the possibility that the leader's values may be different than followers' values. Clearly, at this time this theory is still under development. Virginia Hall was an authentic leader, highly self-aware and guided by moral principles of democracy and by selflessness.

Conclusion

Each of the leaders described in the following chapters demonstrate different aspects of these theories. Some theories better describe a specific leader than others. Regarding leader traits, all the leaders (great and bad) were *determined and driven* to achieve their goals showing exceptional energy, initiative, and perseverance. Most leaders were *self-confident* with *assertive* personalities. Most great leaders demonstrated *integrity* by being truthful, trustworthy, and loyal to their people and cause. Many leaders had strong *cognitive* and *social skills*. These leaders also demonstrated several of the leadership behavior patterns found in contingency leadership theories including directive, supportive, boundary spanning, participative, and rewarding leader behaviors. Most leaders showed some elements of charismatic/transformational leadership. Many leaders relied on in-groups of followers while most fit the prevailing leader prototype for their time and type of organization. Some made use of leadership substitutes to influence followers. Nearly all the great leaders demonstrated ethical behavior and fair treatment of followers and other constituents. Ethics and fair treatment were conspicuously absent from the bad leaders.

Most of the leaders were flawed in some way. Steve Jobs' abrasive interpersonal style and willingness to take credit for others' work left much to be desired. Napoleon's ruthlessness and deceptions were countless; Hayek's

Table 1.1 Matrix of Great Leadership and Leadership Theories

GREAT LEADERSHIP	Trait Theories	Fiedler's Contingency Theory	Leadership Grid	Path-Goal Theory	Normative Decision Theory	Situational Leadership Theory	Multiple Linkage Model	Leader-Member Exchange	Charismatic/Transf.	Servant Leadership	Implicit Leadership Theory	Substitutes for Leadership	Principle-Centered Leadership	Complexity Leadership Theory	Cross-Cultural Leadership	Collective Leadership	Toxic Leadership	Authentic Leadership
Harriet Tubman	X			X					X	X			X					
Indra Nooyi	X	X		X	X	X	X		X									
Bill Wilson	X			X	X	X	X		X	X								
Atatürk						X			X				X					
Maria Montessori	X								X	X								
César Chávez	X	X		X		X	X		X	X								
Winston Churchill	X	X		X		X	X		X		X							
Margaret Sanger	X	X		X		X	X		X	X							X	
Angela Merkel	X	X		X		X	X			X			X					
Martin Luther King, Jr.	X	X	X	X	X	X	X		X	X								
Virginia Hall		X			X					X								
Anita Roddick	X			X			X		X	X								X
Mohandas Gandhi	X	X	X	X		X	X		X	X								
Wilma Mankiller	X									X						X		X
Pat Summitt	X	X	X	X		X	X				X	X						

	Trait Theories	Fiedler's Contingency Theory	Leadership Grid	Path-Goal Theory	Normative Decision Theory	Situational Leadership Theory	Multiple Linkage Model	Leader-Member Exchange	Charismatic/Transf. Leadership	Servant Leadership	Implicit Leadership Theory	Substitutes for Leadership	Principle-Centered Leadership	Complexity Leadership Theory	Cross-Cultural Leadership	Collective Leadership	Toxic Leadership	Authentic Leadership
Steve Jobs	X	X		X		X	X		X								X	
Kōnosuke Matsushita	X	X	X	X		X	X		X	X			X	X				
Mary Kay Ash	X	X	X	X	X	X	X		X	X								
Ernest Shackleton		X	X	X		X		X	X	X		X						
Abraham Lincoln	X	X		X	X		X	X	X	X		X						
Leymah Gbowee	X		X	X		X	X		X	X								
Nelson Mandela	X			X	X	X	X		X	X			X					
Geronimo	X	X		X		X	X		X	X	X							
José María Arizmendiarrieta									X							X		
Napoleon Bonaparte	X	X		X		X	X	X	X		X							
Nicolas Hayek	X	X	X	X	X	X	X		X									
Greg Boyle	X								X	X								
BAD LEADERSHIP																		
Elizabeth Holmes	X								X								X	
Bernie Ebbers	X							X	X								X	
Sepp Blatter	X								X								X	
Adolf Hitler	X	X		X		X	X		X		X						X	

	Trait Theories	Fiedler's Contingency Theory	Leadership Grid	Path-Goal Theory	Normative Decision Theory	Situational Leadership Theory	Multiple Linkage Model	Leader-Member Exchange	Charismatic/Transf. Leadership	Servant Leadership	Implicit Leadership Theory	Substitutes for Leadership	Principle-Centered Leadership	Complexity Leadership Theory	Cross-Cultural Leadership	Collective Leadership	Toxic Leadership	Authentic Leadership
Idi Amin	X	X		X			X	X			X						X	
David Koresh	X	X	X	X		X			X		X						X	
YOU DECIDE																		
Elon Musk	X			X			X		X								X	
Jeff Bezos	X		X						X					X				
Mark Zuckerberg	X	X	X	X		X			X		X			X				
Aung San Suu Kyi	X		X	X					X	X							X	
Travis Kalanick	X								X					X				

bluntness, explosive temper, and tendency to take credit for others' work were well known; Bill Wilson's depression, alcoholism, and infidelities were discouraging to all around him; and Gandhi's treatment of his family and extremist views about Jews sacrificing themselves to the Nazis were unpalatable to most observers. But these leaders exhibited major strengths that they relied on to lead their groups and organizations to amazing accomplishments. Each leader was unique due to their personal nature, background, and context. No single set of traits or behaviors characterize them all. Yet, they are viewed by most observers as examples of great leadership.

Hopefully, the leadership theory descriptions in this chapter, along with the references for each at the end of this chapter, will clarify how the great leaders achieved their amazing feats. If these theory descriptions increase the reader's understanding of the leadership process, then this chapter has served its purpose. The matrix (Table 1.1) relates the great and bad leaders described in this book with the leadership theories in this chapter.

Selected References

Trait Theories

Bass, B. M. & Bass, R. (2008). *The Bass handbook of leadership: Theory, research, and managerial application* (4th ed.). New York: Free Press.

Daft, R. L. (1999). *Leadership: Theory and practice.* New York: Dryden Press.

Kirkpatrick, S. A. & Locke, E. A. (1991). Leadership: Do traits matter? *Academy of Management Executive,* 5(2), 48–59.

Lord, R. G., DeVader, C. L., & Alliger, G. M. (1986). A meta-analysis of the relation between personality traits and leadership perceptions: An application of validity generalization procedures. *Journal of Applied Psychology,* 71, 402–410.

Lord, R. G. & Hall, R. J. (1992). Contemporary views of leadership and individual differences. *Leadership Quarterly,* 3(2), 137–157.

Northouse, P. G. (2004). *Leadership: Theory and practice* (3rd ed.). Thousand Oaks, CA: Sage.

Leadership Grid

Blake, R. R. & McCanse, A. A. (1991). *Leadership dilemmas—Grid solutions.* Houston, TX: Gulf.

Blake, R. R. & Mouton, J. S. (1964). *The managerial grid.* Houston, TX: Gulf.

Hersey, P., Blanchard, K. H., & Johnson, D. E. (1996). *Management of organizational behavior: Utilizing human resource* (7th ed.). Upper Saddle River, NJ: Prentice Hall.

Contingency Theory of Leadership

Ayman, R., Chemers, M. M., & Fiedler, F. E. (1995). The contingency model of leadership effectiveness: Its levels of analysis. *The Leadership Quarterly,* 6(2), 147–167.

Bass, B. M. & Bass, R. (2008). *The Bass handbook of leadership* (4th ed.). New York: Free Press.

Fiedler, F. E. & Garcia, J. E. (1987). *New approaches to effective leadership: Cognitive resources and organizational performance*. New York: Wiley.

Fiedler, F. E., Chemers, M. H., & Mahar, L. (1994). *Improving leadership effectiveness: The leader match concept* (2nd ed.). New York: Wiley.

Schriesheim, C. A. & Kerr, S. (1977). Theories and measures of leadership: A critical appraisal of current and future directions. In J. G. Hunt & L. L. Larson (Eds.), *Leadership: The cutting edge* (pp. 9–45). Carbondale, IL: Southern Illinois University Press.

Schriesheim, C. A., Tepper, B. J., & Terault, L. A. (1994). Least preferred co-worker score, situational control, and leadership effectiveness: A meta-analysis of contingency theory model performance predictions. *Journal of Applied Psychology*, 79 (4), 561–573.

Situational Leadership Theory

Fernandez, C. F. & Vecchio, R. P. (1997). Situational leadership theory revisited: A test of an across-jobs perspective. *Leadership Quarterly*, 8(1), 67–84.

Goodson, J. R., McGee, G. W., & Cashman, J. F. (1989). Situational leadership theory. *Personnel Psychology*, 43, 579–597.

Hersey, P. (1984). *The situational leader*. Escondido, CA: Center for Leadership Studies.

Vecchio, R. P. (1987). Situational leadership theory: An examination of a prescriptive theory. *Journal of Applied Psychology*, 72, 444–451.

Path-Goal Theory

House, R. J. (1971). A path-goal theory of leader effectiveness. *Administrative Science Quarterly*, 16, 321–328.

House, R. J. (1996). Path-goal theory of leadership: Lessons, legacy, and a reformulated theory. *Leadership Quarterly*, 7(3), 323–352.

House, R. J. & Mitchell, R. R. (1974). Path-goal theory of leadership. *Journal of Contemporary Business*, 3, 81–97.

Multiple Linkage Model

Kim, H. & Yukl, G. (1995). Relationships of managerial effectiveness and advancement to self-reported and subordinate-reported leadership behaviors from the multiple linkage model. *Leadership Quarterly*, 6(3), 361–377.

Yukl, G. (2010). *Leadership in organizations* (7th ed.). Upper Saddle River, NJ: Pearson Education.

Yukl, G., Gardner, W. L. III, Uppal, N. (2020). *Leadership in Organizations* (9th ed.). Pearson India Education Services Pvt. Ltd.

Charismatic and Transformational Leadership

Agle, B. R., Nagarajan, N. J., Sonnenfeld, J. A., & Srinivasan, D. (2006). Does CEO charisma matter? An empirical analysis of the relationships among organizational performance, environmental uncertainty, and top management team perceptions of CEO charisma. *Academy of Management Journal*, 49(1), 161–174.

Judge, T. A. & Piccolo, R. G. (2004). Transformational and transactional leadership: A meta-analytic test of their relative validity. *Journal of Applied Psychology*, 89, 755–768.

Mohsin, S., Zoya, X., Song, Sarker, M. N. J. (2020). Effects of transformational leadership on employee creativity: the moderating role of intrinsic satisfaction. *Asia Pacific Management Review*, 25(3), 166–176.

Kahn, H., Rehmat, M., Butt, T. H., Farooqui, S., Asian, J. (2020). Impact of transformational leadership on work performance, burnout and social loafing: a mediation model. *Future Business Journal*, 6, 40.

Shamir, B., House, R. J., & Arthur, M. B. (1993). The motivational effects of charismatic leadership: A self-concept based theory. *Organizational Science*, 4(4), 577–594.

Shamir, B., Sakay, E., Breinin, E., & Popper, M. (1998). Correlates of charismatic leader behaviors in military units: Subordinates' attitudes, unit characteristics, and superiors' appraisals of leader performance. *Academy of Management Journal*, 41 (4), 387–409.

Yukl, G. (2010). *Leadership in organizations* (7th ed.). Upper Saddle River, NJ: Pearson Education.

Normative Decision Theory of Participation

Howell, J. P. & Costley, D. L. (2006). *Understanding behaviors for effective leadership* (2nd ed.). Upper Saddle River, NJ: Prentice Hall.

Vroom, V. H. (2000). Leadership and the decision making process. *Organizational Dynamics*, 28(4), 82–94.

Vroom, V. H. (2003). Educating managers for decision making and leadership. *Management Decision*, 42(10), 968–978.

Yukl, G. (2010). *Leadership in organizations* (7th ed.). Upper Saddle River, NJ: Pearson Education.

Leader-Member Exchange Theory

Fairhurst, G. T. (1993). The leader-member exchange patterns of women leaders in industry: A discourse analysis. *Communication Monographs*, 60(4), 321–351.

Fein, E. C. & Tziner, A. (August2021). Editorial: The future of leader-member exchange theory. *Frontiers in Psychology*, 12, https://doi.org/10.3389/fpsyg2021.73610.

Hogg, M. A. (2004). Leader-member exchange (LMX) theory. In G. R. Goethals, G. J. Sorenson, & J. M. Burns (Eds.), *Encyclopedia of leadership* (pp. 335–376). Thousand Oaks, CA: Sage.

Howell, J. P. & Costley, D. L. (2006). *Understanding behaviors for effective leadership* (2nd ed.). Upper Saddle River, NJ: Pearson Education.

Randolph-Seng, B., Cogliser, C., Randolph, A. F., Scandura, T., Miller, C. D., Smith-Genthos, R. (2016). Diversity in leadership: Race in leader-member exchanges. *Leadership and Organizational Development Journal*. Emerald. doi:10/1108/LODj-10-2014-0201.

Yukl, G. (2010). *Leadership in organizations* (7th ed.). Upper Saddle River, NJ: Pearson Education.

Implicit Leadership Theory

Javidan, M., Dorfman, P. W., Howell, J. P., & Hanges, P. J. (2010). Leadership and cultural context: A theoretical and empirical examination based on project GLOBE. In N. Nohria & R. Khurana (Eds.), *Handbook of leadership theory and practice*. Boston, MA: Harvard University Press.

Offerman, L. R., Kennedy, J. K., Jr., & Wirtz, P. W. (1994). Implicit leadership theories: Content, structure, and generalizability. *Leadership Quarterly*, 5(1), 43–58.

Lord, R. G., Epitropaki, O., Foti, R. J., Hansbrough, T. K. (2020). Implicit leadership theories, implicit followership theories and dynamic processing of leadership information. *Annual Review of Organizational Psychology and Organizational Behavior*, 9, 49–74.

Phillips, J. S. & Lord, R. G. (1986). Notes on the practical and theoretical consequences of implicit leadership theories for the future of leadership measurement. *Journal of Management*, 12(1), 321–341.

Substitutes for Leadership

Devries, R. E. (1995). *Measuring substitutes for leadership using the concept of need for leadership: A cross-sectional research*. Netherlands: Tilburg University, Work and Organizational Research Center.

Howell, J. P. (1997). Substitutes for leadership: Their meaning and measurement— An historical assessment, *Leadership Quarterly*, 8(2), 113–116.

Howell, J. P., Bowen, D. E., Dorfman, P. W., Kerr, S., & Podsakoff, P. M. (1990). Substitutes for leadership: Effective alternatives to ineffective leadership. *Organizational Dynamics*, 19, 21–38.

Kerr, S. & Jermier, J. (1978). Substitutes for leadership: Their meaning and measurement. *Organizational Behavior and Human Performance*, 22, 275–403.

Podsakoff, P. M., MacKenzie, S. B., & Fetter, R. (1993). Substitutes for leadership and the management of professionals. *Leadership Quarterly*, 4(1), 1–44.

Podsakoff, P. M., Niehoff, B. P., MacKenzie, S. B., & Williams, W. L. (1993). Do substitutes for leadership really substitute for leadership? An empirical examination of Kerr and Jermier's situational leadership model. *Organizational Behavior and Human Decision Processes*, 54, 1–44.

Niented, P. & Toska, M. (2022). Leadership Substitutes Theory in present day organizations. *Open Journal of Leadership*, 11, 445–461.

Velez, M. J. & Neves, P. (2018). Shaping emotional reactions and ethical behaviors: proactive personality as a substitute for ethical leadership. *Leadership Quarterly*, 29(1), 663–673.

Servant Leadership Theory

Avolio, B. J., Walumbwa, F. O., & Weber, T. J. (2009). Leadership: Current theories, research, and future directions. *Annual Review of Psychology*, 60, 421–449.

Greenleaf, R. K. (1991). *The servant as leader*. Indianapolis, IN: Robert Greenleaf Center.

Yukl, G. (2010). *Leadership in organizations* (7th ed.). Upper Saddle River, NJ: Pearson Education.

Eva, N., Robin, N., Sendjaya, S., Van Dierendorick, D. & Liden, R. C. (2019). Servant Leadership: A systematic review and call for future research. *Leadership Quarterly*, 30(1), 111–132.

Principle-Centered Leadership

Covey, S. R. (1989). *The seven habits of highly effective people: Restoring the character ethic*. New York: The Free Press.
Covey, S. R. (1991). *Principle-centered leadership*. New York: Simon and Schuster. http://kleczek.wordpress.com/2008/06/14/principle-centered-leadership.

Complexity Leadership Theory

Boisot, M., & McKelvey, B. (2010). Integrating modernist and postmodernist perspectives on organizations: A complexity science bridge. *Academy of Management Review*, 35(3), 415–433.
Burnes, B. (2005). Complexity theories and organizational change. *International Journal of Management Review*, 7(2), 73–90.
Lichtenstein, B., & Plowman, D. A. (2009). The leadership of emergence: A complex systems leadership theory of emergence at successive organizational levels. *The Leadership Quarterly*, 20(4), 617–630.
Marion, R. & Uhl-Bien, M. (2002). Leadership in complex organizations. *The Leadership Quarterly*, 12(4), 389–418.
Stacey, R., Griffin, D., & Shaw, P. (2002). *Complexity and management: Fad or radical challenge to systems thinking*. London: Routledge.
Uhl-Bien, M., Marion, R., & McKelvey, B. (2007). Complexity leadership theory: Shifting leadership from the industrial age to the knowledge era. *The Leadership Quarterly*, 18(4), 298–318.

Collective Leadership Theory

Contractor, N., DeChurch, L., Carson, J., Carter, D., & Keegan, B. (2012). The topology of collective leadership. *The Leadership Quarterly*, 23(6), 994–1011.
Cullen-Lester, K. & Yammarino, F. (2016). Collective and network approaches to leadership: Special issue introduction. *The Leadership Quarterly*, 173–180.
Gronn, P. (2002). Distributed leadership as a unit of analysis. *The Leadership Quarterly*, 13(4), 423–451.
Mendez, M., Howell, J., & Bishop, J. (2015). Beyond the unidimensional collective leadership model. *Leadership & Organization Development Journal*, 36(6), 675–696.
Wu, Q., Cormican, K., & Chen, G. (2020). A meta-analysis of shared leadership: Antecedents, consequences, and moderators. *Journal of Leadership & Organizational Studies*, 27(1), 49–64.
Zhu, J., Liao, Z., Yam, K. C., & Johnson, R. E. (2018). Shared leadership: a state-of-the-art review and future research agenda. *Journal of Organizational Behavior*, 39(7), pp. 834–852.

Cross-Cultural Leadership

Bird, A. & Mendenhall, M. E. (2016). From cross-cultural management to global leadership: Evolution and adaptation. *Journal of World Business*, 51, 115–126.

Dickson, M. W., Castano, N., Magomaeva, A., & Den Hartog, D. N. (2012). Conceptualizing leadership across cultures. *Journal of World Business*, 47, 483–492.

Hanges, P., Aiken, J., Park, J., & Su, J. (2016). Cross-cultural leadership: Leading around the world. *Current Opinion in Psychology*, 8, 64–69.

Steers, R. M., Sanchez-Runde, C., & Nardin, L. (2012). Leadership in a global context: New directions in research and theory development. *Journal of World Business*, 47, 479–482.

Zander, L. (2021). Interpersonal leadership across cultures: A historical espose and research agenda. *International Studies of Management & Organization*, 50(4), 357–380.

Toxic Leadership

Lipman-Blumen, J. (2010). Toxic leadership: A conceptual framework. In F. Bournois, J. Duval-Hamel, S. Roussillon, & J. Searingella (Eds.), *Handbook of top management teams* (pp. 214–223). London: Palgrave-Macmillan.

Lipman-Blumen, J. (2008). Following toxic leaders: In search of posthumous praise. In R. E. Riggio, I. Chaloff, & J. Lipman-Blumen (Eds.), *The art of followership: How great followers create great leaders and organizations* (pp.181–194). San Francisco, CA: Jossey-Bass.

Lipman-Blumen, J. (2011). Toxic leadership: A rejoinder. *Representation*, 47(3), 331–342.

Padilla, A., Hogan, R., & Kaiser, R. B. (2007). The toxic triangle: Destructive leaders, susceptible followers, and conducive environments. *The Leadership Quarterly*, 18, 176–194.

Raghavan, A. (2002, August 26). Full speed ahead: How Enron bosses created a culture of pushing limits. *The Wall Street Journal*, p. A1.

Authentic Leadership

Avolio, B. J. & Gardner, W. L. (2005). Authentic leadership development: getting to the root of positive forms of leadership. *The Leadership Quarterly*, 15(3), 315–338.

Gardner, W. L., Cogliser, C. C., Davis, K. M. & Dickens, M. P. (2011). Authentic leadership: a review of the literature and research agenda. *The Leadership Quarterly*, 22(6), 1120–1145.

Luthans, F., & Avolio, B. J. (2003). Authentic leadership development. In K. S. Cameron, J. E. Dutton, and R. E. Quinn (Eds), *Positive Organizational Scholarship* (pp. 241–258). Berrett-Koehler.

Shamir, B. & Eliam, G. (2005). "What's your story?" A life-stories approach to authentic leadership development. *The Leadership Quarterly*, 16(3), 395–417.

Part II

Snapshots of Great Leadership

2 Harriet Tubman

Anti-Slavery Patriot, Soldier, and Activist

In 2024, the US Mint released $5 gold coins, $1 silver coins, and half-dollar coins honoring Harriet Tubman, the heroic abolitionist and freedom fighter, and commemorating the bicentennial of her birth. Tubman was born into slavery in Maryland. She escaped from slavery and risked her life on many occasions to rescue dozens of slaves through the Underground Railroad. During the Civil War, Tubman served the Union Army as a spy and soldier, helping to free over 700 slaves in the Combahee Ferry Raid. In her later years, Tubman worked alongside Susan B. Antony as an activist for women's right to vote.

Araminta Ross was born circa 1820 as a slave in Dorchester County, Maryland. She was fifth of nine children, whose parents were both slaves owned by two masters. At around the age of five, Araminta's owners hired her out to other families as a nursemaid. As a house slave, Araminta suffered violent beatings and in later life recounted being constantly whipped by one of her mistresses in the mornings. On another occasion, her master attacked her with a brutal blow, breaking her ribs. She suffered with the injury for the rest of her life. At around the age of 11, she was sent back to her masters who hired her out to set muskrat traps. Araminta was removed from those duties after contracting measles and becoming incapacitated. Around this period, Araminta sustained a permanent injury to her head when she was hit with a lead weight as she tried to assist a fleeing slave from his overseer. The injury caused abrupt seizures and frequent vivid dreams. After months of recovery at her master's property, Araminta was sent to chop logs for a lumber merchant.

Araminta had become deeply religious in her Christian faith intermingled with cultural traditions that had survived the transatlantic movement of slaves. She could not read or write, but was familiar with the Bible's teachings in the Episcopal and Methodist traditions. She fasted on Fridays, a practice that she may have found in the Catholic practices at the time. Much has been written on how she was able to reconcile the complexities and contradictions of these practices and beliefs.

Araminta married a manumitted (freed) slave, John Tubman, in 1844. While little detail is known, the marriage was remarkable. Marriages

DOI: 10.4324/9781003333937-4

between free and enslaved blacks were not recognized legally and were subject to the master's intentions. The sale of one spouse or children would cause irreparable harm to the union. In 1712, a Maryland law had dispensed with patriarchal traditions with respect to the black community and if there were children, the children's status would follow that of the mother. For a free black man, the only way he would guarantee that his children would be free was through a union with a free black woman. Slave masters often intervened to stop childless unions and initiate unions that were likely to produce children and supply more slaves. Araminta and John Tubman were not able to have children.

Araminta's father, Ben Ross, was manumitted in 1840 when he reached 45 years of age. Her mother, Harriet Green, remained enslaved by a different master. After paying an attorney to investigate the circumstances, Araminta discovered that according to a will, her mother was entitled to freedom on her 45th birthday, which was long past. All of her brothers and sisters should also have been emancipated. Araminta had few available options. She retreated to prayer and pleas for her master's unchristian and immoral actions of illegal enslavement.

Araminta's plan to escape appears to have been prompted by the death of her master in 1849. The decision heavily weighed on her. She had to leave behind her husband, who was reluctant to accompany her, and most of her family members. Fearing the risk of being auctioned to a new master and relocated to the deep South, Araminta and her two brothers set out to escape, following the North Star. The journey was treacherous with blood-hounds and bounty hunters in pursuit. A bounty of $300 had been published in a local newspaper for their capture and return. Tubman's two brothers developed cold feet and decided to return to their master. Tubman was to recount later that, "… there was one of two things I had a right to, liberty or death; if I could not have one, I would have the other." Three of her sisters that she had left behind were sold to new owners.

During her escape north, Araminta was helped by a white woman who gave her a piece of paper with two names in exchange for Araminta's precious quilt. She used the contacts to seek help along the way. A secret network of black and white individuals and groups often offered aid and comfort to fugitive slaves. This network used code words, hidden messages and symbols such as the "conductor," "stationmaster," "cargo," and "depot" to communicate and provide fugitives with directions and safe houses. This escape route was later known as the Underground Railroad. After traveling north for 90 miles, mainly by foot at night, Araminta arrived in Pennsylvania, a free state. She changed her first name to Harriet in honor of her mother and took her husband's last name, Tubman.

Harriet Tubman quickly settled in Philadelphia, finding domestic work and saving her wages as she planned a new mission. The Fugitive Slave Act, passed in 1850, had created a sense of urgency. The Act allowed slave catchers to apprehend slaves in states that had abolished slavery and return the slaves to their masters. In 1851, she returned to Dorchester County where she rescued 11 slaves, providing them with food and comfort until it was safe to conduct them all the way to St. Catharines, Ontario. She remained in Canada for a few months before returning to Philadelphia to work and raise more funds. Tubman traveled back to Dorchester again where she rescued nine slaves and took them to Canada. During the 1850s, she made numerous other trips, always in the winter, rescuing dozens of slaves and resettling them in St. Catharines. Unfortunately, most records related to her family were burnt in 1852, when an arsonist burnt down the Dorchester County courthouse.

Most details regarding Tubman's travels back to Dorchester County remained secret in order to hide identities of people and places involved in the Underground Railroad, long after slavery had been abolished. However, historians were able to reconstruct details from people she encountered, local newspaper reports at the time, historical records and Tubman's own testimonies in her later years.

After her arrival in St. Catharines in 1851, Tubman set down roots in the community and later rented and operated a boarding house as a transitional point for arriving fugitives. Tubman was determined to rescue all the members of her family. She made more than 13 missions and helped more than 200 slaves to escape. Tubman preferred to travel back to Dorchester County alone to stage mass escapes. She would travel by night and rest and hide during the day. She was a master of deception and often traveled in some form of disguise as an old woman or as a man. She developed useful strategies such as stealing the master's horses on the first leg of the journey and pretending to head south when she encountered slave catchers. She traveled in the winter when the nights were longer and would organize slaves to escape on Saturday nights, since she knew that the news of their escape would not be published in the newspapers until the following Monday. Tubman would secretly organize an isolated rendezvous point, such as a cemetery, and pass the message to selected slaves.

Tubman conducted the fugitives in the hostile terrain through coded messages that were embedded in spiritual songs as they moved along. She bribed slaves along the way to remove reward notices that would be posted by owners of escaped slaves. There was always a danger of being apprehended by slave owners or bounty hunters who were armed with guns, whips, and trained sniffer dogs. Tubman carried a pistol for protection. The pistol was also a precaution against any slave that would panic and attempt to turn back; a dead fugitive would not disclose the secrets of the Underground Railroad. She would use her network to obtain food and clothing for the cold winter nights. Using her basic intelligence, Tubman guided the slaves on the Eastern Shore terrain, as she followed the North Star to St. Catharines, Ontario. She finally rescued her remaining family members, including her parents, in 1857. In 1860, Tubman embarked on her final mission to the East Shore to rescue her sister and children. She was unable to rescue her sister who had died prior to Tubman's arrival. She waited in a raging winter storm to rescue her sister's two children but was not successful. Tubman returned to St. Catharines after rescuing other fugitives.

The Underground Railroad had become more organized as various anti-slavery groups and emancipated slaves set up secret networks to assist slaves to escape and settle in new communities in the north, going as far as Canada. Tubman was already considered a hero in the Underground Railroad network and anti-slavery community. She created important alliances with Frederick Douglass, a former slave who later became an intellectual and statesman. Tubman also established a relationship with sympathetic anti-slavery church groups such as the Quakers and even managed to bribe noncommittal whites along the way. She created an aura of mystique and was highly revered, earning the title of "Moses of their people." Tubman had also cultivated contacts with wealthy and powerful white abolitionists in the north. Awed by Tubman's legendary mass escapes, these activists were instrumental in secretly organizing and providing financial and physical resources such as safe houses, food, and clothing for the Underground Railroad. Abolitionists in England and Scotland recognized her valiant acts and made donations to support Moses's operations.

The anti-slavery movement in the north had been largely dominated by elite white activists. However, by 1855, the black anti-slavery movement was well established in Philadelphia. Tubman, already a legend in these circles, was involved in the movement's activities of organized resistance. She established an alliance with a white anti-slavery activist, John Brown. John Brown had traveled to Tubman's house to meet her in 1858. The two shared a moral outrage against slavery and a mutual respect for each other; John Brown referred to Tubman as "general" and considered her accomplishments not unlike those of a war general.

Brown enlisted Tubman's help in recruiting black volunteers to participate in an uprising in the South. Tubman maintained support but was not involved in the final raid. In the fall of 1859, Brown and a group of 21 insurgents attacked Harpers Ferry, a federal arsenal in Virginia. The raid was a failure; two of Brown's sons were killed, along with eight other insurgents. A few insurgents managed to escape. Brown was arrested and later hanged for treason. Brown's insurgency and martyrdom had historical consequences for the course of slavery. Warrants of arrest were issued for Tubman, Frederick Douglass, and the "Secret Six" white conspirators that had been implicated in the plot. Tubman, who was living in Auburn, New York, was forced to flee to Canada.

While visiting a cousin in Troy, New York in 1860, Tubman was involved in another incident. After hearing that a fugitive slave had been arrested, Tubman decided to attend the court's proceedings to try to assist the fugitive. Disguised in a shawl and carrying a food basket, she was allowed into the hearing room. The fugitive was to be taken back to Virginia. At the right moment, "the frail old woman carrying a food basket" swung into action, wrenching the fugitive free and pulling him down the stairs where anti-slavery activists had gathered. Tubman held on despite beatings with clubs by pursuing policemen. Rescuers hauled the fugitive onto a boat and rowed it across the river. However, when the boat reached the opposite side, the fugitive was re-arrested. Following behind was Tubman along with 400 abolitionists shouting, "Give us liberty or give us death!" Tubman led the crowd to storm the building and retake the fugitive, whisking him away to safety. Tubman was left badly beaten and bruised with her clothes torn. The incident was widely circulated by newspapers around the country, and her heroism celebrated by anti-slavery societies.

Sometime in 1859, William H. Seward, a New York U.S. senator with presidential ambitions, offered Tubman a piece of property in Auburn, New York for $1,200. The Seward family had long supported the anti-slavery movement and sold property to emancipated slaves at discounted prices. Seward asked Tubman to make a down payment of $25 and $10 quarterly payments with interest. Black women did not own property at that time and Seward was breaking the law by abetting and aiding a fugitive slave.

Tubman had an urgent need for funds to pay her mortgage, support her relatives in St. Catharines and Auburn and support John Brown's fundraising efforts prior to the failed raid. Tubman discovered her gift of storytelling when she narrated her personal story of slavery to friends in New England. Her friends, mainly white educated anti-slavery activists, were moved by her courage, faith in God, and unwavering sense of morality. Her simple delivery, dramatic power, ability to change her voice to mimic different people, and wit while describing somber events helped her to connect with her audience. Despite her diminutive five feet and two inches, she had become a larger-than-life figure. She was able to raise money by telling her story to different audiences.

The election of Abraham Lincoln in 1860 and the beginning of the Civil War in 1861 marked a turning point in United States history and slavery in the southern states. Recognizing Tubman's leadership skills, the governor of Massachusetts asked Tubman to join the volunteer corps from Massachusetts and join the war effort in South Carolina. Earlier in the war, Tubman worked as a cook and nurse, providing care for African American soldiers and liberated slaves. Recognizing Tubman's talents, she was reassigned to help recruit former slaves to join the African American Regiment under General David Hunter. Tubman also performed spying missions behind Confederate lines. Though she was illiterate, she carefully memorized information and reported it back to Colonel Montgomery. On the night of June 2, 1863, Tubman led 150 black soldiers down the Combahee River. At the end of the raid, Tubman had led the soldiers in burning down many large plantations. She provided vital intelligence in directing Union ships away from Confederate soldiers and rescuing 750 slaves.

At the end of the Civil War in 1865, Tubman returned to Auburn, New York. Following the ratification of the 13th, 14th, and 15th amendments, anti-slavery movements disbanded. Tubman joined the women's suffrage movements, closely working with Susan B. Anthony and Elizabeth Cady Stanton. Following the death of her first husband, Tubman married Nelson Davis, a Civil War veteran, in 1869. Davis died of tuberculosis in 1888.

During the reconstruction period, Tubman was confronted with health and financial challenges. She had to rely on a group of close friends from the abolitionist movement for financial support. On her way to Auburn after the Civil War, Tubman had been beaten and injured by three train conductors. The conductors had refused to believe that being a black woman, her soldier's pass was authentic. Tubman's home was always filled with her extended family and charity cases. Although Seward had forgiven all her debts, she still owed money on her mortgage. Tubman had also been denied compensation for her role in the Civil War. After numerous appeals, Congress rejected her claims but agreed to increase her pension from $8 to $20 as a war widow.

Despite health challenges, Tubman devoted the rest of her life to her dependent family and philanthropic efforts. She had brain surgery in 1898, but refused anesthesia, opting to bite a bullet like amputees in the Civil War. She bought additional property at an auction and later donated it to the African Methodist Episcopal Zion Church to provide a charity home for old and indigent blacks. One of the buildings on the compound was named after John Brown, anti-slavery activist. The Harriet Tubman Home was opened in 1908. On March 10, 1913, after announcing to gathered family and friends that, "I go to prepare a place for you," Tubman died. She was buried with military honors in Auburn, New York.

Harriet Tubman can be described by Charismatic/Transformational and Servant Leadership Theories. Tubman had a clear *vision and mission* for the society she aspired to live in. She *inspired* courage and hope among the enslaved and those that believed in her *moral values*. Throughout her life, Tubman took *great risks* and *made sacrifices* to achieve her goals. She had great *rhetorical skills* and wit that helped her to cultivate a larger-than-life persona. She had *moral and ethical clarity* and put the needs of her family members and followers above her own throughout her life. She had deep and unwavering *faith* in her religion and felt connected with a higher power. Her *directive and supportive leadership behaviors* during the slave rescue missions reflect the Path-Goal Theory. Tubman's *boundary spanning* behaviors (labeled representation in the Reformulated Path-Goal Theory) were demonstrated with multiple alliances that she cultivated, ranging from fugitive slaves, church leaders, wealthy abolitionists, military generals, and politicians. Tubman had a *high cognitive capacity, determination*, and *fearlessness*; these reflect Trait Theories of leadership.

Discussion Questions

1   How important do you think Tubman's brutal treatment early in her life was in shaping her activities later in life?

2   Why do you think that uneducated Tubman was so effective at gaining support for her anti-slavery activities from influential and wealthy whites in the north?

3   It appears that story telling was an important skill of Tubman's for raising funds. Do you think that story telling is an important leadership skill for other types of leaders?

4   Do you think early experiences in life are generally critical in shaping leaders' later behavior?

Selected References

Anonymous. (n.d.). Harriet Tubman. Retrieved January 12, 2017 from www.pbs.org/wgbh/aia/part4/4p1535.html.

Anonymous. (n.d.). Timeline of the life of Harriet Tubman. Retrieved January 12, 2017 from www.harriet-tubman.org/timeline.

Blight, D. W. (Ed.). (2004). *Passages to freedom: The Underground Railroad in history and memory*. Washington, DC: Smithsonian Books.

Clinton, C. (2004). *Harriet Tubman: The road to freedom*. Boston, MA: Little Brown.

Humez, J. M. (2006). *Harriet Tubman: The life and the life stories*. Madison, WI: University of Wisconsin Press.

Larson, K. C. (2004). *Bound for the Promised Land: Harriet Tubman, portrait of an American hero*. New York: Ballantine.

3 Indra Nooyi

CEO of PepsiCo

Indra Nooyi was chief executive officer and chairperson of PepsiCo Incorporated, the second largest soft drink and food business in the world. PepsiCo major brands include Pepsi, Frito-Lay, Tropicana, Gatorade, and Quaker Oats. It operates in over 200 countries, and earns almost half of its revenue outside the United States. Nooyi was the CEO of PepsiCo from 2006 to 2018. She directed a major strategic shift in direction that diversified the company to overcome poor performance in specific markets and to emphasize healthy products for an increasingly health-conscious world. Her leadership resulted in significant increases in corporate revenues, creating a more sustainable and socially responsible company. Nooyi was rated by *Fortune* magazine as the number one most powerful woman in business in 2009 and 2010 and continues to create impact in society.

Indra Nooyi was born in a middle-class family on the southeast coast of India on October 28, 1955. As a youth she was unusual for the Indian culture, playing in an all-girl rock band and a women's cricket team. She received a bachelor's degree from Madras Christian College and an MBA from the Indian Institute of Management in 1976. After graduating, she held jobs in India as a product manager at Johnson & Johnson and a textile firm. After seeing an advertisement for the Yale School of Management, she applied and was accepted in 1978. After obtaining permission from her parents (who believed her emigration would make her completely unmarriageable), she left for the United States and worked nights as a dorm receptionist to earn a master's degree in public and private management at Yale in 1980. She then joined the Boston Consulting Group and worked on international strategy projects until 1986, moved to Motorola for four years where she directed corporate strategy and planning, and then worked for Asea Brown Boveri until 1994 as senior vice president of corporate strategy and marketing. In 1994 she began at PepsiCo as senior vice president of corporate strategy and development and held this position until 2001 when she was named president and chief financial officer.

As chief strategist at PepsiCo, she worked to make the company's products both profitable and healthy. She pushed then CEO Roger Enrico to spin off its struggling fast food restaurant division of Kentucky Fried

DOI: 10.4324/9781003333937-5

Chicken, Pizza Hut, and Taco Bell in 1997. She saw more future in healthier product lines with beverages and packaged foods. In 1999 she engineered and directed the $3 billion acquisition of Tropicana and in 2001 the $14 billion takeover of Quaker Oats, maker of Gatorade. She led the negotiation team for Quaker Oats and she was described as disciplined, focused, and very firm in her approach. The morning the acquisition was announced, she went to the Hindu temple and prayed. These acquisitions greatly enhanced the company's offerings of functional healthy foods and earnings rose quickly. She also directed the removal of trans fats from PepsiCo products well before other companies.

Howard Schultz, president and past CEO of Starbucks, has worked with Nooyi. He has been especially impressed with her willingness to do the right thing for her customers and employees. He further described her as welcoming input from others who disagree with her, but she is single-minded about following the path she believes is best for the company. Another observer described her as a deeply caring and considerate person who communicates well with people on the front line as well as the board-room. When Nooyi was selected for the CEO position, she immediately flew to visit with the other finalist who was the top operations manager for PepsiCo. They had worked together for a long time and she appealed to him to stay and help her continue creating her vision of the company. She told him she would do whatever was needed to keep him. She then enlisted three other company executives to help her convince the board to increase his salary to almost match her own and he stayed, resulting in what one writer called her team of rivals. This personal approach is characteristic of her leadership style, taking the time to listen to people who need to speak with her regardless of whether they agree with her.

Nooyi allowed her culture to affect her leadership and behavior at work and often wore a sari to official functions. In traditional Indian culture, mothers are often highly involved in their children's lives. After her promotion at PepsiCo, Nooyi (who is married with two children) visited her mother in India where they entertained many family friends. Nooyi noticed the visitors paid the most attention to her mother, congratulating her on doing such a fine job raising such a successful daughter. Nooyi remembered this and began writing thank you notes to the mothers of her major executives. She thanked them for doing such a wonderful job raising their child and how their son or daughter was doing an outstanding job for PepsiCo. The mothers were delighted and the executives appreciated her notes.

Shortly after becoming CEO, she announced her corporate mission for PepsiCo, which she called "performance with purpose." Its intent was to combine financial performance with social responsibility with each element reinforcing the other. She described her vision for the company as having three pillars that support the mission. The first element was human sustainability—providing products that include healthy choices such as low sugar and low-calorie drinks for health-conscious consumers. The second pillar was environmental sustainability—helping maintain the planet through increasingly efficient use of water, energy, and biodegradable packaging for all its products. The third element was sustainability of talent—attracting, training, and retaining the best people by providing a supportive healthy workplace where people can have a life in addition to their work. She encourages people to have fun at work, as she occasionally sings in the hallways, goes barefoot in the office, and sings karaoke at home and at corporate retreats.

With a market capitalization of nearly $100 billion, she noted that PepsiCo is larger than many countries and has tremendous influence in the world. She stated repeatedly that the company had to be a constructive member of the global society by encouraging a healthier future for people and the planet. She believed only this approach would ensure sustainable growth for the company. Nooyi is an inspirational speaker on behalf of her vision. She pledged that half of PepsiCo's revenue from the United States would come from healthy products such as oatmeal and unsweetened tea, they would seek to replace fossil fuels with wind and solar power, and they would actively campaign against obesity.

Nooyi has described herself as a workaholic and the CEO position as more than a job. She often sought help and information from colleagues and maintained close contact with several former CEOs. She had very high goals for herself and others and gave negative feedback when needed, often combining it with humor. She pushed people to solve problems until they found a solution, such as finding a replacement for unhealthy palm oil that was used in PepsiCo's products (rice bran oil was the replacement). She was a strong believer in the importance of boundary spanning as a leader of PepsiCo. She worked to stay connected with important organizations and people in business and government. She often did this through service on boards, foundations, councils, and international business forums that promote the arts, universities, world economic development, and other humanitarian causes. She believes leaders must work with governments and non-governmental organizations to understand their perspective and avoid becoming adversaries. She described much of her job as traveling to different areas of the world to meet employees and customers and spending quality time in these locations to learn the needs, desires, and cultural influences on the consumers of their products. She committed to invest $140 million in a new beverage plant in Russia, which is the tenth PepsiCo plant in Russia. She strongly believes that organizations today must think and act with a global perspective and strived to emphasize this at PepsiCo. Nooyi's socially responsible agenda for PepsiCo reflected in her own plans for the future. She has stated that, after her time at PepsiCo, she hoped to continue her service in Washington D.C. Indra Nooyi stepped down as CEO of PepsiCo in August 2018. She remained as Chairman of the Board of Directors until 2019.

After stepping down as Board Chairman, ending 24 years at PepsiCo and 12 years as CEO, Nooyi has served on several boards of directors of large companies including Amazon and Starbucks. She also served advisory roles at West Point and MIT and authored a book titled *My Life in Full* describing her upbringing in India and her career in the US.

Indra Nooyi's leadership can be described as Charismatic/Transformational due to her clear *vision* and *mission* to change the focus of PepsiCo toward more healthy products and socially responsible actions. While PepsiCo was doing well when she became CEO, she was determined to push her mission of human, environmental, and talent sustainability to ensure the company is a good global citizen and continues to prosper in the future. In addition, her excellent *communication skills, willingness to listen,* and *considerate supportive style* inspire people to join in her efforts to transform the company. These leader behaviors are addressed in models of Charismatic/Transformational Leadership and *considerate/supportiveness* is described in several other leadership models including Fiedler's Contingency Theory, Situational Leadership Theory, and Path-Goal Theory. Nooyi clearly emphasizes *boundary-spanning behavior* in her leadership as she serves on numerous boards and foundations to build networks and travels throughout the world to connect with consumers and producers of PepsiCo products. This behavior pattern is described in the Multiple Linkage Model and Reformulated Path-Goal Theories of leadership. She is also a highly *directive* leader when she determines to pursue a course of action. She focuses on specific issues and assures that her staff members contribute toward the goals she sets. This leader behavior is also described in Fiedler's Contingency Theory, Situational Leadership Theory, and Path-Goal Theory. When facing big decisions, she often consults with others who are informed about the issue and exhibits *participative leadership* in these situations. The Normative Decision Theory describes this behavior pattern. Nooyi's *cognitive capacity, determination, self-confidence, sociability,* and *integrity* reflect most elements of Trait Theories of leadership.

Discussion Questions

1   Why have the vision and mission for PepsiCo outlined by Nooyi been so well received by customers and employees?
2   Why does Nooyi believe she must spend much of her time boundary spanning (especially networking and representing) for PepsiCo?
3   Why did Nooyi believe she needed to change the strategic focus of PepsiCo?
4   Do you believe Nooyi's charismatic/transformational and supportive leadership style will be effective if she enters government service in Washington D.C.? Why or why not?

Selected References

Anonymous. (n.d.). Indra K. Nooyi Biography. Retrieved March 14, 2016 from www.notablebiographies.com/news/Li-Ou/Nooyi-Indra-K.html.

Halpern, T. (n.d.). Indra K. Nooyi. *Reference for Business: Business Biographies.* Retrieved March 12, 2016, from www.referenceforbusiness.com/biography/M-R/Nooyi-Indra-K-1955.html.

PepsiCo. (n.d.). Indra K. Nooyi—Chairman and chief executive officer. Retrieved March 14, 2016, from www.pepsico.com/About/leadership.

Withrow, S. (April 13, 2010). Tuesday Tip Indra Nooyi 11 April 2010. *Mountain Lakes International.* Retrieved June 5, 2011, from www.mountainlakesinternational.com/?tag=indra-nooyi.

4 Bill Wilson
Cofounder and Leader of Alcoholics Anonymous

William (Bill) Griffith Wilson was cofounder with Dr. Robert Smith of Alcoholics Anonymous (AA), the self-help organization of over 100,000 groups around the world. AA is composed of recovering alcoholics who dedicate themselves to staying sober and helping other alcoholics stay sober. Bill Wilson led AA from its inception in the late 1930s until 1955, dedicating his life to staying sober by working with other alcoholics to help them battle their addiction. He worked very hard to remain anonymous and humble by turning down a paid position as an alcoholic therapist when he badly needed money, offers of honorary degrees from distinguished universities, and an invitation to appear on the cover of *Time* magazine. He never saw himself as a role model for other alcoholics. He maintained he was an ordinary man who became an alcoholic and experienced a spiritual epiphany, which led him and Bob Smith to discover a set of steps that has helped many alcoholics stay sober.

Bill Wilson was born in rural Vermont on November 26, 1895. His father left ostensibly on a business trip when Wilson was ten years old and never returned. His mother left shortly thereafter to study osteopathic medicine, leaving Wilson and his sister to live with their grandparents. These experiences resulted in Wilson's first bouts with depression, which plagued him throughout much of his life. He read incessantly, played the violin, and eventually achieved success in athletics at school. Emerging from his depression, he fell in love with a young woman who was a classmate. Life began to look promising, but she died a short time later during surgery. Wilson was 17 and his depression returned. He spent time with his mother outside Boston, did poorly in school, and failed the entrance exam for Massachusetts Institute of Technology. Although he had not graduated from high school, he had enough credits to enroll in nearby Norwich University—a military school.

During the summer he met Lois Burnham whose family was from New York and wealthy. The family all liked Wilson, and Lois pulled him out of his latest depression. In 1917, all students at Norwich were automatically enlisted in the United States reserve forces and Wilson was eventually commissioned a second lieutenant. While in the military, he took his first drink, which relieved him of being self-conscious and anxious when around people

DOI: 10.4324/9781003333937-6

of high status. He became talkative and popular with a magnetic personality and liked the feeling. He and Lois were married in January 1918 before he was shipped to France. He never experienced combat but enjoyed drinking French wine.

At the end of the war, Wilson returned to New York with a drinking problem. He worked doing investigations for an insurance firm and studied law part time, but drinking caused him to put off picking up his degree and he never graduated. He began investigating industrial firms for investment groups and became successful as an astute investor and investment advisor. He and Lois were prosperous until the stock market crash of 1929, but he maintained his job as an advisor until he got fired when his drinking worsened. Wilson was unreliable and abusive to coworkers. On one occasion, he disappeared for two or three days only to be found passed out in the street. Wilson and Lois moved in with her parents in Brooklyn, New York.

In 1933 his sister's husband paid for Wilson to enter the Towns Hospital for detoxification of alcoholics. While at the hospital, he learned about the Oxford Group, a quasi-religious organization dedicated to moral renewal of its members. It included alcoholics and other addicts and had helped an old drinking pal of Wilson's reach sobriety. Its program included confession through sharing one's experiences, religious commitment, strict instructions in all aspects of one's life, and the obligation to "pass it on" by helping other addicts. During his last stay in Towns, he prayed for help with his addiction and experienced a spiritual epiphany, which convinced him he was cured. His doctor indicated that recovery was often brought on by an intense religious experience, and he and Lois both agreed that he looked different after this experience. He never took another drink.

Wilson returned to their home in Brooklyn and began attending Oxford Group meetings. He slowly realized that talking with other alcoholics about his own and their addiction helped him stay sober. The Oxford Group dedicated itself primarily to highly educated elites who became uncomfortable when alcoholic members were unruly. The alcoholics within Oxford began approaching Wilson who they saw as non-judgmental and patient, had experienced their addiction, was a great listener with empathy, and had an inspirational appeal when speaking. He told them his life story and his belief that a spiritual epiphany and surrender of rationality was needed to defeat alcoholism. They became a group of alcoholics within the Oxford Group, but Wilson noticed they only stayed sober for a short time before they relapsed. He spoke with his doctor at Towns Hospital and the doctor told Wilson to stop preaching and to talk with them about the disease of alcoholism.

In 1935, Wilson and Lois needed money. Wilson took a group of investors to Akron, Ohio, to attempt to take control of a small machine tool company. After several days, it appeared they had failed, and the investors returned to New York, leaving Wilson to try to salvage some type of deal. He was discouraged and paced back and forth in the hotel lobby just outside the bar. To avoid drinking, he phoned a local church to try to find an alcoholic to talk with. Eventually he contacted Dr. Robert (Bob) Smith, a physician and member of the local Oxford Group whose struggle with alcoholism was ruining his medical practice. Wilson told Smith he needed his support to keep from drinking. The two met that evening and both were changed forever. They shared their life stories and Smith was inspired by Wilson's ideas about how to become sober. He had read everything available on alcoholism, and they discussed what they had learned far into the night. The Wilsons moved in with Smith and his wife while they worked on a plan for their lives without alcohol. Smith relapsed one time but Wilson and Smith's wife dried him out in time for a scheduled surgery two days later. Bob never drank again. They developed an approach on how to counsel alcoholics and the Wilsons returned to Brooklyn.

After meeting Smith, Wilson became more confident in his speaking ability and was able to describe alcoholism and its effects with a disturbing vividness that touched every listener. He realized that no alcoholic wanted to hear s/he could not drink again, so he advocated "one day at a time." He still believed some type of spiritual epiphany was needed to defeat alcoholism, but he told alcoholics they should define God any way they wanted—as a symbol, a group with Good Orderly Direction, or a Group Of Drunks. They needed to surrender their personal will and place their trust in their own conception of God. Lois's mother died, and her father remarried, moved out, and gave the house to them. Wilson held regular meetings in their home for his group of alcoholics. He began these meeting by saying, "My name is Bill and I am an alcoholic" and this became the norm for each member. Their big house became a flophouse. Few could pay rent and eventually most of their personal belongings disappeared. At this point, he was offered a job at Towns Hospital as an alcoholic therapist, and the hospital owner offered to provide facilities and support for his work with the alcoholics. He was excited but when he described the offer to his group they said "No." They believed if he took money for what he was doing, it would cheapen his efforts and alcoholics would assume he was there for the money and lose faith in him. He took their advice and turned down the job. This consultation with the group became known as the "group conscience" and he used it as part of his regular practice. The will of the group had the final say in his decision making. Wilson and his group were not comfortable with the Oxford Group's evangelism, strict rules, and focus on elite and highly educated membership, so in 1937 they split with Oxford which eventually folded.

Wilson and Smith worked on their approach and became convinced they had the best method yet devised to overcome alcoholism. They combined the members' conception of trust in God and group conscience with complete anonymity of all members. They knew that no member wanted to reveal his entire name due to the stigma of being labeled an alcoholic and the risk of losing one's job. Humility was emphasized so no single member was featured above the group. Wilson tried throughout his life to maintain this anonymity and his actions spoke of his humility. He made plans with Smith for fundraising, missionaries, education centers, leaflets, books, and eventually hospitals that used their methods. But his group nixed all but the fund raising and approved of Wilson writing a book about their approach for those who could not attend meetings. He worked on the book for two years and *Alcoholics Anonymous* was published in 1939. It included the now famous 12 steps for alcoholics to overcome their addiction and the only requirement for membership was the desire to stop drinking.

Through his brother-in-law, he contacted the John D. Rockefeller organization. Rockefeller was a major philanthropist but he rejected their request for a grant of $50,000 and gave them an account for $5,000 with $30 per week salary for Wilson and Smith each. Rockefeller also authorized his advisors to help Wilson set up an alcoholic foundation with a board of directors composed of alcoholics and non-alcoholics. Rockefeller's son gave a dinner for AA that resulted in several donations, although they still needed money. The same year the book was published, the Wilsons lost their home to foreclosure. This began two years of living with various friends. Eventually they rented a converted stable for AA in New York and lived in two small upstairs rooms. Wilson's depression returned and he was visited by a Jesuit priest who told him that saintly men like Wilson were not happy and never would be. For some reason, this cheered Wilson up. Not long after this, a recovering alcoholic in one of their groups sold them a home on very reasonable terms a short distance north of New York City. They lived in this home for the rest of their lives.

In 1941 the editor of the *Saturday Evening Post* (which had over 3 million subscribers) commissioned a tough reporter to do an article on AA. Sensing a scam, the reporter visited the AA office and interviewed Wilson about the program. Wilson told the reporter his personal story and how AA started, then invited him to visit several AA groups in different cities. They did so and the reporter wrote a glowing article praising AA as the best method yet to overcome alcoholism. A similar article appeared in *Reader's Digest* a short time later. At their insistence, Wilson and Smith's names were disguised in the articles. Within a few weeks, thousands of letters of interest poured into the AA office. Wilson had previously answered all letters but this time he had to ask for volunteer help. The book began to sell and AA membership grew in 1941 from 1,500 to 8,000; in 1942 it reached 10,000 with almost 400 groups; in 1946 it had 30,000 members. Royalties on the book eventually eased Bill and Lois's financial problems.

When Pearl Harbor was attacked by the Japanese, Wilson tried to enlist in the army, but his alcoholic past prevented him from being accepted. Sticking to AA's anonymity and humility guidelines, he had neglected to describe his key role as cofounder and leader of the increasingly successful AA organization. Disappointed, he and Lois began visiting AA groups across the country. He was famous at these groups and was always asked to speak. His stories ignited passion in the members and he continued these visits throughout his life. He gathered ideas from these groups about how they operated regarding money, leadership, anonymity, service, and other issues. This later resulted in the 12 traditions he developed for groups to help them manage themselves. He used the word "traditions" to avoid the strictness implied by rules. He believed each alcoholic had his/her own story and path to recovery and he extended this idea of self-control to how the groups governed themselves.

Between 1944 and 1955, Wilson experienced another major depression that sometimes made him incapable of work. Yet during this time he and his staff initiated a regular AA newsletter in which he often wrote articles about alcoholism, he developed and published the 12 traditions, and he developed an organizational plan for AA. The plan included a General Services Office with rotating trustees, a board of directors composed primarily of AA members, and a regular AA conference in which all groups were represented. All of these changes were developed with heavy input from AA members and groups. In 1951, Lois founded Al-Anon, a self-help group for relatives and friends of alcoholics. Wilson continued his travel visiting and connecting with groups throughout the United States and Europe where AA was expanding. At the conference in 1955, he turned over the leadership of AA to the new board of directors and his depression disappeared.

Wilson was always a caring individual and, when he had money, he sent checks to both of his parents and friends who needed help. He believed God expressed his will through the "group conscience" and majority rule, which governed group decision making. He emphasized that all members who were helped by AA should try to help other alcoholics, that the core of AA was one drunk talking with another drunk about their addiction. In 1954 he was offered an honorary law degree by Yale University, which he declined. He also declined an offer to appear on the cover of *Time* magazine, even with only his back showing. His humility was more important.

Wilson knew he was weak in many ways. He was a chain smoker and eventually died in 1971 from emphysema and pneumonia. As he traveled, visiting AA groups, he ignited passions in members and other admirers and apparently engaged in several extramarital affairs. His life was a constant struggle with depression, alcoholism, infidelity, smoking, and the desire for privacy after 1955. His descriptions of his lifelong struggles probably made his communication with other alcoholics more genuine. He constantly tried to discourage the impression that he was a great leader or role model and insisted he had received much help in his battle against alcoholism. His struggles and striving for humility actually made him the role model other alcoholics needed to inspire them to stop drinking. AA current worldwide membership is over 2 million people.

First and foremost, Bill Wilson was a Servant Leader, providing for AA members' needs, *listening* with empathy, being *open* and *honest, humble*, and possessing *self-knowledge* with a clear *connection* to a higher power. His leadership was also *charismatic/transformational* and *participative*. His *inspirational speeches* to alcoholics, his *role model* as a struggling alcoholic, and the *vision* he described for AA are all charismatic behaviors. He also transformed the lives of thousands of alcoholics through the program and organization he cofounded and led. These leader behaviors and impacts are described in Charismatic/Transformational Leadership theories. Not all charismatic/transformational leaders are participative, but Bill's participative leadership is shown in his emphasis on the "group conscience" of the AA groups he led. He regularly submitted his decisions to his groups for feedback and approval, and only went forward with decisions that they approved. Participative leadership is described in the Normative Decision Theory, Path-Goal Theory, and the Multiple Linkage Model. Bill worked hard at *external boundary-spanning* leadership by contacting various organizations where he could locate alcoholics to talk with, meeting with reporters to help build the image of AA, negotiating with possible financial donors to the AA program, and personally answering thousands of inquiries about the AA program. Late in his life, he also engaged in extensive *internal boundary spanning* as he visited AA groups throughout the United States and Europe to strengthen the AA organization and learn from its members. Many of these boundary-spanning behaviors are described in the Multiple Linkage Model and Reformulated Path-Goal Theory of leadership. Bill was clearly a *considerate* and *supportive* leader as he went out of his way to try to help those suffering from alcoholism. These supportive leadership behaviors are described in the Servant Leadership model as well as Situational Leadership Theory, Path-Goal Theory, and the Multiple Linkage Model of leadership. His *determination* and *integrity* to AA reflect Trait Theories of leadership.

Discussion Questions

1   Why was Bill Wilson able to connect so effectively with alcoholics who wanted to stop drinking?
2   Do you think that Bill's efforts to remain anonymous as leader of AA were effective? Or would it have been better to accept awards for his work and create publicity for their program?
3   Why was Bill's idea of the "group conscience" important for the AA program?
4   Do you think that Bill's "flaws" were important to his success as leader of AA? Why or why not?
5   Would Bill have been effective leading a high technology business organization or a professional sports team? Why or why not?

Selected References

Cheever, S. (2004). *My name is Bill: Bill Wilson—His life and the creation of Alcoholics Anonymous*. New York: Simon and Schuster.
Raphael, M. J. (2000). *Bill W. and Mr. Wilson*. Amherst, MA: University of Massachusetts Press.

5   Atatürk

Father of Modern Turkey

Atatürk was a notable military and political figure of the 20th century. During the First World War, Atatürk played a decisive military role in rallying Turkish soldiers to contain Allied forces. Following the defeat of the Ottoman Empire, Atatürk led the remnants of the Ottoman army and ordinary Turks in fighting against invading Greek forces whose goal was to enforce the will of the Allied powers on the war-torn Turks. He successfully repelled British, French, and Italian troops and successfully led a military revolution to depose the sultanate and establish the modern Republic of Turkey. He created a sense of Turkish identity and brought Turkey into the modern world. In the 20 years to follow, Atatürk instituted major reforms to bring Turkey at par with other Western democracies.

The Ottoman Empire, since its origin in the 14th century, had become a multi-ethnic concatenation of Slavs, Greeks, Turks, Arabs, Armenians, Kurds, and others. The origins and rationale for its existence were based on routes of trade in the environs of the Black Sea and the Mediterranean. By the 20th century, the Ottomans were exhausted from a revolution within and ambitions of other empires nearby which had led to war with Italy, war in the Balkans, war with Greeks, and war with Russia along with internal liberal demands for a constitution. In the early 20th century, feeling the need for a Western alliance and support, the Ottoman powers made a treaty with Germany, recently unified and suffering from empire envy and empire ambitions of its own. The end of the First World War and the disastrous losses of the Central Powers (Germany, Austria-Hungary, Ottoman Turkey, and Bulgaria) brought the Ottoman world to an end. Other empires of the West, which themselves were destined for disintegration, would be lusting for its remains. During these events, Atatürk emerged as the most influential military and political leader in the region, changing the trajectory of history.

Mustafa Kemal Atatürk was born in 1881 in Salonika, Ottoman Empire which is presently known as Thessaloniki, Greece. Atatürk was born to a middle-class Turkish family of Muslim faith. Although the Ottoman Empire had been in existence for several centuries, it was not a unified nation and there was no homogeneous language, culture, or civic consistency. According to historians, Atatürk's father may have been of Albanian/Slavic descent,

DOI: 10.4324/9781003333937-7

while his mother was of Turkish descent. His mother, Zubeyde Hanim, was a stay-at-home spouse and his father, Ali Riza, was a minor government official. Atatürk had siblings, but only one sister survived childhood. Atatürk's education started in a religious school. At this early stage, Atatürk demonstrated an aversion to old Muslim customs as well as independence and defiance by his refusal to follow the Muslim practice of sitting cross-legged on the floor during class. Atatürk's father died when he was seven years old, and Atatürk was raised by his mother and close relatives. It has been documented that during Atatürk's birth, Ali Riza placed his sword over his son's cradle and dedicated him to military service. More importantly, he ensured that his son's early education would be in a modern, secular school, as opposed to the religious school preferred by his mother. By doing so, Ali Riza set his son on the path of modernization, for which Mustafa remained eternally grateful to his father.

Following the death of Atatürk's father, Zubeyde Hanim relocated to her stepbrother's farm situated outside of Salonika. Worried that her son would grow up uneducated, she sent Atatürk back to Salonika where he was enrolled in a school that prepared students for careers in the Ottoman civil service. At the age of 13, Atatürk enrolled and passed the entrance examination for the military middle school without his mother's knowledge. Atatürk had long admired the military and Western-style military uniforms worn by military cadets in his neighborhood. This inspired him to pursue a military career. Atatürk knew he was destined to be a leader at an incredibly early age. His sister recounted their childhood where Atatürk was too proud to play leapfrog, as he would not bend down to allow other children to jump over him. In secondary school, Atatürk's mathematics teacher gave him the nickname Kemal, which translates to "the perfect one." Atatürk had started to demonstrate traits of intellectual brilliance, fierce independence, and persuasiveness.

In 1896 Atatürk joined the military high school. Through his instructors, Atatürk became aware of the precarious situation facing the Empire due to military attacks by Greeks, Serbs, and Bulgarians. Atatürk also observed corrupt activities of the Muslim caliphate and undue religious influence on the lives of ordinary Turks. He developed a deep sense of patriotism and an aversion for the caliphate. After completing secondary education, Atatürk joined the military academy in Istanbul. He read extensively on politics, human rights, freedom, and other revolutions, including the French Revolution. German and French-trained military instructors also provided competing ideologies on revolutions.

Atatürk became, paradoxically, a loyal military officer and a young revolutionary thinker. His intellectual curiosity continued following his admission to the war college. He led a group of officers in producing and circulating a clandestine handwritten newspaper, criticizing the sultanate's autocratic regime. Atatürk intensified revolutionary efforts during his time at the Staff College. On passing out from the Staff College in 1905 with the rank of Captain, Atatürk and a group of friends rented an apartment in Istanbul with the intent of organizing their revolutionary activities. Atatürk was arrested and held under solitary confinement for running a clandestine paper and organization. Through the intervention of his friend's father, Atatürk was released, the group was disbanded, and its members assigned to distant parts of the Ottoman Empire. Atatürk was posted to Damascus.

In Damascus, Atatürk was shocked at the corruption and poor treatment of local people by government officials. He became involved in establishing a secret organization, "Society for Fatherland and Freedom." He was transferred to Salonika in September 1907, where he found another flurry of subversive activity. He joined the Committee of Union and Progress (CUP), the leading anti-government organization with connections to the nationalist and reformist Young Turk movement. The Young Turks Revolution of 1908 forced the Sultan to limit his own authority and reinstate the constitutional system of government. Atatürk, however, was not directly involved in that revolution. Atatürk did focus his efforts on military training and combat tactics. He translated German army manuals to Turkish.

During the First World War, Atatürk played a decisive military role in rallying Turkish soldiers to contain Allied forces. Following defeat of the Ottoman Empire, Atatürk led the remnants of the Ottoman army and ordinary Turks to fight against invading Greek forces whose goal was to enforce the will of the Allied powers on the war-torn Turks. He successfully repelled British, French, and Italian troops, and his military victories made him a war hero. This was especially true of the battle at Gallipoli on the straits of the Bosporus which would become a historic event of Winston Churchill's shame. However, during his military career, the profound suffering of ordinary Turks and humiliation of military defeats left a profound impact on Atatürk. He was openly critical of the sultanate and caliphate policies for weakening the Empire. In 1919, Atatürk would resign from the military to lead progressive military forces in the Turkish War of Independence. His goal was to create a strong secular republic, and to restore the dignity of the Turkish people. These struggles led to the establishment of the contemporary Republic of Turkey in 1923. In the ensuing 20 years, Atatürk led the new Republic and instituted substantial political, economic, and social reforms to modernize Turkey. He instilled a sense of pride in Turkish identity, brought the country into the modern world, resulting in a newfound achievement.

After leading Turkey to become a Republic in 2023, Atatürk declared, "... Our nation has crushed the enemy forces. But to achieve independence we must observe the following rule: National sovereignty should be supported by financial independence. The only power that will propel us to this goal is the economy. No matter how mighty they are, political and military victories cannot endure unless they are crowned by economic triumphs." Atatürk embarked on a path of economic transformation in agriculture, manufacturing, and infrastructure. He clarified his vision through public speeches but was also hands-on in ensuring the goals were successfully implemented.

Atatürk's leadership was instrumental in transforming and implementing modern education, social and legal reforms that promoted equality and women's rights. Women gained the right to vote and be elected to public office long before many Western countries. He introduced civil codes and abolished archaic laws that discriminated against women, emphasizing their essential role in the development of modern Turkey. In 1924, Atatürk invited American educational reformer John Dewey to advise him on educational reforms. He introduced Western education and adopted the Latin alphabet to replace the Arabic script. Another of the social changes was the Surname Law adopted in 1934. The law required all Turkish citizens to choose a surname for their family. Mustafa Kemal was then given the surname "Atatürk" (father of the Turks) by the Grand National Assembly,

One of Atatürk's most significant achievements was the establishment of a secular state. He pioneered the separation of religion and state, introducing secular laws and Western-style institutions that helped create a society where citizens' religious beliefs were a matter of personal choice. Atatürk passionately believed that secularism was a prerequisite for the progress of the nation and the freedom of its citizens. He viewed religion as personal and called upon faith to be cleansed of all superstitions and be purified and perfected by the enlightenment of real science.

Atatürk's leadership extended to political reforms that ensured the establishment of a strong and stable modern Turkey. He abolished the sultanate in 1922, bringing an end to the centuries-old Ottoman Empire. In 1924, he abolished the ancient caliphate along with the Sharia court system, and introduced a multi-party democracy, free elections, and constitutional reforms that laid the foundation for a representative government. By promoting democratic principles and institutions, Atatürk guaranteed that Turkey would be governed by the will of the people.

On October 15, 1927, Atatürk delivered a 600-page speech for six days to the Turkish Grand National Assembly. The speech is known as "Nutuk," translated as "The Speech." It has become a document of Turkish culture and is recited still in part and has been published in various translations. There is even a version available for children. Nutuk contained six themes that formed the basis of Kemalism. The first part was a historical background of the decline of the Ottoman Empire and reasons for the decline. The second was the Turkish War of Independence which resisted foreign forces through the suffering and sacrifices made by ordinary Turks, and the unity and resilience that led to victory. The third part described six principles upon which the modern Republic was founded. The "six arrows" consisted of republicanism, nationalism, populism, statism (industrialization of Turkey to become self-sufficient), secularism, and revolution. The fourth part described cultural and social transformation to modernize Turkey. The fifth part emphasized the significance of national identity and unity. The sixth part discussed Atatürk's vision for Turkey's future.

After retiring from the presidency in 1938, Ataturk remained engaged in state affairs. He was actively involved with the Republican People's Party (CHP), the political party he had founded, and provided guidance and support to his successor. He continued to write and deliver speeches articulating his vision for Turkey. Ataturk had gained respect in the international community and continued to maintain relationships with foreign leaders and participated in international diplomacy, ensuring Turkey's place in the international arena. Ataturk's health continued to deteriorate due to various health problems, including cirrhosis of the liver. Despite medical treatment, his condition worsened, leading to his eventual death on November 10, 1938, at the age of 57. Although Ataturk's retirement period lasted less than one year, he continued to exert influence and contribute to the development of Turkey, leaving a lasting impact on the country's trajectory. Ataturk had been married once to a Western-educated woman and divorced without biological children. In his will, he donated his possessions to the Republican People's Party, after providing for his sister, adopted children, the Turkish Language Association, and the Turkish Historical Society.

One of the enduring legacies of Ataturk in today's Turkey is his ideology of Kemalism, based on the six arrows. The Ottoman Empire was a vast multi-ethnic, multi-religious empire and this was a cause of division. In Kemalism, Ataturk secularized the country. This was no mean effort: the Empire had been the largest Muslim country under caliphate law at that time. He unified different ethnic and religious groups to remain part of a nationalistic Turkish Republic under the notion that there was only one ethnic group in the civic sense of Turkishness. To this day, Ataturk's transformational vision and determination continue to shape Turkey's political, social, and cultural landscape. In recent years, Kemalism has been contested due to the rights of minority groups such as Armenians and Christians. Conservative Muslims have also challenged this ideology with their own brand of nationalism. Scholars have also debated Ataturk's autocratic and paternalistic leadership that provided little space for dialogue and a larger-than-life personality cult that continues to loom over modern Turkey. However, Ataturk's legacy because of his sacrifices and heroic achievements of creating modern Turkey from the ashes of the Ottoman Empire has endured.

Several types of leadership theories are descriptive of Ataturk's leadership. He demonstrated Charismatic/Transformational Leadership in his impact on the Turkish people during the wars with Allied forces, the revolutionary war, and in the transformation of Turkey into a modern republic. Ataturk crafted the mission to liberate the remaining parts of the Ottoman Empire from Allied forces in moral terms and as a matter of preservation of dignity and foundations of the Turkish identity. Ataturk traversed different parts of the Empire, giving inspirational speeches to military officers and ordinary Turks on the shortcomings of the Empire, to gather a coalition against the sultanate and caliphate, and to garner support for secular demographic state. Atatürk had extreme self-confidence in his abilities to defeat the Allies with limited resources. He took significant physical and professional risks to launch a violent revolution against the sultanate.

Transformational leaders often inspire followers to uphold high morals and values. Atatürk's moral values and views were widely articulated in his actions, writing, and speeches. A question that has been asked by historians is whether Atatürk was involved in the Ottoman–German alliance during World War I. When Germany and the Ottoman Empire had formed an alliance, prior to World War I, Atatürk was a young military officer and had not become a political figure. As Turkey's president, Atatürk maintained a bilateral foreign policy of friendly relations and avoided alliances and conflicts. He was one of the few statesmen who had read *Mein Kampf* in its German edition. Atatürk was convinced that Germany would one day cause another great war and was horrified at the madness of Hitler's thoughts.

Following declaration of independence, Atatürk turned his focus to transforming Turkey. He had deep emotional intelligence and understood the need to change his leadership style from the autocratic leadership that had served him well during the war period to *situational leadership*. He set about articulating his vision for Turkey through inspirational speeches, coalitions, and alliances that he had developed over the years. The renowned speech, Nutuk, was delivered in 1927 over a period of 36 hours. Atatürk's *boundary-spanning* behaviors were evident early in his military career. He was a passionate student of the classics, Western political ideology, the French Revolution, and learned to speak German and French in addition to mastering Western graces such as the waltz. Atatürk applied these skills to full effect in cultivating lifelong friendships and developing a political network and international allies.

After achieving independence, Atatürk demonstrated aspects of *complexity leadership theory* as he set out to transform Turkey into a modern, secular, and democratic republic. These grand challenges required learning, innovation, and adaptation. Atatürk clarified his vision, invited foreign consultants to lead change efforts, and adapted Western institutional structures to bring Turkey at par with Western European countries. He perceived himself as a change agent and actively participated in national economic projects. Despite acquiring power through the sword, Atatürk made sincere efforts to bring about peace in the region. In 1923, Atatürk negotiated with the Allies and signed the Treaty of Lausanne, a significant pact that recognized Turkey's sovereignty and guaranteed the rights of minorities. Atatürk later declared, "Unless the life of the nation faces peril, war is a crime. If war were to break out, nations would rush to join their armed forces and national resources. The swiftest and most effective measure is to establish an international organization which would prove to the aggressor that its aggression cannot pay." His peace efforts were recognized by other nations and posthumously honored by UNESCO.

Discussion Questions

1 Discuss the various dimensions of Atatürk's effectiveness as a leader during both the Turkish wars and after independence.
2 How did Atatürk adjust his leadership style over the years to be such an effective leader?
3 Which leader behaviors did Atatürk demonstrate?
4 In his quest to transform and modernize Turkey after independence, what influence tactics did Atatürk apply?
5 What is your perspective on criticism of Atatürk's autocratic leadership behaviors and Kemalism in recent years?

Selected References

GüCLü, Y. (2002). Turkey's Relations with Germany from the Conclusion of the Montreux Straits Convention up to the Outbreak of the Second World War. *Belleten*, 66(245), 123–162.
Hanioğlu, M. Ş. (2017). *Atatürk. In Atatürk*. Princeton University Press.
Hughes, L. P. (1992). *Atatürk, Atatürkculuk and political development in Turkey*. The University of Mississippi.
Kinross, L. (1964). *Atatürk: The Rebirth of a Nation*. London: Weidenfeld & Nicolson.
Mango, A. (2002). *Atatürk: The biography of the founder of modern Turkey*. Abrams.
Singer, M. (1983). Atatürk's Economic Legacy. *Middle Eastern Studies*, 19(3), 301–311. www.jstor.org/stable/4282948.

6 Maria Montessori

The Medical Doctor who Revolutionized Early-Childhood Education

Montessori schools are known around the world as elite early-childhood preschools. However, the Montessori method was designed for a group of impoverished children with a purpose of transforming society by educating children to be self-driven, curious, and respectful. The visionary woman behind this method was Maria Montessori, a scientist with an assertive, driven, independent, and curious mind. Her method involved respect for the child, at liberty to act freely, and systematic observation, and it unleashed small children's inherent motivation to learn. In a time when women were not allowed to practice most professions, Montessori was one of the first women in Italy to obtain a medical degree. She was also a celebrated speaker advocating for children and women's rights, a published academic in medicine, anthropology, and pedagogy, and a successful entrepreneur. She failed at reaching every classroom and transforming the fabric of society, but her methods revolutionized early-childhood education and some of her innovations can be found in most preschools of today.

Maria Montessori was born in 1870 to an upper-class family in Chiaravalle, Italy. During her childhood, Montessori was a confident and strong-willed little girl, often the leader of her peers and sometimes a little smug. She had a passion for reading and learning and a strong work ethic, which she acquired from her mother, Renilde, an educated and intelligent liberal woman. Maria's mother would be a pivotal figure in her life, always supportive of her wish for autonomy and her professional aspirations. Both persistent and headstrong, Maria and her mother prevailed against a father who had conservative values and expected Maria to live a traditional life.

Maria was competitive at school and passionate about mathematics and hoped to become an engineer. She was one of the first girls in Italy to join a technical school, often facing pushback and abuse from her male peers, but receiving high marks in all her classes. In her senior year, she had a change of heart and decided to pursue a degree in medicine instead, a career that seemed impossible for a woman at the time. This decision was faced with strong opposition from her father. He arranged for her an interview with the head of the medical faculty at the University of Rome, Dr. Guido Bacelli, who attempted to dissuade her from applying to medicine. A

DOI: 10.4324/9781003333937-8

woman would never be admitted to the School of Medicine, he explained to a smiling Maria, who responded, "But I will become a doctor." Indeed, Maria satisfied all the admission requirements but her application was rejected. However, she persisted. In an interview later in life, she attributed her final admission into the School of Medicine to the active support of Pope Leo XIII, who after a conference with Maria publicly stated that medicine was, in fact, the best profession for a woman.

The University of Rome's School of Medicine was, at the time, a center of progressive thought. Maria learned from her teachers about social reform, care for education, gender equality, and concern for the lower classes. Her interest in social medicine led her to specialize in psychiatry and work in the university's psychiatric clinic with intellectually disabled children. There, she practiced scientific observation and discovery, experimented with recent advances in psychiatric medicine, and collected data for her doctoral thesis. In the clinic, children with diverse conditions (including dementia, autism, deafness, blindness, epilepsy, paralysis, and malnutrition) were committed for life and kept in large, cold, and empty pavilions. Maria noticed that the children were deprived of sensory stimulation, a necessary foundation for the development of basic skills and later abstract learning. She concluded that children did not require a medical solution but an educational one. Her publications advocating for the advancement of the school environment to meet the needs of disabled children quickly gained public interest and were quoted in the general press. In 1896, she became one of the first women in Italy to obtain a doctorate in medicine.

Her already impressive competence and charisma quickly made her a public figure in Europe. In 1896, she championed the defense of women's rights by speaking at Berlin's Women's International Congress. She advocated for equal compensation and women's right to administer property independently. She denounced the double oppression of the working woman, forced to work tirelessly at home and at work, left with no time to cultivate her intellect. In 1897, she was invited to represent the medical profession at the first pedagogical congress in Italy. The congress attendees enthusiastically acclaimed her proposal to create specialized education for children with intellectual disabilities in regular schools. This speech led to media interest and she was regularly invited to interviews and talks. Her auditoriums were full and she was often quoted in the newspapers.

In 1900, Montessori was appointed to co-direct the newly constructed *Scola Magistrale Ortofrenica*, an institute dedicated to training teachers to educate children with intellectual disabilities. The institute included a practice-demonstration school that she used to experiment with existing educational methods and develop new materials based on observation and experimentation. She co-directed the school with Giuseppe Montesano, whom she had met volunteering at the psychiatric clinic. Maria and Giuseppe fell in love and lived a non-traditional partnership based on gender equality, scientific collaboration, and common ideals. They did not get married but promised not to marry anyone else.

From her relationship with Giuseppe, Maria had a son, Mario, who was not recognized as legitimate by either of his parents. Guided by her mother, Maria sent her son to the country with a wet nurse. Though her parents were relieved, this created great distress for Maria and she would regularly travel to observe him from a distance. This decision allowed her to maintain her emancipation during this phase of her life and dedicate herself to her scientific work without the burden of a family. In 1901, Giuseppe recognized Mario as his legitimate son, making it impossible for Maria to see him again or claim any legal rights to the child. A few days later, he married another woman. Maria resigned from her appointment at the institute and discontinued her research work in psychiatry. Losing her son, her partner, and her purpose, Maria was brokenhearted and plunged into a prolonged personal crisis. Despite being a public figure, Maria managed to maintain her private life shielded from the public and the media.

Eventually, she earned a degree in anthropology and became an adjunct professor at the University of Rome, first in anthropology and then pedagogy. However, her legacy would come outside of academia. In 1904, she was approached by Eduardo Talamo, a philanthropist in Rome who had built a housing complex for impoverished people in the San Lorenzo neighborhood. The complex housed nearly 50 preschool children, three- to seven-year-olds, who spent their days running wild without adult supervision. Talamo decided to create a full-time daycare (the first in Italy) for these children and invited Montessori to assume the position of Director. She accepted but had to reconcile this position with her academic job. The appointment came without financial resources, teachers, or even furniture, but Montessori welcomed this limitation as a blank canvas to design the children's learning experience herself. She reached out to the queen, radicals, feminists, nobility, and the masons for financial support, and used these funds to hire a young and inexperienced teacher and commission furniture and other materials for the school. She ordered small-sized chairs and tables, small sinks, and low-placed mirrors that children could use autonomously. Children were given aprons with front buttons that they could put on and remove themselves. Instruments were placed in the bathrooms to track the children's growth. Because of the small furniture, the school came to be known as the *Children's House* or *Casa dei Bambini*.

Montessori's voice was soft and kind. She did not impose authority over the children but let them move and behave freely, always curious about their behavior, transforming every classroom event into a laboratory experiment. Children were presented with learning tasks and then asked to work independently. Montessori would spend all her free time at the school, sitting in a corner, observing the children, and taking detailed notes on what she saw. She systematically experimented with educational tools, keeping the ones that worked and putting together a set of proven materials for the education of preschoolers. Many of these tasks involved practical life skills such as pouring water into a glass, wiping a table after lunch, or fastening a button.

Children quickly became enthused and absorbed by their learning activities, demonstrating an extraordinary capacity for concentration.

One day, the children asked Montessori to show them letters, which she had not intended to do because they were already in the elementary school curriculum. She lacked funds to buy wooden letter blocks, so she cut letters from sandpaper and placed them in a box. Children played for hours with them, grabbing one at a time and tracing it with their finger, naming it, and placing it next to others to build made-up words. Months later, a child in her class exclaimed that he could write and using chalk wrote *mano, camino*, and *tetto* on the ground.[1] His excitement attracted other children who requested chalk to write as well. A curious Montessori then wrote on her board, "If you know how to read this, come up and hug me." Days later, one child came to her and hugged her. She then invented a new game, writing down toy names on pieces of paper and placing them in a box, and asking children to grab a piece of paper, read it out loud, and then go to grab the toy to play with it. Smaller children were offered toys to play with instead but, to her surprise, they ignored the toys and asked to participate in the reading exercise.

The precocity of her pupils' reading ability brought sudden attention to the Montessori method. Newspapers called it the *Miracle of San Lorenzo*. In a public speech during the opening of the second Children's House, Montessori spoke about the important communal service that schools played for families. Schools had the power to be a friendly source of support for families and protect mothers from the imposition of being sole child carers, allowing them to grow other aspects of themselves. Encouraged by an American friend to publish her method, her book *The Montessori Method* would be an instant sensation.

In 1912, following her mother's death, Maria finally reached out to her son Mario, who was 15 at the time. To her relief, Mario was also longing to meet her and they arranged a secret meeting during a boarding school field trip. During the trip, they made an impromptu and risky decision: Mario would drive back to Rome with Maria and live with her. Mario's father Giuseppe realized that he could not oppose this arrangement and mother and son were finally free to be together. From that moment on, they would spend almost every hour together and Mario would eventually become her trusted assistant.

Popular interest in her method led to a series of training courses for teachers. Her students found her lectures deeply moving and she began to build a following of young women who worked tirelessly alongside her. New Children's Houses began to emerge, attempting to reproduce the original results. The British ambassador opened a Children's House for the embassy in Rome with wonderful results even though children often spoke different languages. The Mayor of Rome developed an initiative to extend her method into public schools and elicited Montessori's help in training the teachers. These experiences with early-childhood education in Rome became the center of attention for educators worldwide. People from all over the world would come to her house to meet her. Her mail was so abundant that it was impossible for her and her students to manage. Her students opened new schools in other countries, bringing her to Spain, Britain, the Netherlands, the United States, India, New Zealand, and Australia to advise and train teachers.

In this moment of success, Montessori began to experience contradictory feelings about the popularity of her method. On the one hand, notoriety allowed her to reach out to more children worldwide, bringing her closer to achieving her vision. It also allowed her to quit her academic appointment, which she had neglected, and dedicate herself entirely to studying and disseminating her methods. On the other hand, all of these initiatives made it harder for her to control the results of her work. Often, her method was implemented too quickly and superficially, seeking academic achievements but failing to adopt her pedagogical philosophy. She also found the need to fight for the operative and financial control of her business, often experiencing frustration and a lack of trust in her partnerships. This contradiction is exemplified in her experience in America, where a few magazine articles generated an explosive demand for Montessori's book, methods, and materials among educators and families. Samuel McClure, a dynamic and entrepreneurial businessman, offered to facilitate her access to the American market. Maria's idealism and explosive character would often clash with McClure's pragmatism and continued pressure to monetize her method. The partnership ended badly but it gave her an unprecedented worldwide projection and celebrity status.

Montessori continued working with schools around Europe for years alongside her son. In 1922, the Italian government invited Montessori to return to Italy and oversee the implementation of her method in all nursery and elementary schools in the country. As she began her work that year, Benito Mussolini marched into Rome and overthrew the democratically elected government. Surprisingly, Mussolini's new government decided to continue the implementation of the Montessori method in Italian schools, which they saw as a demonstration of Italy's preeminence in the world. Montessori, with surprising naïveté, accepted the opportunity to pursue the realization of her vision without considering the irreconcilable differences between the fascist ideology and her own philosophy of social reform and pacifism. Her collaboration with Italy's fascist administration would be widely criticized and cast a long shadow over her enduring legacy. However, their opposing views soon began to clash and she did not remain quiet. She refused to order the teachers in her schools to take the fascist oath, making Mussolini furious. She also declared in public talks and newspaper articles that indoctrination turns children into fanatics eager for armed conflict, publicly opposing Mussolini's plans to indoctrinate children as young as three into a fascist ideology. In 1934, during a conference about education for peace, Montessori alerted the audience to the presence of fascist surveillance. She sent Mario to investigate and, upon his return, she abruptly ended the conference and they left the country together that night. The next day, all Montessori schools were closed in Italy, Germany, and Austria, and Montessori statues were burned in the public squares of Berlin and Vienna.

Maria and Mario spent years traveling to Spain, Britain, the Netherlands, and India, where Mario took a prominent role in their joint work. After the war, Montessori would return to a Europe in ruins and begin her work to reconstruct the schooling systems. Only a few years later, she received high honors from a multitude of countries, including France, the Netherlands, Switzerland, England, Austria, Ireland, and Scotland. The UNESCO general meeting welcomed her with warm applause and she was repeatedly nominated for the Nobel Peace Prize. She spent her last days in a coastal city in the Netherlands and died peacefully in 1952, surrounded by her son and his large family.

Maria Montessori had many personality traits associated with effective leaders. She had *assertiveness* and *self-reliance* to find her own purpose and a strong *determination* to succeed in an environment that expected her to be content at home. She was often *dominant* and controlling and exhibited a *high need for socialized power*. Even though these traits led to frequent conflict with her collaborators, they also helped her fight to protect her legacy.

Montessori was also a Charismatic/Transformational leader. She was a *persuasive* and moving speaker who inspired others to work alongside her in the pursuit of a fair and equitable society. This inspiring *vision* took on different shapes throughout her life: equal opportunities for both genders, dignity and growth for the intellectually disabled, and finally, respect and freedom for small children. Her *commitment* to this vision and her *trust in her ability to succeed* were *inspiring* to her followers. She devoted her life to her purpose, relegating everything else to it, including her own family life. She *modeled* the behaviors of the transformed adult that she preached to her students and inspired them to protect children's liberty to find their own motivations. She also showed *individualized consideration* for students and patients throughout her life, often bringing them to her own home for round-the-clock care. However, her charisma was ineffectual in the management of her business partnerships, often unsuccessful and frustrating.

Montessori was assertive and charismatic outside the classroom, but inside the classroom, she was a *servant leader*. She let the children be the leaders in their own exploration and limited her role to showing *support* and *optimism* for their ability to succeed. She relied on *empathy* and *humility* to inspire trust and helped the children be *autonomous* and *committed* to their education.

An estimated 60,000 schools around the world use the Montessori method today. New research is providing stronger empirical evidence of the positive impact that a Montessori education has on children's independence and self-direction, creativity, social skills, and academic performance. However, Montessori's legacy is no longer seen as a force for social fairness and egalitarianism. Maria Montessori's decision to monetize and maintain control over her method precluded her from influencing every classroom and the method is seen today as an elite education, accessible mainly to wealthy white children.

Discussion Questions

1   Do you think that Maria Montessori's unique profile as an accomplished, young, wealthy, beautiful woman helped or hindered her ability to lead successfully?
2   Why do you think that Maria Montessori used such opposing leadership styles inside and outside the classroom?
3   Which of the two styles do you think was more authentic to her true self?
4   Do you think that Maria Montessori's effort to introduce her educational methods in all Italian nursery and elementary schools during Mussolini's fascist dictatorship in Italy was misguided?

Note

1   Hand, chimney, and roof.

Selected References

De Stefano, C. (2022). *The child is the teacher: A life of Maria Montessori*. New York, NY: Other Press.

Robson, D. & Franco, A. (2023, January 31). Montessori: the most influential school? Retrieved from www.bbc.com on June 30, 2023.

Kramer, R. (1976). *Maria Montessori. A biography*. New York, NY: Diversion Books.

Povell, P. (2010). *Montessori comes to America. The leadership of Maria Montessori and Nancy McCormick Rambusch*. Lanham, Maryland: University Press of America.

Winter, J. (2022, March 3). The miseducation of Maria Montessori. *The New Yorker*.

7 César Chávez
American Labor Leader

César Chávez is one of the most prominent labor leaders and civil rights activists in United States history. He fought tenaciously for improving the work and living conditions of farm workers in the United States. He co-founded and led the first truly successful Farm Workers Union which resulted in great improvements for farm laborers. He succeeded in spite of the migratory nature of these workers and tremendous opposition from powerful growers, politicians, legal officials, and another powerful union. He was a forceful advocate of nonviolence and he came to symbolize the history and collective spirit of farm workers in the United States.

Chávez's grandparents emigrated from Mexico in the late 1800s before Arizona became a state. He was born in 1927 on the small family farm near Yuma, Arizona. When he was 11 years old, his family lost the farm and most of their possessions during the Great Depression and they moved to California to work as laborers in the fields. There was a long history of immigrant labor in the farm fields of California. Large banks and industrialists had bought up much valley land to produce food to be shipped all over the country. They used mostly immigrant labor on the farms and the pay and working conditions were miserable. By the 1930s, most of the farm workers were Mexican or Filipino immigrants earning about $0.60 for picking 100 pounds of cotton. Any efforts to gain better wages through strikes were met with violence from growers.

Chávez's family, with six children, moved throughout California following the harvests. All members of the family worked in the fields and lived with the poorest of the poor—often in tents with no running water or toilets available. Chávez grew up amid this backbreaking farm work and observed the injustices of low pay and poor working conditions. He volunteered for military service in World War II and returned to the fields after the war. He soon married Helen Fabela whose family was composed of farm workers and was familiar with the conditions in the fields. While they were living in a barrio (a poor neighborhood of Mexican Americans) in San Jose, he met a civil rights activist named Fred Ross. Ross worked for the Community Service Organization (CSO), which campaigned for the rights of Latin Americans, and he recruited Chávez to help recruit Latinos for their cause.

DOI: 10.4324/9781003333937-9

Chávez learned from Ross how to organize and lead poor laborers. He also learned from Father Donald MacDonald who worked to obtain social justice for Latinos. In the 1950s, Latinos were still discriminated against in restaurants, parks, and theaters, and were usually paid considerably less than white farm workers for the same work.

Father MacDonald introduced Chávez to writings by St. Francis of Assisi (an Italian monk who devoted himself to helping the poor) and Mohandas Gandhi, who advocated nonviolence in his campaign against the British for Indian independence.

Chávez also studied the actions of Martin Luther King, who followed Gandhi's guidance. Chávez realized that to be a successful leader he must be a positive role model for followers and set an example of nonviolence. At first he worked in the fields during the day, and at night he taught farm workers about their civil rights and registered them to vote. Later he became a full-time organizer for CSO, earning $35 per week traveling around California fighting racial and economic discrimination against Latinos. From 1959 to 1962 he was the Executive Director of CSO where he gained the respect of farm workers by advising them about insurance, citizenship applications, translations, and other personal business. He sought out and gained endorsements of Catholic priests for his efforts which increased his legitimacy in the eyes of farm workers. Chávez became frustrated when the CSO membership refused to direct efforts to form a union for farm workers, and moved his family to Delano in the San Joaquin Valley, the heart of California farmland. He rented the cheapest house he could find for his family, which eventually included eight children, he dressed in work clothes, and began driving up and down the valley in his old station wagon talking to farm workers about their wages and working conditions.

Chávez advised workers how to deal with supervisors in the fields and publicized growers' illegal tendency to hire *Braceros* instead of resident farm workers. *Braceros* were temporary farm workers from Mexico who first came to the United States to fill in for resident laborers who were serving in World War II. The program was not discontinued when the war ended, and growers were supposed to use *Braceros* only when resident workers were unavailable. But they often hired them at lower wages and/or used them as strike breakers—replacing resident workers when they were striking for better wages and working conditions. This not only took the jobs of resident workers, it rendered their strikes ineffective. Chávez convinced Dolores Huerta, a talented negotiator and organizer with the CSO, to join him in his efforts.

Chávez and Huerta worked in a garage turning out pamphlets and they traveled throughout the San Joaquin Valley signing up members for a farm workers' union. Chávez again gained the active support of Catholic priests in the area. After six months they held an organizing convention in Fresno, north of Delano, and in 1962 they formally adopted the name National Farm Workers Association (NFWA) with Chávez as president and executive officer. Farm workers were not covered by the National Labor Relations Act, which guaranteed, for other workers, the right to join a union and bargain collectively with employers. They agreed to focus on lobbying the governor for a $1.50 per hour minimum wage, unemployment insurance, the right to bargain collectively as a union, and to set up a credit union for members. Chávez soon borrowed money to start the credit union which eventually loaned out over $5 million in small loans to farm workers.

Chávez's wife and children continued to work in the fields to support the family, and farm workers often gave them food to live on. He started an underground newspaper that advocated for workers' rights and often used humorous cartoons that addressed farm worker issues that illiterate workers could understand. Early in its life, the NFWA supported several groups of unhappy workers who declared strikes with little success. He made all members promise they would be nonviolent in all dealings with growers and others. In 1964, he was offered a job by the Peace Corps as director for Latin America for $21,000 per year. He turned it down to stay with his $50 a week job in the union that he supplemented by working in the fields.

In 1965, Filipino grape workers went on strike over being paid less than other farm workers for the same work. Chávez called an NFWA meeting and spoke in a calm but determined voice. He compared their struggle for fair treatment to Mexico's struggle for independence. He said they were struggling for the freedom and dignity denied to them by poverty. He convinced the members to join with the Filipinos in the strike and directed them to picket, which meant standing at the entrance of the largest grape grower's farm and trying to convince others not to enter. He coached them on how to picket nonviolently. He contacted other unions, churches, and spoke at university campuses to generate support by sending food for the strikers. He invited them to come and see the conditions of the farm workers, and activist students and clergymen began to appear at the strike. More farm workers and activists became involved. Chávez then directed NFWA members to follow the grapes from warehouses to shipping points, and picket, resulting in unionized longshoremen in Oakland refusing to cross the picket line to load grapes on ships. Walter Reuther, President of the AFL-CIO (the powerful federation of dozens of national and international unions), marched with Chávez and the NFWA and pledged financial support for the strikers. A United States Senate subcommittee on migratory labor held hearings in Delano on working conditions at the farms. Senator Robert Kennedy was a subcommittee member and he sided with the strikers, befriended Chávez, and marched with him on one of their picket lines.

Chávez then led a 300-mile march from Delano, up the San Joaquin Valley, to the state capital in Sacramento. The purpose was to dramatize the grape strike and lift the spirits of the union members. They started with around 100 people and much publicity from the press. Chávez suffered bloody blisters, but he limped into the state capital and held a rally with over 10,000 supporters. Shortly before their arrival, the grower who they were striking against agreed to recognize the NFWA and signed a labor agreement. At the rally, Chávez demanded the governor call a special session of the legislature and enact a law, which guaranteed farm workers the right to bargain collectively with growers. He then emphasized to the crowd the importance of their victory, but that they must show humility and remain dedicated to their cause.

Another large grower began negotiating with the union but threatened members when they tried to speak with their workers. Chávez directed them to cut off negotiations and called for a boycott, which urged people not to buy the grower's numerous products. He had a religious altar built on the back of a station wagon and parked it next to the grower's farm where people prayed for the workers. The altar became famous in the press, and publicity increased for the union. On very short notice, the grower announced an election to choose a union for their workers and a short time later announced that the Teamsters union had won the right to represent their workers. The Teamsters had previously organized truck drivers and packers for agricultural products but not farm workers. Chávez saw their action as a takeover of NFWA members and went to the farm advocating a strike. He was arrested and shackled but released the next day. News spread of his arrest and the Teamsters' actions. California Governor Ronald Reagan, Senator Robert Kennedy, and others urged the grower to hold a legitimate election. The grower allowed the new election, NFWA won, and other major growers of wine and juice grapes in California signed contracts with the union.

Chávez then addressed growers of table grapes who refused to negotiate. He held a meeting of union members who voted for a strike. A large grower brought in strike breakers and obtained a court order opposing the strike. So, Chávez declared a boycott of the grower's grapes. When the grower shipped grapes under another name, Chávez initiated a national boycott of all California table grapes, which became the largest most successful boycott in United States history. Violence erupted between strikers and growers' employees, and Chávez worried about how to control his members. He confiscated guns, expelled union members who provoked violence, and began a 25-day fast until members recommitted themselves to nonviolence. The fasting idea came from his studies of Gandhi, who used the fast as an effective symbolic gesture. The fast caused a dramatic decline in his health but it increased the members' dedication and their perception of him as a brother and a leader with tremendous moral stature and authority. *Time* magazine described the boycott, books were written about it, and in 1970 the major growers of table grapes eventually recognized the NFWA and signed contracts with the union. The grape strike and boycott had lasted five years, and 17 million Americans had refused to buy grapes until it was settled.

The same year, Chávez led a 3,000-member march through Salinas and addressed the workers about a secret deal the Teamsters had signed with the salad growers to represent their farm workers. He described how a few white men from the Teamsters and growers could determine the destinies of Latinos and Filipinos in the California fields. He urged them to join the NFWA rather than the Teamsters. Many responded and Chávez lobbied the AFL-CIO and a Catholic Church fund for financial support for a strike, directed a lettuce boycott, and began another fast. The Teamsters then backed off from organizing lettuce workers and the NFWA negotiated much improved wages and working conditions for these workers. Other large growers began meeting with Chávez to avoid boycotts of their produce.

In 1971, the NFWA became the United Farm Workers Union (UFW) and was affiliated with the AFL-CIO. The lives of UFW members were much improved as they saved money, many bought modest homes and settled in one place, and their children finished school. They had toilets in the fields, drinking water, work breaks, pensions, seniority rights, medical insurance, opportunities for advancement, and respect.

In 1973, the Teamsters again tried to organize the grape workers in the San Joaquin Valley. Judges issued injunctions against picketing and the Teamsters tried to incite violence with the UFW members who continued to picket the fields. Chávez visited the picket lines, sought AFL-CIO strike funds, pursued lawsuits against the Teamsters and growers for conspiracy, and went to Washington, D.C., to lobby for a federal investigation into violence against the farm workers. With the press present, he stood in front of huge insulting Teamsters and told them the UFW picketers would not leave. When two UFW picketers were killed, Chávez called off the picketing until federal officials would guarantee the safety and rights of picketers.

In 1975, he successfully lobbied the new governor, Jerry Brown, to help the legislature pass the Agricultural Labor Relations Act (ALRA) of California. It guaranteed the right for farm workers to organize and bargain collectively and set up an office to supervise union elections and to investigate violations. He then successfully fought growers' efforts in the state legislature to block funding for the ALRA and he finally convinced the Teamster leadership to stop all organizing efforts of farm workers.

In the late 1970s his leadership had resulted in significant increases in wages and benefits for UFW members. By the 1980s, union membership was around 100,000 and some farm workers under piece rate systems could earn up to $20 per hour. Union elections were common and workers usually selected the UFW. Chávez became more directive and controlling during this time. He laid off many professional staffers and hired young people from farm worker families, believing that their commitment was greatest and they identified with the members. Chávez kept the union highly centralized without local affiliates because so many farm workers were still migrants. He was viewed as a cultural icon, but some began to question his leadership. Chávez wanted the union to fund a Latino lobby to pursue the interests of all Mexican Americans, but staffers and members insisted they continue their focus on farm workers.

Chávez had opposed the use of pesticides for decades as more cancers and birth defects began to appear among farm workers. Governor Deukmejian, who succeeded Jerry Brown, vetoed a bill to help protect workers from pesticides and cut funding to the ALRA. Chávez responded by making a short film titled *The Wrath of Grapes* that showed the damage pesticide use had on farm workers. The film was shown around the country and generated much support for the union against pesticides. At age 61, Chávez began another fast to force growers to bargain regarding pesticide use. The fast lasted 36 days and was ended due to serious health concerns. He continued speaking out against pesticides over the next few years. In April 1993, Chávez was weakened by the flu and died in his sleep of natural causes. In 2004, California passed a law controlling pesticide use, but it remains a controversial issue. Chávez was awarded the Presidential Medal of Freedom posthumously in 1994.

The leadership of César Chávez has been described as Charismatic/Transformational due to his *role modeling, risk taking*, and *inspirational speeches*. He became a *symbol* for farm workers who identified with his poor background, sacrifices, and his family's hard work in the fields. He was also highly *directive* of union members when quick response was necessary and he continuously *supported* farm workers through strike funding and participating in picket lines, marches, and lobbying efforts to improve their working conditions. These leader behaviors are described by Fiedler's Contingency Theory, Path-Goal Theory, Situational Leadership Theory, and the Multiple Linkage Model. He was constantly active in *boundary spanning* by representing the Farm Workers Union to growers, different levels of government, law enforcement officials, Teamsters, and the public. This leader behavior is addressed by the Multiple Linkage Model and Reformulated Path-Goal Theory. His *empathy, supportiveness, role modeling, competence*, and *connection with poor farm workers* reflected a Servant Leadership approach that was dedicated to the improvement of the living and working conditions of farm workers. Although Chávez was five feet six inches tall and often quiet and inconspicuous, he demonstrated *determination, assertiveness, self-confidence, cognitive capacity*, and *integrity* which are described in Trait Theories of leadership.

Discussion Questions

1   What did César Chávez do to make the farm workers so devoted to him and the union?
2   Why was Chávez's farm worker union so successful against the big growers and the powerful Teamsters union?
3   Do you think Chávez would have been equally successful in leading a profit-making business organization? Why or why not?
4   Give one or two examples of Chávez's actions that reflect the Servant Leadership model.
5   Give one or two examples of Chávez's actions that reflect Charismatic/Transformational Leadership.

Selected References

Ferriss, S. & Sandoval, R. (1997). *The fight in the fields: César Chávez and the farm workers movement*. New York: Harcourt Brace.

Griswold del Castillo, R. & Garcia, R. A. (1995). *César Chávez: A triumph of spirit*. Norman, OK: University of Oklahoma Press.

8   Winston Churchill

British Prime Minister, Wartime Leader, and Statesman

Winston Churchill served as Prime Minister of the United Kingdom during World War II and is known as an outstanding wartime leader. He actively opposed Hitler from the beginning of the German aggression and imposed his imagination and will on the British public to defeat Nazi Germany and the Axis powers. He was also an officer in the British Army, a war correspondent, writer, historian, statesman, orator, and filled many other top-level government positions. He received the Nobel Prize for Literature in 1953 and was the first person to be granted honorary citizenship of the United States.

Churchill was born on November 30, 1874, on a huge family estate in Oxfordshire, England. He was a descendent of the famous first Duke of Marlborough and spent part of his youth in Ireland while his father was Viceroy to Ireland. His father was a flamboyant and outspoken member of the British Parliament who served as Chancellor of the Exchequer. His father also possessed an incredible memory, loved luxury, and had a mercurial personality, traits inherited by his son Winston. His mother, Jennie Jerome Churchill, was born in New York to a wealthy financier and established her status in British high society. Churchill attended three private schools where he showed an early interest in fencing, shooting, and a military career. He was not a good student but loved history and studied English for several years because he could not master Latin or Greek. In school he was competitive and mischievous, stubbornly independent, indifferent to authority, and he developed skill as a public speaker. He attended Sandhurst, the Royal Military College, where he further improved his skills at public speaking and argument, although he had a slight speech impediment that he worked hard to overcome. He was commissioned as a cavalry officer in 1895, the same year his father died at age 46.

Churchill believed he would also die young like his father and became known for his impatience. He obtained an assignment as a war correspondent to observe and write about the Spaniards' fight against Cuban guerrillas. Soon after, he was posted to India, where he was known for his polo playing, and engaged in action against rebellious Indians who were fighting British rule. He received praise and notoriety for rescuing a wounded officer

DOI: 10.4324/9781003333937-10

and for his war-related articles published in Britain. When the action subsided, he wrote his first novel about political intrigue. Churchill's mother was wealthy and socially connected in Britain. She helped him obtain postings to war zones for his war correspondence and to build his popularity and sent him extra money to support his developing addiction to luxury. He obtained a position in the Sudan where a British force was sent to retaliate for the murder of a British officer. He participated in a cavalry charge, killing three enemy soldiers and helping to break the battle of Omdurman. However, Churchill was critical of the British slaughter of enemy combatants. He returned to Britain and published another book on the Sudan campaign, resigned his commission, and ran unsuccessfully for a position in Parliament.

In 1899 a war broke out in British-controlled South Africa between Dutch/German settlers (known as Boers) and the British who wanted to participate in the Boer diamond mines. Churchill obtained a commission as a war correspondent, traveled to South Africa, and accompanied a scouting expedition on a train that was attacked. He helped the wounded escape on the train and was then captured. The Boers learned of his identity and treated him well, calling him "Lord's Son." After numerous attempts, he escaped and traveled nearly 300 miles to Mozambique where he contacted the British Consul. He resumed reporting on the war and criticizing the British military leadership, something he did often throughout his life. Churchill returned to Britain in 1900 to a heroic welcome.

On a second attempt, Churchill was elected to Parliament. Since Parliament was not in session, Churchill went on a lucrative lecture tour in Britain and the United States. His speaking style was self-confident, sincere, and vehement, showing his total belief in his message; he had an excellent sense of humor. His grasp of history, excellent memory, intelligence, and skill with words entertained his listeners, including Members of Parliament who appreciated good rhetoric. He was a favorite at dinner parties and loved the social scene in London. He changed political parties in 1906 and was appointed to his first government cabinet post as Undersecretary to the British Colonies. He championed bills in Parliament dealing with issues that helped working people such as limiting miners' work days, an unemployment act, and an old age pensions act. As President of the Board of Trade he worked harder than any predecessor. In 1908 he married beautiful Clementine Hozier from a distinguished family. She became his frugal partner for life who helped them survive financially, despite Churchill's lavish lifestyle. In 1910 he was appointed Home Secretary, responsible for internal affairs in England and Wales, immigration, citizenship, policing, and national security. He faced several severe strikes. His tactic was to bring disputing parties together, feed them plenty of drink, and usually their mood improved, leading to more friendly talks and an agreement.

In 1911 Germany began belligerent actions with other countries and Churchill began preparing Britain for war. The combination of intelligence and memory gave him a vision of the future course of international events that few others possessed. He directed a push to pass a bill allowing the government to intercept any correspondence, eventually resulting in every major spy being captured during World War I. He wrote a description for Parliament of likely developments with a timetable in case of war, predicting the complete defeat of the French army. The document was criticized and ignored but predicted the course of events three years later almost exactly. When the Prime Minister realized war was unavoidable, he transferred Churchill to become head of the Admiralty. Churchill directed the construction of warships with 15-inch guns, larger than the standard size. Naval officials objected, saying that they might be unworkable, but he persisted, and the British Navy outgunned all German warships throughout the war. He also directed the change from coal to oil in powering warships and the creation of a fast division of battleships used in both world wars. He directed the creation of a Royal Naval Air Service, built the largest navy in British history, and declared a full mobilization to war footing (without the permission of the king or cabinet) just prior to the declaration of war.

Churchill was also placed in charge of Aerial Home Defense and he immediately sent their planes to Europe to take the offense with the objective of winning the war. This resulted in several successful raids on the enemy. He directed the first development of tanks, which were new weapons that would alter future warfare. He spent time at the front encouraging and inspiring soldiers in their fight. He then designed a plan to invade Turkey and help Russia to defeat Germany from the east. The plan failed when the admiral in charge withdrew his ships after three were lost to mines. This resulted in terrible losses for Allied ground troops and a huge defeat on the Gallipoli Peninsula. Churchill was blamed for the defeat and removed from the Admiralty. He then asked for a military commission to command front line troops to re-establish his career. He was appointed Lieutenant Colonel in charge of a Scottish battalion in December 1915.

As a military officer, he took good care of his troops, insisted on their health and cleanliness, made sure alcohol was available, dined with his officers in high style (mostly at his personal expense), and learned all their names and details of their lives. He insisted they sing whenever in motion, commanded several artillery barrages, and insisted on his own method of sandbagging trenches. His men dutifully carried out his orders for sandbagging and then changed to a more effective design after he left. His troops saw little action but they all liked him and cheered him when they were disbanded and sent to other units. Churchill spent days making sure his officers obtained favorable assignments before he left for Britain and a new appointment. A new government had been formed and named Churchill as Minister of Munitions and later Minister of War and Air. For the remainder of World War I, he would often arrive at his office early, work several hours, fly to France to deal with war matters, and frequently then fly in a small plane over the front lines, dropping in on commanders to offer advice—all in one day.

He despised the suppression and mass murder in Russia led by the Communists Lenin and Trotsky. In Parliament he opposed the Communist Revolution and supported the anti-communist White Russians while much of Britain was noncommittal. In 1920 he became Colonial Secretary because the government could see their empire in danger of coming apart.

He quickly hired T. E. Lawrence (the mysterious Lawrence of Arabia) to help him settle postwar disputes in the Middle East. Though the British government was stunned with the presence of Lawrence, he was able to resolve the problems in an amicable manner and then refused any other governmental appointment. As Colonial Secretary, Churchill directed the push for an eventual treaty granting self-rule to Ireland. In 1924 he became Chancellor of the Exchequer. He implemented a return to the gold standard for British currency, which added significant costs to British exports and led to major strikes and economic decline. He was blamed, later stating it was his biggest mistake, and resigned his position.

At age 55 he had fought and/or reported on five wars, held nine cabinet positions, and made 8,000 speeches. Between 1929 and 1939 he wrote numerous newspaper articles, a collection of essays, and engaged in lecture tours. Churchill fought to maintain the British Empire, with England as a benevolent governor of the colonies. His continued opposition to Mohandas Gandhi's peaceful disobedience for Indian independence alienated him from the British government and he held no appointed office for much of the 1930s.

As early as 1932, he actively opposed allowing Germany to rearm to achieve parity with France. Hitler had ignored the peace agreement from World War I that limited the German army, and he formed an alliance with Mussolini in Italy. Churchill advocated rebuilding the Royal Air Force and the creation of a Ministry of Defense, but only a few believed his warnings about Hitler. In 1936, Germany occupied the Rhineland and began its conquest of Europe, but Britain was divided on how to respond. Churchill continued his vocal criticism of Hitler who apparently feared Churchill's power. When Germany's conquests continued and Britain finally declared war, Churchill was reappointed to head the Admiralty. He advocated occupation of Norway and its key iron ore port, which was important to support a war machine. He was opposed, and Germany conquered Norway. In 1940, Prime Minister Neville Chamberlain lost the support of his Conservative Party colleagues. As a result, the king asked Churchill to serve as Prime Minister and form an all-party government. He was now head of the British government and refused to sign an armistice with Hitler's Germany. His tough carefully crafted rhetoric galvanized the British people against Hitler and they prepared for a long war.

As Prime Minister, Churchill directed the creation of a Ministry of Defense and filled the position himself. He placed an industrialist friend in charge of aircraft manufacturing, and production soared. He would sneak up to the roofs of buildings in London to watch the air raids and battles over London. His speeches continued to inspire and stimulate the British people to defeat Hitler's armies. In summer 1940, he initiated the rescue of 338,000 British, French, and Belgian troops when they were cornered by the Germans on the beaches of Dunkirk. Awakened at 6:30 a.m. and alerted to the situation, he immediately began directing a phone campaign that mobilized up to 1,000 naval and private boats and ships to complete the rescue. In addition to the soldiers lost, Britain had left behind huge amounts of equipment and materials, France had fallen, and the United States remained officially neutral. Britain was alone.

During this crisis, Churchill reached the height of his charismatic effects on the British public. With his rhetoric, he inspired them to identify with the noble cause of freeing the world from the threat of totalitarian rule. He dramatized their lives by seeing themselves as carrying out a moral mission. They were somehow better, more noble, and moral than they were before the war. He emphasized simplicity in his speeches and explanations, often using only one- or two-syllable words to assure that his listeners understood. His famous tribute to the Royal Air Force pilots in their defense of Britain is a good example: "Never in the field of human conflict was so much owed by so many to so few."

Churchill courted other nations' leaders to obtain their assistance in the war effort. He loved talking, eating, and drinking and used his personal experience and memory of history to tell fascinating stories. People were curious about him, and his mood always improved when people surrounded him to hear him speak. He was a master salesman for Britain and established a close relationship with U.S. President Franklin D. Roosevelt to obtain needed food, oil, and munitions for Britain. Later, when the United States entered the war, he facilitated the Allied invasion of Europe from England. Roosevelt liked Churchill, but the two were competitive talkers. Roosevelt nagged Churchill to grant independence to India and abandon the British Empire system. When Japan attacked the United States at Pearl Harbor, Churchill immediately issued a statement to the American public that Britain was declaring war on Japan.

Toward the end of World War II, Churchill met several times with the Russian leader, Joseph Stalin. Both were strong willed and competitive, both had insight into the path of political developments, both were patriotic and mutually distrustful, and both loved to eat, drink, and smoke in huge amounts. British supplies had flowed to Russia when Hitler invaded Russian territory. Both knew that Stalin wanted to dominate the world while Churchill wanted to maintain the balance of power and preserve the British Empire. Churchill was effective at negotiating treaty agreements for European and Asian boundaries after the war, although he later spoke decisively against Russian dominance in Eastern Europe.

Churchill loved to visit the battlefront in boats, planes, or on the ground and was often held back by his colleagues. When the war ended in May 1945, he received the greatest ovation ever given in the British Parliament. Two months later he was voted out of office. The public apparently was ready for change from a war leader to one who was devoted to helping the underprivileged. Churchill was always compassionate but viewed complete egalitarianism as a socialist dream. He led the government opposition in Parliament for several years and in 1946, while in the United States, he gave his famous "Iron Curtain" speech at Westminster College in Fulton, Missouri. He pointed out the Soviet dominance and desire to spread their influence throughout the world. He called on the United States and Western allies to oppose the communist movement. His speech marked the beginning of the cold war arms race between the United States and the Soviet Union.

Churchill was re-elected as Prime Minister in 1951 and served until his resignation for health reasons in 1955. During this time a decolonization movement progressed in Europe, starting after World War II and continuing into the later 20th century. Although Churchill used violence at first to try to quell rebellions in the colonies, the British Empire was not sustainable and gradually declined. He experienced a series of strokes, resigned from Parliament in 1964, and died in 1965 at his home. Known primarily for his outstanding wartime leadership, he was also loved as a statesman, historian, writer, and orator.

Two types of leadership theories are descriptive of Churchill's leadership. He demonstrated Charismatic/Transformational Leadership in his impact on the British people during wartime. His *inspirational speeches* describing a moral mission and reflecting his mastery of the English language, his *vision* of future events, his *risk taking*, extreme *self-confidence*, and *foresight* are all charismatic qualities. The fact that he was a heroic leader during wartime and rejected during peace demonstrates the principle behind Contingency/Situational theories of leadership, which predict that different leadership approaches are needed in different situations. Theories such as Fiedler's Contingency Theory, Situational Leadership, and Path-Goal Theory all reflect this principle of effective leadership. The British public's reaction to his leadership after wartime reflects Implicit Leadership Theory's notion of followers' image of an effective peacetime leader. Churchill was also highly *directive* during wartime as the crisis required decisive action. This is described in the Multiple Linkage Model, Path-Goal Theory, and Situational Leadership Theory. His *boundary-spanning behavior* was critical to settling strikes in England and in obtaining cooperation and support from other nations during wartime. This leader behavior is also described in the early Multiple Linkage Model and Reformulated Path-Goal Theories of leadership.

Discussion Questions

1   Why was Churchill such an effective wartime leader?
2   Why do you think the British public did not believe Churchill could adjust his leadership style to peacetime?

3   Which leader behavior do you think was most important in leading wartime Britain: charismatic, directive, or boundary spanning?
4   Why did Churchill find it so difficult to relinquish control of Britain's colonies?

Selected References

Coleville, J. R. (1996). The personality of Sir Winston Churchill. In R. C. Kemper III (Ed.), *Winston Churchill: Resolution, defiance, magnanimity, good will* (pp.108–125). Columbia, MO: University of Missouri Press.

Millard, C. (2016). *Hero of the Empire: The making of Winston Churchill*. London: Penguin.

Pelling, H. (1989). *Winston Churchill*. New York: Springer.

Taylor, R. L. (1952). *Winston Churchill: An informal study of greatness*. Garden City, NY: Doubleday.

9   Margaret Sanger
Leader of the Movement to Legalize Contraceptives

Margaret Sanger was a dedicated activist and leader of the long campaign to make information on birth control legal and contraception available to all women. Beginning in 1911, her decades-long campaign was directed at the Comstock Acts of 1873 which labeled contraceptives as pornographic and obscene and prohibited dissemination of information on contraceptives or their use via the U.S. postal service. Other related acts prohibited the provision by physicians of information or articles related to contraceptives and abortion. Her campaign finally resulted in the prohibition for physicians being overturned in 1936 but birth control was not completely legalized until the 1960s. Margaret established the organization that eventually became the Planned Parenthood Federation of America.

Margaret Higgens was born in 1879 to a poor family of 11 children in upstate New York. She attended boarding school where she worked to pay her tuition and attracted other children, becoming a leader in their activities. In 1899 she quit school to nurse her dying mother who had contracted tuberculosis. Her sisters had left home early and they helped her pay for nursing school tuition after her mother's death. She concentrated on studying obstetrics and gynecology. She contracted tuberculosis, seemed to recover, and met William Sanger who was an aspiring architect, artist, and Socialist. They married and he convinced her to quit the nursing school before graduation—five months later the tuberculosis returned and she was pregnant. She spent a year in a sanitarium with her baby and again recovered. Her husband inherited the money to build a house on the Hudson River where they lived for ten years and had two more children. The house burned down, which seemed to remove her motivation for a quiet life, and they moved to New York City.

Sanger's husband quit his drafting job to be a full-time artist. Though she lacked the Registered Nurse degree, Sanger obtained employment as a visiting nurse working primarily for the poor in New York City. She specialized in obstetrics patients and served as a midwife. Her patients constantly asked her how they could avoid further pregnancies. Wealthy women had physicians who quietly fitted their patients with early illegal contraceptive devices but the poor often had no physicians or knowledge of contraception. She

DOI: 10.4324/9781003333937-11

saw patient after patient suffering from attempted self-abortions or back-street abortions by unlicensed individuals. These cases often resulted in sepsis and sometimes the death of the mother. Many of her patients had multiple children they could not support. They often suffered malnutrition, with babies wrapped in newspapers for warmth. Sanger decided that she would dedicate herself to educating these women about contraception.

She began studying other social movements such as women's suffrage, temperance, and national union drives to learn about activism, resisting criticism, and propaganda. Legalizing contraception was especially sensitive because it involved describing the secret issue of sex which many viewed as obscene. But she believed her movement was preventative medicine and it was the real solution to overpopulation and abortion, which she always opposed except when the mother's health was in serious danger. However, no efficient method of contraception that was within women's total control existed in 1912.

Sanger joined the Socialist Political Party and worked with her husband organizing events, distributing written materials, and assisting strikers. She was jailed for five days for picketing and resisting arrest and she resigned from the Party soon after. She believed the high birth rate was the basic cause of low wages and abusive working hours due to the availability of poor and child labor and these factors maintained the poverty she encountered in her work. She frequented Greenwich Village in New York City, which was an early center for bohemian culture and alternative lifestyles in the U.S. and she began writing and speaking on sex education, feminism, and the "joys of the flesh." She wrote several articles on sex education for a Socialist newspaper and developed a reputation for her writing and speaking. The term "Birth Control" became the label for her campaign to legalize contraceptives. She also obtained an extramarital lover, the first of many.

She continued writing about reproductive physiology, sexual impulses, venereal disease, and pregnancy. Other female activists emerged for the birth control movement but Sanger refused to give them credit, insisting that she was their real leader. She wanted her husband to agree on an "open marriage" with each having other lovers—he refused. She was absent from her family more often, giving their children and her husband little attention—which they eventually resented. In 1913 their family left for Europe—she hoped to learn more about Socialism and he wanted to study painting in Paris and separate her from her lovers. Three months later she returned to the U.S. with the children and almost no money.

She intended to publish a magazine for working women called *The Woman Rebel*. It was published eight months later using loans, grants, and subscriptions from her followers, sold for ten cents per copy and was hand delivered. It was well received by many, though not all. She published a true story about a woman who sold her children because she could not afford to feed and clothe them. She also criticized monogamy and the idea of one sexual partner. She also published an illustrated pamphlet with detailed information on contraception and female reproductive anatomy. She included specific language like penis and vagina which shocked some people. The pamphlet sold 160,000 copies in the U.S. in four years, was translated into several languages and sold throughout Europe. She was soon arrested for violating the Comstock Act so she fled to Europe before the trial. After leaving she instructed associates in the U.S. to release another pamphlet called *Family Limitation* which described six different contraceptive methods with illustrations and instructions on their use. While she was in England her husband was jailed for a month, after being tricked by a female undercover agent into providing her a copy of *Family Limitations*.

In England, Sanger charmed many people, especially men. They introduced her to Malthusians who asserted that population increased geometrically but food production only increased arithmetically so population must be controlled. She met other intellectuals and writers, some of whom became lovers. These included H. G. Wells, Hugh de Selincourt, and Havelock Ellis, author of several volumes entitled *Studies in the Psychology of Sex*. She studied Ellis's writings and spent much time with him discussing the importance and pleasure of sex. While in England, she published 15 articles on birth control in the *New York Times* and decided to divorce her husband Bill, who refused. They fought and were finally divorced seven years later.

While Bill was in jail their three children had no place to live so her supporters paid for them to attend a boarding school. The living conditions at the school were poor and their five-year-old daughter, who had been her favorite, died from pneumonia. Her death shocked Sanger, though she never accepted any responsibility for her death. The case against her was dropped because the court feared it might create a martyr for her cause. This case increased her prominence in news reports and she began a lecture tour across the U.S. citing information about birth control as the solution to abortion and most diseases in the country. The Catholic Church was a major opponent of birth control, though many of her clients were Catholic, and the Church influenced many police officials to disrupt her demonstrations and lectures. Opinions about birth control were changing and many Americans used some type of contraceptive.

In 1916 she opened the first birth control clinic in New York. It was not staffed by a physician but by her sister who was a nurse, Sanger, and a receptionist. She clearly distinguished her clinic as not an abortion mill. Over 500 clients enrolled who all signed a document stating they were married. Authorities shut down the clinic and arrested all its personnel. Always aware of how to promote her cause, Margaret refused to enter the police wagon and walked one mile to jail—accumulating a crowd of supporters and reporters as she went. While awaiting trial she reopened the clinic and was again arrested and found a pro-bono lawyer who soon fell in love with her. This time she was convicted and sentenced to 30 days in jail where she taught inmates about birth control and taught reading and writing to illiterates. During World War I, Sanger blamed Germany and Russia for not controlling their population growth. Arrested again, her lawyer argued that public opinion toward birth control was changing and her publications included comparable information to publications by the War Department and Public Health Service and she was released.

While in England, she was introduced to advocates for eugenics, a belief beginning with the early Greeks. It advocated selective breeding to improve heritable characteristics in a population. It became popular in England and in the U.S. in the early 20th century and was supported by Theodore Roosevelt and other well-known Americans to increase the births of healthy Anglo Saxons while breeding out undesirable traits. Sanger began supporting eugenics during the 1920s in order to gain its supporters to help with her birth control movement. But during her lifetime, Nazi Germany, the U.S., and Canada authorized involuntary sterilization in some institutions for the "mentally deficient," as well as some who were deaf, blind, and diseased. It is relevant that at this time that the U.S. was becoming a major destination for other immigrant races. The U.S. Congress established immigration quotas that discriminated against darker races and eugenics beliefs became selective and often based on prejudice and social class.

Sanger lived on her own in a small apartment in New York City and often went out on the town with her lovers. Her two remaining children attended boarding schools paid by her friends and she had little contact with them. She worked more hours than anyone else in the birth control movement—writing, editing, dictating letters, doing interviews, debating with critics, and lecturing. In 1918, Sanger and her lawyer/lover appealed her earlier conviction and the court ruled that physicians could prescribe birth control methods for married women. This was a huge win for her movement.

She spent the next five years in England writing, lecturing, and attracting men. She wrote two books that became best sellers, *The New Method* and *Pivot of Civilization*. She wrote that with women planning their families by using birth control, a healthier race would be created by their enlightened maternity. She thus believed that eugenics was a female cause with a female solution although she opposed forced sterilizations. She met a British millionaire named Noah Slee who fell in love with her. Returning to the U.S., she engineered the formation of the American Birth Control League (ABCL) and initiated the first conference in the U.S. on birth control. The Catholic Church influenced the police to bar her from speaking at the conference but she sneaked in anyway and was again arrested. When this became public in the *New York Times* she was released and the *Times* became her supporter. She eventually married Noah Slee in London and traveled around the world, lecturing by invitation in Japan, Korea, and China. Slee provided funds for her children's support and for the birth control movement. She continued her free lifestyle and maintained that mothers should never give up their freedom to become attendants to their young.

Slee built a mansion for them north of New York City and she enjoyed a wealthy lifestyle. She opened new birth control clinics which were then legal when staffed by a physician who defined disease liberally. A survey showed that most couples used condoms but she felt that this kept men in control and women must control their own bodies. By 1920 there were 20 birth control clinics in the U.S. and by 1930 there were 55 with 10,000 clients. From 1928 to 1935 Sanger continued writing, lecturing, opening new clinics, and lobbying against allowing only physicians to provide information and items used for contraception. She was charismatic and clever in public speaking and at responding to her critics, which clearly benefited her movement. Her name had become symbolic for birth control.

Mary Ware Dennett was the other major advocate for repeal of the Comstock Act. Although Sanger refused to give her credit, in 1930 Dennett's continued lobbying and legal efforts eventually removed enforcement of contraception as part of federal statutes that defined obscenity. There was not enough organized pressure to repeal the Comstock Act but the American Medical Association endorsed birth control in 1937 and its enforcement became rare.

By the late 1930s, Sanger was generally free to lecture on birth control and she began comparing Lincoln freeing the slaves to contraceptives freeing women from the slavery of unwanted pregnancies. She became estranged from her second husband, found another lover, and sailed for India. There she gave over 60 lectures on population pressures and tried to convince Gandhi to support birth control but he favored abstinence. Her letters sent to the staff at her clinic were widely published in the U.S. She convinced followers in India to open birth control clinics, educate women, and sell spermicides. She traveled to Japan where she recovered from a gallbladder attack, lectured, and engineered a clever plan to have a Japanese physician mail a birth control device to a friendly doctor in the U.S. As she expected, it was confiscated under the Comstock Act and they filed a lawsuit against the U.S. government. A liberal judge decided the device was for research purposes to cure or prevent disease and ruled in her favor—the confiscation was reversed. Labeled the "One Package Ruling," this marked another victory against the Comstock Act. By this time polls showed most Americans favored birth control and the number of clinics was doubling every three years, but some states still confiscated her books and closed clinics and lecture venues. These state level bans were not struck down until the 1965 Supreme Court decision Griswold vs. Connecticut which established the right to privacy as a constitutional doctrine.

In the late 1930s, Sanger began advocating for a single birth control pill. She had established several organizations over the years to support her cause. The organizations' activities overlapped and she was convinced by followers to combine them. The resulting organization eventually became the Planned Parenthood Federation of America. Planned Parenthood became a significant enduring organization supporting sex education, family planning, and contraception in much of the world. She was made honorary chairman, although the new organization now had primarily male leaders who apparently believed they would be more influential with legislators. She attended conferences where she received honors and became a pacifist during World War II. She claimed the lack of birth control and resulting population growth was the major world problem, not fascism or Communism. Between 1939 and 1945 several of her friends who had supported her died, as did her husband and older brother who had helped pay for her education.

When World War II ended, Sanger made several overseas trips to support international efforts to support birth control. In 1949 she had her first heart attack and developed coronary artery disease which inhibited, but did not stop, her activity. In the 1950s she organized conferences on birth control and population growth in several countries. She was described as unyielding, imperious, and egotistical and these characteristics affected her relationships with others in the movement. She was nominated for the Nobel Peace Prize and was interviewed by Mike Wallace (later featured on the show *60 Minutes*) who badgered her and criticized her personal life—this when she was 78 years old. Frank Lloyd Wright designed a home for her next to that of her son, who had six children, and she spent much time with her grandchildren. She continued advocating for research to develop a contraceptive pill. When Dr. John Rock, Sanger's associate, found that progesterone stopped ovulation, her wealthy friends funded a laboratory for human studies. The first birth control pill became available in the late 1950s. She attended her last conference on family planning in India in 1959, when she was 80 years old.

She never abandoned support for eugenics, even after the Nazis used it as an excuse to murder millions of Jews and other unwanted people and the U. S. continued institutional sterilization of "dysgenic" individuals. Some states authorized involuntary sterilization of poor black women, and white women were refused when they requested sterilization. In 2020, Planned Parenthood of New York removed her name from its Manhattan clinic because of her connections with the eugenics movement.

In 1960 the Federal Drug Administration approved the first birth control pill. In 1964 President Lyndon Johnson proposed and passed the Economic Opportunity Act which included federally funded birth control programs. Although she has been accused of supporting abortion, Sanger actually opposed abortion except when the mother's life is in danger from the pregnancy. She always maintained that birth control was the solution to abortion. In 1966 the Supreme Court ruled that the Comstock Act was unconstitutional. Margaret Sanger died that same year of leukemia, shortly before her 80th birthday.

Sanger was clearly a Charismatic/Transformational leader with her desire to improve the lives of women who suffered with issues involving unwanted pregnancies. She showed elements of Servant Leadership by her caring and empathetic response to poor women whose health and wellbeing was damaged by backstreet and self-abortion attempts and their struggle to support numerous children. She was also extremely directive with followers, which reflects behavioral/ contingency theories such as Situational Leadership and Path Goal Theory. She also possessed a few elements of Toxic Leadership through her narcissism and lack of support of other leaders in the birth control movement. Her determination and drive, cognitive capacity, and self-confidence are described in Trait theories of leadership.

Discussion Questions

1   Do you think Sanger's early life history affected her desire to help poor women in need? If so, in what ways?
2   Did her behavior toward her children and other leaders in her movement influence her effectiveness? If so, in what ways?
3   Is there any other aspect of Sanger's behavior that may have decreased her effectiveness? If so, what aspects?
4   Why was Sanger so successful in her movement to legalize birth control?

Selected References

Margaret Sanger (1879–1966). *American Experience PBS*. www.pbs.org.
Kennedy, D. (1970). *Birth Control in America: The Career of Margaret Sanger*. Yale University Press, September 1971.
Baker, J. H. (2011). *Margaret Sanger: A Life of Passion*. New York: Hill and Wang.

10 Angela Merkel
Chancellor of Germany

Angela Merkel was the Chancellor of Germany from 2005 to 2021. By the time she left office, Merkel had served as Chancellor for 16 years and worked with four U.S. presidents. As president of the European Council, which determines the priorities and strategic agenda for the European Union, Merkel had led the European Union in navigating through numerous challenges, including Russia's annexation of Crimea, the global pandemic, and the financial crisis. She was listed twice by *Forbes* as the most powerful woman and the second most powerful person in the world.

Merkel is the oldest of three children, born in West Germany in 1954 but her family moved to East Germany in 1957. The East German government erected the Berlin Wall in 1961 which sealed off East Germany from the West. Her father was a Lutheran minister who was assigned as pastor of Waldhoff, a church operated complex for physically and mentally disabled people. Waldhoff was located in the forest north of Berlin. Angela excelled academically; her intelligence and willpower were evident when she won local and national competitions in the Russian language and mathematics. Her parents were well educated, gave her much freedom, and engaged in lively political discussions at home. Merkel had a quiet nature, did not participate in sports (she describes herself as physically clumsy), and she adopted her parents' Christian faith. Her teachers described her as shy, wearing plain clothes, and often sitting in the back of the class—"almost invisible." She learned self-discipline, determination, and personal drive but was able to enjoy life in an officially atheistic country filled with strict controls over its citizens. With a huge secret police for domestic surveillance and a vast network of undercover domestic informants, she learned to keep silent about her political opinions. This may have helped her eventual quest for a graduate education. She studied physics for four years, married another scientist, and eventually received a doctorate in chemistry. Angela then worked as a scientific researcher for several years in Berlin where she honed her intellectual diligence and constant search for reliable data.

In 1981, Angela separated from her husband and met her future husband, Joachim Sauer, who is a well-known chemist. They eventually married in 1998. She continued to work for the Academy of Sciences until the Berlin

DOI: 10.4324/9781003333937-12

Wall fell in November 1989. Merkel was 35 years old and had grown up and lived in a society where many books were banned, newspapers censored, and much travel was forbidden. Liberty and the free pursuit of one's happiness became basic to Merkel's values. Her preferred leadership style of holding back her opinions, carefully observing and analyzing whatever confronts her, not stating publicly her plans and strategies, and adapting her behavior as things unfold all reflect her early life in East Germany. These cautious behaviors were essential for survival in East Germany before 1989.

When the Berlin Wall came down, Angela joined a group called the Democratic Awakening. Her work there resulted in an appointment as spokesperson for East Germany's only democratically elected prime minister. She actively participated in discussions of German unification. When East and West Germany were unified in 1990, Merkel was elected to a position in the Bundestag (the German parliament). She quickly managed an introduction to the German Chancellor (Helmut Kohl) and was appointed Minister of Women and Youth. In this role she often traveled with Kohl and became known for her ability to absorb information as well as her directness. As in her youth, she was still seen as discreet and shy of public appearances although she was gaining confidence and becoming accustomed to her public role. In 1994, Merkel was appointed Minister of the Environment and in 1998 she became General Secretary of the Christian Democratic Union (CDU) which had merged with the Democratic Awakening. In 2000, after careful political maneuvering, she was appointed party chairperson. In 2005 Merkel was elected Chancellor of Germany.

Critics describe Chancellor Merkel as a gifted tactician without a larger vision. In fact, the German public is suspicious of leaders with grand visions for their country. They remember Adolf Hitler, with his grand vision of a purified master race of white Aryan people who would conquer the world and eliminate other groups they disliked or blamed for their economic problems. Hitler resulted in nothing but horror and destruction for Germany. Today Germans seem more comfortable with a leader who quietly reacts in well thought out ways to international situations and domestic conditions. She was quoted as saying that politicians with a vision should have their eyes examined. One advisor described her long-term view as around two weeks. She prefers compromise to competition and is not dogmatic. Neither is she self-important or condescending. She listens to others carefully and thinks about their message. Angela is a master of self-control. She believes that individual freedom, within the rule of law, is the basis of democracy. Germans have given her the nickname "Mutti" which is a familiar term for "mother."

Merkel was the longest serving head of government in the European Union. She had a close-knit group of advisors and she insisted on absolute confidentiality regarding their discussions. Her foreign policy emphasized strengthening Europe's cooperation and international trade agreements. She believed these issues were critical to Germany's economic welfare. Merkel was familiar with life in East Germany where hard work often did not produce a decent living. She believed a healthy economy where hard work produced a good living was key to competition between countries and ideologies. She was on good terms with Presidents Bush and Obama and spoke regularly with Russian President Vladimir Putin whom she had known for years. She stated that she did not trust Putin but did not detest him. Germany has considerable economic trade with Russia and China and she led numerous trade delegations to China. Domestically, she often cited the high level of Germany's social spending including benefits to the elderly, sick and disabled, unemployed and low-income families. However, she emphasized that remaining competitive was critical to Germany's economic welfare and there must be a limit to social spending.

An economic crisis began to develop in the European Union in 2010. Greece became unable to repay or refinance its government debt, or bail out its over-invested banks, while maintaining its pattern of government spending. It needed financial assistance from other European Union countries to avoid bankruptcy. Wealthy people in Greece avoided paying taxes and the government spent lavishly. As the strongest economic member in the European Union, Merkel delayed committing Germany to a bailout of Greece, insisting that the Greek government severely curtail its spending. When Portugal, Spain, Cyprus, and Ireland also became in danger of bankruptcy, Merkel supported a plan for the European Central Bank to assist these countries in resolving their financial problems. However, she required that they submit to European Union oversight of some of their central banks, and strict government austerity which caused losses in employment. This also damaged demand for some of Germany's exports. At that time, many Europeans saw Merkel as rigid and self-righteous. But her support of the European Union Central Bank's action stabilized the European Union and prevented a major economic catastrophe. She recognized that a healthy European economy was good for Germany. Angela's reaction to the debt-ridden countries was typical of her style. Perhaps due to her scientific training, she was an analyst. She was highly reliant on data, commissioning over 600 public opinion surveys in one four-year period. She approached problems methodically, studying different aspects, making comparisons, developing scenarios, weighing risks, anticipating reactions and addressing each one, and then settling on a decision before she acted. She was not highly emotional, believing that too much emotion disturbs reason and logic. Once she had implemented a decision, she observed carefully the results and adapted her strategy as needed.

Merkel condemned Russian aggression in Ukraine in 2014, but refused to commit to a military response. Many Russians and Germans have memories of war that are too terrible to imagine. She worked for months organizing international sanctions by Europe against Russia without cutting important economic ties between the two countries.

Merkel was a key contact between Putin and the Western world. She is able to converse in Russian, he speaks fluent German, and she could be firm with him in their weekly conversations. Putin clearly valued her as a critical communication link with the West. Merkel hesitated committing Germany to another round of economic sanctions on Russia until the Malaysian airliner was shot down in eastern Ukraine. It soon became clear that Russian weaponry was used and Germans watched on television as Russian-supported separatists looted dead passengers' belongings. She now had the German people behind her and she declared new economic sanctions against Russia.

Merkel warmed up to President Obama during his term. They are both often described as analytical, cautious, and remote. When Germans discovered the U.S. National Security Agency was recording Merkel's cell phone calls, and German officials arrested a German bureaucrat on spying for the United States, she seemed annoyed but maintained her strong relationship with the United States. Her relationship with President Trump was clearly distant. After their first chilly meeting, she stated that Europe could no longer rely on support from elsewhere.

In 2015, droves of refugees and immigrants began arriving in southern Europe from war-torn countries such as Syria, Iraq, Afghanistan, and Pakistan. Several countries restricted their entry but Merkel helped an estimated one million refugees enter Germany. She pleaded with German residents to welcome the refugees and most responded well—converting gymnasiums, classrooms, and airport hangars to refugee shelters. Merkel's generous action directly reflects her hatred of walls and her continuous pursuit to facilitate freedom at every opportunity. German social service centers became overloaded and many Germans began questioning the huge inflow of foreign nationals. More objections surfaced when several terrorist attacks in Germany were blamed on foreign perpetrators. Her popularity in Germany declined, with demonstrators calling her a traitor and worse, while President Trump labeled her as insane. Angela apologized to the German people for not carefully planning for the flood of refugees but she maintained that all want to live in a country that is free and open, and they must not be paralyzed by fear. It is amazing that what may be the most empathetic and openhearted action by a head of state in recent years came from Germany. This is the country that living people recall blowing apart Europe with genocide and heartless invasions of non-belligerent countries. As Merkel sought a fourth term as Chancellor, she was pressured to take a harder stance on admitting refugees and immigrants.

In 2018, Merkel was elected German Chancellor for her fourth term. This last term was to be the most tumultuous. After being Chancellor for 16 years, Merkel retired from politics in 2021. As she left office Merkel was credited with elevating Germany's leadership role in the EU and around the world, and navigating numerous challenges including, EU sanctions against Russia following annexation of Crimea, the global pandemic, and subsequent financial crisis. Merkel identified climate change, digitization, and migration as three grand challenges. She had worked with four U.S. Presidents, four French Presidents, five British Prime Ministers, eight Italian

Prime Ministers, and Vladimir Putin. Merkel was recognized around the world as a role model to women and was named "The World's Most Powerful Woman" by *Forbes* magazine for ten years in a row.

Speaking to reporters on her retirement, Merkel announced she would spend her retirement reading and sleeping. In 2022, Merkel turned down a job offer from the United Nations and announced that she was in the process of writing her political memoirs.

In 2023, Merkel stepped down from the influential board of the Konrad-Adenauer-Stiftung (KAS), a think tank directly tied to the Christian Democrats. Merkel indicated that she had grown out of the role and wanted to be free from political obligations.

Angela Merkel's leadership does not fit the Charismatic/Transformational Leadership Model that is currently popular in the U.S. and many other Western countries. She is generally viewed as an uninspiring speaker with no charisma. She is *unassuming* and *private* with a strong *sense of duty*. When she arrives at a decision, she gives clear *direction* to her ministers to implement her decisions, such as supporting the bailout of debt-ridden European countries and admitting crowds of refugees. She fully *supports* her close advisors and confidants, many of whom have been with her for years. She has shown complete *loyalty* to Germany with all her policies, which are oriented to benefit her country and its people. They have learned to trust her *integrity, patience*, and *intelligence* reflecting Trait Theories. Her "governing by baby steps" approach reflects Path-Goal, Situational, and Contingency Theories of Leadership, because she adapts her approach as events unfold. And her careful *listening, caring*, and *empathetic* responses to the refugee crisis reflect the ethical approaches of Servant Leadership Theory, and Principle-Centered Leadership. Merkel did much *boundary spanning* as she spent considerable effort representing Germany's interests to other countries, reflecting elements of the Multiple Linkage Model of Leadership.

Discussion Questions

1 How do you think Merkel's life history has affected her leadership style and policies?
2 With her apparently poor public speaking skills, why has she been such a successful leader?
3 What do you think of her statement that politicians with a vision should have their eyes examined?
4 What do you think are the strongest aspects of her leadership?

Selected References

Anonymous. (2017). Germany: Trusting in "Mother Merkel." *The Week*, May 26, 16.
Gibbs, N. (2015). The Choice: 2015 person of the year. *Time*, December 21, 49–50.

Kornelius, S. (2013). *Angela Merkel: The Chancellor and her world—the authorized biography*. London: Alma Books.

Packer, G. (December 1, 2014). The quiet German: The astonishing rise of Angela Merkel, the most powerful woman in the world. *New Yorker*. Retrieved December 14, 2017, from www.newyorker.com/magazine/2014/12/01/quiet-german.

Vick, K. (2015). Angela Merkel: Chancellor of the free world. *Time*, December 21, 52–96.

11 Martin Luther King, Jr.
American Civil Rights Leader

Martin Luther King, Jr. was a Baptist minister who became the preeminent leader of the American civil rights movement in the 1950s and 1960s. Using the nonviolent methods of Mohandas Gandhi, he led boycotts, demonstrations, and marches that publicized in dramatic terms the practices and effects of racism and segregation in the United States. His efforts led to important legislation that changed the lives of millions of Blacks and minorities in the United States. Later in his career he expanded his activities to focus on obtaining social and economic justice for all poor and disadvantaged people. He also actively opposed the United States' involvement in the Vietnam War. In 1964 he became the youngest recipient of the Nobel Peace Prize for his work to achieve the end of racial segregation and discrimination through nonviolent means.

King was born on January 15, 1929, in Atlanta, Georgia, to a comfortable middle-class family. His father was an autocratic Baptist minister who named his first son Michael, then later changed it to Martin Luther in honor of the German priest who began the Protestant Reformation. Martin was bright and precocious and became his father's favorite of three children. He learned to speak publicly from the Baptist preachers who enthralled their congregations with their grand rhetoric and young Martin began to develop his own speaking skills. At about five years old, he learned about discrimination when he was slapped and called a "little nigger" in a department store by a white customer who claimed he stepped on her foot. He saw his father rebel vociferously at these affronts, and Martin quit his first job when his supervisor kept calling him "nigger." Biographers assert that these early experiences and his thoughtful moody nature combined to create the quiet, formal, and serious reserve he maintained in public throughout his life.

He skipped two grades in high school and entered Morehouse College, where he studied sociology, was an average student and a lady's man. He became fascinated by Thoreau's essay on Civil Disobedience that Gandhi had studied in his nonviolent revolt against British occupation of India. In his last year of college he decided to enter the ministry as a means of serving humanity. He studied philosophy, scripture, and the life of Gandhi at Crozer Theological Seminary, continued to practice his rhetorical skills, and

DOI: 10.4324/9781003333937-13

was elected student body president and valedictorian for his graduating class. From there, he enrolled in Boston University, where he began developing socialist views with a Christian perspective, met and married Coretta Scott, and was granted a doctoral degree in theology. It was later found that he plagiarized parts of his dissertation. It was common practice for Baptist ministers to use past sermons and written material by others for their own sermons, and King often did this in his speaking and writing. In August 1954 he accepted a position as minister of a small church in a relatively prosperous area of Montgomery, Alabama. He spent hours preparing, memorizing, and practicing his sermons.

In the late afternoon of December 1, 1955, a tired 42-year-old seamstress named Rosa Parks boarded a bus in downtown Montgomery as she headed home after work. She sat toward the back in the section reserved for Blacks, but as the bus filled she was told by the driver to give up her seat for a white man. Other Blacks had complied, but Rosa repeatedly refused and was arrested. In the previous year, the United States Supreme Court had held in *Brown versus Board of Education* that racial segregation in public schools was unconstitutional. Civil rights activists declared a boycott of the Montgomery bus system, which was the major means of transportation for Black citizens. They invited King to help support the boycott and asked him to address a large rally as their leader and spokesman. King's metaphorical rhetoric focused on the struggles of long oppressed people throughout history and inspired the human spirit in his listeners.

The boycott lasted an entire year with carpool operations organized by the boycotters replacing the buses. Local officials suspected communists were behind the boycott and supporters were harassed and often arrested, including King. His vision for the boycott was a moral theater of direct confrontation that must appeal to America's conscience and the powers in Washington through the press. He emphasized nonviolence by boycotters to defeat physical force with moral or "soul" force and appealed to democratic principles contained in the Constitution. This 26-year-old Black minister, who spoke of loving the white oppressors to help redeem them from their evil ways, caught the fascination of the press. During the boycott, he was constantly threatened, his home was bombed and front door shotgunned but no family members were hurt. A state court finally declared bus segregation unconstitutional and was supported by the Supreme Court, ending the boycott with a victory.

Publicity during the boycott made King the symbolic leader for the new civil rights movement in the South. He directed the establishment of the Southern Christian Leadership Conference (SCLC) to facilitate a voter registration campaign for Blacks in the South to encourage them to vote and obtain representation in government. Bogus literacy tests and other forms of discrimination had long been used in the South to prevent Blacks from voting. He began traveling throughout the country giving up to four speeches a day to huge crowds and attending fundraisers to finance the SCLC.

He traveled at least 25 days per month to appeal for support for their civil rights movement. During these trips, he was constantly expected to inspire the crowds who flocked to see and hear him speak, his life was frequently threatened, and he was stabbed in the chest by an insane Black woman in New York.

King had attracted a group of capable lieutenants, and often solicited their advice on his decisions, remaining calm and logical as he patiently listened and considered their views. Decisions were often made together with these individuals after long verbal battles. This participative approach exposed King to opinions that were different from his own, provided new information and ideas, and prevented him from becoming too inflexible in his approach. College students were increasingly involved in demonstrations against segregation, forming their own organization called the Student Nonviolent Coordinating Committee (SNCC). King encouraged their activities and was arrested with them at a demonstration in Georgia. He had forgotten he was on probation for a minor traffic violation and was shackled in the middle of the night, removed from jail, and taken to the violent Reidsville Penitentiary for four months of hard labor. His long-time fear of lynching resurfaced, and he despaired of leaving prison alive.

King was always careful when dealing with the federal government and avoided alignment with specific political parties. The United States Supreme Court had settled the Montgomery bus boycott so he endeavored not to offend federal officials. By not aligning with a specific party, he sought to keep his movement moral and spiritual rather than political. He was friendly with John and Robert Kennedy, who were impressed with King. When he was delivered to Reidsville Penitentiary, his wife Coretta phoned Attorney General Robert Kennedy who phoned the judge who had ordered King jailed and he was released.

J. Edgar Hoover headed the Federal Bureau of Investigation and began investigating King. Hoover suspected him of being controlled by communists due to his friendship with Stanley Levison, who did have communist connections. Hoover had ordered surveillance on numerous influential individuals, including congressional members and presidents. The Kennedy brothers knew Hoover had accumulated a file on President Kennedy's extramarital affairs and could use it to embarrass him, so they agreed to allow Hoover to bug King's phones and the motel rooms where he stayed. However, when he presented the evidence on King's extramarital affairs to the Kennedys, they took no action.

In 1963, Birmingham, Alabama, was a nucleus for racial segregation with cross burnings, abductions and mutilations of Blacks, and bombings of Black churches. King directed a full-scale boycott of the Birmingham downtown merchants. As usual, his goal was to create a dramatic confrontation to bring the national press and demonstrate on television the cruel racial practices of segregation in the South. He often stated that legislators can declare rights, but people must act to make those rights real. King violated a state court injunction against demonstrating and was jailed. He was careful not to violate any federal injunctions in order to allow federal officials to take action favorable to his civil rights movement whenever possible.

During his stay in jail, he composed what became known as his "Letter from Birmingham Jail." It was a response to several white ministers who publicly criticized the demonstration. King described how Blacks had experienced dehumanization in the United States for three centuries. He detailed the danger, fear, and frustration of being Black in America and the ensuing sense of being "nobody." He thus explained why Blacks found it difficult to patiently wait for justice and equal rights in schools, employment, and nearly all aspects of life. His letter was smuggled out of the jail in sections over several days and was eventually published nationwide. It became known as the best statement of the condition of Black America and the urgent need for change.

When he was released on bail, the boycott was weakening and they recruited Black high school students to march in support. This caused the local sheriff to turn fire hoses and a water cannon on the children which tore off their clothes, and snarling police dogs were used to terrify them. All this was caught on national television and broadcast to the entire country. Robert Kennedy responded to the violence and pressured the local government to negotiate with the Black leaders. An agreement was reached to desegregate department stores, lunch counters, and all public facilities and to provide equal opportunities for all job applicants, regardless of race. Hundreds of similar demonstrations began all over the country and President Kennedy proposed federal legislation guaranteeing access to all public facilities for all persons throughout the country.

In August 1963, shortly after the Birmingham boycott, King and his lieutenants organized a march on Washington, D.C., to generate support for Kennedy's public access legislation and demonstrate the size and vigor of the civil rights movement. The march resulted in a huge rally in front of the Lincoln Monument and concluded with King's "I Have a Dream" speech. Using his mastery of dramatic delivery and metaphorical language, he spoke of his vision of freedom and brotherhood among all races and religions. The crowd of over 250,000 was hushed during the speech and erupted in deafening applause when he concluded. President Kennedy congratulated King soon after, and the speech became known as one of the greatest public addresses in United States history. The public access legislation was eventually passed into law, but only after Kennedy was assassinated in November 1963.

Later that summer, a key civil rights leader was assassinated in Mississippi and a Black church was bombed in Birmingham, killing three young Black girls. Many in the civil rights movement, such as Malcolm X, sought violent reprisals. In 1964 a demonstration in St. Augustine, Florida resulted in violence against the demonstrators by local toughs with no efforts at protection by the local law enforcement. King managed to get the protestors into a church after the violence and began contacting Washington authorities for assistance. His devoted lieutenant Ralph Abernathy reiterated King's spiritual nonviolent mission and vision to calm those who advocated violent reprisals. Later that year, while in the hospital with exhaustion and a fever, King was notified he had received the Nobel Peace Prize for his nonviolent actions to end segregation.

In late 1964 King joined with the SNCC in Selma, Alabama in a voting rights campaign. The goal was to stop discriminatory voting practices that prevented most Blacks in the United States from voting. Their demonstration was met by the local sheriff and his deputies with night sticks and electric cattle prods, which they used to herd the demonstrators out of town. King was jailed and a youth was shot to death trying to protect his mother. A subsequent march on the state capital was met with more terrible violence from state and local law enforcement and was shown on Sunday night television. It became known as "Bloody Sunday." President Johnson saw the film and denounced the violence, promising to submit a bill to Congress to assure equal voting rights for all citizens. This legislation was eventually passed by Congress. The Public Accommodations Act and the Voting Rights Act eventually changed life for Blacks in the South and elsewhere in the United States. Within the next few years, restaurants, schools, stores, sports events, and theaters were integrated. Black voter registration increased exponentially, and Black sheriffs, mayors and congressional representatives became increasingly common.

King wanted to broaden his movement to achieve economic and social justice for all poor people. He was amazed to learn that most of the nation's poor were white. In 1967 he directed his followers to Chicago in a Poor People's Campaign to eliminate the slums where the poor were living amid squalor and violence. His efforts were disappointing when he confronted Mayor Richard Daly who ran a corrupt and powerful political machine in Chicago. Daly was clever and tough and agreed to everything they requested thus avoiding major confrontations. Later the agreed changes were lost in the morass of bureaucracy that was charged with implementation.

Major race riots erupted in Newark, Cleveland and Detroit in 1966 and 1967, and violent elements of the civil rights movement were gaining power. King strove to straddle the line between violent tendencies of some groups (such as the Black Panthers) and his own nonviolent mission. After seeing a photograph of a Vietnamese woman holding a baby that had been burned with napalm, he began a crusade to stop the Vietnam War. He declared the war was being waged for the wealthy on the backs of the poor. This assertion broke his connections with President Johnson. King announced that capitalism was not working and advocated a social democratic type of government with assured jobs and a guaranteed annual income for everyone.

In March 1968 King traveled to Memphis to support a strike by sanitation workers when the mayor refused to recognize their union. A planned march turned into a riot and King's followers spirited him away from the violence and out of town. J. Edgar Hoover had his agents spread rumors that King was responsible for the riot. King returned to Memphis four days later to address a church rally for the strikers. He delivered his famous last speech indicating he had climbed the mountain and seen the promised land they were striving for, but he might not be there when it was achieved. When finishing the speech, he fell back with exhaustion and was caught by his advisors during a deafening applause. The next evening he was shot to death by a sniper on his motel balcony. The killer was later caught and convicted of murder.

The civil rights movement was never the same after King's death. It seemed that King became a focal symbol and a leadership catalyst for a social movement that was wide and passionate enough to make a profound social transformation in the South. Although he had multiple affairs with different women, he explained to his lieutenants that they provided an escape from the stress. The inconsistency between his moral message of equal rights for all and his own personal behavior bothered King throughout his campaigns. Regardless of his private failings, he was effective in fulfilling his public leadership role as a symbol and spokesperson for the American civil rights movement and is remembered as a great leader.

Martin Luther King, Jr., is most often described as a Charismatic/ Transformational Leader due to his outstanding *rhetorical skills* he used to describe his *vision* and *mission* of brotherhood and peace among all people. King's other behavioral characteristics that fit the Charismatic/ Transformational Leadership model include his *risk taking* during dangerous demonstrations and marches and his key role as a *living symbol* of the overall civil rights movement in the United States. King also excelled at *boundary spanning* as he represented his movement to governmental organizations, funding sources, and the American people via the press. This leader behavior is described in the early Multiple Linkage Model and Reformulated Path-Goal Theory of Leadership. He used *directive leadership* with followers as he guided them to demonstrations at key points and times in the South that were designed to assure the presence of the press. He also demonstrated *sympathy* and *supportiveness* for followers who were victimized by violence and discrimination throughout his career. These behaviors are described in Path-Goal Theory, Fiedler's Contingency Theory, Situational Leadership Theory, and the Leadership Grid. In strategic meetings with his closest advisors, he used *participative leadership* in gathering information from each of them, patiently listening and getting ideas, and mediating among them when they disagreed. This leadership behavior is best described by the Normative Decision Theory. King's *determination* and *cognitive capacity* reflect Trait Theories of leadership. King's leadership can also be addressed by the Servant Leadership Theory since he was totally *committed to the goal of a better America for all Americans.*

Discussion Questions

1   Why did Martin Luther King, Jr. become so important to the civil rights movement in the United States?
2   How important were his boundary-spanning activities with the press?
3   Why do you think the civil rights movement lost much momentum after King's death?
4   It was well known that King had many extramarital affairs. Do you believe a leader's personal behavior affects his/her effectiveness as a leader?

Selected References

Carson, C. (2001). *The autobiography of Martin Luther King, Jr.* New York: Hachette.

Frady, M. (2002). *Martin Luther King, Jr.* London: Penguin.

Garrow, D. (1986). *Bearing the cross: Martin Luther King, Jr. and the Southern Christian Leadership Conference.* New York: William Morrow.

Washington, J. (1991). *A testament of hope: The essential writings and speeches of Martin Luther King, Jr.* New York: HarperCollins.

12 Virginia Hall

Virginia Hall Was a Spy!

The Allies (Britain, France, and America) of World War II would come to know great need for organization, training, and management of espionage, sabotage, and reconnaissance. Virginia Hall would be ready for this crucial work for the French resistance. Originally she worked in the presence of a puppet Nazi German government headquartered in Vichy, France and later under the full Nazi occupation of France. French resistance was a critical factor in the Second World War. The resistance became the support system for Allied invasions from the coast of Normandy and from North Africa. Ultimately, General Eisenhower estimated that the French resistance reduced the length of the war by nine months. Virginia Hall's story is of the complexities required for resistance as she triumphed over a crippling injury and gender discrimination; paradoxical invisibility cloaks for a dangerous but significant service.

Virginia was born in 1906 to a wealthy Maryland family. In her youth, she was an adventure seeker, loved life on a family farm with its animals and a quirky tolerance for snakes. Her high school career was lively as captain of sports teams and a flair for swashbuckling roles in drama productions. Her capacity for leadership was recognized by her classmates as they elected her their president. All of this was punctuated by her audacious shock of red hair. Virginia's father adored her antics, but they would be the source of consternation and anxiety for her mother's whole life.

Following high school, Virginia experienced a privileged education at American University, Barnard and Radcliffe Institute for Advanced Study. Virginia enjoyed the opportunities of European travel. She extended her education as a student of political science, languages, economics, and journalism in European locations.

At the age of 23 in 1929, Victoria returned home competent in five languages and knowledgeable of European cultures, geography, and politics. She had enjoyed the electricity and diversity of the *l'annees folles* (the crazy years) of Paris in the 1920s and would forever love France. In contrast, she had observed the activities of fascists in Venice and Nazis in Germany and was aware of similar trends in Russia.

Her European studies and experiences may have formed Virginia's dream of a career in the diplomatic service, and although her applications for

DOI: 10.4324/9781003333937-14

diplomatic appointments were always turned down, she did serve in clerk and secretarial-level positions at embassies in Poland, Turkey, Venice, and lastly in Estonia. In Virginia's era, secretarial positions were the appropriate level for women. At the time, only six of 500 foreign service officers were women. There are reports, however, that some of her superiors were quite impressed with her energy and competence.

A mishap during her term in Turkey would forge a distinction in Virginia's persona when she had an accident on a bird-hunting outing. The year was 1933. Stories are that she shot herself in the foot, perhaps as she was climbing a fence. Surgeons amputated her foot, but in an era predating antibiotics, gangrene was a terrible risk, and it did result. There was a further amputation of her leg, and her critical condition would precipitate a return to the United States where she received improved treatment and was fitted for a prosthesis of a better design than a crude and painful wooden leg. The episode was a season of life-threatening trauma. The handicap would define her in the conflicts to come in heroic ways and pejoratively as well on occasions when she was designated a "limping bitch." It was her challenge and circumstantially, her cover. Reactions by others to her disability taught her to be a judge of character. The prosthesis would even become a named presence, "Cuthbert."

Virginia's final embassy assignment was in Estonia in 1939, the year that Hitler invaded Poland, and subsequently Britain and France declaring war on Germany. Estonia was at risk too, of a Russian invasion, so Virginia resigned her post with the State department there and determined to look for opportunities to oppose Nazi aggression. She hurried off to London on a boat as opportunities for departure were waning, hoping to join the war effort by volunteering with the women's branch of the British Army, the Auxiliary Territorial Service. Virginia would find herself defined by her American passport as a foreigner, and foreigners were not trusted for the war effort. So, she was off to Paris where a driver's license sufficed to allow her to resist fascism. She was an ambulance driver on the French front lines during the Nazi German invasion beginning on May 10, 1940. Six weeks later, on June 22, the French government capitulated to the German occupation, enduring curfews, arrests, and surveillance.

In the chaos of her moment, Virginia encountered an undercover British agent who recognized the courage, the dedication, the knowledge, and ability that Virginia brought to the war. He provided her with the phone number of someone who might offer a more crucial role for her service. A British secret service, the Special Operations Executive (SOE), had been quickly established at the war's beginning for sabotage, subversion, and spying. Undercover agents were hard to come by, and Virginia, a woman limping on a prosthesis, might not have seemed promising. There were clear definitions that "war was a man's work," but the desperation of war got Virginia hired to the SOE and trained in espionage trade craft, communications, weapons, organizing and running spy networks and, of course, coded messages which she would be sending under her cover as an American journalist reporting for the *New York Post*.

Her assignment was to Lyon, France which was administered for the Nazi Germans from Vichy, France by Marshal Philippe Petain, a French World War I military hero who was nominally French but of quite an authoritarian mind set. In September 1941, 14 months after the French Third Republic capitulated to the Nazis (and three months before the bombing of Pearl Harbor which would bring the United States into the war), Virginia returned to France and set forth immediately to write articles about the war for the *New York Post* under her journalist cover all the while she began building a network of resistance and intelligence. Intelligence by radio transmission was the lifeblood of the war and a great deal of Virginia's work involved the facilitation and protection of radio operators whose signals could be detected by the equally clever radio detection vans of the Nazis invaders. The operators needed to be constantly vigilant on the move and to take great care to hide their equipment. Safe houses needed to be located and codes designed. All was dangerous! Germany offered generous payments to those who revealed resistors or spying agents undercover. In time she would be identified as "the limping lady."

Virginia's love of France accorded her useful relationships and friendships with Nazi collaborators and resistors alike. Her facility with languages was useful, although her American accent could be a problem. The circles of resistors she developed included nuns and harlots, farmers, bar keepers, entertainers, guerillas—an inclusive list. A story of renown is of the collaboration with a woman who ran a major brothel in Lyon. Intelligence was available from the mixed clientele of Nazi officers and French Nazi collaborators who required the available entertainment. Alcohol loosened their tongues, and they relaxed and slept. Prostitutes must have been resistors as they willingly gathered information and copied the papers carried by their clients. The venue's upstairs rooms were also useful as safe houses for fellow spies. A resisting gynecologist added a service by providing the prostitutes with "free from infection" cards even when they were actually infected with syphilis and gonorrhea, a bit of subterfuge not quite imaginable!

Virginia's capacity for organizing was remarkable. The work to be done was to coordinate and secure finances for such things as ammunition dumps, fuel depots, troop movements, safe houses, false papers, driving permits, food rations, many and any elements of subterfuge on the part of the resistance. One notable accomplishment was intelligence acquired of a secret Nazi submarine base that the Allied powers eventually destroyed. Night drops by parachute of explosives and weapons were planned as radio operators were protected. In her cover as journalist, she frequently visited the American Embassy where she smuggled messages out. Then she received replies of cash to support her work. Significant numbers of French people were Nazi collaborators. Hair-wire judgments of who to trust were life and death decisions, and there are stories of meetings and connections that

Virginia avoided by means of a second sense. Many SOE agents were victims of Nazi traps, but at least for a time the assumptions about gender were a benefit: the suspected agent of resistance was a man! The SOE relied increasingly on Virginia.

Stories of her resistance activities abound, and some reveal a feminist wisdom, free from privilege and ego, the ego and confidence that would lead several essential radio operators for the SOE into a meeting in the city of Marseille. The meeting was a trap, and all were arrested and imprisoned. Their arrest left Virginia in dangerous isolation and increasingly vulnerable: so vulnerable that both the SOE in London and the editor of the *New York Post*, who continued throughout to receive her reports, strongly advised that she leave France.

Virginia remained in France nevertheless, dedicated to the project of an exquisite prison break for the radio operators. It is a war story that challenges anything in the best of spy novels or the imagination of RPGs (Role Playing Games) of current entertainment. It is a war story for the ages! Ultimately, Virginia was clever enough to determine the location of their imprisonment and by exquisite means to organize a notable prison break of the war. Stories abound of Virginia's dangerous moments and clever judgments in the time when she did most of her work for what was known as the F (French) section of the SOE from her location in Lyons, France.

As the bombing of Pearl Harbor on December 7, 1941 brought the war to the world, the United States declared war and joined the Allied cause. Shortly, the United States would craft its own version of the British SOE, the Office of Strategic Services (OSS) which was the nascence of the Central Intelligence Agency (CIA), and Virginia was an American! Her role as an American journalist no longer had the cover of neutrality and it was suspected that Virginia's existence was known to the Nazis, and their intelligence was as clever as clever. Double agency (even triple) could be very lucrative since information had a high value. There were agents whose loyalties were compromised by the allure of the opposite sex who would break and betray their confidences. Virginia prepared to leave France. Agents of the SOE realized that Virginia's capture would be an enormous calamity. Her work was so valuable that her discovery would compromise major efforts of the F section. She was becoming known as "The Limping Lady of Lyon" and had captured the attention of Klaus Barbie who would become known as "The Butcher of Lyon." She was increasingly aware of footsteps behind her and sensed close calls.

Traps will spring, and it was the appearance of a priest, Abbe Robert Alesch, in clerical robes, announcing himself with appropriate code names to the trusted doctor for Virginia's harlots. He came with a request for funds for his Paris branch of the resistance. At the opportunity to meet him in person, Virginia had a reaction of extreme discomfort at a German accent which he quickly explained originated in the border region of Alsace. Time would reveal that this was one of his lies. Virginia did, however, comply with his request as he was able to verify credentials with good knowledge of critical code names. However, it was not long before Virginia received alarming news of arrests and disappearances in the Paris unit of the resistance that indicated a serious breach. Abbe Alesch was spying for the Nazis. He was funded doubly and living lavishly. The supposed intelligence that he provided to Virginia's circle was useless or false. Intelligence that he provided to the Nazis revealed intentions of the Allied operations to come. Alesch was ultimately be tried by a French court of justice and executed by a firing squad on January 25, 1949.

In November 1942, Operation Torch, the Allied Invasion of North Africa, changed everything in the war in France. The Nazi occupation moved brutally over what had been the puppet Vichy government. With grief and concern for her network, Virginia conceded, "I think my time has come." She was able to leave on a train for marginally neutral Spain before Nazi security could seize the railways. At the border, she found a former collaborator who arranged for her escape, much of it over 50 miles on foot across a high pass through the Pyrenees while "Cuthbert" bled. The pass was snowy and glacial, but walking was the safest form of transportation. Back in Lyon, Klaus Barbie was having a tantrum, and posters were out calling for information about her. As the predations of Abbe Alesch continued, trusted resistors were arrested, tortured, and imprisoned. And Virginia resolved that somehow, she must return to France.

Arriving in Spain was as complicated as Spain's mixed neutrality during the war. Virginia would experience arrest, imprisonment, and the aid of a fellow inmate before she could get to the American consulate in Barcelona. There she spent some months doing clandestine operations to assist French resistors and Jews to escape as by this time she was savvy of the means and channels of subversion and escape.

It was months before her celebratory arrival at the "F" section of the British SOE in London. Soon, however, she was pigeonholed by the administrative and perhaps appropriately protective mindset of the SOE into office work and gender appropriate busy work under the direction of superiors. Virginia perceived an opportunity to return to France in training to become a radio operator, one of the most dangerous opportunities of the war. This time, as an American citizen, she would work with the fledgling American OSS, and they saw their opportunity in the knowledge and experience that was gained in the British SOE. She returned to France on March 21, 1944, 16 months after her departure as plans for the Normandy invasion were being designed. She arrived as an elderly peasant woman, a little dirty and distressed. She had had her teeth filed to appear more aged and had devised an elderly shuffle. She carried a heavy suitcase that contained a 30-pound radio. She carried it lightly. (Later in the resistance, she would be supplied with a 15-pound radio.) The Nazi Gestapo was still hoping to find her, and the nature of the war had significantly changed since the Nazis now fully occupied France. French citizens at this point were heavily surveilled and conscripted for service in the Nazi war effort.

In her return, Virginia first worked as a milkmaid in a country setting, radioing from barns, studying the terrain for air drops for the supplies of warfare and recruiting resisters among the locals: the postman, the farm hands, housewives, cooks. She sold dairy products to the Nazis and gathered information through her knowledge of German. As the term of the war progressed, she made frequent changes of location and disguises. The point of Allied efforts was now to prepare the French to meet the D-Day invasion which was becoming apparent from the gathering of troops and ships. The imperative was to blow up trains, bridges, phone lines, and enemy convoys. Brutality was the means of preparation from the Nazi regime. Radios were alive. France was getting ready! It was intense!

Virginia's last spying accomplishment was at Le Chambon-sur-Lignon, in the Jura Mountains of France. The region had a Huguenot history of more than 400 years. They knew of repression, and as World War II progressed, they honored their history as Jews were being hidden by numerous households in the region. Although a resistance was endemic in its stony heights, its need for support and supplies had not received attention. The local guerrillas of the mountains and the woods, called maquisards, were desperate even though the region was a supply route especially useful to the Nazis. Later, the route would be as useful for their evacuation. Virginia arrived in the region only days after the Normandy invasion, hardened with experience, sure of her command and grimly determined. Accounts of these days describe how Virginia displayed an aura of calm, earning her a new title, "Madonna of the Mountains." This was despite the Benzedrine she often used to keep going! Other accounts tell of hair-wire escapes from Nazi detection. A particularly colorful story tells of Virginia escaping detection as a patient covered in blankets on an ambulance.

At this point yet, Virginia faced another round of gender challenges as the hardened men of the woods and mountains found it difficult to bear the command of a woman. This time her management in the OSS assured her authority by supplying their need of radio operators and tons of weapons, explosives, medicines, currency, and even such necessities as shoes, coats, cigarettes, and chocolate. Finally, too, Virginia received a promotion in rank, something far overdue.

The sum of Virginia's accomplishments and the value added by many who contributed with great risk must always be accounted against the cost of the many of her collaborators who were lost to prison, torture, and execution or were mired in grief. Airplanes were shot down and intelligence was betrayed. Following the Allied invasions, Nazi actions were desperate and increasingly brutal, but by the end of August 1944 Virginia's south-east region of France was liberated from their control within days of the liberation of Paris by Allied forces.

The defeat of the Nazis in the Chambon region was significant in the liberation of France, but there were still cleanup operations required. One of the late airdrops from the Allies was an American officer named Paul

Goilliot who became the love of Virginia's life. At the end of the war and after a return to London where Virginia turned in a trove of reports from the resistance. Virginia and Paul returned to the United States where Virginia worked for another 20 years for the CIA. It was to be an era of heavy intelligence concentration on the Soviet Union and the Cold War.

A retrospective of Virginia's career has brought to notice the persistent gender discrimination that deprived the CIA, her employer, of the value of her experience and wisdom. In a report to come, the CIA recognized that lesser men with greater egos were often intimidated by Virginia's undeniable past and hard-earned wisdom. Some suggest that she was overlooked due to her reluctance to attract attention. It was almost that her undercover persona clung to her still in civilian life. Nevertheless, a cause has coalesced around Virginia's story, the cause for women's equality, opportunity, and recognition for their contributions. Currently, a movement is being carried by women who have had careers in intelligence for Virginia to receive a posthumous United States Armed Forces Medal of Honor, its highest award. They determine that the Distinguished Service Cross that she was awarded in 1945 was an inadequate recognition.

Even though Virginia Hall has remained largely unrecognized in historiography despite her unmatched achievements, she stands out as one of the most impactful leaders in the clandestine world of World War II. She was directive in planning military operations and extremely supportive of her fighters, reflecting early Behavioral Leadership models. On the one hand, Hall's leadership style can be analyzed through contingency leadership, demonstrated by her ability to adapt her approach to the unique challenges she encountered during the war. She demonstrated both task-oriented and relationship-oriented behaviors as necessary to navigate complex and dynamic situations. While task-oriented in accomplishing mission objectives, her emphasis on building relationships highlights the significance of both task and relationship orientation in her leadership style. In addition, Hall's leadership style aligns with servant leadership principles, characterized by her selflessness and dedication to serving others. Her goal was to serve her beloved France by ridding it of the ruthless Nazi occupation, and she prioritized the well-being and safety of her fellow agents and the resistance fighters she worked with, often placing their needs above her own.

Virginia possessed a deep sense of self-awareness, understanding her strengths, values, and beliefs, which allowed her to lead authentically and purposefully. She was able to inspire resistors to take incredible risks by appealing to their vision of a free France, by encouraging innovation in their activities against the Nazis, and by her own role modeling for followers by taking huge risks herself. Virginia was a transformational leader, demonstrated by her ability to inspire and motivate others toward a common goal. Her charisma, determination, and vision enabled her to inspire those around her to persevere in the face of adversity and foster a sense of camaraderie among her team members. She demonstrated inspirational motivation through her ability to communicate a noble mission and vision, and she reinforced her commitment through symbolic actions that deeply resonated with her followers. She encouraged her team to challenge conventional thinking and approach problems with creativity and innovation, fostering an environment of intellectual stimulation. With high self-confidence and dramatic emotional rhetoric, Virginia radiated strong charisma, captivating and inspiring those around her.

Discussion Questions

1   Why do you think Virginia Hall was so effective in organizing and leading French resistance fighters in World War II?
2   Do you think Virginia's gender affected the response to her by French resistors?
3   After being rejected from the United States foreign service multiple times, why did Virginia keep trying to "get in the fight" against Nazi Germany?
4   Do you believe the story of Virginia's leadership during wartime conveys lessons can apply to leadership in other situations? What have you learned from her story?

Selected References

Central Intelligence Agency (n.d.). Virginia Hall: The Courage and Daring of the "Limping Lady". Retrieved on January 15, 2022, www.cia.gov.

Helvering, A. (2016). An Unlikely Hero: how Virginia Hall became the most feared allied spy in occupied France, and why you've never heard of her. Open Works. https://openworks.wooster.edu/independentstudy/6977.

Katz, B. (2020). How a Spy Known as the "limping Lady" Helped the Allies Win WWII. Retrieved January 20, 2022 from www.smithsonianmag.com.

Purnell, S. (2020). *A woman of no importance: The untold story of the American spy who helped win World War II*. New York: Penguin.

13 Anita Roddick

Founder and CEO of The Body Shop

Born in 1942, Anita Roddick, a British entrepreneur, was often referred to as "Mother Teresa of Capitalism" or the "Queen of Green," due to her efforts on environmental consciousness and ethical consumerism. Roddick founded The Body Shop, a small cosmetics store in Brighton, England in 1976, and turned it into a multinational corporation with over 1,900 stores in over 50 countries. Roddick's reputation was related to her activism in advocating for environmental issues, human rights, and opposition to product testing on animals. She used The Body Shop as a powerful platform to pursue her agenda for social and environmental change. Described as "loquacious, wacky and opinionated," she never wavered in her moral outrage at the actions of some corporations and governments, her anti-establishment idealism, and dedication to the causes she championed.

Trained as a teacher, Anita spent time early in her life traveling and working abroad in a library, a labor organization, and an Israeli Kibbutz. She traveled in the South Pacific before returning to England where she met her future husband, Gordon. The two of them ran a bed and breakfast and a restaurant for a time, but they grew tired of working seven days a week and having little time for their two children. Anita then hatched her idea for the cosmetics shop with natural products, Gordon helped her obtain her first loan for £4,000, and The Body Shop was born. Gordon then took off on a horseback adventure in South America.

Gordon eventually returned and began helping with the business, but Anita *was* The Body Shop from the beginning. The business grew quickly, and in 1984 they had the initial public offering for The Body Shop. Anita was determined to use their success for the benefit of society. The first item in her mission statement read: "To dedicate our business to the pursuit of social and environmental change." She never wavered from her active pursuit of this mission. The business of The Body Shop, providing women worldwide with cosmetics, lotions, and soaps that are created from natural ingredients and are not tested on animals, became a vehicle for pursuing her true passion for change. She traveled extensively and created trading relationships with disadvantaged communities throughout the world to assist them in becoming self-reliant and sustainable.

DOI: 10.4324/9781003333937-15

In 1986, The Body Shop established an Environmental Projects Department and engaged with Greenpeace to support the "Save the Whales" campaign. Soon after this, they partnered with Friends of the Earth to combat acid rain and to preserve the ozone layer. Two years later, Anita led a "Stop the Burning" campaign to end the massive burning of rainforests in Brazil. Her organization collected a million signatures from their customers, and Anita presented this petition with signatures to the Brazilian embassy. In 1990, The Body Shop Foundation was created to help fund human rights and environmental protection groups. One effective initiative was to help (with her husband) establish *The Big Issue* magazine, which provided a platform and political presence for homeless people. Her organization helped finance the London headquarters for Amnesty International, initiated the use of biodegradable plastic bags, gathered over 4,000,000 signatures resulting in the British government's decision in 1998 to ban animal testing for cosmetic ingredients and products, campaigned to fight domestic violence, fought against carbon emissions in the mining industry, and the list goes on. She emphasized how these programs made employees proud of The Body Shop and had a huge effect on motivation and morale.

Roddick envisioned The Body Shop as a *stakeholder corporation* that was accountable not only to shareholders, but to all stakeholders including employees, customers, and communities. The stakeholder corporation would focus on three bottom lines—financial, social, and environmental. The Body Shop was expected to deliver superior performance that benefited all of these stakeholders. Her sales force held "Body Shop at Home" gatherings that provided word-of-mouth advertising. Anita believed that the absence of a marketing department at The Body Shop was a moral statement, and her public image was all that was needed for marketing her products. Her organization invested in a wind farm to use environmentally friendly electricity (ecotricity) in their headquarters and stores in the United Kingdom. It also supported a new management degree at the University of Bath that combined training in business, environmental, social, and ethical issues. In 2000 the Foundation established a human rights award to give recognition to grassroots individuals and groups working on social, cultural, and economic problems around the world. The award provided financial support for the recipients. The first theme for the award addressed child labor and those who help children receive a basic education.

She was committed to leading an environmentally and socially responsible company that represented her values and she challenged other corporate leaders to be "true planetary citizens." Roddick modeled her socially active role by sacrificing profits—she would not do business in countries she believed were not attempting to address her social and environmental causes. She was considered an inspirational leader and generated passion among Body Shop employees. She invited ideas for the business and social programs from all employees through their Department of Damned Good Ideas (DODGI). She spent as much time with employees as possible and continually emphasized an image of female beauty that was realistic and not socially constructed by the media. She regularly sent video messages to employees regarding their organization's most recent advances in social causes and reminded them that their work efforts made an important contribution to larger environmental and social issues. Her organization financially supported employees who spent time working in community programs.

Her charismatic leadership style was focused on the future and the need for change from the status quo. Her office contained a sign that read "Welcome to the Department of the Future." Roddick referred to her style as "benevolent anarchism." She inspired creativity by inviting employees to examine what they were doing and how they were doing it, hoping to find better work methods. She encouraged employees to make their work enjoyable and to try novel and unique approaches to problems. Her passion for environmental and social causes, her personal belief and message that all women are beautiful, and her future-oriented inspirational leadership style all contributed to The Body Shop's amazing success.

In 2005 Anita announced she was giving away her £51 million fortune through her Foundation to support ethical entrepreneurs. In 2006 the Roddicks agreed to a buyout by the French company L'Oréal. Although she was criticized for this because of L'Oréal's record, she was later featured in a survey of the most admired powerful women. Anita Roddick died in 2007 from liver problems due to contracting Hepatitis C during blood transfusions in 1971.

Several leadership theories are demonstrated in Anita Roddick's leadership. Reformulated Path-Goal Theory and the Multiple Linkage Model are reflected in her *boundary-spanning* behaviors as she was a constant advocate with employees, customers, and governments for environmental issues, human rights, and eliminating product testing on animals. She regularly corresponded with all employees through videos emphasizing the importance of their efforts for society and the latest environmental efforts of her organization. She embodied aspects of Servant Leadership by her total *commitment to her mission* of addressing the role of business corporations and individuals in tackling environmental issues, human and animal rights, and ethical issues. She displayed Charismatic/Transformational Leadership by constantly portraying a *vision* of women's beauty different from that defined by the popular media, by *inspiring* other organizations to be environmentally responsible, and by inspiring her employees to help create a better future for the world. Her *determination, self-confidence,* and *integrity* reflect Trait Theories of leadership.

Discussion Questions

1   Why do you think Anita Roddick focused her behaviors and efforts so heavily on social and environmental issues?
2   Was her focus on social and environmental issues "good leadership" in her industry?

3   Which leadership theory do you believe best characterizes Roddick's leadership approach?
4   Would her leadership approach be effective in other contexts, such as automobile manufacturing, extractive industries (oil or mining), or tobacco?

Selected References

Adler, N. J. (1997). Global leadership: Women leaders. *Management International Review*, 37(1), 171–196.

The Body Shop (September 3, 2002). Retrieved November 20, 2008 from http://every thing2.com/index.pl?node_id=1131866&displaytype=printable&lastnode_id=0.

Howell, J. P. & Costley, D. L. (2006). *Understanding behaviors for effective leadership* (2nd ed.). Upper Saddle River, NJ: Pearson Prentice Hall.

Kochran, N. (1997). Anita Roddick: Soap and social action. *World Business*, 3(1), 46–47.

Roddick, A. (1991). *Anita Roddick: Body and soul*. New York: Crown.

14 Mohandas Gandhi
Indian Political and Spiritual Leader

Mohandas Gandhi is frequently known as the father of the Indian nation and is often referred to as "Mahatma," meaning Great Soul. He was the most influential Indian leader of the movement that freed India from almost 200 years of British rule. His humorous, cheerful, and optimistic manner made him easy to like, although his tactics were often difficult to understand. He emphasized human rights and self-sacrifice as the basis of his movement and consistently taught and modeled nonviolent civil disobedience as the correct path for Indian independence.

Gandhi was born on October 2, 1869, in Porbandar, India. He was the sixth child of a father who was a provincial administrator and a very religious mother. He began learning negotiating skills at an early age by observing his father and spent much time helping the sick and poor with his mother. At 13 he was married to Kasturbai Makhanji in an arranged marriage and when Gandhi was 15 his first child and his father both died. He was expected to be successful and help support the family. After one year in college, a family friend suggested he study law in England. Gandhi's brother raised the money and he spent the next three years in London completing his legal studies. While in England, he showed early signs of the asceticism that characterized his later life by not drinking alcohol, eating only vegetarian foods, and rigorously studying religious and philosophical texts.

Upon returning to India, he learned his mother had died. He opened a law practice, but it did not flourish. When he tried to intervene in a dispute for his brother, he experienced his first major insult by a British administrator who had Gandhi pushed out of his office. Shortly thereafter he was offered a lucrative contract by an Indian company doing business in South Africa. In 1893 he traveled there alone and was thrown off a train for being a "colored" riding in a first-class compartment. Later, he was prevented from riding in a stagecoach until other passengers intervened. Prior to this he had attributed prejudice and discrimination to individuals, now he experienced these insults as part of an institutionalized legal system. Indians had been brought to South Africa as contract labor to work in the mines. When Gandhi arrived in South Africa, there were sections of the country where Indians needed a special pass to walk on the street after 9:00 p.m., they

DOI: 10.4324/9781003333937-16

could not own land or engage in business, they were forced to pay a resident tax and live in slums, and were forbidden from using public facilities such as sidewalks.

He began studying and informing Indian residents of the government practices and advising them of their legal rights. When he completed his contract, he was persuaded to stay and help fight further discriminatory legislation aimed at Indians in South Africa. Gandhi then founded the Natal Indian Congress of South Africa to pressure the government for Indian civil rights, to help train Indians in how to organize themselves and to serve as a political party. He ran the Congress by collecting dues, keeping records, publishing newsletters, and raising funds. In 1896 he returned to India for his wife and four sons and discovered he had become a symbol of Indian suffering overseas. Upon returning to South Africa, he was assaulted and beaten by a mob but refused to press charges—blaming the government discriminatory policies for the mob's actions.

Sometime in 1900 he began his transformation from a well-dressed professional lawyer to an ascetic celibate lifestyle, eventually rejecting all symbols of wealth and wearing simple clothing of the poor. He began volunteering two hours a day in a Christian mission to help nurse the sick and took leprous people into his home for care. His changes were undoubtedly difficult for his family members. He insisted his entire family do menial tasks cheerfully, including cleaning the chamber pots for those staying in their home. His wife was unaccustomed to this chore, and when he saw her frowning while carrying a chamber pot, he screamed at her. She reacted, and he dragged her out of the house and started to push her into the street. Her weeping question of how he had forgotten himself made him hesitate, and he realized how his anger had taken control of his actions. He began cutting his own hair, washed and ironed his clothes, and refused to allow his sons to attend a local European-run school. He planned to teach them himself, even though he had little time, and they later regretted their lack of schooling. Gandhi studied home-based medicine, diets, and fasting for healing and used them to treat himself and family members. He later organized and led an ambulance corps during the British military campaigns against the Zulus and Boers. In 1908 he decided to return to India and insisted his entire family donate their valuable jewelry, which they had received as gifts, to a fund for the needy. His wife objected, but he demanded that she comply.

Soon after arriving in India, he attended the All-India National Congress, which was a political party, a platform for Indian public opinion, and a vehicle for social reform that eventually became instrumental in gaining Indian independence. While at the Congress meeting, Gandhi met other influential political leaders but he was soon called back to South Africa to meet with the British Council Secretary. He decided to stay again in South Africa to lead the fight for Indian rights. He helped start an Indian newspaper and set up a hospital for plague victims in a Johannesburg ghetto. He then led a resistance campaign against a proposal to require fingerprinting and registration for all Indians. He had carefully studied Henry David Thoreau's *Essay on Civil Disobedience* and he planned his campaign accordingly. He called a mass meeting and delivered an inspirational speech advocating death rather than compliance with the proposal—but the resistance must be nonviolent. This passive resistance became his trademark tactic and was known as *satyagraha*—meaning "insistence on truth" or "soul force."

The registration act passed and Gandhi began directing a campaign to oppose its implementation. He used his newspaper to issue directives to followers and to notify government officials of his actions, he organized peaceful picketing of registration offices, burning of registration cards, and sent a representative to India to generate world opinion for their cause. Gandhi went to England for the same purpose. Returning to South Africa, he was arrested and jailed for a short time, which boosted morale for Indian protestors. He was then given the opportunity to negotiate with the governor of their district, who agreed to repeal the law but did not carry through.

Gandhi opposed other legislation that provided legal recognition for only Christian marriages—effectively making non-Christian wives concubines. He directed strikes and long protest marches resulting in beatings of protestors by police and thousands of arrests, Gandhi among them. The British and Indian press expressed outrage, resulting in a British investigative commission coming to South Africa. Gandhi was released and negotiated with the governor, resulting in the repeal of the marriage and registration laws and the resident tax on Indians.

Returning to India, he gave an invited address at a new Hindu University and surprised wealthy VIPs and benefactors by directing them to quit their high-paying positions and begin working in the villages of India to serve the poor. He also told them to commit to massive civil disobedience against the British colonial government and to work toward an independent India. He role modeled his directives, wearing the clothing of the Indian poor as he walked and spoke through most of India. Wherever he went he nursed the sick, opened primary schools, persuaded doctors to visit rural villages and clinics, and tried to prepare Indians for home rule. He used donations to start a commune (*ashram*) to help poor families through subsistence farming. He advocated for the elimination of "untouchables"—the lowest members of the Hindu caste system who were prohibited from participation in many aspects of Indian society. He investigated injustices to sharecroppers from British landowners and was arrested. A huge crowd gathered and he was released—demonstrating the power of peaceful civil resistance to the peasant farmers. He negotiated a major dispute between textile workers and their employers and fasted to obtain workers' compliance with his position.

When the British government implemented censorship of the press and limits on free speech and assembly to quell the movement for Indian independence, Gandhi called for a general strike. Violence ensued between strikers and the police and Gandhi began a fast to protest the violence. British troops fired on an unarmed crowd at a meeting, killing over 350 and wounding over 1,000. Gandhi met with the Indian National Congress and proclaimed independence as their goal. He traveled with Muslim leaders throughout India advocating peaceful civil disobedience and refusal to pay taxes. He directed Indians to burn all foreign-made clothing and to use spinning wheels to make homemade fabric for their clothing. He used drama by beginning each speech asking everyone to strip off all foreign-made clothing, to make a large pile and burn it. His vision for India emphasized the popular goal of independence from Britain, but he added elimination of untouchables and a peaceful unified country. His mission to achieve the vision featured nonviolent civil disobedience in the form of protests, strikes, boycotts, and noncompliance with unfair laws and taxes. Gandhi's sincerity, self-sacrifice, good humor, and optimism created a flow of donations. But his followers were beaten with metal-tipped sticks when they protested a sham British investigation of India's readiness for home rule. Gandhi directed Indians to refuse to pay a 22% increase in taxes, donations flooded in and the tax was withdrawn.

The British held a monopoly on salt processing and sales in India and imposed a significant tax on salt sales. This had long been a source of irritation for Indians as the poor often used more salt than the wealthy, due to their hard physical labor and the warm climate which increased perspiration. At 60 years of age, he began a 240-mile salt march to the Arabian Sea, the source of high-quality salt for India. The march gained thousands of additional followers along the way. When he arrived at the sea, he picked up a piece of sea salt. Indians all over the country began gathering, processing, and selling their own salt. Gandhi directed demonstrations, strikes, and boycotts related to salt resulting in 60,000 arrests and some killings among the primarily nonviolent demonstrators. He then informed the government that he would march to and raid a major British salt works in another city, resulting in his arrest. The raid was carried out by his followers who were unmercifully beaten and seriously injured by police with metal-tipped sticks. Waves of protestors came forward for several days to be beaten without even raising their hands in defense. Gandhi had publicized the march, and the world watched through the eyes of journalists who witnessed the beatings. World opinion was mounting against British control of India. Gandhi directed Indians to boycott British shipping, insurance, and banking organizations and many Indians stopped paying taxes. Britain could no longer maintain law and order and their revenues were declining in India. The government decided to negotiate with Gandhi and they eventually agreed to allow Indians to produce salt, to release all nonviolent prisoners, to return confiscated properties, and to allow the boycott of foreign cloth.

Shortly thereafter, Gandhi attended a conference in London where he spoke to many working-class groups and told them that one fifth of the population of India was on the edge of starvation. His optimism, sincerity, and sense of humor made him popular wherever he went. He returned to

India and was again arrested and jailed by the new Viceroy, who planned to crush the Indian National Congress Party. More civil disobedience, violence, and arrests occurred. The British planned separate elections for untouchables, separating the electorate from other Hindus and Muslims. Gandhi objected and started a "fast to death" to eliminate the designation of "untouchable" from Indian society. He became ill very quickly, a compromise was reached and approved by the British in London, and Gandhi stopped his fast. Over the next several years, he was in and out of jail and fasted frequently as an example of willing suffering and a means of influence to keep his followers nonviolent. He traveled throughout India and shook hands with untouchables in violation of age-old traditions. He built a small hut for himself with no electricity that would be his home for the remainder of his life.

In 1939, Great Britain declared war on Germany and the British Viceroy did the same for India without consulting any Indians. Gandhi advocated nonviolent civil disobedience against the Nazis and he actually urged voluntary sacrifice by Jews, homosexuals, and gypsies who were being murdered in German gas chambers. When the Indian National Congress offered to fight the Nazis in return for independence, Winston Churchill refused and the Congress asked Gandhi to take charge. He realized Japan, which had invaded the Asian continent, was a threat to India and believed Indian independence was essential in order to defeat the Japanese. So he directed more civil disobedience, was arrested, and riots erupted with fires, destruction of railroads and telegraphs, and killings of both British and Indians. In 1943 a famine in Bengal killed over 1.5 million people and while in prison, Gandhi began another fast, announcing that the British were willing to die for their freedom but would not grant India its freedom. He quickly became ill but recovered with his wife's nursing only to have his longtime secretary, and his wife, both die a short time later. He later contracted malaria and was released after almost two years of imprisonment.

By this time, most of Britain had decided trying to control India was too expensive and no longer possible. Gandhi wanted a unified India free from prejudice with equality and justice for all citizens. But Muslims feared being dominated by the Hindu majority and wanted their own country, to be called Pakistan. In 1945 a new prime minister in Britain announced support of self-governance for India but that two countries was unrealistic. Terrible violence erupted in India between Hindus and Muslims and the Muslim leader then announced in London that they would wash the Indian continent in blood if a separate Muslim state were not created soon. Weary of the struggle and violence, officials agreed to the creation of a separate Muslim nation. In spite of achieving Indian independence that he had fought for so long, Gandhi felt he was totally defeated and refused to attend Indian Independence Day celebrations on August 15, 1947.

The government of the new India reneged on their promise to pay Pakistan a share of the Indian treasury, violence between Muslims and Hindus became rampant, and over half a million died. Gandhi traveled to help quell the violence and started his last "fast to death" in January 1948 at 78 years of age. As he weakened, the new Indian cabinet agreed to pay Pakistan. The violence decreased and Gandhi stopped his fast. He announced his next peace journey would be to Pakistan, but on January 20 his prayer meeting was interrupted by a bomb. Ten days later he was shot to death by a member of a radical Hindu organization that advocated military conquest of Pakistan and elimination of all Muslims from India. Through his dedication and unusual tactics, Gandhi achieved one of his two major goals—the independence of India from British colonial governance. His other goal of a unified India with equality and justice for all and without prejudice had eluded him. In later years, his leadership became a model for other great leaders—including Nelson Mandela and Martin Luther King, Jr.

Gandhi's leadership is probably best described by Charismatic/Transformational and Servant Leadership theories with a strong emphasis on *boundary spanning*. His charismatic leadership is shown by his *inspirational rhetoric* and a *clear vision* and *mission* for Indian independence. He also exhibited *self-sacrificial behavior* in the form of repeated fasts, arrest and imprisonment, and a poor lifestyle as well as continued *role modeling* of nonviolent civil disobedience. His Servant Leadership is shown by his lifelong *concern* and *service* to the poor, *providing for followers' needs* through giving away worldly possessions and establishment and *support* of ashrams, as well as his *empathy, openness, humility,* and *optimism*. His *boundary-spanning* behaviors are demonstrated by his successful *negotiations* with governing officials in South Africa and India, his effective *use of the media* to publicize to the world the condition of his followers, and his amazing success at *fundraising* for his campaigns. These behaviors are described in the Multiple Linkage Model and the Reformulated Path-Goal Theories of leadership. He also clearly used *directive leadership* in organizing and conducting campaigns of civil disobedience, strikes, marches, and boycotts. He was *supportive* of his followers financially and spiritually throughout his life. These behaviors are described in several leadership models including Path-Goal Theory, Situational Leadership Theory, the Leadership Grid, and Fiedler's Contingency Theory. His *determination, sociability,* and *cognitive capacity* are addressed in Trait Theories of leadership.

Discussion Questions

1 Why was Gandhi successful in gaining Indian independence when Indians had longed for freedom from British domination for so long before Gandhi's time?

2 What was the purpose of Gandhi's fasting and why was it important for his leadership?

3 Do you believe Gandhi's type of leadership can be used in other organizational contexts, such as business or educational organizations?

4 What can you learn from Gandhi's leadership that you can use as a leader?

Selected References

Kytle, C. (1982). *Gandhi: Soldier of nonviolence*. Washington, D.C.: Seven Locks Press.

Severance, J. B. (1997). *Gandhi: Great soul*. New York: Clarion Books.

15 Wilma Mankiller

The Chief who United the Cherokee Nation

Wilma Mankiller was the first woman elected as Principal Chief of the Cherokee Nation, the second-largest Native American tribe in the United States. An unlikely leader of her time, particularly in conservative rural native communities, she had a vision of a self-reliant Cherokee Nation that inspired her work as a community developer in Oklahoma. She understood at a very personal level the importance of preserving Cherokee rural communities to protect the Cherokee culture and language. To accomplish her vision, she empowered communities to decide, plan, and execute community development work using "gadugi" crews, a Cherokee tradition by which groups of organized unpaid workers work together towards a common collective goal. During her tenure as Principal Chief, the Cherokee Nation thrived. She was instrumental in doubling tribal membership and revenues, and she played a pivotal role in attracting high-paying industries to the region. Her administration achieved unsurpassed improvements in key areas such as infant mortality, housing, and adult literacy. While Chief and until the end of her life, she championed Indigenous people and Indigenous women. Some doubted that a woman would be able to succeed as Principal Chief, but she hard-earned the respect of her people by showing unwavering trust in Cherokees' traditional wisdom and capacity to resolve their own problems.

Wilma Mankiller was born in 1945 in Tahlequah, eastern Oklahoma, the middle child of 11 boys and girls. Her father was Cherokee and her mother Irish-Dutch. They lived in a home without a stove, electricity, or running water. She acquired a deep love for reading from her father and a close connection with nature from her mother. Wilma grew up a happy child surrounded by a tight-knit, mutually supportive Cherokee community and the beautiful nature that decorated the Mankiller Flats, her family land. The Mankiller Flats had been allotted to her grandfather John Mankiller by the federal government after the Allotment Act of 1887 forcibly redistributed tribal land and relocated Native American individuals and families. Wilma's great-great-grandfather, Ka-skun-nee Mankiller, had himself survived the forceful relocation of 1839 known as the "Trail of Tears," during which approximately 4,000 Native individuals lost their lives. In 1953, the Termination Act removed tribal sovereignty and terminated federal health care,

DOI: 10.4324/9781003333937-17

education, and social services for Native American tribes. Many Indigenous families were again being forced to move. The federal government incentivized family relocations to large cities by offering assistance in finding housing and employment. As their ancestors did before them, Wilma's family left their land behind, seeking a new home in San Francisco.

The government's promise to help with housing and employment never materialized. Wilma's family moved to a project neighborhood, surrounded by neon signs, prostitution, gang violence, broken glass, and loud siren noises. She was insulted in the street for the first time by a woman who used a racial slur. At school, she was bullied for her last name and her accent, and some accounts indicate that she may have suffered a sexual assault during this time. In her own words, she felt "surrounded by wolves." She became deeply homesick and lonely and grew insecure about her adolescent body and her Native identity. She was only happy while working on her grandmother's farm and volunteering for the San Francisco Indian Center with her father. With time, Wilma became street-savvy and witnessed the power of community activism, often led by invisible mothers, in the fight against urban poverty. In 1963, she finished high school and met Hector Hugo Olaya, a charming and sophisticated Ecuadorian college student. They quickly fell in love and got married, soon realizing that they were very different people. Three years later, they were parents to two baby girls, Felicia and Gina.

Wilma was overwhelmed and unfulfilled by her life as a mother and housewife and longed to be a part of San Francisco's cultural transformation and grassroots movements. Eventually, she would participate in activities organized by the women's liberation movement, the American Indian movement, the civil rights movement, the Chicano movement, the Black Panthers, and the anti-Vietnam War protests. Then, she began a degree in political science. In 1969, a group of representatives from 20 different tribes occupied the abandoned Island of Alcatraz, off the coast of San Francisco, to highlight the historical federal government's abusive expropriation policies of Native American land. Through her volunteering for the Indian Center, Wilma worked to secure donations for the occupation and brought supplies to the Island regularly. During these visits, she caught up with friends and family on the Island and connected with inspiring Native American leaders whose voices gave her a language to express her lifelong feelings and experiences. The occupation was a learning experiment that taught Wilma about direct democracy, gender inclusion, and bottom-up organizing. It also helped establish Wilma's leadership style, which recognized the importance of differences of opinion, finding common ground, and maintaining a positive and kind mind (being of a "good mind") to motivate others. After Alcatraz, Wilma continued volunteering for other occupations, meeting community organizers, and bringing her daughters with her. Later, she directed the Oakland Native American Youth Center and became a social worker, working to prevent the all-too-common removal of Indigenous children from their families.

Her husband, a traditional man, strongly disapproved of her activism, her studying, and her involvement with Indigenous people. Clashes between them were frequent. After living in a tense relationship for years, they got divorced in 1974. Her father had recently passed, and her ex-husband's continued manipulative and threatening behavior convinced Wilma to leave the Bay Area and return to Oklahoma with her daughters in 1977. This move allowed her to reconnect with the Cherokee community and made her feel whole again. Her old home had burned, so Wilma and her daughters camped on the Mankiller Flats. They participated in stomp dance ceremonies, joined the Four Mothers Society,[1] and listened to elders' stories. Wilma began job searching and building a new home on the Mankiller Flats. Her first job was as director of the Cherokee Nation's economic stimulus program. Her dedication and her ability to secure challenging federal grants caught the attention of Principal Chief Ross Swimmer. She helped fund several community centers, a daycare center, and home renovations in impoverished areas. During this time, she completed a social studies degree and began a master's program in community planning. Finances were tight, so she took a graduate assistantship and did occasional consulting for the tribe. Her schedule was impossibly busy, but she was resolved to show her daughters the power of perseverance to achieve one's goals.

One day, on the way to a consulting meeting, Wilma's car collided with another car that had invaded her lane on a slope with poor visibility. She came close to dying and the other driver, her best friend, died in the crash. Wilma was brokenhearted and underwent a large number of surgeries to repair her crushed face and leg. A few months after her devastating accident, she began experiencing symptoms of muscular dystrophy. She needed extensive physical and emotional healing and was forced to stay home for approximately a year. During this time, she reflected on her life, and through this mindful exploration, she lost her fear of death, and also her fear of living life to the fullest. Tribal healers taught her how to be of "good mind," a Cherokee attitude of positivism, self-confidence, calm, measure, kindness, and care for others. When she was finally allowed to work again, Wilma had developed a new vision for the Cherokee community. She understood, like very few did in the Cherokee Nation government, that an important portion of the Cherokee population lived in rural communities like her own, underdeveloped, under extreme poverty, mistrustful of administration, and politically conservative. They were proud, tight-knit communities where neighbors relied on each other for help and were closely connected to their Cherokee traditions and language. The preservation of these communities, she realized, was essential to the cultural survival of the Cherokee people.

In 1981, Wilma founded and became the first director of the Cherokee Community Development Department, built to facilitate grant applications for rural community development. She decided that development projects needed to follow the "gadugi" Cherokee tradition of collective action; more specifically, gadugi crews are unpaid organized groups of people working together for the collective good. Wilma believed that working to develop their own projects would give the Cherokee rural communities pride in themselves and trust in their power to self-help. Bell was then a poor and rural community of about 350 people, 95% Cherokee, not far from the Mankiller Flats. Wilma thought that Bell was the ideal place to start. She was warned that the area could be unsafe at night and that the neighbors would never collaborate in development projects. Unfazed, Wilma organized several town meetings. There was no attendance at the early meetings, but every new meeting brought in a few more people. She asked them just one question: "What single thing would change this community the most?" She carefully avoided making suggestions or being the leading voice during meetings, but let them discuss and reach their own collective decision: constructing a water line that served every home with fresh water. A water line, they explained, would reduce water collection time and allow their children to bathe more frequently, avoiding ridicule in the nearest high school, and likely reducing the dropout rate.

Wilma offered them a partnership. The people of Bell would develop the plans for the project and complete the construction of the water line. Cherokee Nation staff would facilitate coordination and provide funding through government grants. Chief Swimmer assigned Wilma a co-coordinator for this project; a Bell native who worked for the Cherokee Housing Authority named Charlie Soap. Nobody, not even the residents of Bell, believed that the project would be successful, but Wilma's earned their trust and they committed to the project. The 16-mile waterline project cost a million dollars. Residents marked the ground, transported materials, ditched, and laid pipe. Almost each of the 300 Indigenous families in Bell laid two miles of pipe, competing to see which family could lay pipe faster. Their enthusiasm was palpable and attracted visitors from neighboring communities. It also brought the attention of a television crew from CBS who, expecting scenes of powerlessness, found an exciting story of community self-help and engagement. Seeing their collective work on "CBS Sunday Morning with Charles Kuralt" gave the community of Bell national visibility and a powerful sense of pride in their collective achievement. Community meetings were now booming with excitement and new projects were developed to rebuild homes, an old community center, education programs for senior citizens, and a bilingual education program. The success of the Bell project validated Wilma's beliefs about people's capacity to take responsibility for their communities. Similar projects followed in Kenwood, Burnt Cabin, Wild Horse, and Briggs. Wilma and Charlie continued working together and eventually realized that they truly liked each other and had very similar values. Charlie was secure, bright, and unassuming, and a wonderfully positive influence on young people, including her daughters. They got married in 1986. They made a wonderful couple and a marriage of equals, and Charlie would be her best friend and supporter throughout her life.

In 1983, Chief Swimmer asked Wilma to join his campaign as Deputy Chief. Although she feared brutal tribal political confrontation, the dire needs of her people convinced her to run. Swimmer and Mankiller were odd running partners: he was a Republican with a background in law and banking; she, an extreme liberal feminist with a background in community development. Many opposed her for her gender and her ideology, and she faced great confrontation from the Cherokee Nation's Council. However, her known work in rural community development, her can-do attitude, and her hard door-to-door campaigning led her to win the election. She worked with Chief Swimmer to grow the Cherokee Nation's membership and assets and establish alliances with the Eastern Cherokee tribes. Wilma also continued to work on rural community development projects and, two years later, virtually all the community development projects in the Cherokee Nation were completed by gadugi crews of volunteers.

In 1985, President Reagan appointed Chief Swimmer as his new Assistant Secretary of the Interior for the Bureau of Indian Affairs. Wilma, who was 40 at the time, was automatically appointed Principal Chief of the Cherokee Nation, the first woman to hold this position. The appointment took her by surprise but she had a clear mission: building the economy of the Cherokee Nation from the bottom up. She explored new streams of revenue and jobs for the community and developed health care and educational programs designed to preserve the Cherokee language and culture. Wilma's leadership style was honest, reflective, positive, nurturing, and aligned with her Cherokee identity. She had no time or patience for political games, and she built trust through excellent listening skills and a great sense of humor. From her time at Alcatraz, she learned about the importance of diverse options to make effective, collaborative decisions. She also trusted the power of being of a good mind, gender equality, and gadugi Cherokee historical traditions, which she believed were useful tools for self-determination that would help the tribe stay true to itself.

In 1987, Wilma decided to run for Principal Chief. Wilma and Charlie campaigned incessantly, reminding voters that women had played a major role in the Cherokee government until the arrival of the white man. Her car was vandalized multiple times and they received threatening phone calls at home. During this time her kidney failed and she had to undergo kidney transplant surgery. Phone calls were made suggesting that she was dying, forcing her to appear in public during her convalescence to quiet the rumors. She won by only a few hundred votes. During her first term, she spent long hours in her tribal complex office, visited the Cherokee communities to learn about their problems and advance community development, and lobbied in Washington for Indigenous people's independent self-government. Under her leadership, the Cherokee Nation enacted a tax code, built its own tribe's judicial courts and law enforcement, and constructed multiple casinos that became important sources of revenue. In 1991, she ran for reelection, this time winning with 83% of the vote. During her second term, she worked alongside other tribal leaders and national politicians in defense of environmental protections, built a Cherokee code of ethics, and established a separation of powers between the Cherokee Nation's industries and the tribal government. She also worked to decentralize tribal services to bring them closer to the community. She was now a visible national figure who would speak frequently at universities, conferences, news interviews, etc., challenging Indian stereotypes and educating the general public about Native American history. Some found this popularity unsettling, and others challenged her decision to invest industrial earnings into health care, education, and home construction, rather than investing in building further industrial growth.

In 1995, tired of criticisms and in poor health, Wilma Mankiller decided not to run for office a third time. In the years that followed, she survived second-stage lymphoma, another kidney transplant, and overcame breast cancer. Still, she remained fearless and active, writing and lecturing about Native American identity, history, and rights, and giving voice to Indigenous women. In 1998, she received the Presidential Medal of Freedom from President Bill Clinton. She died from pancreatic cancer in 2010, surrounded by her family and close friends. Her funeral was attended by 1,200 people. Indigenous leaders around the world built fires on mountaintops in her memory.

Wilma Mankiller's identity was central to her leadership, and she can certainly be characterized as an *authentic leader*. She was, above all else, a Cherokee and all the steps that led to her growth as a young adult were inspired by her commitment to her people and her vision of a self-reliant Cherokee people. Her leadership style was driven by Cherokee traditions of collective leadership and work, women's central role in leadership, and being of a good mind. As a leader, she spoke truth to power and carefully listened to diverse voices with an open mind to make effective decisions. She exhibited traits associated with effective leadership, like *drive, energy*, and *honesty*, and she did not fear *taking action* to follow her vision. From a Path-Goal Theory perspective, Wilma used *participative leadership to* consult with different parties to make collaborative decisions and *shared leadership* to develop gadugi projects in which organized teams work together to develop rural communities. She can also be characterized as a *servant leader*, with a great understanding of who she was as a Cherokee, *caring, empathetic, optimistic*, and an excellent *listener*, dedicated to serving the Cherokee community, particularly those who lived in dire conditions. Her early life in the Mankiller Flats taught her that traditional Cherokee communities would not trust top-down leadership, but that she had to build on social networks and mutual support to facilitate the *emergence* of collective leadership towards a *common goal* of community self-development. As a formal leader, Wilma Mankiller provided the vision and the context to inspire others but she also understood the power of collective leadership and knew when to remain on the sidelines to empower others to emerge as leaders.

In recent years, her figure as an Indigenous female leader has received renewed attention. In 2022, the first American Women Quarters Program released a series of quarters with her portrait. In 2023, Mattel added a Wilma Mankiller Barbie to the Inspirational Women Barbie Dolls series. However, her legacy transcends breaking the glass ceiling. She was the most visible tribal leader in the United States and used this position to fight negative stereotypes and educate Americans about Native history. Her inspirational vision profoundly affected the Cherokee Nation, doubling its membership and revenue, reducing infant mortality, and improving educational achievement. Her focus on gadugi work would later inspire the Gadugi Project, which provided resources for Indigenous community self-help development projects around the nation, and the Gadugi Corps, a volunteer program dedicated to strengthening the Cherokee Nation. Gadugi Corps was signed into Cherokee law in 2023 with an annual $3 million budget.

Discussion Questions

1   What leadership traits are reflected in the Cherokee term "being of a good mind?"
2   Is the Bell pipeline project an example of collective leadership? Justify your response.
3   What specific behaviors did Wilma Mankiller use as a formal leader to facilitate the adoption of collective leadership in Bell?
4   Wilma Mankiller chose to facilitate the development of self-led gadugi projects in the underdeveloped and impoverished rural communities of Cherokee Oklahoma. Do you think that she could have been successful as well using charismatic leadership to inspire her followers by talking to them about her vision, rather than letting them take the leadership of their projects? Justify your answer.

Note

1 Religious, political, and traditionalist Native American society created in the late 1800s that opposed land allotment and other abusive federal laws.

Selected References

Cushman, E. (2023). *Cherokee Syllabary: Writing the People's Perseverance*. University Of Oklahoma Press, pp. 197.
Herda, D.J. (2021). *Wilman Mankiller: How one woman united the Cherokee Nation and helped change the face of America*. Helena, MT: TwoDot.
Mankiller, W. & Wallis, M. (1993). *Mankiller. A chief and her people*. Griffin.
Swafford Bliss, T. (2023). *Wilman Mankiller: A life in American History*. Santa Barbara, CA: ABC-CLIO.
Verhovek, S. H. (2010, April 6). Wilma Mankiller, Cherokee Chief and First Woman to Lead Major Tribe, Is Dead at 64. *The New York Times*. www.nytimes.com/2010/04/07/us/07mankiller.html.

16 Pat Summitt
Women's Basketball Coach

Pat Summitt was the head basketball coach for the University of Tennessee Lady Volunteers (Vols). She coached at Tennessee from 1974 and was one of only two collegiate coaches with over 1,000 victories. Her teams won more games than any other NCAA basketball coach in history. Summitt was a consummate competitor who won eight NCAA national championships (second only to John Wooden from UCLA who had ten titles) and 27 Southeastern Conference championships. Her program has produced 19 Olympic athletes and 43 professional players. She was admitted to the Basketball Hall of Fame the first year she was eligible and she was the first women's basketball coach to break the $1,000,000 salary ceiling. Perhaps most importantly for her players, every Lady Vol who completed her basketball eligibility at Tennessee graduated with a degree.

Patricia Head Summitt was born in 1952, the fourth of five children, in Clarksville, Tennessee. She spent most of her early years working with her family from sunrise to sunset on their dairy and tobacco farm. Her father was a strict disciplinarian who built a small plot of farmland into a 1,000-acre farm before branching into several other businesses. Pat described her early days as filled with school, church, and fieldwork. But her father did build a basketball court in the hayloft of their barn and strung lights so Pat and her brothers could play at night. The entire family was tall in stature, and Pat grew up playing against her athletic brothers. When she was in high school, her father moved the family to another county so Pat could play for a school basketball team. By then she could dribble circles around the boys.

She excelled on the court and attended the University of Tennessee at Martin where she was selected as an All-American. In 1974, her senior year, she severely injured her knee and was sidelined. That same year she became a graduate assistant basketball coach at the University of Tennessee, Knoxville. When the head coach left, Summitt was named head coach of the Lady Vols. She was not much older than her players. They were all from Tennessee and had played only six-person women's basketball in high school, three on defense and three on offense, which required very little running. They were now playing five-person full-court basketball, a new game for these players. The athletic funds for the team were minimal so Pat drove

DOI: 10.4324/9781003333937-18

them to their games and washed their uniforms. She told the under-graduates who showed up for the first tryout how demanding it would be to be a Lady Vol and many never returned. She was accustomed to hard work, she role modeled this for her players, and she expected their maximum effort at all times.

In her first year of coaching, the Lady Vols finished with 16 wins and eight losses, this was followed the next year with a similar record. During this time Pat finished her master's degree and served as co-captain of the 1976 Olympic basketball team, earning the United States a silver medal. Billie Moore coached the Olympic team that year and she drove Pat like a tough taskmaster with harsh words and challenges. Pat attributes her aggressive verbal and physical style of coaching to Moore. It is also likely her upbringing with a domineering father influenced her style. After her first two years of coaching, Summitt's teams never won less than 20 games per season.

Summitt believed that life is competition and those who believe they will win, usually do. She stated that winners are not born, they are made, and told her players they must always go for what they want and have no fear of failure. They must learn from mistakes and correct them for the next opportunity. She was animated, intense, and demanding during practice and games—shouting directions and waving her arms. She met with each player at least four times per year to direct them in how to perform their roles. She then held them accountable for meeting her expectations, as such they learned self-discipline and began to "own their role" on the team. She also met with the team captains early in the year to set goals for the team in writing. She believed the goals must require great effort to achieve, but not be so high that the players lose morale and self-discipline. She set goals for the team each day and held them accountable, with rewards for achieving the goals and punishment for non-achievement. One example was decreasing the number of turnovers during practice scrimmage, which was often against male players. If this goal was met, they ended the practice with an easy shooting drill. If the goal was not met, they ran sprints. She had few rules for her teams but enforced them consistently with negative consequences for violations. One key player who was destined for a successful professional career was dropped from the team when she repeatedly violated team rules. Summitt insisted that her players always gave their best effort and maintained that this made others respect them. She constantly challenged her players by scheduling a large percentage of their games against nationally ranked opponents. She noted that the pressure of these games prepared her team for NCAA tournament competition.

She learned from her parents that you win in life with people, so she consulted with her players and listened. Early in the year, she asked the players what style of play they wanted to use during the season. They nearly always said they wanted to run, press, play hard, fast and smart. Later in the year, when they were gasping for breath after running sprints, she reminded them of their decision. She also used her captains' input in setting team goals and establishing rules. John Wooden stated that Summitt knew people as well as she knew basketball. She got to know each player and tried to understand their goals and motivation. Early in her career, she realized that her constructive criticism and aggressive style was destroying some of her players' confidence and ability to play to their potential. At her husband's suggestion, she instituted a program called Rebound and Two Points. Whenever a Lady Vol received a compliment from Summitt, they responded with "Two Points!" When they received a criticism, they stated "Rebound!" This made them keep track and realize that they received compliments along with the criticism. By being honest, she built mutual trust and respect. She showed that she cared for her players, who called her "Pat," and she always gave them the major credit for their successes.

Summitt knew that to be successful, she must constantly change and update her strategy and tactics. Tennessee has a long-standing rivalry with the University of Connecticut, a basketball powerhouse. When the Lady Vols lost to Connecticut in the final game of the NCAA tournament in 1995, Summitt studied the triple-post offense UConn used to defeat her team. She then took her staff to Chicago and met with coaches for the Chicago Bulls who used that offense at the professional level. They learned the Bull's strategy and implemented portions of this offense in their team's play the next year, resulting in three consecutive NCAA national championships.

Pat Summitt knew that all leaders have weaknesses and believed they should surround themselves with people who are better than the leader in those areas. They should then rely on those people for decisions and guidance when needed. She believed in role modeling good citizenship and was extremely active in representing her program and university to the local, state, and national community. She was an active fund raiser for University of Tennessee and served in numerous capacities for the Smithsonian Institute, United Way, Verizon Wireless Hopeline (which benefits domestic violence advocacy organizations), Big Brothers Big Sisters, Easter Seal Society, American Heart Association, Race for the Cure of Juvenile Diabetes, Basketball Hall of Fame, United States Olympic Committee, and other organizations. She was a popular motivational speaker for numerous organizations such as the CIA, Federal Reserve, and Victoria's Secret, and she served as consultant to the Women's National Basketball Association. Summitt's achievements and service brought her widespread recognition and numerous national leadership awards. Her players describe the life lessons they received from her as just as important as their coursework and degree from University of Tennessee. Pat Summitt was diagnosed with early-onset dementia in 2011 and stepped down as head coach in early 2012. She died on June 28, 2016 at the age of 64 from complications due to Alzheimer's disease.

Pat Summitt was a highly *directive leader* when she assigned roles and clarified expectations for individual players. She also used *participative leadership* by consulting with her captains on goal setting, rule specification, and style of play. She was *supportive* of her players by getting to know them and showing she cared for them as individuals. She used *reward* and *punishment behaviors* by implementing a system so they remembered how she complimented them for meeting goals, gave them credit for their successes, and punished them for rule violations. These leader behaviors are discussed in the Multiple Linkage Model, Situational Leadership Theory, Path-Goal Theory, and the Leadership Grid. Her fundraising and volunteer activities for worthy causes demonstrate effective *boundary spanning* for her university and sports program. This leader behavior is described in the Reformulated Path-Goal Theory and the Multiple Linkage Model. Her aggressive verbal and physical style fits with common expectations for a leader in highly competitive sports, demonstrating the Implicit Leadership Theory for this type of leader. She made use of *substitutes for leadership* in hiring staff members who could fill in for her weaknesses and provide leadership in their areas when needed. Her *determination, self-confidence,* and *integrity* reflect the Trait Theories of leadership.

Discussion Questions

1　Do you believe Pat Summitt's highly aggressive verbal and physical style is necessary in leading a national contender in university level sports competition? Why or why not?

2　Do you believe there are athletes who would be unable to play for Summitt? If so, why?

3　How important were Summitt's boundary-spanning activities for the success of her program at University of Tennessee?

4　In what ways did Summitt make use of substitutes for leadership in the teams she coached?

5　What are the leadership characteristics and behaviors that make up an implicit leadership theory for a top-level university sports coach? Are these characteristics and behaviors any different for a professional sports coach?

Selected References

Frick, L.Summitt, Patricia Head. Notable Sports Figures, 2004. Retrieved August 6, 2011 from www.encyclopedia.com/people/sports-and-games/sports-biographies/pat-summitt#3407900547.

Pat Summitt and the Tennessee Lady Vols. (n.d.). Retrieved November 6, 2009, from http://thethunderchild.com/LadyVols/Photos/BioPhotos/Biography.html.

Summitt, P. H. & Jenkins, S. (2014). *Sum it up: A thousand and ninety-eight victories, a couple of irrelevant losses, and a life in perspective.* New York: Three Rivers Press.

University of Tennessee (n.d.). Pat Summitt: Women's basketball head coach emeritus. Retrieved on January 20, 2017 from patsummitt.org/our_role/pats_story/her_story.aspx.

17 Steve Jobs

CEO and Cofounder of Apple Inc.

Steve Jobs was cofounder and CEO of Apple Inc. and founder and former CEO of Pixar Animation. He was a complex human being. Described as a brilliant megalomaniac, his vision for the personal computer and information technology combined with his intense focus on style and function made Apple "the temple of techno-cool." He was innovator, agitator, and egotist. Most importantly, he was a charismatic speaker who captivated employees, potential employees, and crowds of technology buffs exactly like an evangelist or demagogue. He excited people to buy into his vision and inspired them to work absurd hours, days, and months to meet ridiculous deadlines to create what he termed "killer products" that would change the world. The teams he created and inspired were usually successful.

Steve Jobs was born in San Francisco on February 24, 1955 and was adopted by Paul and Clara Jobs. He attended school in the San Francisco bay area and became interested in electronics. When he was 14, a friend introduced him to Steve Wozniak (known as Woz) who was five years older and was already building an early personal computer.

Jobs was fascinated, and the two became friends. Both were solitary and self-absorbed individuals who could focus on a project they chose to work on and become lost in their work. Woz had the real engineering knowledge and Jobs had the drive and guts to do anything to achieve his goal. After graduating from high school, Jobs attended Reed College in Oregon for a short time, dropped out, and returned to California where he joined a computer club with Woz. Jobs took a job with Atari, manufacturer of computer games, to earn money. He was affected by the anti-Vietnam War era with its hip drug culture and he later spent several months backpacking around India with a friend from college.

Back in the United States, he returned to Atari and was assigned to reduce the number of chips on a circuit board for a game called *Breakout*. He made a deal with the tech savvy Woz to reduce the number of chips, and they would split the commission evenly. Woz completed the project with incredible success, and Jobs paid him $350. Jobs did not reveal that Atari had actually paid him several thousand dollars for the job.

DOI: 10.4324/9781003333937-19

In 1976, Jobs and Woz formed a business partnership called Apple, which would sell their first computer—Apple I. It was actually a circuit board that could be used to help hobbyists build their own computers. Jobs succeeded in selling the boards to an early computer parts store. Meanwhile, Woz was busy designing the Apple II—their first freestanding computer. Jobs worked hard at finding deals on parts, looking for investors, and promoting their computers. Together they attended the first personal computer festival and made key decisions about their next computer. In 1976 they met Mike Markkula who provided financing and in January 1977 they founded Apple Inc. There were four shareholders—Jobs, Woz, Markkula, and Rod Holt who specialized in power supplies. Jobs had wanted a business to build and now he had one.

When Apple became a corporation, Steve Jobs' management style came into focus. He was a perfectionist and very impatient. He could not wait for things to be completed and introduced to the public. At Markkula's insistence, an outside executive was hired as president. However, Jobs, Woz, and Markkula were the major owners and they had the power. Power was an issue that recurred throughout Steve's life. Over the next year, the friendship between Jobs and Woz deteriorated. Jobs was described by an early employee as primarily focused on the end user—he was most concerned with the appearance of the computer screen and the computer case. But the interpersonal style he used in conveying his desires often angered employees. At the West Coast Computer Faire, Jobs insisted the cases for Apple II be sanded and repainted the night before the show. They were a sensation and Apple received several hundred orders.

Jobs was insistent on having his ideas implemented at Apple. He fought with the president to include a one-year warranty to promote customer loyalty and won after crying to have his way. He was a very tough negotiator with suppliers and bested many people with more experience. He repeatedly set unrealistic goals for product development, yet he had an almost unbelievable power of persuasion. People would "drink Steve's Kool-Aid"—a reference to LSD mixed with Kool-Aid and served at rock concerts in the 1960s. They believed in his perception of reality—that they could change the world—and accepted his ridiculous timetables. They called this Steve's "reality distortion field." He could infuriate and inspire small groups of hand-selected engineers to do the impossible. One coworker described Jobs' power of vision as almost frightening. In the early years, Apple staff were not there for the money, they were changing the world.

In the late 1970s Apple had made the originators wealthy. Two years later Apple had its first public offering of stock, and they made extremely rich. Jobs refused to offer stock options to loyal employees who had worked hard for Apple for years. He seemed determined to show his power. Woz initiated a private sale and gave away some of his own stock to deserving employees. Jobs insisted on a small computer case for Apple III, too small for the electronic configuration. It never worked well, and the engineers were blamed. Problems with the next Apple computer, titled Lisa and driven by Jobs, resulted in a revolt by the management. In 1984, Jobs was moved out of an operational role and given the titular role of chairman of the board. Jobs then found another project to build called the Macintosh. He had opposed this project as originally conceived, but now needed something to push and he was enthused about creating a small inexpensive computer for the masses. Through political maneuvering and tearful confrontation, he took over the project from its originator, Jef Raskin.

He micromanaged the project and insisted that the Macintosh be ready for market in 12 months. He interrupted on-going work and was interested in every detail. His people said he would typically reject a new idea when first presented, but he would often return two weeks later with the same idea and claim he just thought of it. They could then incorporate "his" idea in their designs. They eventually used this tendency to influence his decisions. Steve made a dramatic presentation of the Mac at Apple's 1984 annual meeting, and the computer used a voice synthesis program to introduce Steve as "like a father to me." The early sales of the Mac were very good but they soon lagged due to problems with storage space. Steve had insisted on specifying the exact configurations without market research and he had missed key user needs.

Continued sales declines and unhappiness with Steve's management led to his ousting as head of Macintosh. In May 1985 he tried to have John Sculley, then Apple CEO, ousted but failed. Jobs was then labeled "Chairman," and "Global Visionary," and was stripped of any management role at Apple. Woz had already left Apple; it was a different place now.

Steve then started a new company, NeXT Computer, with Ross Perot as a major investor. The new computer would provide advanced technology for the scientific and academic fields. He described the new machine as an "interpersonal computer" to facilitate communication and collaboration between people, and it sported improved email features. Jobs insisted on a small magnesium cube to house the machine, which caused hardware problems, and it never sold well. The new company eventually transitioned to software development. In 1986, Jobs bought the Graphics Group from George Lucas for one-third the asking price (due to Lucas' impending divorce). He named the graphics company Pixar. It was originally a sophisticated graphics hardware developer, but frustration in selling their graphics computer ended with signing a contract with Disney to produce several computer-animated films. Its first product was *Toy Story* followed by several other box office hits that won Academy Awards. Jobs and Michael Eisner, Disney CEO, could not agree on renewing their partnership, but Eisner was ousted by the Disney board in 2005, partly due to Jobs' criticism. The new CEO patched things up with Jobs and Disney acquired Pixar from Jobs for 7% of Disney stock. Steve was now the largest shareholder of Disney.

In 1996 Apple bought NeXT for $429 million, and Steve was back at Apple as an advisor. Shortly thereafter, Apple was having trouble competing in the rapidly growing PC market and the board, with Steve's help, ousted the CEO. Steve was made interim CEO of Apple. He quickly terminated several projects and people and tried to implement other cost cutting measures. The board disagreed so he managed to force most members to resign, including Mike Markkula. He replaced them with some old friends. Employees developed a renewed fear of Steve, that he would fire them on the spot. He would lash out unexpectedly, even at his closest friends and commanded loyalty. He craved respect yet he would often leave turmoil and bad feelings in his wake.

NeXT brought technology and skilled engineers back to Apple and they developed the iMac for the home consumer market which helped Apple's competitiveness. This was followed by iTunes music software, the iPod portable music player, and the iTunes music store which made use of the new technology at Apple and revolutionized music distribution. Apple then entered the cell phone business with the iPhone—a touch display cell phone, Internet device, and iPod. Throughout, he continually reminded his employees that "real artists ship," meaning they must produce functional stylish products on time.

Jobs dropped the term "interim" from his title in 2000. He never desired or emphasized a salary for his work, some years he took $50 and other years he took nothing. He did believe in stock ownership and the power it bestows. He always sought to place Apple and his other companies at the cutting edge of information technology by anticipating and setting innovative and stylistic trends. He loved to quote Wayne Gretsky, "I skate to where the puck is going to be, not where it has been." He was temperamental, aggressive, and demanding and he radiated zeal for "killer" products while instilling fear in his employees. He was an egotistical perfectionist who craved approval, as well as an insightful and masterful communicator. He had tremendous successes and huge failures, but his extreme self-confidence never waned. Perhaps most of all, Steve Jobs was an entrepreneur who saw that computers could be more than business and scientific tools; they could unleash human creativity and provide enjoyment for everyone. He had the ability to harness the most creative talent available and motivate employees to change the world. In early 2011, Jobs took an extended leave of absence from Apple to recover from an illness. In August of the same year, he resigned his position as CEO of Apple but remained as chairman of the board of directors. Steve Jobs died in October 2011.

Steve Jobs' leadership can be viewed from several theoretical perspectives. He was clearly a Charismatic/Transformational leader by providing a convincing *vision* of the importance of information technology in today's society, he reframed or *stimulated our thinking* about computers as more than scientific and business tools, and his *speeches inspired* audiences to create, write about, and buy his products. He might also be viewed as partly a *negative charismatic* by exhibiting narcissistic characteristics of extreme self-promotion and lack of consideration for coworkers. His leadership can be described by the Path-Goal Theory, Fiedler's Contingency Theory, Managerial Grid, or the Situational Leadership Theory due to his precise *directive* leadership regarding product specifications and appearance. He can be criticized for his *lack of support and consideration* for coworkers. His effective negotiating skills also reflect *boundary spanning* leadership from the Reformulated Path-Goal Theory and the Multiple Linkage Model. Jobs' leadership might be criticized from the Servant Leadership perspective regarding his frequent *lack of openness* and *honesty* in dealing with others. His *coercive threats, dominating style,* and *personal need for power and prestige* often undermined the quality of life for Apple employees, reflecting elements of Toxic Leadership. His *determination, cognitive capacity,* and *self-confidence* clearly reflect Trait Theories of leadership.

Discussion Questions

1 What do you think of Steve Jobs' charismatic leadership style?
2 Would you be comfortable using Jobs' leadership style? Why or why not?
3 In light of his severe treatment of some colleagues and coworkers, why do you think he was so successful?
4 Are there unique characteristics of the computer/information technology and animated film industries that make Jobs' leadership style especially effective? If so, what are they?

Selected References

Deutschman, A. (2000). *The second coming of Steve Jobs.* New York: Broadway Books.

Isaacson, W. (2011). *Steve Jobs.* New York: Simon & Schuster.

Young, J. S. & Simon, W. L. (2005). *iCon Steve Jobs: The greatest second act in the history of business.* Hoboken, NJ: Wiley.

18 Kōnosuke Matsushita
Japanese Industrial Leader

Kōnosuke Matsushita was less than 5 feet 5 inches tall, thin and sickly, not considered handsome and seldom recognized. His youth was filled with tragedy and poverty. He was neither a good speaker, nor a good student and was not considered extremely intelligent. But he motivated many thousands of employees to achieve socially worthwhile goals through his inspiring and caring leadership and his insight into the role of private business organizations in society. He supplied high-quality household appliances to billions of people at affordable prices and was a key person in helping to rescue the Japanese economy after World War II. He started with nothing and created an organization with $42 billion in revenue at the time of his death. In Japan, he was more admired than movie stars and professional athletes and was considered a national hero.

Matsushita was born in 1894 in Wasamura, Japan, to a family of eight children. He was the youngest child, and his father was a relatively prosperous farm owner. His earliest years were very happy, but his father lost everything by speculating in commodities when Kōnosuke was four years old. The family was forced to move to the city where they lived in a three-room apartment and tried to survive. His father failed at a small business, three siblings died in 1901, and Kōnosuke became the oldest living son with hopes that he would help rebuild the family's respect and fortune. At nine years of age, after only four years of schooling, he was apprenticed to a charcoal heater maker in another city where he lived and worked with the owner's family and other apprentices. Three months later his employer downsized and no longer needed young Kōnosuke. His father found him another apprenticeship in a bicycle shop in Osaka (a larger city) where he lived and worked seven days a week with a stern boss who allowed no laziness. However, his master cared for him and taught him his trade. He worked there until he was 15 and with encouragement and support from his master, he learned how to control costs, to buy and sell merchandise, and to care for customers.

In 1906 his father and two sisters died. In the same year, Matsushita became interested in electricity, which was becoming widespread in Japan. He saw it as a technological breakthrough that signified the beginning of a

DOI: 10.4324/9781003333937-20

new age. He left the bicycle shop and obtained a job in an electric light company to learn about electricity. He began as a wiring assistant but his openness to learning, curiosity, and ambition led to several promotions over the next few years. By the age of 19 he was supervising several large projects at one time. He tried returning to school part-time but his writing was inadequate, he fell behind and quit. His self-confidence at work grew steadily and at one point he convinced a crew to work around the clock for three days to finish a project on time.

His mother died in 1913 and two years later he entered into a marriage arranged by his sister. His wife, Mumeno, was 19 and she and Kōnosuke were not acquainted before the marriage. About this time, he designed a new light socket, which he presented to his employer who showed no interest. Matsushita was hurt by this response and resolved to quit and start his own company to manufacture light sockets. His original design had several flaws, which he eventually corrected, and in 1917 he quit the light company and began his own business. He was 22, had little savings, a new wife and 13 years of work experience. He began with four assistants—his wife, two previous coworkers, and his 14-year-old brother-in-law. None had a high school education. The business occupied a two-room apartment, and Kōnosuke and his wife slept in the corner of one room. They had little money for supplies and only made a few items, which they were unable to sell to wholesalers. Two employees eventually quit for other jobs to support themselves. Kōnosuke and his wife pawned their clothes and personal belongings to keep the business going. One wholesaler liked them and advised them to make 1,000 insulating plates for electric fans which were in demand. They did so, sold them immediately and received an order for another 2,000. This revenue allowed Kōnosuke to rent a larger house with more floor space where they made the plates, electric sockets, and another attachment plug. The plug was needed in most Japanese houses that had only a single electric outlet. By emphasizing very low overhead and long working hours, he kept costs low and sold good quality products at 30% below the market price. All his products began to sell.

As demand increased, they worked 12 to 16-hour days and eventually hired more workers who specialized in different aspects of production. A distributor approached him for exclusive rights to sell the attachment plug. Kōnosuke then showed his shrewd negotiation skills. He agreed, in return for a loan to finance his further expansion. He began taking in young apprentices who lived with the Matsushitas and were fed by Mumeno. Kōnosuke was stern but paternalistic, and Mumeno became their surrogate mother. His overall business strategy which he adhered to during most of his life was to create improved versions of existing products, produce them at low cost with minimum overhead and long hours (which were common in Japan) and sell them at below market prices. This required close attention to detail during production and no one in his organization worked harder than Kōnosuke. He was fiercely independent, optimistic, and determined to make his company prosper. He was also very willing to take risks.

In 1919 another sister died, and in 1921 his last sibling passed away. At 27, Kōnosuke was the only survivor of his family and continued to devote himself to his business. At first, he did all his own product designs, later he hired others to work under time pressure to satisfy perceived customer needs. He opened an office in Tokyo in 1921 and built a larger plant in 1922, which was financed through a loan he negotiated from his contractor. Matsushita Electric now had modern equipment and 30 employees and was developing one or two new products every month. They developed a much-improved battery-powered bicycle lamp that he first sold through a creative marketing strategy in bicycle shops. The shop owners were not required to pay for the lamps until they were sold to satisfied customers. Lamp orders increased, more money flowed into the business and they began making radio parts.

Matsushita was not considered a good public speaker but he was sincere, with infectious energy, and earned increasing credibility from his success in business. He began to devote his energies to training and developing his workers. He believed that a "collective wisdom" would make his company successful and this required empowering employees with the information they needed to continually improve performance, and managers having faith in their employees' capabilities and development. These capabilities must be nurtured by leaders through a caring attitude, as well as an inspiring vision and mission that motivated them to meet and exceed goals. He modeled a strong work ethic for his employees as well as a willingness to experiment, learn continuously, and take risks as they developed new products. He urged his employees to do likewise. He created a Matsushita employee organization that sponsored cultural, recreational, and sporting events for employees.

Kōnosuke and Mumeno had two children born in the 1920s. Their daughter was healthy but the son died before his first birthday. This was a great tragedy for Kōnosuke as sons were very important in Japan at that time. He continued to work incessantly and built a bigger plant in 1929 just as the world economy crashed into a depression and sales slumped. He refused to lay off workers, but decided to reduce them to half time while continuing to pay their full wages and eliminating all holidays. He asked all employees to try to sell the huge backlog of products when they were not working. They responded and sales increased, resulting in their plant returning to full-time work only three months later. Radios were unreliable at that time. Matsushita built their radio business in the 1930s by buying a radio factory and working to improve their reliability while opening their own stores with qualified personnel who could repair the radios. In ten years they were the biggest radio producer in Japan. By 1931, Matsushita Electric produced over 200 products and continued to grow during the depression. Kōnosuke expected much from his employees, but he showed concern and support for them by treating them well and with respect.

In an employee meeting in 1932, Kōnosuke presented his vision and mission for Matsushita Electric. He described their mission as creating useful household products that are as plentiful, inexpensive, and high quality as clear tap water. When they achieved this mission, his vision was a world in which poverty had vanished and his employees could enjoy their lives while benefiting future generations. He created ideal principles and asked employees to recite them together aloud each morning before beginning work. They included resolutions to serve the public, treat everyone with fairness, honesty, courtesy, and humility, and emphasize teamwork and continuous improvement. At first, most employees saw the mission and ideals as very idealistic. But over time, as they recited them and saw how Kōnosuke and his managers modeled their behavior to fit these principles, employees began to see them as useful general guides to their behavior. They also began to see their business as noble and just and to put more energy and dedication into their work.

Matsushita Electric was incorporated in 1935 and Kōnosuke immediately developed several plans to encourage employees to own stock in their company. He also reorganized the company into major product divisions that allowed him to delegate authority to each division to adapt to their market as needed. They began opening manufacturing plants in other countries. He constantly monitored financial and other reports, asked questions, and offered advice to his division managers. If a manager was reluctant to address a problem, Kōnosuke often yelled at the manager. If a manager failed to take action that was needed, he usually moved the manager to another position with a minimum of loss in pride and found a new manager. He opened a sales training institute in 1934 and a factory workers' training facility in 1936.

During World War II, Matsushita was required by the Japanese government to produce products to support the war. He complied and focused strictly on production while his marketing organization deteriorated. At the end of the war, he lost 39 foreign plants and 17 Japanese plants, which the occupying forces required to be spun off into separate businesses. This was part of the occupational force's plan to restructure the Japanese economy and Matsushita Electric was selected as one of the large conglomerate businesses to be broken up. The major executives were required to leave their jobs, and this included Kōnosuke, until a petition and repeated pleas by Matsushita employees changed the ruling for Kōnosuke. He was allowed to stay on as president.

He began rebuilding the company, and by 1951 it was profitable again. He then decided he needed to learn from more advanced industrial societies such as the United States and Europe. He visited the United States, spent much time in New York, and returned to Japan with plans for their own research laboratory. This was built in 1953 and began developing new Matsushita technology for televisions, microwaves, mixers, recording equipment, refrigerators, rice cookers, and other household products. Their product sophistication grew and their reputation increased worldwide as they marketed products under several brand names including Panasonic.

In 1956, Kōnosuke told employees that Japan was behind the United States and Europe in standard of living. He wanted all Japanese homes to have washing machines and other labor-saving devices at a reasonable cost. So he set the goal of quadrupling their sales in five years. Employees thought he was crazy, but they adopted techniques such as statistical quality control and product development teams and reached the goal in four years. In 1960 he told them in five years he wanted to reduce their workweek to five days (from the traditional six days) and keep wages at the same level. This was to catch up with United States living standards and let workers enjoy their prosperity. Again, the managers thought he was crazy, but they worked at developing more efficient work methods and automating plants, to become the most efficient organization in Japan. By 1972, Matsushita employee salaries were approximately equal to those in the United States and exceeded those in Europe.

In 1977, Kōnosuke was 82 years old and he promoted an independent and creative product manager to be president of Matsushita Electric. The new president adopted his predecessor's technique of challenging managers with high goals that reflected humanitarian values and giving them independence to act on these goals. Kōnosuke spent more time with the Institute for Peace, Happiness and Prosperity, which he founded in 1946. Its purpose was to prevent Japan from ever repeating the mistakes that led to World War II. He wrote and published books about private business organizations being "public trusts" with broad social responsibilities. He wrote that a humble person was not arrogant or reckless, kept a focus on the mission, always listened to others, and did what was right. He repeatedly emphasized the collective wisdom of people working together toward goals that benefited society and the importance of leaders who created inspiring missions that motivated people to place all their efforts to achieve the mission. He also created the Matsushita Institute of Government and Management to promote government leaders for the 21st century. In April 1989, Kōnosuke Matsushita died of a lung infection at age 94.

Kōnosuke Matsushita's leadership style reflects several popular leadership models. His *supportiveness* and *concern* for employee development and prosperity reflect Fiedler's Contingency Theory, the Leadership Grid, Path-Goal Theory, Situational Leadership Theory, and the Multiple Linkage Model. His challenging goal statements and insistence on efficient production also reflect *directive* leader behaviors discussed in these theories. His *inspirational vision, mission statements*, and *role modeling* are discussed extensively in Charismatic/Transformational Leadership theories. His negotiation skills and information gathering abroad are part of *boundary spanning* discussed in Reformulated Path-Goal Theory and Multiple Linkage Model. His *reward behavior* with employees in allowing them to own stock in his successful company and in raising their wages also reflects these theories. His *integrity, sharing attitude, enthusiasm, service orientation, optimism*, and *belief in the importance of his organization's mission* represent Principle-Centered and Servant Leadership theories. Matsushita's emphasis on the strength and value of the *collective wisdom* of organizational members, *continuous learning*, *delegation*, and *empowerment* reflect Complexity Leadership Theory. His *determination* and *drive, self-confidence, integrity*, and *cognitive insight* reflect Trait Theories of leadership.

Discussion Questions

1 In what ways do you think Matsushita's leadership style reflected his culture and personal experiences during his childhood and youth?
2 No one who knew Matsushita described him as especially intelligent or a good speaker. So how do you explain his inspirational effects on his employees?
3 Which of his leadership behaviors do you believe was most important in motivating his employees to work so hard and be committed to his goals?
4 Why was Matsushita able to remain effective for so long while society and the world went through many changes?
5 Do you believe his leadership approach would be effective today in highly developed economies?

Selected References

Kotter, J. P. (1997). *Matsushita leadership: Lessons from the 20th century's most remarkable entrepreneur.* New York: The Free.
Panasonic (n.d.). Retrieved on July 15, 2017, from www.panasonic.com/global/corp orate/history/Kōnosuke-matsushita.html.

19 Mary Kay Ash
Founder and CEO of Mary Kay Cosmetics

Mary Kay Ash was born in 1918 in Hot Wells, Texas to a family of modest income. As a young girl, she helped care for her father who had tuberculosis, while her mother worked. She was a good student, but the family could not afford to send her to college. She married at 17, eventually had three children and began working in direct sales for Stanley Home Products in Houston, Texas. She possessed tremendous energy and learned quickly, while conducting demonstration "parties" for homemakers where she sold Stanley's cleaning and personal care items. She eventually became a unit manager and held this position from 1938 until changing companies in 1952.

After her divorce from her first husband, she began working for the World Gift Company, another direct sales firm in Dallas. She became national training director for this firm and developed her own ideas about managing a sales organization. She held this position until 1963 when she was passed over for promotion in favor of a man she had trained and who had less experience and job knowledge than her. Tired of being underrewarded, she retired and decided to write a book to help women in business deal with the discrimination they faced on a daily basis.

Her planned book turned into a business plan for an "ideal company" that would help women succeed and flourish while maintaining a healthy family life. The plan emphasized the need for work-life balance by advocating three priorities for all employees—God, family, and career—in that order. She believed all managers must model these priorities, even though she eventually began rising at 5:00 a.m. to extend her workday. Mary Kay purchased formulas for specialized skin care products developed by the family of a previous customer. She knew they were excellent products and a good base from which to start her business. Her second husband helped her plan her new business but died of a heart attack before it opened. Her son then stepped in and helped her open Mary Kay Cosmetics in a Dallas storefront in 1963 with her total savings of $5,000 and nine saleswomen who she termed "beauty consultants."

From the beginning, Mary Kay emphasized a caring and supportive style in managing her employees and sales force. She believed that caring for people was completely consistent with a profit-making organization as long

DOI: 10.4324/9781003333937-21

as its operations added value to her beauty consultants, customers, suppliers, and the business. She was a vocal advocate of the moral principle known as the Golden Rule: Do unto others as you would have them do unto you. Although she speculated that women might be more responsive to a caring supportive leadership style, she believed that this approach would yield positive results in nearly any organization. Her company had a flat organization structure with most of its people operating as independent entrepreneurs in direct sales through "parties" or "shows" they presented in private homes. These beauty consultants bought their products from Mary Kay (everyone paid the same prices) and sold them for twice their cost. They worked as hard as they wanted and earned as much as they could. There was very little management hierarchy so promotions were not emphasized—only sales. Mary Kay provided extensive and continuous training and coaching as well as ideas for sales presentations. Beauty consultants recruited new salespersons and earned a percentage commission on the sales of those they recruited. This encouraged recruitment and built Mary Kay's business.

Mary Kay Cosmetics grew quickly as women seized the opportunity to be in business for themselves. Regional directors were appointed to help with training and coaching in their areas. Mary Kay invited groups of directors to her headquarters once a month for sales training and always had them to her home where she cooked and served them homemade cookies. She always emphasized treating people fairly and helping them achieve their goals. She believed strongly that praise and recognition as well as substantive rewards were powerful motivators. She looked for things people were doing right and praised them, emphasizing that this showed appreciation and helped build the person's self-esteem. She noted that this was critically important for new salespeople just starting out.

She gave pink Cadillacs to salespersons for reaching specific sales goals, referring to these awards as "trophies on wheels." She also awarded diamond bracelets and first-class trips to foreign cities. She believed these awards should be things the salespeople would not buy for themselves and they should demonstrate to others their success. Over the years she awarded literally thousands of Cadillacs.

She clearly emphasized financial rewards as a motivator because of the profit margin built into the products they sold. But she believed that public recognition was a more powerful motivator than substantive rewards. At her regular sales conferences, her salespeople wore designer suits and color-coded outfits to signify the level of sales they achieved. She published a company magazine titled *Applause* where top sellers were described and publicized. At times she speculated about whether this type of recognition was most powerful with women. Within two years of opening Mary Kay Cosmetics, her beauty consultants had sold over $1 million in products, and by 1992 it was one of the Fortune 500 largest companies in the United States.

Mary Kay was very free with advice and directions about how to conduct sales shows, but she respected her consultants as independent entrepreneurs and did not force them to use her techniques. She did require that they always be well groomed and dress appropriately. Pants suits were not encouraged. She emphasized that all Mary Kay personnel must be proud of their products, the company, and themselves and show this in their appearance and demeanor. She believed this was an important part of role modeling for customers and salespeople. She was always enthusiastic and emphasized a positive attitude, believing that a positive interpersonal style was contagious, and salespeople would mimic this style if it was shown by directors. She made extensive use of her directors in solving problems, often asking questions during meetings until they developed a solution. She believed that new ideas originated primarily from the salespeople, and taught her directors that people will support programs and changes that they participate in creating.

Mary Kay's vision for her business was to fulfill two needs—to allow women to achieve success and still have time for their families, and to provide beauty products that would make women feel good about themselves. She emphasized this vision at every opportunity and made frequent speeches about her business model as her fame spread. The saleswomen owned their own businesses; they were not in partnership with their spouse. However, at her conferences she provided seminars for husbands to teach them how to help their wives in their Mary Kay business. There were no sales territories in Mary Kay; salespeople and directors could sell and recruit new beauty consultants anywhere. Regional directors helped train all salespeople in their district, whether they received a percentage of their sales or not. They did this because they knew other directors were training their recruits in other areas. The organizational culture she created is often described as "can do" and frequently involved salespeople asking, "What would Mary Kay do in this situation?"

Mary Kay authored three books and received dozens of national and regional awards, including distinguished recognition from major business schools and *Fortune* magazine for her business leadership. Her company is often discussed in a case at the Harvard Business School. She frequently helped raise money for charities and established the Mary Kay Ash Charitable Foundation to combat domestic violence and to support research on cancers that frequently affect women. She suffered a stroke in 1996 and this affected her overall health.

She had over 800,000 salespeople in 37 countries with total revenue of over $2 billion when she died in 2001, leaving $15 million to her Foundation. In 2008 her company had over 1.7 million salespeople worldwide. She had become a symbol for many women in how to achieve success on their own, especially those who felt discriminated against in strongly male corporate cultures. Her inspirational speeches, determination, hard work, enthusiasm, and passion for helping women succeed became her legacy for many women around the world.

Mary Kay Ash was a truly *supportive* leader. Her message of God, family, and career in that order carried an *ethical* tone and her positive behavior to support her salespeople were prominent in her leadership style. Her caring and *supportive style* reflects Situational Leadership Theory, Multiple Linkage Model, Path-Goal Theory, the Leadership Grid, and Fiedler's Contingency Theory. Her *inspirational speeches, role modeling, vision* for her company, and *symbolic role* clearly represent Charismatic/Transformational Leadership theories. Her *empathy, caring attitude, optimism, competence*, and *connection with housewives* reflect Servant Leadership. Providing constant *recognition* and *rewards* for high sales performers are also described in the Multiple Linkage Model and Reformulated Path-Goal Theory. Her use of *participative* decision making is addressed in the Normative Decision-Making Model. Mary Kay's continual emphasis on increasing her associates' training and knowledge to improve their independent sales presentations reflects Substitutes for Leadership. Her *determination, sociability, integrity*, and *self-confidence* all reflect Trait Theories of leadership.

Discussion Questions

1   What are the main reasons Mary Kay Ash was able to create and lead such a successful business organization?
2   Why did she emphasize such a caring and supportive style with Mary Kay salespeople?
3   What elements of charismatic/transformational leadership did she demonstrate in her leadership?
4   Did Mary Kay utilize substitutes for leadership in her organization? If so, which ones and how did they work?

Selected References

Ash, M. K. (1984). *Mary Kay on people management*. New York: Warner Books.
Stefoff, R. (1992). *Mary Kay—A beautiful business*. Ada, OK: Garrett Educational Corporation.
West, S. E. (2011). *Mary Kay Ash*. Retrieved May 10, 2016, from http://theleadership resource.com/?s=Mary+Kay+Ash.

20 Ernest Shackleton

Antarctic Explorer

The Antarctic expedition of 1914–1917 led by Ernest Shackleton became one of the most amazing feats of adventure and leadership in the 20th century. Shackleton was an Irishman born in 1874 who sailed as a naval lieutenant on Robert Scott's first expedition to the South Pole in 1902. Shackleton became ill early in the Scott expedition and was forced to return to England. Shackleton later led the Nimrod expedition to the Antarctic in 1908 but was forced to turn back for lack of food.

Undeterred, he organized a third expedition in 1914 with the goal of crossing the Antarctic continent from one coast to the other via the South Pole. Although this expedition also failed, Shackleton's determined leadership and dedication to the welfare of his crew became the focus of an incredible story of survival and rescue under the harshest conditions imaginable.

Shackleton was inundated with volunteers for his third expedition and chose the Norwegian ship *Endurance*, which was built for Arctic cruises. They left England bound for the Antarctic in August 1914. After stops in Buenos Aires and a whaling station on the sub-Antarctic island of South Georgia, they left on December 5, 1914 for the Weddell Sea on the northern edge of the Antarctic continent. The *Endurance* struggled through 1,000 miles of icy seas over the next six weeks and was 100 miles from the Antarctic continent when the ice closed in and froze her solid. The ship drifted southwest with the ice and all efforts to free her failed. Temperatures fell to minus 20 degrees Celsius, yet the crew had faith in "the boss"—their nickname for Shackleton. They played soccer and hockey games on the ice and hunted for seals and penguins for meat until the long dark winter set in. The sun returned in July along with blizzards, more low temperatures, and ice floes that "rafted" atop one another posing a severe danger to the ship. In October 1915, the *Endurance* had become so badly damaged they were forced to abandon ship. Shackleton then wrote in his journal that his task was to reach land safely with all members of his expedition.

Their ship had drifted nearly 1,200 miles during the 281 days they were lodged in the ice. They were about 350 miles from the nearest land and possible shelter. They had no chance of contacting the outside world or of rescue in their present position. They had limited supplies and the ice was

DOI: 10.4324/9781003333937-22

starting to break up—making their position even more perilous. During their first night camping on the ice, they had to move camp three times due to cracks appearing beneath them. When their ship broke up in the ice, Shackleton made a characteristic speech to encourage the men. He spoke simply and briefly, but told them not to be alarmed; through hard work, cooperation, and loyalty they would reach land. The speech immediately caused the men to adopt a more cheerful view of their situation, even though they had only thin linen tents that did not keep out the cold and had to sleep on the ice in sleeping bags that were not waterproof. They simply believed that if any man could lead them to safety, it was Shackleton.

On December 20, 1915 Shackleton and his 27 men began a march westward on the ice, pulling three 22-foot lifeboats in relays as they went. He knew that if the ice began to disappear under them, the boats would be essential to their survival. Many times they took to their boats and hauled them up onto large ice floes to pitch their tents for the night. On April 12 they discovered that instead of actually traveling westward, the drifting ice had carried them 30 miles eastward during nearly four months of their march. This produced frustration, irritability, and outbursts of anger among the men. But Shackleton had a keen sense of how one man or a small group could influence the morale of the entire crew. He tactfully redistributed certain men among the tents on different pretexts, reminded them they needed to work together, and insisted on an optimistic attitude that was contagious. At one point they were camped on a long ice floe and, while sleeping, the ice turned so the sea swell began to crack the ice through the middle of their camp. They heard this and ran outside to see a tent being split in half, one half on each side of the crack. Shackleton immediately looked into the crack and saw a man in his sleeping bag that had fallen in. He quickly leaned down into the crack and pulled the man out before anyone realized the situation.

Seconds later, the two pieces of ice were jammed together again with a huge thud. Actions such as this became symbolic and solidified the men's faith in their leader. On April 14, after several days of rowing through treacherous icy seas, they sighted Elephant Island and the next day they reached the island—497 days since they had last set foot on land. Shackleton's dedication to his men and understanding of the importance of maintaining their morale kept them together through months of pulling their laden lifeboats across broken ice floes and in and out of the water.

The crew was safer than they had been since leaving the ship, but Shackleton realized they would not be rescued from Elephant Island. No ships used that passage and they had no radios to call for help. Winter had set in again and they did not have enough supplies to last the winter. Shackleton had a patriarchal view of his crew and believed everything that happened to them was his responsibility. The men had trusted him and he felt morally accountable for their welfare. He decided he needed to travel to the nearest habitation to get help. This was the whaling station on South

Georgia Island, which was 800 miles away and across the stormiest expanse of ocean in the world. Waves as high as 50 feet, known as "Cape Horn rollers," frequented these seas and their navigation would rely on a sextant and chronometer. However, these tools required sighting of the sun that may not be visible for weeks at that time of year. It was clearly a very risky trip but essential if Shackleton was to save his men. When he told the men of his plan to go for help, all 28 immediately volunteered to accompany him. He was almost overtaken with emotion from their faith in him, and finally managed to say only, "Thank you, men."

He chose five experienced seamen and the lifeboat, *James Caird*, for the trip. The men worked on the boat to make it as seaworthy as possible, using canvas and odds and ends to create a partial covering. The canvas required thawing over a seal blubber fire before it could be sewn in place. The wooden boat seams were caulked using lamp wicks, oil paints from the ship's artist and seals' blood. Launching the boat was difficult because of all the supplies needed for the estimated 30-day trip and the rough seas. The boat rolled over on the first attempt, throwing two of the men overboard. Those remaining on the island used the other two boats to make a hut because the wind had shredded their tents. They heated the hut and cooked with a smoking seal blubber stove.

The six men left Elephant Island on April 24, 1916, the day before the ice closed in on the island. The sea constantly washed into the boat, making the reindeer-hide sleeping bags and everything else wet. They were soaked with seawater an average of every three to four minutes. Reindeer hair from their sleeping bags clogged the manual pump they used to empty the seawater. Ice formed on the boat that was 15 inches thick, making it sluggish in the enormous waves, strong winds, and "cross seas" that battered them about. They chipped away at the ice but eventually had to throw items overboard including all but two sleeping bags to lighten the load. Shackleton insisted on hot meals every four hours using a tiny stove that two men had to hold in place while boiling water for the "hoosh" they drank from mugs. After seven days they determined they had traveled 380 miles toward their desti- nation and concluded they would make South Georgia Island in good time—if their navigation was correct. On the 11th day they were nearly swamped by the most enormous wave any of them had ever seen. All six bailed water for dear life and after ten minutes they realized they would not sink. On the 14th day they sighted South Georgia Island, half as long as they expected the journey to take. They were out of drinking water because their last container had been contaminated with seawater. They finally landed two days later after fighting their way through treacherous surf and reefs and were able to obtain fresh ice to melt for drinking water. They had navigated the 800 miles using only four sightings of the sun—an amazing feat. If they had missed South Georgia Island, they would have been swept into the south Atlantic to perish and the men on Elephant Island would have had no chance of survival.

When they finally landed on South Georgia Island it was nearly dark. They stripped the boat of all supplies and hauled it up as far as possible on the rocky beach. Finding a cave in the rocks fringed with 15-foot icicles, they rested, ate, and slept. The boat was nearly destroyed that night, and they all had to hold it onto the land for the rest of the night. Shackleton got a laugh from the men by thanking them for joining his little party. The next day the boat received further damage, and they decided they had had enough of sailing.

They needed to travel overland 22 miles to reach the whaling station and obtain a ship to rescue their crewmates on Elephant Island. This required crossing the main mountain range on the island, which was totally unmapped, covered with snow and ice, and had never been traversed. Some of the men were too weak for the trip so Shackleton set out with two others to cross the mountains. They crossed glaciers, icy slopes, and snowfields with fog closing in behind them. As night fell, they knew they had to descend to a lower altitude or freeze, since they had no sleeping bags. Because they were so high and the slopes so steep, Shackleton proposed they take a chance and slide down a very steep snowy slope in the dark, hoping they did not go off a cliff or hit rocks. He took the lead and they survived without injury. They then warmed a hot meal of hoosh and the other two exhausted men fell asleep. Shackleton realized they would freeze and never wake up, so after five minutes he awakened them and told them they had slept for an hour and it was time to go. The two then noticed that Shackleton was not wearing the warmest boots designed for their trip, but a lighter weight boot that was less warm. They realized this was typical of their leader, as there had been a shortage of boots on their trek and his rule was any deprivation should be experienced by him before any of the men.

At first light, Shackleton climbed a ridge and thought he heard a steam whistle from the whaling station. It was repeated at 7:00 a.m. and they rejoiced. They roped themselves down and cut steps in the ice to get off the ridge, they then had to lower themselves down through a drenching waterfall in the ice cliffs to reach solid ground. When they approached the whaling camp with unkempt beards and hair, tattered clothing, and unwashed for a year, the first two people who saw them were young boys who ran in terror. But the manager recognized them, took them in, and helped them recover.

After recovering, they first took a boat to rescue the three men on the other side of South Georgia Island. Shackleton sent them home to England as soon as possible. He then arranged for a ship to rescue the rest of the crew on Elephant Island. But the ice pack forced them back to the Falkland Islands, where Shackleton got another ship from the Chilean government. Once again the ice was too much and they had to turn back. British and Chilean citizens then donated enough money to Shackleton to commission another ship, which broke down on route. Shackleton then petitioned the Chilean government for a fourth ship, which was finally successful in reaching the men on Elephant Island. When the first lifeboat was lowered to rescue the men on the island, Shackleton was one of the first in the boat. As it neared shore he yelled, "Are you all well?" The men answered immediately, "All well!" All had survived 105 days on the island in spite of hardships, which included amputation of one young crewman's toes. Shackleton was surrounded by his men who pummeled his back and arms in gratitude. Within half an hour they were all on the ship headed north and eventually back to England.

Frank Worsley, skipper of the *Endurance* and close confidant of Shackleton, attributed their survival to Shackleton's constant care for the men and his general watchfulness concerning their welfare. He would attend personally to the smallest details and had unending patience and persistence regarding their well-being. He was viewed by the men as exceedingly brave but never foolhardy. He always approached dangerous tasks with caution and careful planning. In 1921 Shackleton returned to Antarctica on a scientific expedition but died suddenly from a suspected heart attack while at anchor on South Georgia Island. He was 47 at the time of his death.

Fiedler's Contingency Theory, Path-Goal Theory, the Leadership Grid, and Situational Leadership Theory can be used to discuss Shackleton's extreme concern, *supportiveness*, and *consideration* for the safety, welfare, and survival of his crew. He was also highly *directive* in the dangerous and highly uncertain situation they faced when their ship broke up in the ice. He exhibited Charismatic/Transformational Leadership by *inspiring* his men with short speeches and personal *risk taking*. This caused them to cheerfully carry out his directives and maintain their supreme confidence in his leadership. His absolute belief in assuming *moral responsibility* for their situation, in assuring their safety and escaping danger reflects elements of Principle-Centered and Servant Leadership. One might also consider him from a Leader Member Exchange perspective in that he had an *in-group* of confidants he frequently consulted on important decisions, but he always included all the men in any benefits possible—*out-group* members did not suffer under his leadership.

Discussion Questions

1   How did Shackleton's situation and environment on the Antarctic expedition affect his leadership approach?
2   Why was Shackleton's supportive and considerate leadership approach especially important to the crew?
3   Do you believe Shackleton's leadership style would be effective in organizational environments such as government, business, labor, or sports? Why or why not?
4   Which leadership theory do you believe most accurately characterizes Shackleton's leadership approach?

Selected References

Cool Antarctica. (n.d.). Shackleton, Sir Ernest (1874–1922) Trans-Antarctica Expedition 1914–1917. Retrieved December 7, 2008 from www.coolantarctica.com/Antarctica %-20fact%20file/History/Ernest%20Shackleton_Trans-Antarctic_expedition.htm.

Worsley, F. A. (1931). *Endurance*. New York: W. W. Norton.

21 Abraham Lincoln

16th President of the United States

Abraham Lincoln is often described as the greatest president in United States history. He was first elected to the presidency in 1860 when the United States was on the brink of being torn apart. Economic strife between Northern and Southern states, changing attitudes toward slavery, and rapid western expansion all combined to create an explosive social and political division in the country. This situation eventually led to a civil war that destroyed over 600,000 lives as well as countless families, livelihoods, and the collective fabric that holds a nation together. The Civil War began one month after Lincoln took office and occupied his entire time as president. His insightful and skilled leadership held the Northern states together and eventually ended the war, while showing empathy and compassion for all the soldiers and families involved.

Lincoln was born in 1809 in a frontier log cabin in Kentucky. His father farmed, and Lincoln described his early life as poor but apparently rich in affection, especially from his mother who died when he was nine. His father remarried and his stepmother encouraged Abraham in his efforts to educate himself. He developed a lasting fondness for her. His youngest brother died in infancy and his last sibling, a sister, died when he was 19. These early tragedies undoubtedly affected the young Abraham, creating a somewhat melancholy demeanor and philosophical perspective on life.

Lincoln had very little opportunity for formal schooling, but he showed persistence early in life as he read and reread anything he could find. His love of literature and fondness for reading aloud for an audience continued throughout his life. He held many jobs in his early years including storekeeper, postmaster, and surveyor while he studied law. He was popular and respected due to his honesty and sincerity, his physical strength, and his ability and willingness to tell humorous stories that delighted his audiences.

He ran unsuccessfully for the Illinois state legislature in 1832 but was elected in 1834. That same year he became a partner in a law firm, the first of three law partnerships that allowed Lincoln to develop a high level of legal competence and a reliable income. He married Mary Todd, daughter of a successful banker, in 1842. He served for eight years in the state legislature where he voted and spoke out against slavery. In 1846 he was elected

DOI: 10.4324/9781003333937-23

to the United States Congress where he opposed the war with Mexico. The issue of slavery emerged in a proposed amendment to legislation banning slavery in any territory acquired from Mexico. Lincoln supported the amendment, and it became a battle with Southern states that feared eventual abolition of slavery. He drafted legislation banning slavery in the District of Columbia but did not receive the needed support and it was never introduced to Congress.

In 1849 he did not seek reelection and returned to his law practice. He ran unsuccessfully for the United States Senate two times and helped organize and lead the new Republican Party in Illinois. In the second Senate race, he participated in the famous Lincoln-Douglas debates over slavery in the new territories. Public speaking and debating were major forms of entertainment at that time, and Lincoln was gaining fame and confidence as a master orator. In 1859 he positioned himself for a presidential nomination through long speaking tours where he exposed himself to thousands of voters. He deftly engineered the nominating convention toward Chicago, in his home state of Illinois. At the convention in May 1860 he managed to secure the presidential nomination over several major rivals, all of whom had longer and more distinguished careers. He did this by letting the more famous candidates fight it out with each other and positioning himself as the second choice for everyone. His election team also packed the hall with his supporters. Using friendly and complimentary requests, Lincoln convinced his former rivals to speak on behalf of his campaign for election. They did a magnificent job while Lincoln worked on keeping the party factions together through writing letters, resolving disputes, carefully avoiding commitments for patronage, and gathering and sharing information for the election. He was elected in November 1860 as 16th president of the United States. He had finally reached his lifelong goal of being respected and esteemed by his fellow men. He now needed to prove himself worthy of that esteem.

Lincoln immediately set about establishing his cabinet of close advisors. Lincoln knew the country was in jeopardy and that incredibly difficult problems lay ahead. He wanted individuals who were highly intelligent and experienced, were well respected, and represented different factions in their new Republican Party. He chose as his top cabinet members the three individuals who had also sought the Republican Party nomination for president—his former competitors. His self-confidence allowed him to select men with more education and longer records of public service than his own. He knew he would need their information, perspective, and insight to help solve the problems they faced. He selected the remainder of his cabinet with the same criteria in mind. He constantly consulted with these advisors, individually and as a group, throughout his presidency. He became especially close with Secretary of State William Seward and relied on his advice and suggestions many times.

Lincoln had shown his ability and willingness to mediate among powerful factions within his party to maintain its cohesion throughout the election.

Now he needed to fulfill the same function to span boundaries among Northern states and keep them together as Southern states began to secede from the Union. Seven Southern states seceded between Lincoln's election in November 1860 and March 1861. Lincoln had consistently maintained he did not seek to eliminate slavery in states where it existed, but only in the new territories. He believed that slavery would die if not extended to these territories where Southern growers planned new plantations. On his first day in office, the first item on his desk reported that the federal Fort Sumter in South Carolina was being threatened by Confederate troops and a resupply ship had been fired upon and forced to turn back. The military recommended surrendering the fort and Lincoln polled each member of his cabinet separately for their opinion. He then gathered more information, shared it with his cabinet, and polled them again. They decided to try to resupply the fort again with the support of their best warship.

Unfortunately, a communication error resulted in the ship being misdirected and the fort was attacked and eventually surrendered. The South had fired the first shots, the country was now divided and engaged in a civil war. Lincoln had shown his willingness to listen carefully to his advisors and to use them to help make major decisions, a pattern he would demonstrate repeatedly during his administration. He was a skilled communicator and now realized the critical importance of accurate communication in the war effort.

He frequently acted as mediator between military generals and among members of his cabinet, who differed in their opinions of the correct actions during the Civil War. He supported individuals even when he disagreed with them and defended officers who were attacked by the press or other officials. He often took personal responsibility for mistakes that were caused by others, to show his support. He visited the Union troops often and after every defeat, showing his kindness and concern, sometimes taking his young son Tad on these visits. At 6 feet 4 inches tall, plus his tall stovepipe hat, he looked comical atop a horse with his long legs dangling down when he made these visits. The overall effect was to endear him to the troops and develop great loyalty from the military and his advisors.

A key factor in the North's war effort was preventing Britain from recognizing the Confederate States as a separate country. Lincoln diplomatically softened Seward's approach in negotiating with Britain to successfully prevent their recognition of the South. Early defeats of the Northern forces caused resentment among military officers and cabinet members, which Lincoln continued to mediate. He became frustrated with General McClelland, his main military commander, for lack of action against the South's forces. McClelland continually insisted on the need for more personnel and supplies with predictions of future victories, while living a lavish lifestyle in camp and overestimating the enemy's forces. In January 1862 Lincoln issued a General War Order directing McClelland to move on the South. His directive was soon followed by the death of his beloved son, Willie, who succumbed to Typhoid Fever. Lincoln and his wife suffered incredibly in their grief. His melancholy persisted when the Union Army suffered several defeats.

Lincoln replaced General McClelland with General Burnside who was then out-maneuvered and badly defeated at Fredericksburg. Lincoln consulted Seward on how to raise more troops. He eventually accepted Seward's idea of having the Northern governors offer the additional troops from their states, thereby removing Lincoln from any public criticism for wanting more troops. It became clear that slaves were being used by the South to build defensive positions for the Confederate forces, freeing up Southern whites for active combat. In January 1863 Lincoln issued the Emancipation Proclamation freeing all slaves in the Confederate States and allowing them to join the Union armed forces. He countered significant Northern feelings of discrimination by publicly pointing out that Blacks were needed for the war effort. The Emancipation Proclamation resulted in huge numbers of former slaves entering Northern lines and joining forces in military companies of their own. These companies soon distinguished themselves in battle and became highly respected by other soldiers and officers.

These were difficult times for all those involved with the war effort including Lincoln's administration. Cabinet members and many generals were proud men under stress, and often resented it if Lincoln did not take their advice. In addition to his reputation as a great speaker and humorous story-teller, Lincoln was a master at "smoothing their feathers." He was always charitable and showed kindness, respect, and provided generous compliments for offended individuals. He showed tremendous emotional control and understanding of those around him by never retaliating against those who attacked his ideas and never holding a grudge (even though Secretary of War William Stanton had humiliated Lincoln early in his political career). Although outwardly he appeared melancholy, Lincoln dealt effectively with stress by frequently reading great and popular literature and poetry (often aloud to friends), by visiting Seward and his two secretaries, and trips to the theater. As the war dragged on, his appearance became more careworn, pensive, and haggard. However, his face would always lighten and often smile in the presence of friends and acquaintances who he usually entertained with his never-ending repertoire of humorous stories and anecdotes.

Lincoln continued to try new generals until he appointed General Meade three days before Union forces confronted Lee's army that had invaded the North. It was July 1863, and Meade held the high ground near the town of Gettysburg. In a horrible three-day battle that claimed over 60,000 lives, the Union Army defeated Lee's army and forced a retreat. Lincoln's hopes for hastening the end of the war were dashed when Meade failed to follow up and capture Lee's army. The Gettysburg victory was quickly followed by the capture of Vicksburg as well as a large Confederate force by Union General Grant. At last the tide was turning in favor of the North. In November 1863 Lincoln delivered the famous Gettysburg Address at the site of the battle. Many believe this brief address is the greatest speech in United States history.

His overall goal from the beginning was to preserve the Union and he eventually resolved to end slavery throughout the country. With excellent writing skills, he wrote public letters addressing policy issues to be read by officials at gatherings. These complemented press releases and speeches which he and cabinet members gave on tours of the Union states. Lincoln often inserted material in the speeches delivered by his advisors. He continued to support Secretary of the Treasury Salmon Chase, when he criticized Lincoln and the administration's handling of the war during his own pursuit of the presidency in 1864. Chase had done an outstanding job financing the war and Lincoln was grateful, while realizing that keeping him close and involved in the war effort would likely minimize the damage he could inflict on Lincoln. He regularly obtained input from influential individuals including congressmen and senators, governors, military officers, cabinet members, and those outside the government such as anti-slavery advocate Frederick Douglass (who spoke very highly of Lincoln).

Lincoln placed General Grant in charge of the Union Army in March 1864. Grant avoided the public eye, lived very frugally, and took the initiative against the South. He soon fought a seven-week battle of attrition against Lee's army in Virginia, inflicting major damage on the Confederate forces. General McClelland opposed Lincoln as the Democratic candidate for president, but Union victories at Atlanta, Mobile, and in Virginia made peace imminent and confirmed Lincoln's reelection.

Lincoln and Grant worked together to develop a program to give land and assistance to freed slaves. Lincoln pushed the Thirteenth Amendment of the Constitution through Congress abolishing slavery throughout the United States, using patronage to sway Democratic senators to vote for the amendment. The Thirteenth Amendment was ratified after Lincoln's death. He negotiated from strength with Southern peace commissioners, insisting on three points—all the states were part of a single country, with no slavery, and any suspension of hostilities must include the Confederacy's full surrender and a complete end to the war.

Lincoln was reelected in November 1864 and in March 1865 he gave a conciliatory inaugural address directed toward the Southern states—"with malice toward none, with charity for all." Grant and Sherman pursued Lee's army and occupied Richmond, Virginia, the Confederate capital. Lincoln followed Grant's progress and visited Richmond where Blacks called him their savior. He left Richmond in a joyful mood. Secretary of State Seward, who had become Lincoln's close friend and ally, had worried about Lincoln's safety as the war was ending. Seward was seriously injured in a carriage accident. Lincoln returned to Washington to see Seward, and Robert E. Lee surrendered the following day.

Always self-confident, Lincoln became more cheerful and neatly groomed in the following days. He read literature and writings by his favorite humorists aloud to visitors and planned a visit with Mary to his favorite playhouse, Ford's Theater. On April 14, 1865, five days after Lee's surrender, they visited the theater and Lincoln was fatally shot by a well-known actor who easily gained admittance to the theater. Seward was also attacked but survived his injuries. Lincoln died the next morning. He had stated his ambition was to be esteemed by his fellow men and to prove himself worthy of their esteem. History shows Lincoln clearly achieved his ambition, since his reputation as an honest, caring, and intelligent leader, who was a great speaker and abolitionist, has spread throughout the world.

Lincoln's leadership has often been described as Charismatic/Transformational due to his *vision* for preserving the United States Union, his outstanding *rhetorical skills*, and his ability to create loyal and devoted followers to support his candidacy and programs as president. His *boundary-spanning* activities are clearly evident in his political maneuvering during his candidacy and time in office, as well as his effective mediation among politicians and military generals. His *caring* and *consideration* for all people were evident in his *supportiveness* for troops, widows, and concern for the Southern states as he opposed all punitive actions against Southern states once the war ended. He exhibited *directive leadership* by issuing General War Orders requiring specific action by the Northern forces. These actions demonstrate important leader behavior patterns described in Reformulated Path-Goal Theory, the Multiple Linkage Model, Situational Leadership Theory, and Fiedler's Contingency Theory. Lincoln demonstrated Leader-Member Exchange Theory by developing an *in-group* of trusted advisors composed of several members of his cabinet. These men became fiercely loyal to Lincoln despite having been his rivals during his first presidential election. His reliance on this cabinet also demonstrated *Substitutes for Leadership*. He demonstrated a *participative* approach in making complex decisions with trusted cabinet members during the Civil War. This approach is addressed in the Normative Decision Theory. Lincoln's *cognitive complexity, determination, self-confidence, sociability*, and *integrity* all reflect Trait Theories of leadership. His *integrity, empathy*, and *commitment* to preserving the United States Union are described in Servant Leadership.

Discussion Questions

1 Try to think of specific situations in Lincoln's life where he demonstrated Charismatic/Transformational Leadership. Describe these situations.
2 In what ways did Lincoln show his consideration and concern for people?
3 Why was Lincoln's boundary-spanning behavior so important for his administration and the country?
4 Why was a trusted in-group of individual advisors, as described in Leader-Member Exchange Theory, so important for Lincoln during his presidency?

Selected References

Goodwin, D. K. (2005). *Team of rivals: The political genius of Abraham Lincoln.* New York: Simon and Schuster.

History.com Staff. (2009). Abraham Lincoln. Retrieved July 10, 2017 from www.history.com/topics/us-presidents/abraham-lincoln.

The White House. (n.d.). Abraham Lincoln. Retrieved December 10, 2010 from www.whitehouse.gov/about-the-white-house/presidents/abraham-lincoln.

22 Leymah Gbowee
Liberian Leader of Women in Peacebuilding Network

Leymah Gbowee is a Liberian social worker who initiated and led a mass movement of Christian and Muslim women to end many years of civil war and carnage between fighting factions in Liberia. The movement succeeded in ousting the despot Charles Taylor from the presidency and exiling him from the country. Gbowee's efforts contributed to peace talks among warring political factions, and formation of a transitional government, which held democratic elections resulting in the first popularly elected female head of state in Africa.

Leymah was born in Liberia and grew up in the capital, Monrovia. Her parents were Liberian and poor, and she experienced civil war from the time she graduated from high school. Taylor had been a major African warlord who launched a rebellion against the president of Liberia in 1989. He had a checkered past, having been educated and arrested in the United States twice and was fired for embezzlement when serving as an official for the Liberian government. Beginning in 1989, the population was subjected to a continual campaign of rape, mutilation, and murder of non-combatants by child soldiers with automatic weapons from both sides of the conflict. The "boy soldiers" (9–15 years old) were given guns and drugs and told to take what they wanted—resulting in horrible atrocities committed in front of families. Taylor eventually emerged as the victor and was elected president in 1997. Liberians voted for him because they feared him and a continuation of the war. His administration was marked by diamond smuggling, gun running, supporting terrorism, conscription of children as soldiers for the war in Sierra Leone, as well as abduction, torture, and murder.

Shortly after Taylor became president, another rebellion began in northern Liberia to overthrow him. The war continued with boy soldiers decimating the population and hacking off limbs of civilians to prevent them from fighting. Innocent civilians fled to Monrovia for protection as the rebels took over most of the countryside. The refugees were placed in camps of displaced persons where they faced lack of drinking water, sanitation facilities, and food. Many other Liberians faced these issues as well, including Leymah and her family. She had become a social worker in 1994 and her young children had felt hunger all their lives. She saw the horrible conditions in the camps

DOI: 10.4324/9781003333937-24

and how the children suffered. She had counseled former child soldiers and the damage done to Liberia's children was becoming too much for her. By 2003, over 200,000 people had died in the wars.

Leymah had a dream in which someone told her to organize the women in her church to pray for peace. She spoke to her Christian church congregation and described the terrible life of the Liberian people. They were tired of war and what it was doing to their children, and it was time to rise up and speak together about the need to end the fighting. A Muslim woman, an official in the Liberian National Police, was in the church and became inspired by Gbowee's speech. She offered to carry the message to the other Muslim women in her mosque. They listened and agreed that bullets did not discriminate, so they joined with the Christian women and formed the Women in Peacebuilding Network (WIPNET) with Gbowee as their leader.

Taylor's government was embarrassed by the refugee camps, and he told the inhabitants to return to where they were born. They refused because there was still fighting in the countryside and he threatened them. He hypocritically professed to practice Christianity and the rebels were largely Muslim. So the women pressured their ministers, bishops, and imams to pressure government officials and rebels to conduct peace talks. Gbowee had the women meet to demonstrate for peace at an open-air fish market in Monrovia, where Taylor's convoy drove past every day. They all dressed in white (to symbolize peace) with placards and banners saying that the women wanted peace now. On the first day, 2,500 women overcame their fear and demonstrated as Taylor's convoy slowed but did not stop. She led them in singing, and their words rang out that they were tired of running, suffering, and dying and that they wanted peace for their children. They demonstrated every day for a week and Taylor announced that no one would be allowed to embarrass his administration. The women became more cohesive and declared a sex strike—denying sex to their men until they did something to help stop the war. Husbands began to join the women in praying for the end of the war.

Rebels were getting close to Monrovia and apparently attacked the refugee camps. Taylor sent soldiers supposedly to protect the inhabitants, but both sides committed atrocities against the people living there and the camp populations fled. The international community began to call for peace talks, but both Taylor and the rebels refused. WIPNET decided to submit a position statement to the government demanding they meet with the rebels to discuss peace. It stated that they must stop the carnage, rape, hunger, and disease and save the children's future. They insisted on an unconditional ceasefire and a fruitful dialogue to end the war. Taylor realized the women were supported by the Liberian population and the international community and he agreed to meet with them. Gbowee read their statement and presented it with careful respect to a government representative who gave it to Taylor. Gbowee knew Taylor could smile one minute and have them killed the next. But she vowed they would continue sitting in the sun and rain at the fish market until Taylor responded. The women left the meeting with Leymah leading them into the street. As they marched, more women joined them at every intersection, all dressed in white. The march grew and grew and Taylor knew he could no longer ignore them. He agreed to attend peace talks in Ghana.

Gbowee and her followers then needed to convince the rebels to attend, so they conducted a fundraising campaign to send WIPNET representatives to Freetown, in Sierra Leone, where the rebels were meeting. Money came in from all over Liberia, and in Sierra Leone they organized women from that country. Together they lined up outside the hotels and along travel routes— all dressed in white to symbolize their solidarity and all calling for peace. Some of the women knew several rebels and told them their mothers and sisters had traveled a long distance to talk with them. The women told the rebels that if they did not attend peace talks that many innocent people would die in Monrovia and that they would be responsible for the deaths. The women of WIPNET were there to demand that all human rights abuses must stop and the rebels eventually promised to attend the peace talks.

The women knew they needed to keep up the pressure, so they raised money to send a group to Ghana to mobilize the refugee women there. Peace talks began with pressure from many other countries to stop the fighting that was destabilizing much of Africa. The women in white demonstrated across the street from the conference center where negotiations took place—singing and holding placards. Gbowee described the demonstrators as the "conscience" of the negotiators and called on them to do the right thing for Liberian women and children. Several African leaders spoke at the conference calling for an end to the fighting. On the first day, the BBC reported that Taylor (who was attending the conference) had been indicted for war crimes in Sierra Leone. Fearing arrest, he fled back to Liberia and left his delegation to negotiate. Rebel leaders gave orders to attack Monrovia and full-scale war began around the city while the negotiations proceeded. Taylor's boy soldiers rampaged through the city and threatened to destroy Liberia if Taylor was arrested. His forces repelled several incursions by the rebels and the war continued.

In Ghana, Gbowee talked with the mediator (the former president of Nigeria) who saw the women as an important ally. They went to different hotels and spoke with the warring parties, asking them what they could be comfortable with in a settlement. They realized the real issues were power, positions in government, and control of resources that would allow them to profit from any settlement. A high-level rebel officer told the women they planned to kill all the people in Monrovia, bring in more women and replenish the population. After six weeks, the talks were stalled with little or no progress. Both sides wanted more power and control in Liberia.

Gbowee and the other women despaired for their families in Monrovia where they heard of mass graves and soldiers leaving the front to return and rape civilian women. She sent for more women for a showdown. She instructed them to engage in a "sit in" at the entrances and exits to the main conference room, to lock arms, and to allow no one to leave until a peace accord was signed, even if it took days. Security guards told Gbowee that the women were obstructing justice, and she exploded, telling the guards she would make it easy to arrest the women. In Africa, it is considered a curse to see the naked body of your mother, especially if she disrobes deliberately. Gbowee began removing her clothes and stated they would all do so unless a peace accord was signed. At this point the mediator arrived to calm the situation. Gbowee pointed out that many of the negotiators were having a dream vacation, after sleeping in the bush for most of their lives. She told the mediator about the rebels plans to kill the population in Monrovia and replenish the population. She stated the women wanted the negotiators to feel the hunger and thirst that Liberian people were feeling.

At this point, one rebel warlord tried to jump over the women and they pushed him back into the conference room. He prepared to kick them, and the mediator dared him to try it. The mediator told the warlord the women were treating him like a boy because he was not acting like a real man. He was told to return to the conference table and no one could leave until the women were satisfied. Then the security officer, who had threatened to arrest Gbowee, came to her and told her they needed to send some women to block a window where some negotiators were trying to escape. They did so. Gbowee and the mediator talked and she decided to give the negotiators two weeks to reach an agreement or they would return with more women and block the doors again. She insisted that the talks must move forward, all delegates must attend every session, and they must not insult the women demonstrators. From this point on, the talks became very serious and sober. The international community continued to apply pressure and threatened financial reprisals if no peace agreement was reached. A peace agreement was finally signed two weeks later. As part of the agreement Taylor was exiled to Nigeria, United Nations and other peacekeepers entered Monrovia to supervise the disarmament, and a transitional government was set up to supervise democratic elections of a new permanent government.

The women of WIPNET returned to Liberia as heroes. The transitional government contained many rebel leaders, and the women immediately let them know that they would carefully monitor implementation of the peace agreement. They continued demonstrations for the implementation, wore their white clothing, and displayed placards. Disarmament did not go well until the women asked for calm and began talking with the fighters to assure them of their safety and that the women would help them receive their benefits under the agreement. Many of the fighters told the women they appreciated them and surrendered their weapons. The women worked at accepting former young combatants, knowing they must forgive to move forward. Gbowee counseled them and realized they too had been victimized by the military leaders. Gbowee and WIPNET worked to support the democratic elections—registering voters and supporting peace candidates. In 2005 Liberia elected Ellen Johnson Sirleaf as president—the first popularly elected woman head of state in Africa. In her inauguration speech, she acknowledged the women of WIPNET who brought peace to Liberia.

Gbowee later earned a master's degree in conflict transformation from Eastern Mennonite University in Virginia and received a Blue Ribbon Peace Award from Harvard University, the John F. Kennedy Profile in Courage Award, as well as other awards for her leadership role in bringing peace to Liberia. She is currently a director of the Women Peace and Security Network—Africa (based in Ghana). This organization works to build relationships and peace in West Africa by supporting women's efforts to prevent and resolve conflicts. Leymah is also a founder and president of the Gbowee Peace Foundation based in Liberia—providing educational and leadership opportunities for girls, women, and youth in West Africa. Gbowee was awarded the Nobel Peace Prize in 2011.

Leymah Gbowee is an effective *boundary-spanning* leader, as she represented the women of Liberia in confrontations with Charles Taylor's government and the negotiators in Ghana. This leader behavior is discussed in the early Multiple Linkage Model and Reformulated Path-Goal Theory. She also exhibits Charismatic/Transformational Leadership in her *inspiring speeches, risk taking, emotional appeals*, and focus on a *vision* and *mission* to achieve peace in Liberia. Her compassion for women and children during the struggle for peace and her activities since then demonstrate a *considerate* and *supportive behavior* pattern addressed in the Situational Leadership Theory, Path-Goal Theory, Fiedler's Contingency Theory, and the Leadership Grid. Her *determination* and *integrity* clearly reflect Trait Theories of leadership. Her *role modeling, altruism, openness, connection* to the Liberian people, and *importance she placed on their mission* all demonstrate Servant Leadership.

Discussion Questions

1   Why do you think Leymah Gbowee chose to appeal primarily to women in the peace movement in Liberia?
2   Why was her leadership strategy with WIPNET successful in finally ending the fighting?
3   Which of Gbowee's leader behaviors do you believe were most important? Why?
4   Would Gbowee be successful as a business leader? Labor leader? Military leader? Why or why not?

Selected References

Disney, A. E. (Producer), & Reticker, G. (Director). (2008). *Pray the devil back to hell* [Motion picture]. United States: Fork Films.

Macaulay, S. (2008). Women create peace in Liberia. *Amazing women rock.* Retrieved May 16, 2010, from www.amazingwomenrock.com/role-models/womencreate-peace-in-liberia.html.

Reeves, S. (February 3, 2011). Liberian activist tipped to win 2011 Nobel Peace Prize. *Nordic Africa News.* Retrieved from www.nanews.net/MAIN.asp?ID=4304.

23 Nelson Mandela

Human Rights Leader and President of South Africa

Nelson Rolihlahla Mandela was the primary leader of the decades-long anti-apartheid movement in South Africa, which opposed the systematic segregation and subjugation of Black Africans by an all-white minority. He led a largely peaceful, but sometimes violent, movement to establish equal rights for all South Africans and was imprisoned for 27 years for his activities. He sponsored negotiation and reconciliation with the dominating and often ruthless white minority and led the transformation toward a democracy for all races in South Africa. He eventually became the president of that country in the first truly representative democratic election with all South Africans' participation.

Nelson Mandela was born July 18, 1918, in the village of Mvezo in the Union of South Africa. His father, Nkosi (Chief) Mphakanyiswa, was a descendant of the Xhosa kings in Eastern Cape Province; although not in line to become king, he served as the king's advisor. The nation was only eight years old at the time and Black Africans were controlled and restricted by the white former British colonials and Afrikaner population. Afrikaners were former northern European settlers (mostly Dutch and German) who spoke their own language and made peace with the British after several years of war. Nelson's father died when he was nine and he was adopted by the acting king who became a role model for Nelson's leadership. He watched as this tribal leader listened patiently to members as they criticized and argued and he then tried to render a consensus decision that showed respect to all parties. Mandela later described this as a true democracy that allowed voicing of diverse views and kept the tribesmen together. This type of participative leadership style reflects the African cultural value of *ubuntu*, a belief in the brotherhood of all people, compassion, mutual respect, and openness to others, and the idea that nothing important can be accomplished without the support of others.

Mandela attended Methodist missionary schools run by the British and was given the name Nelson by a teacher, following the colonial practice of naming African boys after famous British citizens. He then enrolled in Fort Hare University, the only Black university in the country, which was heavily attended by bright students from aristocratic tribal families. He began to

DOI: 10.4324/9781003333937-25

flourish and eventually led a boycott to protest poor food. This resulted in him being expelled after refusing to give up his objections, which were supported by the students. His adoptive father arranged marriages for Nelson and the future king, and they both fled to Johannesburg to avoid them. There he worked in a law office, completed his BA degree, and began studying law. He also met members of the African National Congress (ANC), which was established in 1912 by tribal chiefs and religious leaders to promote the rights and freedom of African people. Like most Black Africans, he had always viewed whites as interlopers who unfairly suppressed the Black majority. He joined the ANC in 1944 and began his political career protesting extreme segregation of Black Africans by the ruling white government through their program of apartheid. He was married the same year to Evelyn Ntoko Mase who belonged to the same Xhosa tribe as Mandela. She was a very religious woman who later stated she thought Mandela was a student and did not approve of politics.

When he was 25, he helped form the ANC Youth League to encourage more mass action by the organization for the rights of Africans. The white government viewed the ANC members as communists, violently cracked down on strikes by Black miners, and began limiting the ability of Indian residents to acquire property. The ANC supported the Indians, who practiced the peaceful resistance of Gandhi, and they joined forces in demonstrations. The same type of alliance occurred later between the ANC and the communist party when the latter was outlawed in South Africa. Gandhi's peaceful tactics were followed by Mandela during much of his early political activities, to be changed later when he decided they had been ineffective. Nelson rejected communism but did advocate nationalization of large industries prior to running for president.

In 1948 a new Afrikaner government was elected with severe segregation policies to combat what they saw as "Black peril" and communism among Black Africans. Every person was to be classified by race, different races were required to live in separate parts of the cities, mixed marriages were forbidden, non-whites were removed from voting rolls, and "pass laws" severely limited the movement of non-whites when they left designated areas. Mandela helped organize a Defiance Campaign to protest the new restrictions, resulting in his arrest with many other ANC protestors. He was charged under the anti-communist laws and found guilty but given a suspended sentence. Arrests became a badge of honor in the ANC, but Mandela was banned from attending their meetings. In 1952 he became a legally qualified attorney, established a practice with an old friend and ANC colleague Oliver Tambo, and began representing the ANC and other Black clients for little or no fees.

He developed a flamboyant speaking style in court, assertive and theatrical. He treated racist magistrates with contempt and defied apartheid restrictions. He became prominent in courtrooms and in politics, but was banned from holding public office and public speechmaking. He relied on his court appearances and image to stay visible. In 1953 he was restricted to Johannesburg and required to resign from all organizations and he began to believe that violence was needed to change apartheid. The same year a former professor of Mandela's proposed a conference for African people of all races to develop a "freedom charter." This charter eventually denounced racist policies and laws, asserted that the state government must be based on the will of all the people, and argued for public ownership of large monopolistic business organizations ("nationalization"). Apartheid continued to spread to schools and universities, cutting off opportunities for young Blacks. In 1956 Mandela and other supporters of the freedom charter were arrested and charged with treason. This widely watched trial lasted until 1961 and gave Mandela the opportunity to present carefully prepared and inspiring descriptions of his own and the ANC's experience of subjugation and their goals of equal rights for all Africans. All were acquitted but he knew the government would not stop their apartheid policies.

In 1961 he co-sponsored an armed wing of the ANC, Umkhonto we Sizwe (The Spear of the Nation), which carried out sabotage against government offices and facilities, but avoided attacks on people. He stated it was a last resort when nonviolent tactics made no progress. He had divorced his first wife who disapproved of his political activities and married Winnie Madi-kizela—a strong-willed social worker who became an activist and political revolutionary herself. Both dressed extremely well (he had acquired this habit from his adoptive father), and the handsome couple developed a glamorous public persona. Demonstrations, arrests, and killing of protestors increased and Mandela decided to go into hiding, knowing the government-sponsored security officers who constantly followed him would eventually move in. He helped organize a national stay-at-home strike of trains and buses which hurt the government, coordinated sabotage bombings, and was eventually arrested (probably from a CIA tip to the South African government). Nelson was charged with inciting an illegal strike and leaving the country without a passport. When he entered the court, he noticed the magistrate in charge appeared spellbound by his appearance and he realized his own power. He represented himself in the courtroom to increase the symbolism of his work, delivering inspiring speeches to justify his actions and those of his colleagues. He was found guilty and given five years in prison, the heaviest penalty ever given in the country for a political offense. He became the militant martyred leader who had defied the apartheid system, was hunted, and remained devoted to his people. To Black Africans, he was the primary symbol of the injustices to native Africans by the white South African government.

Nine months later, the government seized ANC papers that proposed a violence campaign and overthrow of the government. Mandela and others were charged in the Rivonia Trial where he held the court spellbound. He used the courtroom as his theater, retracing his background and the ANC objectives of equal rights, multiracialism, and the end of white domination. His speech was reported throughout the world and ended with the following words:

> ... during my lifetime I have dedicated myself to this struggle of the African people. I have fought against white domination, and I have fought against Black domination. I have cherished the ideal of a democratic and free society in which all persons live together in harmony and with equal opportunities. It is an ideal which I hope to live for and to achieve. But if needs be, it is an ideal for which I am prepared to die.

Mandela and eight others were found guilty of sabotage, but not of conspiring to overthrow the government, and were sentenced to life in prison. He had become a powerful spokesman and symbol of the anti-apartheid movement and his sacrifice for this movement was unquestionable. They were imprisoned on Robben Island. For the next 27 years he was largely cut off from the world, but was surrounded and supported by his ANC colleagues. He now had the time to examine himself as others saw him— an aggressive and militant revolutionary—and he learned to control his temper and strong will, to use persuasion and emphasis to convince others, and to slowly build his influence over other prisoners and the white guards. He was treated with respect, probably due to his connections and his royal family, and was able to continue his legal studies through correspondence with the University of London. His legal background, court experience, past leadership in the ANC, and assertive personality made him a natural leader of other prisoners. He was visited by dignitaries, explained ANC policies to visiting officials, wrote to prison officials about the poor treatment of prisoners, and inspired others to take courses and continue their education. Robben Island became known informally as Mandela University. This atmosphere of self-improvement and education gave them confidence and a type of authority over the white guards who were as young as 17 and not well educated. Mandela listened to others' life stories and learned to appreciate and understand their perspectives, including the guards'. He impressed them with his assertiveness, respect, and legal knowledge and he learned to maintain his dignity in all situations. He respected the guards as fellow humans, but carefully refused to be subservient and he made sure that he and other prisoners worked in the rock quarry at their own pace.

Nelson heard about the increasing violence by other anti-apartheid groups outside the prison. He recognized the need for reconciliation in South Africa to achieve a true democracy. He developed the capability to see the best in people, emphasized respect for all people, and advocated forgiveness. He became less arrogant and autocratic, and more democratic in his dealings with others. He stayed in excellent physical condition and always maintained self-control while being sensitive to others' insecurities and resentments.

Winnie struggled with government harassment of her and their children and was becoming increasingly rebellious and violent in her associations and actions. But she kept Mandela informed of the anti-apartheid movement, which now included white liberals, church officials and many students in South Africa. A Free Mandela campaign was building around the world, which involved other countries limiting investments and loans to South Africa. This and the increasing violence were seriously damaging the economy and whites were leaving the country. Nelson was moved to a nicer location with more visits from journalists and eminent individuals. In a closely held government report, he was described as the number one Black leader in South Africa whose influence as a charismatic inspirational leader had increased while in prison. He was celebrated in songs, international concerts, street names, and was adored by African children. The government decided he was helping the ANC and anti-apartheid movement more as a symbolic martyr in prison than if he were free. A team of government officials began several years of negotiations with Mandela concerning the creation of a more democratic South Africa.

In 1989 a new white president took office in South Africa. F. W. de Klerk represented the Afrikaners and knew that Mandela must be released to save the country from civil war and economic collapse. In February 1990 he stunned his party by unbanning the ANC and other political organizations, releasing all political prisoners not guilty of violent crimes, and suspending all executions. Mandela and others were freed as the world watched. He had won but he humbly gave credit to the ANC for all the work they did during his imprisonment. He entered prison when he was 46 and emerged when he was 71. He returned an eminent moral leader who had stood by his fundamental principles of liberty and equal rights for all and he gave hope to all oppressed people around the world.

Mandela began traveling the world speaking and asking for financial support for the ANC. His relaxed charm and serious moral arguments commanded respect and disarmed listeners. He was successful at fund raising, was elected president of the ANC, and resolved to reorganize that organization to attain political power. He was more moderate and pragmatic than prior to his imprisonment and younger ANC members worried about his effectiveness. Mandela and the ANC members met with the government and offered to cease their violent campaign. He also withdrew his call for nationalizing large industries and supported a development program to generate foreign investment. Independent groups within the South African police and security forces continued terrorizing and killing anti-apartheid workers. His wife Winnie was implicated in violent activities involving torture and murder that hurt the movement, and Mandela eventually divorced Winnie in 1995.

In December 1991, a conference with all political parties in South Africa was held in Johannesburg where de Klerk spoke of the need for power sharing in government. The eventual result, after months of negotiation, was a new constitution and a planned popular election with all major parties represented, including the ANC. When another Black ANC leader was fatally shot by a white man, a white Afrikaner woman saw the assassin's license plate and reported the number to the police who caught the killer (a European immigrant) within 15 minutes. Mandela's speech described her actions and asked for calm, which avoided widespread rioting and made it clear that most South Africans wanted peace and equality. Mandela and de Klerk were jointly awarded the Nobel Peace Prize and Mandela was elected president of South Africa at the age of 75. The constitution provided that de Klerk would be one deputy president and Mandela picked Thabo Mbeki, his long-time ANC colleague, as his other deputy president. Mandela was inaugurated in May 1994, four years after leaving prison, determined to show that Africans could govern effectively.

During his presidency, he quickly won the respect and support of his staff, many of them from the previous administration. He was noted for his humility and preferred one-on-one meetings and personal contacts with other leaders, thereby skipping bureaucratic protocol. He thus made use of his convincing and supportive interpersonal style honed during his many years in prison. His speeches were written by a multiracial staff and were often stiff, but he always followed the scripted material with his own stories, often making fun of himself ("I'm just a sinner who keeps on trying"). This caused his audience to continue to identify with him as a man of the people. He was inclusive with his multiracial cabinet, listening carefully to their discussions before stating his position or decision, which generally reflected much of the cabinet members' discussion (similar to his adoptive father's participative style). His friendly, smiling style was often contagious, and his multiracial cabinet members worked surprisingly well with a focus on problems and issues rather than partisanship and ideology. His vision and mission as president was to transform the nation from a white oligarchy to a multiracial democracy. In 1995, he actively supported the Springboks, a largely white South African rugby team, who hosted and won the World Cup final game in Johannesburg. Mandela presented the cup to the Springboks captain after the game, Francois Pienaar, wearing a Springboks jersey with Pienaar's number on the back. This symbolic act became a critical turning point for the reconciliation of the white and Black populations in the new multiracial democracy of South Africa.

Although Nelson liked to socialize with business executives and movie stars, he lived a relatively simple life. He gave one third of his salary to the Nelson Mandela Children's Fund, which he founded in 1995 to improve the conditions of children in the world. He visited high-profile Afrikaners, Afrikaner churches, and met with widows of deceased Black and white leaders. He adamantly supported a free press, even though he sometimes disagreed with the reporting. He directed the creation of a Truth and Reconciliation Commission in 1996 to investigate past crimes involving apartheid policies and ANC activities. If perpetrators revealed the truth, they were granted amnesty if they could prove their actions were politically motivated. This Commission was chaired by Archbishop Desmond Tutu and caused tremendous pain for families of tortured and murdered victims, but it revealed violent acts by both parties and helped resolve long-term resentment.

In 1996 de Klerk's party withdrew from the government, making Mbeki the sole deputy president. De Klerk's party lost coherence when he later resigned from public office due to personal issues. Mandela stepped down as president of the ANC and in his last speech he warned the members against the corruption and greed of "predatory elites" in Africa who looted their country's national wealth and he called for moral renewal as part of an African renaissance. In 1998 he married Graca Machel, widow of the former President of Mozambique, who helped him relax from the strains of office. He traveled extensively with Graca and saw his moral mission as spreading peace and tolerance around the world.

Graca described him as being very aware of his basic values and many of his colleagues pointed to his strong sense of human dignity. Others view Mandela as a symbol of moral authority and a peacemaker in a continent rife with racial and tribal conflict. He set the direction for South African diplomacy, insisting that human rights must be the core of international relations. He became a charismatic symbol for all of Africa seeking to escape the colonial past to achieve a fair and democratic society. He negotiated and forged economic alliances with Asia and other countries and often criticized the United States for its actions in the United Nations and elsewhere. He confronted powerful myths of Black inferiority, white invincibility, and incompatibility between races and gave confidence to people in the world who had been conditioned into submission. He also personified African dignity and self-respect by avoiding the arrogance, pretension, and paranoia that characterized many leaders in developing countries. He used the term "we" in speeches, much more than "I." His mistakes were often in trusting and seeing the best in people who later disappointed him, but he was able to bring the best out of some former enemies during reconciliation. He also adapted his leadership style as the situation dictated, shifting from an early aggressive militaristic approach to a negotiating and conciliatory style after his release from prison. This latter style included participation of all parties while recognizing their fears and respecting their dignity and sensitivities. He served his five-year term as president and chose not to seek another term in 1999, being succeeded by Thabo Mbeki.

In retirement, he became an important advocate of social causes—especially those focused on poverty and children's living conditions. He acted as mediator for numerous conflicts and disputes outside South Africa. He received awards and acclaim throughout the world. Above all else, Mandela's integrity, values, and dedication speak more about him as a leader than any other aspect of his life. Mandela died on December 5, 2013 from a respiratory infection.

Mandela is often described as a Charismatic/Transformational leader because of his *inspirational sacrifice, moral rhetoric,* and *symbolic role* in Black Africans' struggle to overcome apartheid. He emphasized a clear *vision* and *mission* for the anti-apartheid movement with which he was identified. He modified this vision when released from prison to allow for reconciliation and a true democracy for all South Africans. He therefore also reflects contingency/situational leadership theories such as Situational Leadership Theory, Path-Goal Theory, or the Multiple Linkage Model, which advocate modifying a leader's style to fit the situation. These leadership theories also address Mandela's *directive leadership* in initiating early militant campaigns of sabotage and demonstrations and eventually negotiation and reconciliation. His *supportive behaviors* are clear in the respect shown for all persons, encouraging fellow prisoners to pursue their education in prison, support for colleagues in court and after imprisonment and interpersonal relations as president. His inclusive *participative leadership* as president is described in the Normative Decision Theory. Mandela's negotiating behavior, reflecting *boundary-spanning leadership*, was critical to overcoming anti-apartheid policies after his imprisonment and in gaining foreign support for the ANC movement. The Multiple Linkage Model and Reformulated Path-Goal Theory address this leader behavior. His *self-reflection* and awareness, as well as *self-regulation* and careful *listening* behaviors are included in the Servant Leadership model. His *character, competence, trustworthiness,* and *empowerment* reflect Principle Centered Leadership and aspects of Trait Theory.

Discussion Questions

1   Which leadership theory do you believe most accurately describes Mandela's behavior prior to his imprisonment? What about after his imprisonment?
2   What do you believe are the most important things Mandela did to overcome the apartheid policies of the white government of South Africa?
3   As president, some criticized Mandela for tolerating government inefficiencies in favor of reconciliation. Was this good leadership? Why or why not?
4   How important was Mandela's supportive and friendly interpersonal style to his long-term success as a leader?

Selected References

Mandela, N. (1994). *Long walk to freedom: The autobiography of Nelson Mandela.* New York: Little Brown.

Sampson, A. (1999). *Mandela: The authorized autobiography.* New York: Alfred A. Knopf.

24 Geronimo

Apache Native American War Leader

Geronimo was a brave and shrewd Apache warrior. After Mexican soldiers killed his entire family, he led violent raids in Mexico for decades. He also defied U.S. government efforts to force his tribe onto restrictive reservations, embodying the spirit of Apache warriors and their nomadic culture. Geronimo (whose birth name was Goyathlay, meaning "one who yawns") was born in about 1829 in the mountains of what is now eastern Arizona and southwestern New Mexico. He was fourth in a family of eight children and was part of the Bedonkohe group of the Apache Indians. He grew up in the traditional Apache culture, learning to pray to their high God Usen and hearing stories of brave deeds of warriors and glories of the warpath. The Apaches were nomadic and lived primarily on wild game, berries, acorns, roots, and other foods available in their surroundings. They also traded with other tribes and villages. They typically traveled throughout the mountains of eastern Arizona, New Mexico, and the Mexican states of Chihuahua and Sonora. Until 1852, these were all part of Mexico. His father died when he was young and he assumed responsibility for his mother.

Geronimo was admitted to the council of warriors when he was 17 as he had met the requirements of killing dangerous animals alone and participating in raids on those outside the tribe. He immediately married his first wife, Alope, who was from the Chiricahua band of Apaches, and they had three children during the next five years. In spring of 1851, their group traveled to Mexico and camped near a small Mexican town to trade with the locals. While most of the men were in town, Mexican soldiers raided the camp and killed nearly all who were there, including Geronimo's wife, three children, and mother. Left with nothing, the survivors immediately returned to their homeland in the Arizona-New Mexico mountains. Geronimo described himself as unable to speak or act, he simply followed his tribesmen home. He burned all the possessions he had shared with his wife, children, and mother. He had lost more than anyone else. He had nothing.

Geronimo's small Bedonkohe band joined forces with the Mimbreno Apaches whose chief, Mangus Colorado, called a council; all members wanted war. Geronimo was sent to other Apache groups (including the Chiricahuas who were led by Cochise), and they agreed to join his group in seeking vengeance on the Mexicans.

Apache raids on Mexicans dated from the 17th century. In the early 1800s, Mexico began paying a $100 bounty for each scalp of an Apache

DOI: 10.4324/9781003333937-26

warrior, $50 for an Apache woman, and $25 for an Apache child. The Apaches willingly traveled to the town where Geronimo's group had been attacked and his family murdered, and they lured the soldiers out to meet them. Geronimo was allowed to direct the battle because he had lost so much. In the fight that followed, the Apaches wiped out the Mexican soldiers. Geronimo was so fierce that he attacked the soldiers with his knife after he ran out of arrows and was without his spear. The soldiers called on their saint so often during this and later battles with these Apaches that he was labeled Geronimo, which is Spanish for Jerome, the patron saint of the Mexican soldier. He later reported that he was given the title Apache War Chief after this battle—a sign of great respect.

Although many other Apaches were satisfied with their vengeance, Geronimo could not get enough. Repeatedly over the next 25 years, he convinced various groups of warriors to accompany him on brutal raids to Mexico. At times the Mexican soldiers attacked Apache villages with equal brutality. Many of Geronimo's raids were successful and he would return with booty of cattle, horses, mules, and other supplies to be distributed to his tribe. This earned him great respect among his people.

Britton Davis, a United States Army lieutenant who later lived with Geronimo's tribe on the reservation, came to know Geronimo, and eventually pursued him through much of Mexico. He wrote that Apaches viewed raids as an exciting adventure, a way to attain glory and respect from their people. Geronimo's raids in Mexico were that and more—he sought revenge on the Mexicans throughout his free life after the death of his family.

Geronimo reported that his first meeting with white men was in the 1850s when a group of surveyors came through their country.[1] He described them as friendly. They traded with the Apaches and were well liked. In the early 1860s a column of Union soldiers came through to protect supply lines from Confederate forces. The United States had obtained possession of Arizona and New Mexico territory in the Gadsden Purchase of 1852, and the soldiers claimed the areas traditionally occupied by Apaches for the United States government. Some historians report that soldiers were instructed to kill Apache men but not women and children. This set the Apaches against the white soldiers and settlers.

Geronimo's mistrust of whites was permanently fixed by two incidents. One involved an invitation by United States soldiers to meet peacefully with Chiricahua Apache Chief Cochise and other subchiefs regarding a missing white boy. When the Indians entered the soldiers' tent, the soldiers tried to place them in chains. Cochise and others cut their way out of the tent and escaped, but others were taken prisoner and executed. Geronimo and his group had always been close to the Chiricahuas, and he was later married to Cochise's niece. The other important incident occurred when white miners lured Geronimo's chief, Mangus Colorado, with a peace offering but imprisoned and eventually murdered him. These incidents cemented Geronimo's hatred and distrust for white people.

The Mescalero Apaches, who occupied land east of Geronimo's band, resisted the white invasion first. They were defeated and forced onto a reservation where they were unable to support themselves and were inadequately supplied and fed. Geronimo now expanded his list of enemies to include whites, and conducted hit-and-run attacks on soldiers, miners, and settlers throughout southern Arizona and southwestern New Mexico. He also continued his raids into Mexico. He was viewed by Apaches as epitomizing their male warrior culture. Time and again he was courageous in battle, he was cunning in planning his raids, and he never relinquished his desire for his people to live their free nomadic life.

In 1876 the United States government tried to move the Apaches to reservations, which were barren desert and completely unlike their mountain homeland. When the Chiricahuas were forcibly removed to the San Carlos Reservation in Eastern Arizona, Geronimo fled to Mexico with a group of followers. He was arrested soon after and taken to San Carlos. Indian agents were assigned by the U.S. Indian Bureau to manage government supplies for the Indians when the Indians were sent to the reservations. Many agents were political appointees and unqualified for their positions. This was true for Geronimo's band and many supplies intended for the Indians were siphoned off to whites and sold for private profit. When an Apache prophet was slain by whites in 1881, Geronimo's band left the reservation and went to the Sierra Madre Mountains of Mexico to continue their traditional way of life. They also continued their raids against Mexicans and whites.

In 1882 General George Crook was called to Arizona to conduct a campaign against the Apaches who were still outside the reservation and waging war. Through continuous pursuit and harassment, Geronimo was persuaded to surrender and return to the reservation. He did so with 350 Mexican cattle, which were taken from him at the reservation to be used by the Indian Bureau. He resented this for many years. Life on the San Carlos Reservation, where Geronimo and his tribe were located, was not pleasant. Although they were allowed to select a location in the mountains of their homeland, their hunting grounds were restricted and they were subjected to inadequate supplies and further graft by the Indian agents. The reservation Apaches resented being prohibited from making and drinking Tiswin, a Native American alcoholic drink made from corn. The men protested at not being permitted to discipline their wives through physically beating them or cutting off their nose when they were unfaithful. They protested that they had kept their bargain with the military by living on the reservation and keeping the peace. Nothing had been said in their agreement about how they lived and conducted their private affairs. They were not allowed to raise stock, which appealed to their skills, but were told they had to farm.

The country they inhabited was not well suited for farming and farming was not a major part of their traditions. Although General Crook and some of his officers recognized these difficulties, they enforced the government requirements and battled with the Indian Bureau to try to assure the Indians received their promised food and supplies. The Apaches were often losers in these bureaucratic battles. They were idle much of the time, which was totally foreign to their nomadic subsistence-oriented culture. These factors bred mistrust and defiance by the Indians. In spring 1885, Geronimo and about 150 other Apaches again left the reservation.

Many of the Apache chiefs who had first resisted the whites had died by then, and although he was not a hereditary chief, Geronimo was a respected leader due to his courage, unwavering determination, and skill as a war chief. He was viewed by his people as having special powers such as walking without leaving any tracks and having visions of the future. It was believed that guns could not kill him, and he reported late in life that he received eight gunshot wounds during his war years. He had also been related to several of the great chiefs by marriages subsequent to his first family's death. Geronimo's group conducted several raids on white settlers before again entering the mountains of Mexico. General Crook was replaced by General Miles in pursuing the Apaches along with 5,000 soldiers who had permission to follow the Indians into Mexico. Several groups split from Geronimo in the months that followed over disagreements and the fact that they were constantly harassed by both Mexican and United States troops. The Indians knew that smaller bands would be harder to locate by the soldiers. But they were worn down by constant pursuit and attacks that continued to decrease their numbers. Apache women, children, and young boys were frequent casualties of the soldiers' attacks.

In fall 1886 Geronimo let it be known he would meet with General Miles to discuss surrender. Lieutenant Charles B. Gatewood first met with the Indian leader and arranged the meeting with the general. Miles told Geronimo that many Apaches had already been moved to Florida; these included many relatives of Geronimo and his band. The Apaches were very concerned about their families and wanted to be with them. Miles said Geronimo's group would be sent to the east where they would be reunited with their families. After two years, they would be returned to the reservation, which included many of the mountains of their native homeland. Geronimo and his band surrendered and several days later were placed on a train for Florida.

The United States government did not keep its word. Geronimo and his followers were placed in hard labor and were not reunited with their families for nearly a year. Later they were all sent to Alabama for seven years where they suffered badly from disease. They were ill suited for the humid climate and living conditions in the south and many died. Eventually the Comanches and Kiowas, who had been traditional enemies of the Apaches, invited Geronimo's band to share their reservation in Fort Sill, Oklahoma. They arrived in Fort Sill, and Geronimo lived there the remainder of his life. He appeared in a presidential parade and at state fairs and dictated his life story to S. M. Barrett in 1905. After much wrangling with the United States government, his story was published in 1907. Despite repeated requests, he was never allowed to return to his homeland. He died of pneumonia in 1909 after drinking heavily and lying overnight on a cold wet road.

Geronimo's leadership can be considered using several leadership theories. He was highly *directive* with followers, especially during the raids they conducted. Path-Goal Theory emphasizes *directive leader behavior* in high stress situations. Fiedler's Contingency Theory, Multiple Linkage Model, and Situational Leadership Theory also describe similar leader behaviors. Reformulated Path-Goal Theory is also seen in his *boundary-spanning behavior* through negotiations with other Apache groups to join in his raids and in his repeated negotiations with United States soldiers over their surrender. Charismatic/Transformational Leadership is evident in his *inspiration* of warriors to accompany him on his continued raids, especially against Mexican soldiers. As a *charismatic* leader, he was viewed as having special powers which were greater than other Apaches. Implicit Leadership Theory can also be applied to Geronimo's leadership, since he embodied the traditional Apache beliefs and values of an ideal warrior-leader. He was fearless in battle, unrelenting in the face of adversity cunning in his planning, and generous with his tribal group with booty obtained on his raids. His *determination* and apparent *cognitive capacity* reflect Trait Theories of leadership.

Discussion Questions

1   Some writers believe a specific experience early in a leader's life is critical in shaping the leader's behavior throughout his/her life. Why was this true for Geronimo? Explain.
2   Some Indian leaders acquiesced to the U.S. government demands and struggled to make a life on their reservation. Do you think Geronimo's defiant stance toward the military and Indian Bureau was good for the Apaches?
3   Given the situation facing the Apaches in the mid-1800s, what type of leadership behaviors by Apache leaders do you believe would have been most effective?
4   Try to describe an Implicit Leadership Theory for the ideal Apache leader in the mid-to-late 1800s.

Note

1   In this chapter, we follow Geronimo's telling of his own story where he contrasts Mexicans and White people as separate groups. While this distinction reflects the context of Apache experiences during his time, it is important to note that contemporary understandings of these identities are nuanced and intersectional.

Selected References

Barrett, S. M. (1907). *Geronimo's story of his life*. New York: Duffield and Company.
Davis, B. (1929). *The truth about Geronimo*. Lincoln: University of Nebraska Press.

25 José María Arizmendiarrieta

The Priest Who Built the Largest Industrial Cooperative in the World

Father José María Arizmendiarrieta, a Basque Catholic priest from Spain, inspired and guided the creation of an impressive network of cooperatives in the town of Mondragón, Northern Spain. Mondragón Group is made up of 98 mutually supportive cooperatives in multiple industries. With nearly 80,000 employees, it is the world's largest industrial cooperative and the tenth-largest business group in Spain. Most remarkably, these cooperatives inspired by Arizmendiarrieta's vision of wealth redistribution and democratic decision-making were created during the difficult early years of General Franco's anti-socialist authoritarian regime. The longevity and success of the Mondragón Group are a testament to the impressive leadership of this modest but determined priest.

José María Arizmendiarrieta was born in 1915 in the Basque Country, a historic and administrative region located on Spain's northern coast with a unique culture and language (Euskara). He grew up in the countryside speaking Euskara and had a strong connection with his Basque culture and identity. An early childhood accident left him blind in his left eye, a disability that would prevent him from joining rougher play with other children and made him a calm, reflective, and mindful child. He was the oldest of four children in a family of farmers, so he was meant to inherit his family 's big farm or "caserío." Instead, his strong religious vocation compelled him to join a Catholic seminary at the age of 12. This education would be foundational for his convictions, influenced by principles of social justice, wealth redistribution, and social organization. Stimulated by a Basque national culture renaissance, he published works in Euskara regularly: poetry, theater, philosophy, ethnographic studies on oral narratives, and literary critique, among others.

In 1936, General Francisco Franco led a military coup that divided the country between those who defended the democratic Republic or "republicanos" and those who supported the fascist insurrection or "nacionales." The Basques, including the Basque Church, joined forces for the Republic. Arizmendiarrieta was not allowed to participate in armed combat because of his visual impairment, but he joined the Basque Forces as a journalist for the Basque newspaper Eguna. His writings dealt with social concerns and were

DOI: 10.4324/9781003333937-27

aimed at the Euskara-speaking population in the front. When Bilbao fell to the insurrectionists in 1937, and realizing that fleeing to France was nearly impossible, Arizmendiarrieta turned himself in to the new authorities. Had he informed them of his journalistic work during the war, they would have given him a death sentence. Instead, he presented himself as a soldier and was acquitted after a month in prison.

After the war, the Basque Country felt to Arizmendiarrieta like an occupied region. Its cultural, political, and religious leaders were executed, taken to concentration camps, deported, or exiled. He returned to the Vitoria seminary to complete his theology studies and was ordained a priest in 1941. The new diocese administration, now aligned with General Franco's authoritarian regime, denied his application to further his education at the University of Louvain and assigned him instead to join the parish of Mondragón, close to his own hometown, where they could observe his activities. He was assigned a coadjutor[1] position, tasked to provide spiritual guidance to young people in Mondragón. He was a skinny 25-year-old newly ordained priest who used dark glasses to hide his left eye. He was also (and would be throughout his life) an appalling public speaker, particularly so in Spanish[2] (as Euskara was his first language). Contrasting with his eloquent and capable predecessors, he delivered monotone sermons made of long, complex sentences that were difficult to understand. He rarely spoke about individual salvation but about the dignity of work for a person's self-realization. He discussed the need for cooperation and collective solidarity in their community, and the importance of professional education as the natural foundation of a more equitable economic and social order. His parish found his sermons tedious and uninteresting and failed to understand the implications of his ideas. He quickly developed a reputation as a "socialist" priest.

Mondragón was at that time a deeply impoverished town that was lacking in bread, meat, sugar, oil, coal, and electricity. The people he had known in town before the war were either dead, imprisoned, or exiled. Society was broken by pain and resentment between families and by social struggle. The city had become a dangerous place for young activists and labor unionists, who engaged in underground activities. Cognizant of these challenges, Arizmendiarrieta reflected on the needs of post-war Spain. He understood that much of the hurting working class was disinterested in religion. In his writings, he describes the principles that would guide his work from the moment that he arrived in Mondragón: rather than waiting for workers to come into the Church, he needed to go and find them where they worked, lived, and socialized; he needed to free himself of the Church's formulaic demands and truly live in the community, adapting to those around him rather than imposing his own values and practices; and, finally, he had to work harder than anyone else, to show hard-working people that they could trust him and that he was, in essence, a working-class person himself.

Despite his poor public speaking skills, he was very good at building personal relationships, frequently stopping as he moved around town to catch up with the villagers, using these conversations to push his social projects. He was also driven and tenacious to the point of stubbornness, a pragmatic problem solver, an excellent listener, and had contagious self-confidence. He built some following with some of his early social initiatives, organizing the community to create a medical clinic and a soccer field. He then focused his energy on Mondragón's most pressing need: a school that would grant every child in town a professional education to improve their economic conditions. A local locksmithing factory had an apprenticeship program for their workers' children. Arizmendiarrieta attempted to negotiate an expansion of the apprenticeship program to accept other local children but his proposals were repeatedly rejected.

Left with no alternative, Arizmendiarrieta set out to open a new professional school that would welcome all children in town who were 14 and older. He built popular interest in the school through the soccer club, organized fundraising initiatives, and reached out to local enterprises. Boxes were placed in the town streets to collect the names of those interested in providing either money or personal services to the school. Nearly 600 people, a surprising 15% of the adult population in Mondragón, and some local and medium-sized businesses supported this initiative and became members of the parents' association. Membership in the association earned them a right to vote in policy decisions and the election of officials. The school board was elected among representatives of the parents' association and included contributing enterprises and the Mayor of Mondragón.

A democratically run school in a dictatorial Spain raised concerns and suspicions from authorities and the Church, but Arizmendiarrieta carefully designed its activities to ensure that they fell within the limits of the law. The Zaldispe Polytechnic School opened its doors with a capacity of 250 students, but enrollment quickly rose to 800 students. They had scarce resources, but professors and students were tight and energized to succeed together. When the first cohort graduated from the school, Arizmendiarrieta negotiated with the University of Zaragoza the offering of a long-distance industrial engineering program for the more advanced students. They were helped at the school in the evenings as they completed their degrees, becoming a great source of pride for the townspeople.

The school and its democratic organization would constitute a transformational seed for the town of Mondragón. Graduates from the school would continue to meet with Arizmendiarrieta regularly for discussions and study circles. Over time, these discussions led to the collaborative crafting of a shared vision of cooperativism for Mondragón. His closest followers remember how these conversations inspired a transformation from a society ruled by capital to one ruled by labor; he also urged them to build professional identities that integrated values of professional mastery with their personal and social values. Before a cooperative could be created,

Arizmendiarrieta concluded later, it was necessary to build "cooperativists." His insistence on labor reform and his presumed leadership in the 1956 labor strikes led to serious warnings from the authorities but his work also earned him the respect of some government officials who appreciated his constructive social influence.

During those years, Arizmendiarrieta's followers started to explore paths for employee growth and ownership in the locksmithing factory in town but their initiatives were systematically turned down by the company and they grew frustrated with capitalistic business practices. In 1955, a group of five graduates from the Polytechnic School left their jobs at the locksmithing factory and set out to create the first industrial cooperative of Mondragón: Ulgor[3] (the name would change in the 1990s to Fagor Electrodomesticos). He helped the founders build financial support for the cooperative by leveraging his contacts and recommending that they used the traditional "txikiteo"[4] after work every day to spread the word in the community through the bars. The founders had no experience or assets to their names, but they were cared for by their community for being part of the Polytechnic School's first cohort of graduates and they had the endorsement of Father Arizmendiarrieta. Through these efforts, they built an impressive 12 million pesetas pledge (nearly 2 million dollars in 2023), which allowed them to start their operations.

Despite the tradition of cooperativism in the Basque Country, dictatorial Spain lacked blueprints or legal provisions for cooperative organizing. The founders met with Arizmendiarrieta regularly to design their newly formed cooperative. After three years of deliberations, he was also the one who carefully crafted the final version of Ulgor's bylaws to ensure they were consistent with the law. These bylaws would be subsequently used by every other cooperative in Mondragón. The ultimate power of the cooperative would rest on the general assembly, in which all worker-owners had a vote. The governing council would be elected in two to four-year terms by the assembly and would be responsible for management policy decisions and for the selection of the management council, made up of the general manager and chief department heads. An elected three-member audit committee would audit financial operations regularly. Finally, a Social Council would further the communications of the company, question possible abuses from the management council, and give worker-owners the opportunity to represent their departments and learn about day-to-day challenges.

When the existing cooperatives encountered difficulties, a new cooperative was created to resolve them. Arizmendiarrieta urged Ulgor's founders to create Caja Laboral Popular (Popular Labor Bank), a cooperative bank, to help them finance Ulgor's expansion, an idea that they initially rejected as absurd. Later on, Caja Laboral's business division would become the main promoter of cooperative organizations in the Basque Country. He also insisted on the creation of an efficient cooperative supermarket by integrating seven existing consumer cooperatives: Eroski. With time, Eroski would become one of Spain's most important supermarket chains (fifth-largest in

Spain in 2022). He also led the constitution of the League for Education and Culture, which transformed the Polytechnic School into a mixed cooperative where teachers, students, and business organizations were participating members. In 1997, the League became part of the new Mondragón University, also structured as a cooperative.

Despite his active involvement in deliberations and discussions about the cooperatives, Arizmendiarrieta purposefully avoided any form of formal legal power and never attended official meetings. Thinking back on those times, Arizmendiarrieta affirmed, "I was the one who reserved myself the easiest task—to think aloud. All that I did was to raise ideas and provoke young people, and nothing more." Arizmendiarrieta was seen as a communist by the more radical conservatives and as a collaborationist (with the dictatorial authorities) by the radical progressives in Spain. Navigating these challenging waters, he successfully mobilized the community of Mondragón and transformed it into a collaborative and thriving economy primarily owned by the workers.

Arizmendiarrieta prioritized the interests of the community over the interests of the individual, including his own. He maintained a frugal and modest lifestyle, rejecting unnecessary material belongings or money from a community that flourished under his leadership. He refused to buy a car (or let others buy one for him) despite his followers' insistence that he found a more comfortable means of transportation to move around town than his old road-style bike. In 1967, Arizmendiarrieta began to suffer from heart disease, for which he underwent a series of cardiac surgeries over the years as his health deteriorated. He discreetly endured pain and medical treatment until his death in 1973, without any possessions, and still occupying the coadjutor position that was assigned to him when he first arrived in Mondragón.

A systematic thinker and a pragmatist, he crafted a *vision* that guided his work in Mondragón over the years and ultimately led to a dramatic transformation of his community. He showed *individualized consideration* for the people of Mondragón, dedicating time in the day to building strong personal relationships as he crossed paths with the neighbors in town. However, he does not entirely fit the model of a Charismatic/Transformational Leader. Arizmendiarrieta lacked the ability to craft an inspiring message to motivate his community to follow him in his vision, a limitation of which he was painfully aware. Instead, he gained support for his vision using unusual charismatic behaviors. He was a *role model* of hard work and self-sacrifice for the benefit of the community and impressed the young people of Mondragón with unwavering confidence in himself and in his followers' collective ability to succeed. He did not have a *high need for power* but empowered others to execute their joint vision. In fact, he rejected power when it was offered to him and much preferred engaging in *intellectual stimulation*, listening attentively to his followers in group and individual conversations over the years, and then challenging them to think beyond modest changes and strive for profound transformations in their community. In fact, Arizmendiarrieta could be characterized as a *servant leader*, reflected in his constant *optimism*, his *firm belief in the importance of his vision*, and his *modeling of values of great importance for the attainment of that vision*, such as *altruism, humility,* and *trust* in their collective ability to succeed.

Critical voices today question the Mondragón Group's commitment to its foundational principles of collaboration and democratic power. Possibly due to global competition or failure to nurture its founder's values to the new generations, Mondragón has experienced a decrease in the rate of cooperative members among the total number of workers, particularly in foreign countries and the Group's subsidiaries. Studies have found stark governance and working conditions similarities between Mondragón's subsidiaries and those of more traditional multinationals in China and Poland. In 2013, Mondragón's flagship and first cooperative, Fagor Electrodomesticos (Ulgor's company name since the 1990s) declared bankruptcy during Spain's housing sector crisis that followed the 2008 global financial crisis. The Mondragón Group, having bankrolled Fagor for years, decided to stop supporting its poor decision-making. Cooperative members were able to either request early retirement or transfer to jobs in other cooperatives, but the jobs of non-member workers and workers of subsidiary companies were not protected.

Discussion Questions

1   Which of the two models captures Arizmendiarrieta's leadership better: charismatic leadership or servant leadership? Why?
2   Do you think that Arizmendiarrieta's vision of worker-owned and worker-led organizations can be sustainable without his leadership?
3   Mondragón leadership roles are shared and rotated among worker-owners during limited terms. Are the cooperatives in this business group an example of collective leadership?

Notes

1 Assistant.
2 There are four co-official Spanish languages in Spain: Castellano, Catalán, Euskara, and Gallego. For this reason, the term "Spanish" is less common in Spain and is often replaced by "castellano" or "Castilian Spanish."
3 The name ULGOR is an acronym created with the names of its five founders.
4 Traditional practice in the Basque Country (and other parts of Spain) in which people socialize with friends and acquaintances by walking together from bar to bar, drinking very small amounts of wine ("txikitos") with small appetizers ("pintxos") in each bar.

Selected References

Aruzmendi, J. (1984). *El hombre cooperativo. Pensamiento de Arizmendiarrieta*. Caja Laboral Popular.

Goodman, P. S. (2020, December 29). Co-ops in Spain's Basque Region Soften Capitalism's Rough Edges. *The New York Times*.

Errasti, A. (2013). Mondragon's Chinese subsidiaries: Coopilalist multinationals in practice. *Economic and Industrial Democracy*, 36(3), 479–499.

International Cooperative Alliance (2021). World Cooperative Monitor. Report 2021. Retrieved from https://monitor.coop.

Romeo, N. (2022, August 27). How Mondragon became the world's largest co-op. *The New Yorker*.

Urresti, G. (Director). (2018). Arizmendiarrieta, el hombre cooperativo [Streaming video]. Available from www.famiplay.com.

Whyte, W. F., & Whyte, K. K. (1991). *Making Mondragon*. Ithaca, NY: Cornell University Press.

World Cooperative Monitor (2022). Exploring the Cooperative Economy. Report 2022. Retrieved from https://monitor.coop.

26 Napoleon Bonaparte
French Military and Political Leader

Napoleon Bonaparte was a military leader and eventually Emperor of France whose conquests determined much of the European geopolitical landscape during the late 18th and early 19th centuries. He may be the best example to demonstrate that major events are frequently determined by the personal drive and leadership of men and women rather than by environmental forces such as economics and geography. Napoleon was a highly talented opportunist who took advantage of the French Revolution to propel himself into a position of great power. He used force and political maneuvering to expand his power throughout Europe. He also made significant contributions to judicial law and public administration. He is credited with cultural advances, many of which resulted from art works that were looted by his armies and brought to France. His military campaigns demonstrated true genius at strategy and tactics and are studied in military academies throughout the world.

Napoleon was born in 1769 on the island of Corsica, just one year after France obtained the island from the city-state of Genoa. At age nine he benefited from family connections and obtained an appointment to the royal military school in France. This was followed by four years at the military college and one year at the officers' academy in Paris. At 16 years of age he became a professional military officer in the French king's army, specializing in artillery. He was gifted in mathematics and learned to take a calculative approach in effectively planning military campaigns and in placing and using cannons during battle. He also became a master at map reading and was able to visualize and exploit terrain to develop battle strategies better than any other officer. His father died the same year he was commissioned, and he took charge of the family with seven siblings.

Over the next few years he returned to Corsica several times, occasionally engaging in political wrangling, until his family was forced to flee by the insurgent leader, Pasquali Paoli, who obtained dictatorial power in Corsica. But Napoleon observed that Paoli imposed order and passed legislation that benefited Corsicans—thus giving a reason for his revolutionary success. Napoleon kept this model in mind during his career, though his penchant for military campaigns and conquest overshadowed his role in governance.

DOI: 10.4324/9781003333937-28

In the 1780s, change was thriving in Europe. Legal reforms were instituted, outdated tariffs eliminated, feudal labor and slave trade were abolished, and commerce was promoted peaceably in Denmark, the Netherlands, and Germany. But France's King Louis XVI was slow to respond and was dedicated to France's image as "the Great Nation." The King provided financial support for the Americans in their revolution and prepared for a war with Britain while severely taxing his own people. Food prices increased steadily causing major financial hardships and in 1789 an assembly of representatives from the three classes in French society (commoners, clergy, and noblemen) was called by the Minister of Finance. From this point, the French Revolution gained momentum. The assembly of representatives became the National Assembly to form a French constitution, the nobility refused to pay more taxes, and the Bastille (the royal prison in Paris that symbolized the King's tyranny) was attacked by a mob and its seven prisoners freed. Larger mobs formed, other prisons were stormed to obtain guns, and Paris became the scene of general insurrection with many French soldiers joining the revolutionaries. Eventually, King Louis XVI was stripped of his powers and the National Assembly declared France to be a republic and the end of the monarchy.

Napoleon watched these developments until it was clear the monarchy was doomed and then he took the side of those supporting the Republic. France declared war on Austria and Sardinia in 1792, which delighted Napoleon since war meant promotion and a larger command. He was promoted to captain and sent to Toulon where royalists, who supported the King and were joined by British troops, had taken possession of that important French port. His ingenuity and aggressive nature gave him control of the assault, which he directed to retake the port. This action propelled Napoleon to brigadier general, skipping the ranks of major and colonel, and started his rise to power.

Napoleon's desire for power is reflected throughout his life. He saw his cannons as a source of power that inspired fear in opponents. He was not patriotic, in fact he considered himself Corsican. He viewed the French as frivolous and volatile, with short attention spans, and believed they were easily diverted from major issues by temporary excitement. He exploited these traits later in his career when he gained control of the media and used clever propaganda campaigns to bolster his heroic image with the French people.

He led several successful military campaigns against the Austrians and Prussians capturing enormous amounts of land and looting treasuries, which were removed to France. His personality was belligerent in nature and he viewed war and battles as his way of gaining and exerting power. He saw people with detachment and believed they needed competent leadership to accomplish anything worthwhile. He inspired his troops to believe in his military campaigns and tactics. His approach was always to attack and never assume a defensive position. He emphasized rapid movement of troops and artillery, the element of surprise by attacking before the opponents were deployed, the use of ruse to confuse the enemy, and rapid improvisation with high-risk maneuvers. He visited his troops before a battle to show his confidence in them and his infantry wore hats that were nearly two feet tall to make the soldiers appear larger and intimidate the enemy.

As Paris was shaken by riots and bloody coups, those in power realized Napoleon was their most dynamic and influential general. Fearing his aspirations for power, they plotted to keep him away from Paris. They thus approved his plans to invade Egypt and the Orient to take India from British control. He landed in Egypt in early July 1798 with a major naval fleet, troops, and 200 scientists and artists to document their expedition. He won a major battle near Cairo, but three days later his entire naval fleet was destroyed by the British Admiral Nelson at Alexandria. His army was then without naval support and he proceeded to invade Syria but was repulsed at Acre. Retreating to Egypt, he lost many of his remaining troops in sand-storms. In Egypt, he presented several carefully prepared speeches to his generals outlining how he was needed in Paris and they eventually agreed he must leave. He returned to Paris where he carefully spun a story of the cul-tural successes of his "scientific" expedition, which included discovery of the Rosetta Stone and incredible artworks that documented ancient Egyptian civilization. The following year he participated in a coup and was given control of the army. He also managed to get himself appointed First Consul of the Republic, which was really a dictatorship with Napoleon at the top. All of the restraints on political power had been swept aside during the Revolution—church, courts, aristocracy, and universities—leaving all the power to Napoleon. He led the French military to other victories against coalition forces from Russia, Austria, Sweden, Prussia, and other parts of Europe. He was made First Consul for life in 1802 and appointed himself Emperor in 1804.

His soldiers identified with Napoleon and trusted their future to him. He demonstrated amazing energy as he wore out his officers in long meetings to plan his battles. He was totally self-confident in his decisions and actions and he delivered carefully planned speeches to inspire his troops to victory. He exploited the terrain effectively by choosing his battlefields carefully and implemented an effective signaling system for communication among officers during battles. He directed his armies from a high hill or rooftop to view the battles as they developed, and during the action he wore a dark green uni-form with a gray overcoat, with no decorations to attract enemy fire. His daring and aggressive style of warfare became his trademark and Wellington (who finally defeated Napoleon at Waterloo) described him as the greatest general in Europe.

In addition to his aggressive style, inspirational speeches, and repeated victories, Napoleon motivated his troops with the promise of great rewards, which they frequently obtained. He promised them riches from looting, as well as honor and glory in victory. He offered promotion based on merit in battle where an infantryman could become a high-level officer. When he appointed himself Emperor he rewarded successful generals by making them princes and dukes with enormous estates. He also made it easy for soldiers to send home their looted riches so families in France shared in the rewards of his victories. He eventually made the military a privileged class in French society. The entire country benefited from the riches he sent home from looting the treasuries of Europe.

Napoleon was a highly authoritarian commander as he directed his generals to carry out his plans. He had an excellent chief of staff who translated his strategies into clear orders. His generals rushed to obey his directions and were obsequious in their praise. He appointed all his senior officers without consulting other officers.

Wellington believed his commanding type of direction decreased disputes among his generals, something Wellington and other military leaders struggled to resolve. When Napoleon became Emperor, he answered to no one. He was not a considerate leader as he repeatedly deserted his army when his plans were not successful. This happened in Egypt and again when he invaded Russia and was defeated in a long winter campaign. He later deserted his troops again when he was defeated at Leipzig and he returned to Paris, allowing 100,000 French troops to be captured. He constantly drove horses to death, whipping them as well as the horses his aides rode. He urged his cavalry to do the same, which depleted the French horse population and caused his cavalry to become less effective over time.

Scholars indicate that Napoleon learned during the terror of the Revolution that people did not bother to keep their word, honor was not respected, and treachery and murder were commonplace. Napoleon and his troops did not spare the populations they invaded—rape, murder, and pillage were commonplace. One general looted the Swiss treasury and murdered 500 citizens who objected—men, women, and children. In Syria, Napoleon had over 4,000 prisoners slaughtered because he feared they might rise up against him. He had at least one innocent individual murdered because he suspected him of plotting another coup. His armies lost 50,000 men a year during his campaigns, and he stated he would gladly sacrifice a million lives to attain the power he sought.

Napoleon was active in revising administrative and legal systems of the conquered territories. He implemented a new legal code in all countries he conquered, abolished the remains of the feudal system in Europe, and theoretically made all persons equal before the law. But he also reversed progress on women's rights that had been attained during the Revolution, reinstituted slavery in French possessions, and solidified powers of the central government. Wellington said that Napoleon was much too impatient to govern over a long term. This impatience also prevented him from fighting a defensive campaign against coalition forces that defeated him at Leipzig and later, at Waterloo. If he had done so, he may have been able to negotiate a settlement with these forces and remain in power.

After his defeat at Leipzig and the coalition forces invaded France, Napoleon was exiled in 1814 to the small island of Elba in the Mediterranean near Italy. He had a small force of 1,000 soldiers and a staff. He was not provided with the financial support France promised and became bored. In France, the monarchy had been restored but the King did not treat the people well, a major recession occurred and the remaining soldiers had lost their status and were unemployed. Napoleon sensed an opportunity, secretly left Elba and marched to Paris. French soldiers joined him en route after he lied to them that members of the government and several European powers wanted his return. As they approached Paris, the King and his family fled to Belgium. Napoleon gathered the army together and moved north where he was met at Waterloo by Wellington and the coalition forces. The fighting raged for three days with Napoleon's army finally retreating. He left the army two days later and eventually surrendered to the British. He was exiled to St. Helena, a small island in the Atlantic, when he was 45 and lived there six years before he died of stomach cancer.

Napoleon has been described as an incredibly talented military leader without a trace of humility and no patience for governing. His pattern of dedication to force and war, a totally powerful state government, centrally controlled propaganda to justify a single head of state, and marshaling an entire society behind a single dictator was followed by numerous leaders in the 20th century. In the end, the people subjected to this type of leadership generally suffered.

Napoleon's military leadership can be viewed as highly *charismatic*— whether or not it is transformational is debatable. He reflected the Multiple Linkage Model and Reformulated Path-Goal theories with his soldiers by *rewarding* them for their conquests. Leader-Member Exchange Theory could be used to analyze his relationship with his troops. His *directiveness* was extremely authoritarian. Elements of directive leadership are addressed in contingency leadership models such as Situational Leadership Theory, Path-Goal Theory, Fiedler's Contingency Theory, and the Multiple Linkage Model. However, these models generally avoid authoritarian elements in their prescriptions for directiveness. Implicit Leadership Theory might be invoked to analyze how his leadership style matched the expectations of military leaders at the time of Napoleon. His *determination* and *dominance, cognitive capacity*, and *self-confidence* demonstrate Trait Theories of leadership.

Discussion Questions

1 What aspects of Napoleon's leadership would you describe as charismatic/transformational? Would you consider him a "dark" charismatic? Why or why not?

2 What other leader behaviors or traits do you see in Napoleon's leadership that can be linked to specific theories of leadership?

3   In what ways did Napoleon likely fit an Implicit Leadership Theory for military leaders in his time?
4   Would you describe Napoleon as a Principle-Centered Leader? Why or why not?

Selected References

Anonymous. (August 30, 2017). Napoleon Biography. Retrieved September 12, 2017 from www.biography.com/people/napoleon-9420291.

History.com Staff. (2009). Napoleon Bonaparte. Retrieved September 12, 2017 from www.history.com/topics/napoleon.

Johnson, P. (2002). *Napoleon*. New York: Penguin Books.

27 Nicolas Hayek

Swiss Watch Executive

Nicolas Hayek was the major founder, CEO, and Chairman of the Board of Directors of the Swatch Group, the largest manufacturer of finished watches in the world. He and his staff engineered one of the most amazing industrial turnarounds in the world and saved the Swiss watch industry from oblivion. He also played a major role in the creation of the Smart Car, a small green European automobile built by Mercedes Benz for city driving. Hayek's strategic leadership is at odds with contemporary thinking about how companies must compete in the global marketplace, but his strategic vision and outstanding communication skills resulted in Switzerland retaking the leading role in the global watch industry.

Hayek was born on February 19, 1928 in Beirut, Lebanon to a prosperous family. He attended a Lebanese Christian university and graduated with a diploma in math, chemistry, and physics. He was a nonconformist in his youth and fell in love with a young Swiss woman who was working as an au pair in Beirut. His parents did not approve of their marriage, so Hayek immigrated to Switzerland when she returned home shortly after his graduation. They were married two years later. In Switzerland he faced suspicion and hostility as an outsider so he chose to downplay his background and focused on becoming a Swiss citizen. His fierce independence made him comfortable with risk taking with little fear of failure. Throughout his career he was never discouraged by opposition or setbacks, using them as energizers to work harder to achieve his goals.

Shortly after moving to Switzerland, his father-in-law, who owned and ran an iron foundry, had a major stroke. The family asked Nicolas to take over management of the foundry, even though he had no management experience. He accepted and began working in the shop where he had much direct contact with staff and foundry workers. As his Swiss German language skills improved, he slowly overcame the early lack of acceptance. He eventually attended an international foundry fair in Germany where he concentrated on networking with customers and others in the industry, landing a large contract with the Swiss Railway system. This allowed their family foundry to carry out a much-needed expansion and improvement of their facility. His father-in-law soon recovered and returned to the foundry, resulting in a

DOI: 10.4324/9781003333937-29

significantly reduced role for Hayek, who had enjoyed his new management experience and the independence he had as head of the company.

Throughout Hayek's career, he excelled at networking and representing himself and his organizations to other businesspeople, governments, and unions. While working at the foundry, he met an American engineering consultant named Lester B. Knight who respected Hayek's capabilities. When his role at the foundry became too confining, Knight suggested that Hayek start a branch office of his consulting firm in Switzerland. Hayek obtained a loan and rented office space and in 1957 began as a consultant in Zurich. His wife and two children joined him later when he could afford a living space for the family. At this time, Germany was still rebuilding from the destruction it experienced in World War II. Hayek had made many contacts in the foundry industry in Germany and was able to obtain contracts there. His reputation grew and so did his business. He added staff members to support the growth and six years later he parted with Knight to open his own consulting firm, taking many of the staff members from the branch office with him. His networks and consulting practice continued to grow with Swiss and international contracts and offices in other countries. His associates described him as highly intelligent with an excellent memory, a master at analyzing production, cost, and financial data, extremely energetic and diligent in his work, with an intuition for market trends and developments. He also preferred to be in control of his operation by making all major decisions himself and using an autocratic type of directive leadership. He was highly self-confident in his judgment and enjoyed public recognition for his accomplishments.

In 1981, Hayek was asked by major Swiss bankers to undertake an analysis of the two major Swiss watch manufacturers that were almost bankrupt. The Swiss watch industry dated from the early 1800s when jewelry and watchmakers fled religious persecution in France to live in Switzerland. After an early concentration on expensive luxury watches, less expensive models were developed that were affordable to a larger market. At this point the watch industry became a major industrial sector in Switzerland. During the economic depression of the 1930s, the Swiss government began protecting the watch industry through legislation and investment, which provided monopoly power to a few companies. They were protected from international competition and the management became complacent, concentrating on accuracy and precision in watches that sold themselves. They failed to adopt new technology as it became available and in the late 1960s they did not recognize that new electronic and quartz watch movements produced adequate accuracy for most consumers. In the 1970s Asian manufacturers mass-produced and marketed these inexpensive electronic watches worldwide and the Swiss market share declined rapidly. The Swiss concentrated on luxury watches, but this market niche was decreasing in size. Many Swiss watch manufacturers went out of business and the others were in trouble. Major Swiss banks were the dominant shareholders of the two biggest Swiss manufacturers and they were considering selling their best brands to Japan. At this point, they asked Hayek to evaluate the companies and advise them of the best course of action.

With his colleagues, Hayek identified problems in products, policies, and distribution as well as outdated leadership that required changing. He advised merging the two watch companies to avoid duplication and recommended establishment of three divisions—finished watches, parts and components, and diversified industrial products. He also recommended replacing the entire leadership group with a five-member committee containing a senior member of his consulting group—Ernst Thomke. He opposed selling the best brands to foreign watchmakers and emphasized keeping watchmaking knowledge in Switzerland. His proposals were implemented, and within a year improvements in performance were visible. Within three years the merged company (Swiss Corporation for Microelectronics and Watchmaking—SMH) was showing a profit. Hayek's consulting firm was quite successful and he started to look for investments when a major banker suggested he invest in SMH. Hayek assembled an investment group and eventually bought 51% of the company. As originator of the group, he arranged to have the major leadership role in SMH, and in 1986 he became president and operations manager. The market value of the company began to climb.

A major product of SMH at the time of the merger was the Swatch—an inexpensive plastic watch, produced in different colors, which was becoming a fashion accessory. The Swatch had been developed by two company engineers under the guidance of Ernst Thomke. It was produced in fully automated production lines and was very successful in the low-price segment of the global watch market with many models under $100. When Hayek assumed his leadership position, he became the Swatch champion and nurtured its further development and marketing. He consulted with designers and increased the advertising budget in the United States and Europe. The Swatch became a lifestyle product, and Hayek hired celebrities to promote the watch—including Jack Nicholson, Cindy Crawford, Andy Warhol, and actors portraying James Bond. Advertisements emphasized fun activities and new Swatch collections were launched each year. SMH skipped distributors and shipped the watches directly to retailers. In the first five years over 250 Swatch models were produced and by 1992, production had exceeded 100 million. The Swatch eventually created billions in revenue for the company. Hayek presented himself as Father of the Swatch and held a huge party to celebrate its success. His business acumen had certainly helped promote, distribute, and expand the production of the Swatch, but he did not originate the concept or begin its development and production. Ernst Thomke later gave credit to the creative engineers who originated the Swatch idea, but they received only small bonuses for their extra efforts.

Another successful watch brand acquired by SMH in 1983 from a small watch company was the Rado, which sported scratch proof metal, a ceramic face, and sapphire crystal. It sold well in the middle to high-priced market segment ($700 to $30,000) and was very well accepted in Middle Eastern countries. Hayek wanted to develop the Omega brand, the luxury line of watches produced by SMH, to challenge Rolex. Omega had been producing over 100 models with over 1,500 variations in all price brackets. The meaning of its brand had become unclear and it was losing its appeal to customers. Hayek asked Thomke to take control of Omega and restore its position in the luxury market. Thomke reduced the number of Omega models to fewer than 20 and reduced the staff to 33% of its former size. Production and sales increased and it began to be profitable. The same result occurred with the SMH Longine brand, which was a luxury watch just under Omega.

Hayek's strategic vision was to be strong in all segments of the watch market. He had an excellent management team with Ernst Thomke and other colleagues. Hayek set the strategy while Thomke and others carried it out. Thomke loved to start new projects and move on to other things; Hayek wanted to build his own business empire with all the recognition that went with it. Both were extremely talented, egocentric, combative, and reacted emotionally to unpleasant news. They were either loved or hated by employees. Hayek was a patriarchal leader who emphasized autocratic leadership over his employees. Although often blunt, he was a persuasive communicator and able to make people like him. He was approachable and people who worked with him indicated they learned tremendously from their experience. He was loyal to his people, although sometimes tough on his executive managers. Those who left the company were usually *persona non grata*. Eventually Hayek's tendencies to exert control of all activities became intolerable for Thomke, and he left to form his own companies. SMH was eventually renamed the Swatch Group and board members indicated that Hayek controlled the board of directors.

Hayek told interviewers from *Harvard Business Review* that his strategy demonstrated how high-wage countries could manufacture high-quality products for the mass market and be competitive. He did this not by decreasing wages, but by decreasing the proportion of labor costs to total costs through automation and increased efficiency. If mass production was shipped to other countries, he asserted that the United States and Europe risked losing key skills and the loss of these skills for low-cost items endangered the production of high-quality items. He lobbied Swiss and international labor organizations to allow for night work so the Swatch automated production facility could run around the clock. Throughout the 1990s he continued to expand through the purchase of small watch companies that focused on the extreme luxury market with brands such as Patek Phillipe, Blancpain, and Breguet. These watches sold primarily to collectors and royalty for $500,000 or more each. With these purchases he realized his vision of a major market presence in all segments of the global watch market. He also developed a relationship with Tiffany in the United States to produce luxury watches for their stores.

In the late 1990s, Hayek developed an interest in producing an eco-friendly hybrid powered car for European cities. He saw a similarity between watches and cars—both were consumer goods with strong emotional appeal. He partnered with Mercedes Benz to produce the car, planning to call it the Swatch Car. He helped promote the new car through clever publicity events and interviews. Although Hayek is credited for the original idea, the final result produced by Mercedes was called the Smart Car and was far from his planned creation. He eventually withdrew from the project due to its size and possible financial endangerment to his watch company. He did, however, establish a company to conduct research on clean power for cars and named actor George Clooney to the Board of Directors to help promote green projects in the United States.

Although Hayek professed no interest in politics, he often made controversial public statements that reflected his beliefs. He was an anti-militarist, opposed nuclear energy, and condemned extremely high executive salaries. Considering his great personal wealth, he was personally thrifty and believed management must consider all corporate stakeholders in making decisions—including stockholders, employees, and the public. He cultivated excellent relations with labor unions in the watch industry.

He continued representing his company throughout his life, appearing as a torchbearer in the 1996 Olympics in Atlanta, Georgia as the only business representative. From the mid-1990s he bought company stock and consolidated his holdings, while the Swatch Group remained debt free with a market value of $10–20 billion and over 24,000 employees, mostly in Switzerland. He received numerous awards and honorary degrees and is viewed as a classic model of the modern entrepreneur/leader and savior of the Swiss watch industry. Hayek died of heart failure in his office in June 2010.

Nicolas Hayek was a *visionary strategic leader* with excellent *communication skills*, as addressed by Charismatic/Transformational Leadership. He also excelled at *boundary spanning* by networking and representing his companies to important outsiders. This behavior pattern is addressed by the Multiple Linkage Model and Reformulated Path-Goal Theory. He was highly *directive* of followers in assigning them to carry out his decisions, although he was often authoritarian. Directive leadership is described by Path-Goal Theory, Fiedler's Contingency Theory, and Situational Leadership Theory. In decision making he was *autocratic* and *patriarchal* which are addressed in the Normative Decision Theory and Leadership Grid Model. He was *supportive* of his factory workers by maintaining high wages and avoiding layoffs whenever possible. This behavior is also included in Path-Goal Theory, Fiedler's Contingency Theory, and Situational Leadership Theory. Hayek's *intelligence, determination*, and *self-confidence* are addressed by Trait Theories of leadership.

Discussion Questions

1   Was Nicolas Hayek's autocratic and directive leadership style necessary to save the Swiss watch-making industry? Why or why not?
2   There were two major elements to Hayek's vision for the Swatch Group: preserving Swiss watch-making skills in the country, and establishing a major presence in all the price segments of the global watch market. Was one of these elements more important than the other to his success? Why or why not?
3   How important were Hayek's boundary-spanning efforts at networking and representing in building the Swatch Group's success?
4   What do you think of Hayek's practice of controlling the Board of Directors and making all major decisions himself?

Selected References

Pope, S. (June 29, 2010). Swatch billionaire Nicolas Hayek, who saved the Swiss watch industry, dies. Retrieved June 10, 2012 from www.forbes.com/sites/bil lions/2010/06/29/swatch-billionaire-nicolas-hayek-who-saved-the-swiss-watch-ind ustrydies/#70d2c3bc40f4.

Swatch Group History. (n.d.). Retrieved February 18, 2010, from www.swatchgroup. com/en/group_profile/history/yesterday.

Wegelin, J. (2010). *Mister Swatch: Nicolas Hayek and the secret of his success.* London: Free Association Books.

28 Father Greg Boyle

Founder of Homeboy Industries

Father Greg Boyle is the founder and leader of Homeboy Industries, the world's largest program for rehabilitating and reintegrating gang members recently released from incarceration. Homeboy, located in one of the poorest areas of Los Angeles, has helped Father Greg (Father G) lead thousands of gang members out of a life of poverty, violence, and hopelessness. Former gang members receive services like anger management, job training, domestic violence support, tattoo removal, and employment in its various social enterprises. Homeboy Industries is primarily funded by its social enterprises but also by public funding and sizable private donations. Father G has received numerous humanitarian awards, including the Presidential Medal of Freedom, and police chiefs have singled the work of Homeboy as the primary factor behind the significant decrease in gang homicides in Los Angeles since 1992.

Greg Boyle was born in Los Angeles in 1954 to an Irish Catholic family with eight children. After high school, he joined the order of the Jesuits and obtained master's degrees in English, divinity, and theology from top-tier universities. He was ordained in 1984 and spent a year in the Bolivian Andes mountains, working with impoverished communities and learning to speak Spanish. This impactful experience motivated him to continue seeking opportunities to serve the poor. In 1986, he returned to Los Angeles to serve as assistant pastor for the poorest parish in the city, Dolores Mission Church, the youngest pastor to ever work for the diocese. The church was located between two of the largest public housing projects in the United States and served an area with eight gangs at war against each other. The county had over 1,000 gangs and more than 100,000 gang members, locally known as "homeboys." If Los Angeles was at the time the gang capital of the world, the Dolores Mission served the area with the highest concentration of gang activity in the city.

In 1988, Father G started a church-supported alternative school to educate a large number of middle schoolers who were being expelled from public schools and eventually joining gangs. The school welcomed all kids, regardless of gang affiliation, and kids received free food at church gatherings. Father G started to walk and bike through the neighborhoods,

DOI: 10.4324/9781003333937-30

approaching groups of gang members uninvited, with very little success. He attempted to mediate a truce between gangs, but this strategy was unsuccessful and helped solidify gang identity. Then, he began focusing on individual gang members, but only those who wanted to change their lives. He would visit wounded homeboys and homegirls during their hospital stays and conduct church services at juvenile halls, probation camps, jails, and state youth facilities in Los Angeles County. During these visits, he would hand out his card and offer to help them get a job upon release, knowing that having a job was a main concern for homeboys.

He and church members started the program Jobs for the Future by contacting nearby factories to line up jobs for homeboys and homegirls. At the same time, Father G and other volunteers counseled them about the importance of coming to work on time and following directions from abrasive supervisors. That same year, and using support from the church and small donations, Father G turned the Jobs for the Future program into Homeboy Industries. Homeboy hired groups of homeboys to build a local childcare center for neighborhood clean-up crews, landscaping, and graffiti removal. Homies were required to work with members of other gangs. When they responded well to counseling and supervision and cooperated with coworkers, Homeboy would find them jobs outside the program. Father G's first office was in the church. Later, a local hospital rented a storefront for Homeboy with an office for Father G. He added a few staffers, including job developers, to find employment for successful trainees in the private sector. Every time they located a job for a gang member, eight more would show up at Homeboy Industries wanting a job. They began receiving gang members from over 40 different gangs.

In 1992, a Hollywood producer purchased a local bakery for Homeboy. Homeboy Bakery, run by gang members, started selling tortillas but soon received a contract from a large company to bake bread for restaurants. Father Greg was offered a grant to buy an automatic dough mixer but rejected it because hand kneading ensured employment for more homies. They soon opened Homegirl Café, a safe space run primarily by female gang members, many of them victims of domestic violence. They eventually began a tattoo removal service to remove symbols of gang affiliation for trainees and started a silk-screening operation that sold Homeboy t-shirts, backpacks, and coffee mugs. By 2000, they had added mental health and substance abuse professional counseling, case management, and legal services. They served 1,000 homies each month from over 800 gangs throughout Los Angeles County. Homeboy Industries provides no religious services and does not describe itself as a religious organization.

By 2002, Homeboy Industries had expanded its services well beyond its financial resources. They appointed a volunteer business executive to bring more resources into Homeboy. His job focused on making its service enterprises more viable and ensuring Homeboy's sustainability. This executive quickly realized that all Homeboy enterprises were overstaffed, so he implemented employee cutbacks, job furloughs, and pay cuts to economize their operation. He soon learned that the major objective of these enterprises was to hire as many homies as possible. Many employee trainees were not very productive because they were still learning to work effectively and to hold a job. He decided to focus on job training and develop those who showed potential into enterprise managers. He also learned that many of his trainees did not trust that hard work would pay off for them, so high-potential homies would receive pay raises and promotions before more was asked of them as motivation. Homeboy Industries became a more efficient and financially sustainable operation.

First-time Homeboy visitors are often greeted by an employee covered in tattoos. The reception room has seating around the walls and sits together gang members, prospective volunteers, business contacts, media personnel, and others seeking a tour. Mixing these diverse groups begins to blur the line between gang life and the "outside world." Homeboy has developed an 18-month training program that includes time with counselors, mentors, case managers, mental health professionals, and community leaders, who provide support for their lives and participation in the program. It also provides temporary financial assistance and a job at one of Homeboy's social enterprises—thus beginning an individualized recovery and development plan. As trainees become more comfortable with their assigned jobs, they help newly entering trainees. They currently welcome over 10,000 people and graduate over 400 from their training program yearly. Many of their senior staff members are graduates of Homeboy Industries.

Homeboy has become a symbol of gang member rehabilitation and hope. Its members' recidivism or reincarceration rate is 30%, significantly below the 70% statewide average in other programs in California. Homeboy is also recognized by police chiefs as the main factor behind the continued and very important reduction in gang homicides in Los Angeles since 1992. Homeboy Industries is raising $15 million for a Homeboy Ventures and Jobs Fund to help their social enterprises grow and to acquire similar businesses to employ more trainees.

Father G views gang membership as an addiction and inspires staff members to feel the pain and the shame of gang members. Homies have often been abused as children, and many have been abandoned by one or both parents, often heavy drug users. They have no strong family attachment or support, nothing to help them move into the future, and they see themselves as marginalized and rejected by society. Homeboys do not expect to live past the age of 30 so, rather than planning their future, they often plan their untimely funerals. Many homegirls seek to have children young because their expectation is that they will die young. Father G argues that their surly and belligerent behavior is the vocabulary of the deeply wounded, whose burdens are more than they can bear. They need someone to give them complete acceptance, individual attention, and kind compassion. He seeks to include them in a community of unconditional love and caring—no matter what. Father G receives hate mail, death, and bomb threats for his work.

He is often asked to speak about Homeboy at meetings and conferences. When he does, he brings along Homeboy trainees who tell their stories and explain what Homeboy has meant for them. Father G hosts a Global Homeboy Network gathering in Los Angeles for those interested in learning more about Homeboy Industries. Many attendees go on to develop therapeutic organizational communities patterned after Homeboy to help poor and marginalized men, women, and youths in their own areas. Father G's inspiring work has resulted in over 250 partner organizations throughout the United States and in several other countries. In 2024, President Joe Biden awarded Father Greg the Presidential Medal of Freedom in recognition of his work as founder and director of Homeboy Industries, helping thousands of people turn their lives around.

Father Greg Boyle is seen as a legendary charismatic leader by gang members, families, Homeboy staff, volunteers, donors, city administrators, and law enforcement. Indeed, he exhibits many characteristics of a Charismatic/Transformational leader. He demonstrates a *socialized need for power* in his constant efforts to create large-scale solutions that improve the lives of thousands of people. He *communicates a vision* of kindness and compassion through his work, conferences, and TED talks, emphasizing the need for compassion for those who are hurt and have lived difficult childhoods. His personal behavior in his community with families and gang members and his presentations to potential donors, supporters, and other groups are described as truly *inspirational*. He offers *individualized consideration* and supportiveness to gang members and their families, regardless of their violent past, identifying him also as a Servant Leader. He is seen as *trustworthy* by his entire community and, most importantly, by gang members. He shows a *conviction* in his mission, empathy and altruism, a never-ending positivity, and confidence in homies' ability to succeed, instilling in them a determination to make changes in their own lives. Father G also exhibits *traits* characteristic of effective leaders, as he is clearly intelligent, determined, sociable, and reflects a high degree of integrity and empathy.

Discussion Questions

1   How important do you think Father G's intelligence and behavioral modeling are in his effectiveness in rehabilitating gang members and those recently released from incarceration?

2   What are the major reasons for Father G's effectiveness with gang members? How does Father G help build gang members' trust in their ability to change their own lives?

3   Would Father G be effective in leading a for-profit business organization?

Selected References

Boyle, G. (2010). *Tattoos on the Heart: The Power of Boundless Compassion*. New York: The Free Press.

Simon, T. (2021). Father Greg Boyle: The Answer to Every Question is Compassion. Retrieved June 11, 2022, from http://resources.soundstrue.com.

Vozzo, T. (2022). *The Homeboy Way: A Radical Approach to Business and Life*. Chicago: Loyola Press.

Part III

Snapshots of Bad Leadership

29 Elizabeth Holmes

Innovation through Blood and Deception

On June 15, 2018, the Department of Justice reported that a federal grand jury had indicted Elizabeth Holmes with two counts of conspiracy to commit wire fraud and nine counts of wire fraud. The charges stemmed from allegations that Elizabeth had engaged in a multi-million-dollar scheme to defraud investors, and a separate scheme to defraud doctors and patients. Elizabeth had been the founder and Chief Executive Officer of Theranos, a private health care and life sciences company in Silicon Valley. Elizabeth had grown Theranos to become a multibillion-dollar unicorn, making her the youngest self-made female billionaire. This is a story of Elizabeth's emergence from a college dropout to a CEO and billionaire, leader in the healthcare technology industry, the collapse of Theranos, the company she founded, and her own criminal conviction and incarceration.

Elizabeth Anne Holmes was born on February 3, 1984, in Washington, D.C. As the eldest child in her family with only one younger brother, Elizabeth came from a well-educated and affluent background as her parents had diverse professional experiences. Her father, Christian Rasmus Holmes IV, was vice president of Enron, which closed its doors in 2007 after being involved in one of the largest accounting frauds in U.S. history, to later work in executive government agencies. Noel Anne Daoust, Elizabeth's mother, worked as a Congressional committee staffer and later quit to become a stay-at-home mother. According to Richard Fuisz, a Georgetown educated psychiatrist, inventor, and former CIA agent who claimed to have known Elizabeth since childhood, Elizabeth was heavily influenced by her parents. With a great desire to make more money and earn prestige, Holmes' parents pushed her to be an inventor, to do something great.

Elizabeth Holmes completed her high school by graduating from St. John's School in Houston, where she started to develop her interests in computer programming and her first business, as she sold C++ compilers to Chinese universities. Elizabeth's parents encouraged her to learn a new language and tried to improve her capabilities to get into Stanford by sending her to study abroad in China. In addition, she started to take Mandarin home tutoring to later attend Stanford's University's summer Mandarin programs.

DOI: 10.4324/9781003333937-32

At age 18, Elizabeth was admitted to Stanford University School of Engineering where she enrolled for chemical engineering and worked as a student researcher. Her charisma, discipline, and hard work gave her the opportunity to do an internship at the Genome Institute of Singapore where she helped develop a computer chip designed to detect the presence of the SARS virus in the body. While short, this experience played a key role in her interest in healthcare technology and diagnosis, which later contributed to the founding of Theranos. Elizabeth was able to patent a device that, when in contact with a person's body, could measure the effectiveness of a drug by comparing parameters of chemical markers produced by a diseased area with those of the therapeutic agent. Elizabeth dropped out of Stanford, which was before her sophomore year, to pursue her business endeavors and develop her startup idea. Initially, Elizabeth founded Real-Time Cures, with the goal of democratizing diagnostic testing by performing multiple blood tests with a few droplets of blood.

In 2004, Elizabeth incorporated the company as Theranos in Los Altos Hills, CA. Theranos had stated its mission as to revolutionize medical laboratory testing through allegedly innovative methods for drawing blood, testing blood, and interpreting the resulting patient data. Elizabeth sought to transform medical testing by developing a diagnostic testing device that could perform an array of blood tests through a drop of blood. Her initial idea was to develop medical devices and methods capable of real-time detection of biological activity and the controlled and localized release of appropriate therapeutic agents. The idea was marketed to investors as an adhesive patch that would painlessly draw blood through the skin using microneedles. A microchip in the TheraPatch would analyze and make decisions on how much drugs to deliver. The concept of TheraPatch involved a wristband that would simultaneously detect people's ailments by drawing their blood with microneedles and cure them by injecting them with the appropriate drug. TheraPatch would also communicate its readings digitally to the patient's doctor. TheraPatch never became a viable product. Elizabeth abandoned TheraPatch and decided to develop a miniaturized blood testing kit named "Edison."

A significant employee at Theranos was her then boyfriend, Ramesh "Sunny" Balwani. Balwani met Holmes in 2002 while traveling to Beijing. Balwani, who was already a tech millionaire, became Holmes' mentor before they started dating in 2003. It seemed they were both able to keep their relationship secret from investors. Balwani did not join Theranos until 2009, though he had maintained a constant presence at Theranos. Balwani, who had become wealthy after spinning off a software company during the dotcom years, became the Chief Operating Officer and President after personally guaranteeing a $12 million credit line to Theranos. Balwani played a significant role in hiring and operational decisions until he was fired by Elizabeth in 2016.

With seed funding from her parents, Elizabeth embarked on creating Theranos. She recruited her professor, Channing Robertson, as the first board director. Robertson and others connected Elizabeth to venture capitalists, and by 2004, Theranos had raised $6 million. Theranos had many prominent early investors and sophisticated venture capitalists that invested in the company. One of Elizabeth's earliest investors was a family friend, Tim Draper, the famous venture capitalist from Draper Fisher Jurvetson. Other famous investors included Don Lucas and Larry Ellison. Another early investment group was the family of Betsy DeVos. Her family invested $100 million in Theranos. Other investors were members of Atlanta's billionaire Cox family and billionaire industrialist, Carlos Slim. Walmart founders, the Walton family, gave $150 million to Theranos. Media mogul Rupert Murdoch invested $125 million in Theranos, and eventually lost all the money. It almost seemed Elizabeth was adept at talking many (mostly) wealthy old men out of their money while failing for 15 years to produce any actual results. In addition, Theranos raised a total of $1.6 billion from a total of 16 sophisticated venture capital investors. When Eizabeth was later indicted for fraud, it was discovered that conspicuously absent from the package that went to potential investors were income statements, balance sheets, and cash-flow statements that had been audited and signed by a qualified public accounting firm.

In addition to successfully raising capital, Elizabeth had hired prominent scientists, software and hardware engineers from Ivy League universities including Stanford, MIT, and Cambridge. Elizabeth had also hired prominent employees from major corporations that included Apple and NASA. Many of these hires had left promising careers to work for Theranos because they identified with Holmes' vision of transforming medical laboratories and saving lives. By 2015, Elizabeth had also assembled a powerful and influential board of directors that included the most prominent statesmen, financiers, corporate executives, and politicians. Board members included George Shultz, former U.S. Secretary of State, William Perry, former U.S. Secretary of Defense, Sam Nunn, a former U.S. Senator, James Mattis, a retired U.S. Marine Corps general, Richard Kovacevich, the former CEO of Wells Fargo, Henry Kissinger, former U.S. Secretary of State, and William Frist, a heart and lung transplant surgeon and former U. S. senator. The board members had certain common characteristics. They were all older white men with past success in their respective fields. For the most part they were in awe of Holmes' brilliance, sense of purpose, and a vision to transform the healthcare industry and save lives. However, none had a medical background.

By 2009, Elizabeth had developed Edison, a blood testing kit, for use by corporate clients, including pharmaceutical companies, foreign governments, and grocery stores. One of the earliest pharmaceutical companies to form a partnership with Theranos was Pfizer. Pfizer walked away from the collaboration after realizing that Theranos' blood testing kit was producing inaccurate results. At the same time, Elizabeth tried to sell the kits to the Mexican government, Thailand, and Belgium. The deals fell through following failure to validate their accuracy. In 2010, Elizabeth made a business proposition to Walgreens, claiming Edison could conduct more than 192 blood tests with a drop of blood. In addition, it would cost half the price of laboratory tests and be more easily available to customers, thereby detecting diseases early and saving lives. Walgreens executives ignored the advice of an internal testing consultant and signed a contract to purchase $50 million worth of Theranos equipment in addition to extending a $25 million bridging loan to Theranos. Walgreens was not the only one chasing Elizabeth's invention. Safeway and CVS were interested. In 2010, Safeway, with no evidence of due diligence, signed an agreement with Theranos, extending $30 million debt financing to Theranos and undertaking to revamp its grocery stores where customers would get tested on Theranos devices. After signing the two big contracts, Elizabeth realized that clients had their suspicions about Edison. However, none of the clients seemed aware of the magnitude of the problem. The clients did not know that Edison was incapable of performing 192 blood tests; in fact, it could only conduct a handful of tests. Elizabeth decided to commission a new blood testing device, miniLab. In 2011, Elizabeth, through her connections in the military's Central Command, tried to get the Defense Department to procure Theranos testing equipment for use in the battlefields of Afghanistan. However, the army found out that Theranos equipment did not have FDA approval. Subsequently, the army contracting unit awarded a no-bid contract worth up to $75,702 to Theranos in April 2012.

By the end of 2011, miniLab was still a prototype with no proof of concept. In the meantime, Safeway had invested millions of dollars in retrofitting 1,700 stores, in preparation to host Theranos' blood testing devices. Alarm bells started to go off when a Safeway employee discovered that, during a pilot test, Theranos did not have the testing equipment in the stores and was sending blood samples to a remote location for testing. By 2013, miniLab was yet to be installed in Safeway stores. Safeway's CEO, Steven Burd, who had hedged Safeway's survival on the wellness clinics, resigned from the company. By 2015 Theranos had rolled out wellness centers in Walgreens stores in Arizona and patients could order their own blood testing. Theranos was offering 240 tests ranging from cholesterol to cancer by testing a few drops of blood.

Two regulatory agencies responsible for regulating Theranos were Centers for Medicare and Medicaid Services (CMS) and Federal Drug Agency (FDA). Prior to 2015, Theranos appears to have used a loophole in the FDA regulations that did not require lab-developed tests to get prior approval. Despite questions regarding the accuracy of its finger-prick test results, the FDA had continued to provide approval for its products. When the FDA granted Theranos approval to test for the herpes virus using the finger-prick method, it led some to raise questions about the arbitrariness of the state of medicine and the lack of information to the scientific community. Following a tip-off by a whistleblower, the FDA had launched investigations into lab activities at Theranos. In September 2015, the FDA declared the tiny vials used by Theranos to collect finger-pricked blood an "uncleared medical device" after inspecting the company's California facilities.

CMS had been tipped off about Theranos' activities by another whistleblower and had started a federal investigation into the practices of Theranos' main facility in Newark involving erratic test results and unqualified personnel. By March 2016, CMS found Theranos' main lab continued to side-step compliance issues and decided the startup's reasoning for compliance was unsatisfactory. The Centers for Medicare & Medicaid Services (CMS) revoked the Clinical Laboratory Improvement Amendments (CLIA) certificate of Theranos' Newark, CA, laboratory and banned the company's CEO Elizabeth Holmes from owning, operating, or directing a lab for at least two years.

By April 2016, Elizabeth was being investigated by the Securities Exchange Commission (SEC) on whether she had made deceptive statements to investors while soliciting funding. Elizabeth's net worth was downgraded from $4.5 billion to nothing by Forbes. Industry analysts had downgraded the value of Theranos from $9 billion to $724 million based on company credit for its intellectual property and the $724 million that it has raised from venture capitalists.

In August 2016, Elizabeth made an appearance at the American Association for Clinical Chemistry, where she presented a sophisticated minilab capable of carrying out an array of tests, including detecting the Zika virus, from a finger prick of blood. Elizabeth's efforts to relaunch Theranos were met with skepticism by the scientific community. Eleftherios Diamandis, a researcher at Mount Sinai Hospital, wrote in the Clinical Chemistry and Laboratory Medicine article that, "any claim made by the company will be speculative until validation shows that it is true."

At Theranos, Elizabeth had instituted a high level of secrecy and sophisticated security systems that ensured even employees at Theranos did not have access to areas that were not related to their immediate jobs. Employees were under digital surveillance and had to sign confidentiality agreements. Visitors were carefully monitored by professional security guards. Tyler Schultz was a Theranos employee and grandson to George Schulz, board member at Theranos and former Secretary of State. Early in 2014, Tyler Schulz had noticed inferior quality control in the Edison testing equipment and falsified research data. When he complained to Holmes about it, he was berated and threatened by the company's president Baswani. Schulz resigned from the company and filed a complaint regarding the lab proficiency tests with laboratory regulators in New York's Department of Health. Holmes found out and sued Schulz for violating a confidentiality agreement and stealing trade secrets. Schultz stood firm against Theranos, convinced that fraud was not a trade secret. However, Schultz and his parents had to spend $400,000 in legal fees fighting off Theranos lawsuits. Another medical researcher, Erika Cheung, who had worked with Schultz, had noticed disturbing activities in the labs, describing Theranos as "the Wild Wild West of blood diagnostics." Cheung had begun noticing anomalies whereby she would run tests of patients and get different sets of results. These results were subsequently given to patients to make medical decisions. Theranos was also experimenting on patients without their knowledge or consent, making them believe their tests were going before a well-vetted doctor. When Cheung reported the anomalies to Baswani, Baswani dismissed the concerns. Theranos threatened litigation after finding out that Cheung had spoken to a *Wall Street Journal* journalist, Carreyrou, about the anomalies. Cheung was forced to resign from Theranos, and, fearing for her life, filed a whistleblower complaint with the Centers for Medicare and Medicaid Services.

On July 14, 2018, Elizabeth Holmes and her partner Ramesh "Sunny" Balwani faced legal charges related to their involvement with two multi-million-dollar schemes to promote their company Theranos. They were accused of using false advertisements to encourage doctors and patients to use these services, despite knowing that Theranos could not consistently produce accurate and reliable results for certain blood tests. The indictment alleged that Elizabeth and Balwani defrauded doctors and patients by making false claims on Theranos' ability to provide accurate, fast, reliable, and cheap blood tests and test results, and omitted information concerning the limits of and problems with Theranos' technologies. A federal grand jury issued an amended indictment, accusing Elizabeth of two charges of conspiracy to commit wire fraud and ten charges of wire fraud. Following a trial that lasted four months, Elizabeth was charged with one count of conspiracy and three counts of wire fraud, and later sentenced to 11 years and three months in prison and ordered to pay $452 million in restitution to investors. Elizabeth never admitted guilt and even expressed regret for letting down the people who believed in the company. On May 30, 2023, Elizabeth started her sentence at a federal prison in Bryan, Texas where she remains incarcerated. Elizabeth is permitted family visits every weekend and allowed to hold her children on her lap. The U.S. Bureau of Prisons credited her with 608 days of Good Conduct Time (GCT), reducing her total sentence to just over nine years.

Elizabeth possessed a remarkable set of qualities that facilitated her rise as an influential entrepreneur and leader. First, her exceptional sociability enabled her to forge instant connections with investors and followers. By presenting herself as an intelligent, innovative, and self-confident woman, she successfully attracted investors and instilled her vision and mission, which, even if untruthful, projected her interest in revolutionizing the medicine industry. Elizabeth's leadership style can be examined through the lens of various leadership theories. She embodied the qualities of a charismatic leader. She had an optimistic vision of the future and wanted to revolutionize the healthcare industry. Elizabeth was confident in herself, and had amazing communication skills characterized by her ability to deepen her voice and a penetrating eye contact. Charismatic leaders, by nature, exert a profound influence on their followers by appealing to their individual emotions, aspirations, needs, and values. Elizabeth leveraged this dynamic by presenting investors, clients, and employees with a life-changing product that promised to reduce costs and improve the patients' well-being. Elizabeth's formidable social skills and intelligence established her as a trustworthy entrepreneur from the beginning and her ability to articulate and sell her vision to investors captivated them to the point of following her almost blindly.

Elizabeth can also be defined as a visionary leader as she was driven by the ambition to make healthcare more accessible and affordable for everyone. Elizabeth rapidly ascended to a position of extraordinary prominence and became a very influential entrepreneur, as evidenced in her nomination as one of the hundred most influential people by *Time* magazine. Elizabeth was even compared to Steve Jobs, known for being one of the most influential charismatic leaders, as she also encouraged her followers to have innovative and creative behavior. However, she also possessed the negative aspects of a charismatic leader, characterized by having a high need for power and a desire to exert control over her environment, often including other individuals. Elizabeth exhibited a personalized need for power, diminishing her followers' autonomy and reserving decision-making almost exclusively for herself. By it, she can also be considered an authoritarian leader as she oversaw Theranos' decisions and accepted little input from her team. Elizabeth installed a culture marked by fear and intimidation, both emblematic traits of a fear-based leader. She was ready to do whatever it took to cover up her product's flaws and keep her much desired power. Theranos had massive layoffs as Elizabeth fired those who opposed her and forced all employees to sign numerous non-disclosure agreements, threatening them with substantial financial penalties for any disclosure of information related to the company. Elizabeth's leadership can also be assessed under different ethical theories. Her lack of transparency and humility disrupted the trust proper of a caring leader. She was indifferent to the career and professional well-being of her employees. Elizabeth's narcissism and obsession for power and admiration led her down a path of deception that spiraled out of control, creating a lie that she continues to defend to this day.

Discussion Questions

1 How would you describe Elizabeth's leadership characteristics and behaviors?
2 What aspects of Elizabeth's leadership attributes and personality may have led her to refuse to admit guilt or regret?
3 What were Elizabeth's leadership mistakes? Is it possible for a great entrepreneur to be an effective leader of a large organization?
4 What leadership lessons can be drawn from Elizabeth's actions at Theranos? Does she deserve a second chance?

Selected References

Carreyrou, J. (2018). *Bad Blood: Secrets and Lies in a Silicon Valley Startup*. Alfred A. Knopf.

Lancet, T. (2022). Theranos and the scientific community: at the bleeding edge. *Lancet* (London, England), 399(10321), 211.

Straker, K., Peel, S., Nusem, E., & Wrigley, C. (2021). Designing a dangerous unicorn: Lessons from the Theranos case. *Business Horizons*, 64(4), 525–536.

Williams, M. (2022). Elizabeth Holmes and Theranos: A play on more than just ethical failures. *Business Information Review*, 39(1), 23–31.

30 Bernie Ebbers

Corporate Executive

Bernie Ebbers was a Canadian-American who rose from a high school basketball coach to become the CEO of WorldCom, the second largest telecommunications company in the U.S. by 2002. WorldCom collapsed and filed for bankruptcy in 2002 when it was discovered that Ebbers had staged the largest accounting scandal in the United States at the time by fraudulently inflating WorldCom's assets by billions of dollars. Ebbers was sentenced to 25 years in prison, and died in 2020 after being released early due to poor health.

Bernie Ebbers was born on August 27, 1941 in Edmonton, Alberta, Canada. The second of five children, Ebbers' working-class family was rooted in strong Christian beliefs and a strong work ethic. After Ebbers completed first grade, his father, who was a traveling salesman, moved the family to California and then New Mexico before moving back to Edmonton. In high school, Ebbers was a 6-foot-4 star basketball player and helped his school to win the city championship. His schoolmates described him as an aggressive athlete and said that even his own teammates stayed out of his way. Ebbers' academic success was less remarkable. He dropped out of the University of Alberta after failing in the sciences. He failed a second time after re-enrolling at Calvin College, Michigan. Ebbers returned to Edmonton to work as a milk deliveryman and a bouncer.

Ebbers decided to join two high school friends from Edmonton who had moved to Mississippi. On his decision to move to Mississippi, Ebbers remarked later, "delivering milk in 30 degrees below zero isn't a real interesting thing to do with the rest of your life." Ebbers did not have a job when he arrived in Mississippi and started out by helping to coach a local basketball team. His former high school coach, who had also moved to Mississippi, helped him to obtain a basketball scholarship at Mississippi College, a Christian university. Ebbers' basketball scholarship and career quickly ended when an inebriated assailant hit him with a bottle and ruptured his Achilles tendon. He was determined to finish college and was able to raise money through a scholarship fund.

After graduating with a degree in physical education, Ebbers moved north to Hazlehurst High School where he taught science and coached high school

DOI: 10.4324/9781003333937-33

basketball. During the summer, he coached Little League baseball. Through coaching contacts, Ebbers was offered a managerial job at a local family-owned garment factory, Stahl-Urban. Ebbers had good social skills that helped him to rise fast in managerial ranks and he stayed for five years at Stahl-Urban. After saving enough money, Ebbers bought Sand's motel and restaurant in Columbia and became the onsite owner-manager. Within a few years, Ebbers had expanded the business to eight motels under flagship chains such as the Hampton Inn and Courtyard by Marriott.

In 1983, two entrepreneurs who knew Ebbers through a prayer group came to pitch the idea of starting a telephone company in Hattiesburg, Mississippi. Ebbers liked the idea but was not convinced that they had a good business plan. In 1982, the Justice Department had issued a consent decree announcing the breakup of AT&T, following violations of the Sherman Antitrust Act. Provisions of the agreement allowed other firms to compete with AT&T in the long-distance business, while AT&T would cede control of local telephone services that were broken down into seven independent companies, "baby bells." Ebbers and his friends agreed to invest in Long Distance Discount Service (LDDS). The concept was to lease long-distance phone lines from AT&T and sell them to underserved customers around Mississippi.

By 1985 LDDS had a debt of $1.5 million and was yet to break even. The board asked Ebbers to become the CEO following his success in managing motels. On the CEO's role, Ebbers pointed out, "If we're going under, I at least want to pilot the ship." Ebbers embarked on an aggressive acquisition and cost cutting strategy and for the first time, LDDS made a profit. On August 14, 1989, LDDS went public after acquiring Advantage Companies, Inc., which was also in telecommunications. LDDS was grossing $116 million in revenues and its stock was valued at 84 cents. A notable event was the hiring of Arthur Andersen as independent auditors. Andersen was also the auditor involved in deceptive accounting practices at Enron. Ebbers decided to focus on expanding the company through acquisitions.

By 1992, LDDS had acquired 35 companies and become a major competitor in the national telecommunications market. Besides acquisitions, Ebbers focused on cost cutting and management of earnings. In 1995, LDDS had a workforce of more than 7,000 employees and 160 offices around the world. Ebbers decided to change the company name to WorldCom to reflect its global reach. WorldCom further diversified to fiber optics and internet services. As part of its branding and marketing strategy, Ebbers contracted Michael Jordan, the NBA legend, to be WorldCom's spokesperson. The following year, WorldCom joined the Fortune 500. Ebbers had dazzled Wall Street and was considered a master in telecom mergers and acquisitions.

Ebbers' leadership started to emerge as combative and uncompromising. Within the company, one either played by Ebbers' rules or would have to leave the company. In an era where suit and tie were the norm in the corporate world, Ebbers had defined his own unique dress code. He preferred to wear jeans, alligator boots, turquoise jewelry, and drove a pickup truck. He was an avowed fan of Willie Nelson and would show up at WorldCom's headquarters in Jackson, chomping a cigar. On one occasion, a new employee thought he was a fax machine technician. He ate in local restaurants and lived in a trailer while building a $1.8 million home. Ebbers supported the local community financially and even worked in a local homeless shelter. He donated millions of dollars to his alma mater, Mississippi College. At WorldCom, Ebbers inspired deep loyalty and had a rock star presence. He was highly revered for creating a lot of wealth. Outside the company, he was considered flamboyant and became known as the telecom cowboy.

Over the years, Ebbers had demonstrated strong Christian devotion in the Baptist Church. He was a designated deacon in the local church and often taught Sunday school. He would start board meetings with a word of prayer; this endeared him with many older WorldCom shareholders in the Mississippi area. WorldCom was now a dominant player in the telecom industry and Mississippi. However, as Ebbers became more powerful, WorldCom executives observed that he appeared to lose his "Christian conscience."

The Telecommunications Act of 1996 further liberalized the telecommunications industry by allowing a single company to offer long-distance and local telephone services. Within the industry, many competitors had built their own infrastructure with more advanced technology. WorldCom, which had also acquired UUNET and MCI, started to experience over-capacity and a clash of corporate cultures. Ebbers continued on the path of aggressive acquisitions. In one ego-driven acquisition, Ebbers bought Digex Inc., at a cost of $6 billion after finding out that Global Crossing was in the process of acquiring it. Ebbers sealed the deal after a 35-minute conference call without approval of the board. A WorldCom executive later suggested that Digex may have been worth $50 million.

By 1997, the WorldCom stock was performing exceedingly well. Those who had invested in the company in 1990 had a 225/1 return on their investment. In 1997 alone, WorldCom's stock appreciated by 66%. Ebbers had become wealthy with 14 million shares worth $500 million. By 1999, WorldCom was the 14th largest company in the U.S., reporting $37 billion in revenues. Ebbers was the 174th richest man in the U.S. with a fortune worth $1.4 billion. Mississippi had become a magnet for other technology companies and real estate investments. What was not reported were internal problems at WorldCom. Aggressive acquisitions had led to slack, integration difficulties and poor customer service. The U.S. economy was also going through the internet bubble. There were ominous signals in World-Com's accounting practices that went unnoticed or were ignored. Ebbers had promoted Scott Sullivan to the position of Chief Financial Officer in 1994 and over the years, they had developed a close working relationship. Ebbers exerted immense pressure on Sullivan to manipulate revenue figures to align with targets. Sullivan was the highest paid CFO in the U.S. in 1998 with a compensation package of $19 million per year. At a time when technology companies were declaring bankruptcy and there was increasing over-capacity in the industry, WorldCom seemed to be doing exceedingly well. But a careful scrutiny of the company would have painted a different picture. For instance, WorldCom reported $16 billion earnings between 1996 and 2000, but only showed $1 billion in taxable income—the real results.

Ebbers set his eyes on acquiring Sprint. In order to provide a full suite of communication services, WorldCom needed Sprint's wireless network. Sprint had also developed packet switching that allowed multiple phone connections simultaneously, a significant improvement from circuit switching. The Justice Department and the European Commission on Competition opposed the merger on antitrust grounds. Ebbers, whose company had benefited from antitrust action, was highly critical of the decision by the Justice Department and Federal Communication Commission, accusing them of unnecessarily interfering with the marketplace.

By 1999, Ebbers' stock value at WorldCom was in excess of $1 billion. As CEO, Ebbers made $36 million in 1999 and $31 million in 2000. Using his company stock as collateral, Ebbers had borrowed almost $1 billion from WorldCom and invested in personal business ventures. These included a 164,000-acre ranch in British Columbia, a hockey team, a yacht building company, and a rice plantation in Louisiana. Besides these ventures, Ebbers invested in personal properties, including a yacht named *Aquasition*.

When WorldCom's stock started to tumble in 2001, the banks issued payment demands to Ebbers for the difference between the loans he had borrowed and the minimum share price of the stock he posed as collateral. Ebbers asked the Compensation Committee of WorldCom's board of directors for additional loans to fill the gap and was given $50 million. The decision by Ebbers to sell 3 million shares of WorldCom caused the market to react negatively with a further freefall. The board used this reaction to justify issuing more unsecured loans to Ebbers totaling $408 million at a below-market rate of 2%. After pressure from some board members, Ebbers agreed to provide external collateral for the loans. The information on these loan agreements was not disclosed in WorldCom's financial reports.

In March 2002, the Securities Exchange Commission opened an investigation of financial fraud at WorldCom. The board found that Ebbers had failed to secure loans issued by WorldCom with his personal assets as he had agreed. Ebbers was stunned when the board dismissed him from WorldCom on April 30, 2002. Ebbers' severance package included a guaranteed $1.5 million each year for life, as long as he fulfilled his personal loan obligations. Other perquisites included the use of WorldCom's corporate jet for 30 hours a year, medical insurance, life insurance, and stock options.

During his tenure as CEO, Ebbers had acquired 70 companies and increased the value of WorldCom's stock by 7,000% at its peak. The stock price dropped from $96.74 to less than $2 per share after Ebbers' departure in 2002. Another accounting firm was hired to replace Arthur Andersen as independent auditors. WorldCom stock was in junk status and 25 banks filed a lawsuit to freeze WorldCom's assets. On July 21, 2002 WorldCom filed for the largest bankruptcy in the world. An audit of WorldCom's books revealed that Ebbers had pressured Scott Sullivan to engineer accounting malpractices that included capitalizing operating expenses, fraudulent computer expenses, fictitious revenue figures, reclassification of customer credits, excessive accruals, and unjustifiable bonuses among others. The value of fraudulent profits reached $11 billion; another $79 billion worth of assets and goodwill was written off. Other class action lawsuits against WorldCom and its senior executives started streaming in.

It took two years for the federal prosecutors to build a criminal case against Ebbers. This was in part because Ebbers hardly used technology to communicate although he managed a technology company. Ebbers had always perceived this as a strength: "The thing that has helped me personally is that I don't understand a lot of what goes on in this industry." When Scott Sullivan decided to testify against him, prosecutors decided to move forward with the case. In March 2004, federal prosecutors indicted Ebbers and other former WorldCom executives with fraud. Ebbers decided to testify in his own defense. In his folksy style, he pleaded innocence and maintained that he had delegated accounting activities and did not know what was going on. Speaking in court, Ebbers stated that he had performed poorly in college, and his marks "weren't too good." He went on to say that, "I don't know anything about technology, and I don't know about finance and accounting."

In March 2005, a jury convicted Bernie Ebbers on nine counts of conspiracy, securities fraud, and other crimes. In an agreement with the court, Bernie Ebbers agreed to forfeit all his personal assets, other than $50,000 and a modest house in Mississippi that were left to his wife. On July 13, 2005, Bernie Ebbers was sentenced to 25 years in federal prison. The judge observed that "this is likely to be a life sentence for Mr. Ebbers; I find anything else would not reflect the seriousness of the crime." Coming on the heels of the Enron case, the sentence was the most severe in U.S. corporate history. Bernie Ebbers died in his home in 2020, after being released from prison for health reasons.

Ebbers' leadership of WorldCom demonstrates distinct leadership traits. Ebbers was clearly a *determined* and *driven* individual. He pursued his goals with a high degree of *energy, competitiveness*, and *perseverance*. He did not give up completing college despite academic and financial obstacles. One of his primary goals at WorldCom was to continuously increase the share price at all costs. He was *ambitious* and often *dominated others* socially and at the workplace. Ebbers appeared to be *sociable, friendly,* and *extroverted*. Wall Street analysts and investment bankers thought he was a great deal maker and did not envisage a scenario where he would fail. His actions and public statements suggest that he was *self-confident, assertive,* and *self-assured* of his abilities.

During his tenure, Ebbers demonstrated some elements of Charismatic/ Transformational Leadership. Many employees, shareholders and the local community *revered* Ebbers for his financial performance and were *inspired* by him. Even when WorldCom was on the path of collapse, local stock-holders refused to offload their stock, believing he would turn the company around. Ebbers used his *charisma* to influence some board members and accounting executives to commit accounting malpractices and lend him ille-gal loans. He had a *high need for power* and often demonstrated this by selectively rewarding his favorite employees with bonuses and stock options. He had *strong beliefs in the correctness of his own values and beliefs*. He clearly believed that acquisition was the only strategy that was effective. Ebbers seemed to have misguided faith in himself and WorldCom's pro-spects and decided to hold onto his stock even when the price was in free-fall. He was ruthless and frequently dismissed senior executives who had sold their WorldCom shares. He clearly transformed WorldCom into a huge company—and caused its final bankruptcy. His aggressive *dominating behavior, extreme self-confidence*, and *unethical financial activities* reflect Toxic Leadership.

Leader-Member Exchange Theory is another relevant aspect of Ebbers' leadership. WorldCom was made possible by an old boys' network that Ebbers had developed through sports and church membership. Over the years, the *network* grew strong and highly cohesive. At WorldCom, Ebbers enjoyed complete *loyalty* from Scott Sullivan, the CFO, and a few board members that seemed to be under his spell. Ebbers felt comfortable in these in-groups with *high quality exchanges* and may have exploited these rela-tionships as well as those with favored employees to pursue selfish motives.

Discussion Questions

1   Why do you think WorldCom employees were so loyal to Ebbers, even though he had a combative and uncompromising leadership style?
2   As Ebbers' power increased, he seemed to engage in more unethical behaviors. Yet need for power is a characteristic of positive Charismatic/ Transformational leaders. What does this mean about need for power?
3   Do you believe that relying on corporate acquisitions is an effective business leadership strategy?
4   In light of Ebbers' unethical behavior, do you believe his professed strong Christian faith was genuine?

Selected References

Belson, K. (March 1, 2005). Ebbers Mounts an "I Never Knew" Defense. *New York Times*. Retrieved October 14, 2017, from www.nytimes.com/2005/03/01/business/ ebbers-mounts-an-i-never-knew-defense.html.

Clikeman, P. & Lemon, W. (2010). Called to account: Fourteen financial frauds that shaped the American accounting profession. *The Accounting Review*, 85(5), 1811–1814.

Faber, D. (September 9, 2003). The rise and fraud of WorldCom. *CNBC TV*. Retrieved October 14, 2017 from www.nbcnews.com/id/3072795/ns/business-cnbc_tv/t/rise-fraud-worldcom/#.WswRIdPwZL4.

Goodman, P. & Merle, R. (June 30, 2002). End of its merger run led to WorldCom's fall. *Washington Post*. Retrieved October 15, 2017 from www.washingtonpost.com/archive/politics/2002/06/30/end-of-its-merger-run-led-to-worldcoms-fall/5230e607-54f0-4753-88e6-302f5e1d5f2d/?utm_term=.0e0d8cc4df32.

Hamilton, S. & Micklethwait, A. (2016). *Greed and corporate failure: The lessons from recent disasters*. New York: Springer.

Jeter, L. (2004). *Disconnected: Deceit and betrayal at WorldCom*. Hoboken, NJ: John Wiley & Sons.

Markham, J. W. (2015). *A financial history of modern US corporate scandals: From Enron to reform*. Abingdon, UK: Routledge.

Neff, T., Citrin, J. & Brown, P. (1999). *Lessons from the top: The search for America's best business leaders*. New York: Broadway Business.

31 Sepp Blatter
Past President of FIFA

On the afternoon of June 5, 2015, Sepp Blatter called an international press conference to announce his resignation as president of Federation International de Football Association (FIFA). Blatter's resignation followed dramatic corruption investigations and the arrest of FIFA executives by the U.S. and Swiss law enforcement authorities. Swiss police had raided a Zurich luxury hotel, arresting 16 FIFA executives on charges of wire fraud, racketeering, and money laundering. FIFA had long been plagued by corruption allegations. Blatter, like a well-curved free kick, had always managed to get around such allegations and was not arrested on either occasion. The leadership career of Sepp Blatter was closely connected with the development of modern soccer around the world by the premier governing body, FIFA, from 1975 when he joined the organization until he stepped down in 2015. While at the helm of FIFA, Blatter had globalized soccer, but also monopolized its governance around the world.

Sepp Blatter, a Swiss national, was born in 1936 in Visp, a scenic alpine town in the canton of Valais, Switzerland. Blatter has often claimed humble roots that gave him a fighting spirit; nonetheless, his family was determined to give him a good education. During his youth, he was a soccer forward and played in the Swiss amateur league. He failed to turn professional when his father refused to endorse a contract on his behalf. His father had better ambitions for Sepp, who did odd jobs when he was not attending school, including performing as a wedding singer. In 1959 Blatter obtained a degree in business and economics from the University of Lausanne. His childhood friends have described him as charming, highly competitive, well dressed, and ruthless to disloyal followers and those who stood in his path. He has been married and divorced three times and is known to be very close to his daughter, who often accompanied him on FIFA activities. Now suspended from soccer, Blatter lives in Zurich and Visp.

Blatter's early career involved working as a sports writer, head of public relations for the Valais Regional Tourism Office, departmental director for Longines (the Swiss watch company), and General Secretary for the Swiss Ice Hockey Federation. Blatter was introduced to FIFA by Horst Dassler, the CEO of Adidas and founder of International Sports and Leisure

DOI: 10.4324/9781003333937-34

Company (ISL). Credited with revolutionizing the concept of sports marketing, ISL later acquired exclusive TV broadcasting rights to FIFA events. ISL was subsequently linked to paying kickbacks to FIFA officials and declared bankruptcy in 2001. Dassler was impressed by Blatter's charm, but also recognized Blatter's unique social skills as an asset. In addition to his charm and sharp dress, Blatter was fluent in five major languages: German, English, French, Italian, and Spanish. When Blatter joined FIFA as the Technical Director in 1975, FIFA had 12 employees. In 1981 he became FIFA's Director-General and worked alongside his mentor, João Havelenge, who was FIFA's president at that time. Since taking over FIFA's leadership in 1974, Havelenge had initiated its transformation into a multi-million-dollar entity, by commercializing World Cup TV broadcasting rights. Havelenge had long been suspected of corruption by news organizations, though he was revered and considered a national treasure in Brazil, his country of origin. In 2011, Havelenge resigned as FIFA's honorary president when FIFA's ethics committee opened investigations of bribery allegations against him.

FIFA was founded in 1904 in Paris by European soccer representatives who wanted to unify the game and make the rules clear and fair. In 1930, FIFA united the soccer world by hosting the first World Cup in Uruguay. Modern FIFA transformation did not start until Havelenge and his protégé, Blatter, tapped into its marketing potential. Blatter was elected FIFA's president in 1998 and immediately embarked on transforming FIFA to align with his vision; with the same autocratic style of his mentor. Through ISL, FIFA sold TV and marketing rights, turning it into a global entity with more than 400 employees and a firm grip on each organization that played competitive soccer. Blatter has been credited with growing the game, introducing international youth soccer, the Women's World Cup, and providing financial assistance to soccer confederations and states. Each year every member association from more than 200 countries received $250,000 in addition to other monetary assistance to regional confederations and associations. Blatter introduced additional tournaments for the World Cup competition in different continents and reinforced the perspective of soccer as the people's game in many countries.

Allegations of corruption at FIFA predate Blatter. The combined force of ISL, Havelenge, and Blatter had a cozy and corrupt working relationship that former executives and sports journalists frequently compared to a mafia family. Accusations of bribery and Machiavellian tactics started hounding Blatter immediately after taking over FIFA's leadership. In 1997, Blatter is said to have returned $1.5 million to FIFA's marketing partner, ISL, after realizing the payoff was intended for Havelenge. During the 1998 elections, Blatter and individuals associated with him were accused of buying votes from the delegates. In a book and news columns, David Yallop, a famous investigative journalist, alleged that Blatter had spent $100,000 to buy votes from delegates representing third-world countries. Blatter sued for the book to be banned, and it was banned in Switzerland; however, it was widely available in other countries. Prior to the 1998 election for presidency of FIFA, Blatter used a private jet belonging to the Emir of Qatar to travel to different countries soliciting delegates' votes.

In the 2002 elections, FIFA's secretary-general Michel Zen-Ruffinen tabled a report accusing Blatter of corruption and mismanagement. Zen-Ruffinen was quickly forced to leave the organization. FIFA's own executive committee members filed a criminal complaint of corruption in a Swiss court against Blatter, but it did not lead to an indictment. When Blatter was accused of bribing a referee with $25,000 to run a smear campaign against his opponent, Blatter's explanation was that he was only guilty of charity. Blatter won subsequent re-elections in 2007, 2011, and 2015. It was estimated that FIFA generated four billion U.S. dollars in revenue from a single event—the 2014 World Cup hosted by Brazil. This revenue was mainly generated through corporate sponsorships, TV rights, and other fees. It was also alleged that FIFA's executives had engaged in corrupt activities estimated to be worth 150 million dollars in the process of bidding and awarding contracts.

In order to understand Blatter's tenure at FIFA, it is important to understand the FIFA institution. FIFA governs every aspect of soccer through its six continental confederations. Confederations are responsible for soccer associations in more than 200 countries. Within each country are the soccer clubs ranging from private clubs to professionally managed soccer organizations. Blatter often lamented that he had no authority over the confederations and soccer associations. However, he wielded considerable influence through rule-making, compliance, and financial rewards. Blatter's opponents had complete loathing for his leadership and often made comparisons to *Cosa Nostra*. Andrew Jennings, an investigative journalist who conducted decades-long investigations, had long accused FIFA of lacking oversight and transparency in the management of its affairs. Executives with close ties to Blatter who supported his election bids over the years appeared to be embroiled in perpetual corruption. The list included Michel Platini (a celebrated French soccer player who Blatter had recruited), Mohammed Bin Hamman (a former Qatar delegate), Ricardo Teixeira (president of the Brazilian football association and son-in-law of Havelenge), Jack Warner (former president of Northern, Central American and Caribbean Association—CONCAFA), and Chuck Blazer (secretary-general of CONCAFA). All these executives were eventually indicted for corruption-related crimes.

In December 2015, FIFA's ethics committee issued its first verdict by suspending Blatter from football activities for eight years (the suspension was later reduced to six years) over an illegal payment of $2 million to Michel Platini in 2011. The payment was based on a verbal agreement between Blatter/FIFA and Platini that had been made almost a decade earlier. While there was insufficient proof of bribery regarding the French election vote for Blatter, the committee determined that both men had demonstrated an abusive execution of their respective positions. Blatter still faced investigations related to bribery and TV rights over the years and controversial decisions to host the World Cup in Russia (2018) and Qatar (2022). The current FIFA president, Gianni Infantino continues to repair the image and reputation of FIFA.

Since his resignation in 2015, Sepp Blatter has stayed out of formal leadership roles but is a vocal presence on football governance and FIFA's activities. He has criticized the new leadership, especially FIFA President Gianni Infantino on numerous occasions. For instance, he called Infantino's plan to hold the World Cup every two years an imbecility. Blatter continues to fight legal battles and charges related to corruption and financial misconduct during his tenure at FIFA. His suspension from football activities will end in 2028.

Blatter is considered transformational in his contributions to the global expansion of football, the development of women's football, and the financial growth of FIFA. During Blatter's tenure at FIFA, the global game saw significant expansion through the introduction of new competitions such as the Club World Cup, Women's World Cup, beach soccer, and futsal (indoor soccer). He built extensive worldwide connections, particularly in Asia and Africa, where he established his power base by generously distributing attention and FIFA funds to members in those regions.

Blatter's leadership of FIFA was controversial. When Sepp Blatter took over, he set out an ambitious *vision* of transforming the organization into a global rule-making body with influence on each football confederation around the world. Following on from his mentor and predecessor, Havelenge, Blatter extended the financial success of FIFA through multibillion dollar TV rights and marketing promotions. Blatter was also committed to transforming soccer from a European sport to a global sport played by both women and men of all ages. He was intent on ensuring that each state had equal representation regardless of size and status.

Setting out this *vision* to *transform* FIFA combined with Blatter's personal *charm, rhetorical skill*, and *ability to generate deep emotional reactions* from diverse individuals cast him as a Charismatic/Transformational leader and is consistent with Trait Theories leadership. Certain decisions and actions by Blatter have cast a cloud on his achievements. Over the years, Blatter secretly awarded himself significant bonuses that FIFA later claimed were not included in his employment agreement. A case in point involves $23 million retroactive bonuses after the 2010 World Cup in South Africa. Blatter often consumed other perquisites, including the use of a private jet belonging to the Emir of Qatar. It has been asserted that this might have influenced the decision to host the 2022 World Cup in Qatar, a country with a population of 2.3 million, triple-digit summer temperatures, poor labor practices, and lack of sufficient infrastructure. Blatter is a subject of multiple corruption investigations by different entities. He generously rewarded confederations and executives that were loyal, but was brutal to disloyalty and spoke openly against those that he perceived to be enemies, including FIFA executives, politicians, and the news media. A dark side of charismatic leadership involves the use of charisma for *selfish personal gain, intolerance for opposing views,* and reliance on *convenient moral standards* to satisfy self-interests. Blatter's *grandiosity, arrogance* at the media and investigative authorities, and deployment of FIFA funds and *financial largesse* to gain adulation in third-world countries may be indicative of *narcissism.* Over the years, Blatter denied involvement or knowledge of corruption at FIFA. When confronted with facts regarding corrupt executives, Blatter stated he had no authority over elected officials from the confederations. In recent years, Blatter has acknowledged that FIFA needed to reform and become more accountable to its stakeholders. Condoning *unethical behavior* within FIFA and a *lack of clear moral values* are indicative of Toxic Leadership.

Discussion Questions

1   Sepp Blatter was apparently very popular in the international soccer community around the world. This was in spite of his autocratic style of leadership. Why do you think he was so popular?
2   Do you think that personal charm and social skills are critical for all types of leadership?
3   It seems that unethical behavior became endemic to FIFA during and even prior to Blatter's tenure as president. Do you think this type of behavior is infectious to an organization?
4   Do you think that Blatter's tenure with FIFA helped or hindered the international popularity of this sport?

Selected References

Borden, S., & Das, A. (June 3, 2016). Sepp Blatter and deputies arranged huge payouts after indictments, FIFA says. *New York Times.* Retrieved August 12, 2017, from www.nytimes.com/2016/06/04/sports/soccer/fifa-corruption-sepp-blatter-jerome-valcke.html.

Boudreaux, C. J., Karahan, G., & Coats, M. (2016). Bend it like FIFA: Corruption on and off the pitch. *Managerial Finance,* 42(9), 866–878.

Cuttler, T. (February 2, 2017). Sepp Blatter defiant over FIFA legacy as successor Gianni Infantino approaches anniversary. *Newsweek.* Retrieved March 10, 2017 from www.newsweek.com/sepp-blatter-gianni-infantino-fifa-sport-552152.

The Guardian. (December 18, 2015). Sepp Blatter: how the machiavellian master of FIFA power politics fell. Retrieved March 10, 2018, from www.theguardian.com/football/2015/dec/21/sepp-blatter-fifa-power-politics.

Jennings, A. (2007). *Foul!: The secret world of FIFA.* New York: HarperCollins.

Jennings, A. (2011). Investigating corruption in corporate sport: The IOC and IFA. *International Review for the Sociology of Sport,* 46(4), 387–398.

Jennings, A. (2014). *Omerta: Sepp Blatter's FIFA organised crime family.* London: Transparency.

Katwala, S. (May 25, 2002). For the good of the game. *The Guardian.* Retrieved March 10, 2017, from www.theguardian.com/world/2002/may/26/worldcupfootball2002.sportfeatures.

32 Adolf Hitler

Chancellor of Nazi Germany from 1933 to 1945

Adolf Hitler led Nazi Germany on the most destructive and violent military campaign in modern history. During the world depression of the 1930s, he transformed Germany into a totalitarian dictatorship using ruthless and violent tactics against many of his own countrymen. He originally gained support as leader of the National Socialist Workers Party through charismatic oratory advocating anti-Semitism, anti-communism, anti-capitalism, and ethnic purity with extensive use of propaganda and theatrics in his speeches. He pursued a policy of rebuilding the German military and eventually dominated Europe through military conquest. His territorial expansion began in the mid-1930s using political threats and lack of action by the international community and culminated in the invasion of Poland in 1939. In the next three years, he and his allies overran most of Europe and northern Africa, threatened invasion of England, and began a prolonged attack on the Soviet Union. His conquests and rule were filled with treachery, ruthless slaughter, and extermination of civilians. He was likely responsible for the deaths of 40 million people.

Adolf Hitler was born on April 20, 1889, in a small Austrian town near the German border. His father was a customs official and the family lived, at different times, on both sides of the border. There were two older children in their family, one half-brother and one half-sister, and another boy and girl were born after Adolf. Their father was a strict authoritarian who expected his commands to be followed immediately. Adolf was closest to his mother and was apparently a happy prankish boy who did well in school and aspired to be an artist. He was outgoing, learned to enjoy arguments at school, and became a ringleader among the other boys. In about 1899, Adolf's younger brother contracted measles and died. This tragedy apparently shocked Adolf and his demeanor and behavior changed abruptly. He became gloomy and sullen and his schoolwork declined. His father refused to allow him to study art, causing Adolf to be more remote and rebellious at school. Finding magazines devoted to warfare in his father's small library, he became infatuated with organizing war games with other boys. He used his powers of persuasion and demanded obedience to his orders. He read fantasy stories of warriors fighting American Indians and became lost in a dream world in which he was an artist and a great military figure.

DOI: 10.4324/9781003333937-35

In 1903 his father died and in 1904 he was expelled from school. His mother enrolled him in school in a different town where he boarded with another student. One year later after a serious confrontation with school authorities and an illness, he left school, never to return. He lived with his mother and sister in a large city and read, attended opera, drew, painted, and lived on a small legacy from his father and pocket money from his mother. He was enthralled with an opera by Wagner and identified with his proud, great, and remote hero. When he was 18, he decided to move to Vienna to study at the Academy of Fine Arts. He relocated and prepared for the entrance examination but failed twice and spent the next several years living in dingy apartments and a poorhouse, selling painted postcards and taking charitable donations for a meager living. He became interested in politics and often made frenzied speeches to other residents in the poorhouse. He was erratic, he dominated conversations, and would often become sullen and leave. He consumed political writings that advocated the future of Europe ruled by Germany, the power of human will, and the supremacy of the Aryan race. In 1912 he visited his brother in England and was impressed with British engineering and industry. The following year he returned to Vienna and received another inheritance. He then moved to Munich, Germany to avoid military service in Austria.

At the outbreak of World War I, he joined the German army and served as a runner delivering messages among military units. Others remembered him as a solitary soldier who would occasionally jump up and begin yelling about some military or political issue. He was wounded and decorated before the war ended and was appalled at the punitive conditions imposed on Germany during her surrender at the Treaty of Versailles. He remained in the army for a short time doing menial tasks and later wrote that this was when he decided to become a politician and punish those who were responsible for Germany's defeat. The political and economic situation in his home state of Bavaria was in turmoil, and a communist group (whose leaders were Jewish) seized power for a short time. Hitler became an undercover army agent and informer, identifying communist sympathizers who were arrested and executed. He attended classes in Munich on political philosophy and delivered speeches on preserving German racial purity and attacking Jews whom he associated with communists. He soon realized he had a gift for oratory, giving speeches with conviction on the spur of the moment with no preparation. He could hold his listeners' attention and sway an audience, and he became an instructor of indoctrination classes for returned prisoners of war. When he spoke against the Jewish people, he obtained a roar of approval from veterans who needed to blame someone for their defeat and poverty.

In 1919 Hitler was assigned to investigate a small political party (the German Workers Party) that advocated fierce nationalism and anti-Semitism. He attended their meeting and read a pamphlet by their leader that described a new socialist world order. It claimed the Jews were responsible for all of Germany's disasters and a savior was needed to sweep Jews and communists from Germany and preserve it for pure-blooded Germans. Hitler soon joined the party and began learning from its leader who apparently saw him as the German savior. He gave Hitler books to read, introduced him to society, taught him to dress with a military style that hinted at intimidation, loaned and gave him money. They shared the core belief that Germans represented the master race.

Hitler became the charismatic spokesperson for the party, and he drew growing audiences and attracted membership. He realized speeches are remembered when accompanied by violence so he encouraged interruptions and had his bodyguards initiate violent fights with objectors. He invented terrible visions of poverty and degradation of Germans and pounded his fist on tables before describing a future Germany as the most powerful country in the world, free of Jews and free of international financial obligations. He studied the acoustics and colors of the rooms before his speeches and he would always arrive late so the audience was tired and anxious to see and hear him. He would then enter from an unexpected direction, marching across the hall with a stern fixed expression and a wedge of bodyguards in front and behind. He often attacked the Berlin government, which suited his audiences, many of them believing it was filled with corruption. He wrote much of the party's platform that demanded all Germans be united into a single Germany, the abrogation of peace treaties and reparation payments from World War I, denying Jews the right to German citizenship, and declaring war against parliamentary government. In 1921 he engineered a coup of party leadership by threatening to leave the party. The executive committee knew his name had come to represent the party and reluctantly granted his demands for dictatorial power over all party affairs. He recognized the importance of strong recognizable symbols for influencing large groups of people and he developed the heavy black swastika in a white circle on a blood-red field as the party symbol. It appeared oversized and menacing on posters, flags, and the armbands of his bodyguards. He changed the name of the party to the National Socialist German Workers (Nazi) Party and invented a new title for himself—*Der Führer* (the leader).

With his new title, he increased his violence, including physical attacks on opposing party representatives. Hitler began organizing a private army with red armbands and swastikas. They accompanied him when he spoke and marched in the streets of Munich often with small musical bands. He would bait those who opposed him into objecting to his exaggerated rhetoric. He had directed his troopers to attack the objectors on his signal—especially if they were suspected of being communists. This group of ruffians became known as Hitler's storm troopers, and their violence increased the drama of his speeches and his popularity grew.

In 1923 he attempted a takeover of the Bavarian government with distinguished military figures from World War I and other right-wing groups that also had private armies. When they marched toward the capital, they were dispersed by Munich police who fired into the street. Ricocheting bullets killed several of the plotters and Hitler fled. He considered suicide while in hiding but was soon arrested and tried for high treason. He was given nearly unlimited time to speak in his defense and he claimed strong nationalistic motives for his attempted takeover. He thus became a nationally known political figure and was sentenced to five years in prison. He received favored treatment by prison authorities who were convinced of his nationalistic sentiments. He received unlimited visitors in prison and, with their help, wrote *Mein Kampf (My Struggle)*, his autobiography and description of his political beliefs. Although sales of the book were good at first, they slumped after one year. However, by the end of World War II it had sold 10 million copies. He was released from prison after serving only one year of his sentence.

For a short period, his party was made illegal and he was banned from public speaking. When these bans were lifted, he took direct control of the party and resumed his theatrical speaking performances. He was always able to sway his audience by appealing to German national pride, which he claimed had been disrespected by the terms of the Treaty of Versailles and the huge reparation payments Germany was forced to pay. His revived storm troopers used violence against party rivals. His party leadership was totally centralized with subordinates appointed by him, not elected, and he demanded unquestioned obedience.

The post-World War I government of Germany had never been strong and was opposed by many groups, including the Nazis and communists. The depression, which began in the late 1920s, made economic conditions in a weakened Germany even worse. Hitler exploited these weaknesses in his speeches by blaming the German Parliament and the existing government for the deteriorating conditions. An early election in 1930 gave Hitler's party 107 seats in Parliament to become the second most powerful party in government. In 1932 he ran for president by openly claiming Hindenburg, who was the incumbent president, an octogenarian and his major opponent, was senile and stupid. After a runoff election, Hindenburg won with 53% and Hitler was second with 37% of the vote. Mathematics was never Hitler's strength. He ignored Hindenburg's majority of the vote, and claimed that since a 51% majority was enough to govern and he had 37%, this entitled him to three-fourths of the governing power and his opponents should have only one-fourth. He refused the office of Vice Chancellor and, after considerable pressure from German industrialists and bankers, Hindenburg appointed Hitler as Chancellor (equivalent to a prime minister) but gave his party only three other major positions in government. In that way, he hoped to minimize the influence of Hitler's National Socialist Party on governmental affairs. But Hitler now had power and he stated he would never relinquish his power while still alive.

Hitler proceeded to prevent all others from gaining a majority in Parliament, making governing nearly impossible. He then convinced Hindenburg to hold new elections but before they were held, Hitler apparently directed the Parliament building to be set on fire and he blamed the fire on a communist plot. He already had a list of 4,000 communists and directed that they be rounded up and placed in prison, removing the communist leaders as candidates in the new election. Hitler's party conveniently won a majority of parliamentary seats in the special election. He convinced the aged and confused Hindenburg to sign special decrees that supposedly would protect the people from communist violence. These decrees eliminated constitutionally guaranteed freedoms such as privacy in telephone and postal communications, freedom of assembly and press, rights to hold one's own opinions, and the right to avoid unlawful arrest. Hitler also managed to pass an Enabling Act that gave his cabinet powers to legislate new laws. With Hindenburg's mental and physical capacities failing, Hitler's government had become a dictatorship. He banned the other major political parties and his storm troopers ransacked trade union offices.

Many of Hitler's storm troopers were thugs and criminals, and he worried they might become too powerful and unruly. In 1934, he claimed their leader was plotting a government takeover and ordered their entire leadership arrested as well as opposing politicians, military officers, and clergy who had caused him problems. There were no trials and estimates are that 1,000 people were summarily executed by Hitler's select secret service at this time, most of them in a single day. Later that year President Hindenburg died. Ignoring the constitution, Hitler then forced passage of a law transferring the powers of the president to him as leader and chancellor. He now had absolute power, and no one dared to oppose him. He was supreme commander of the armed forces and he changed the loyalty oath for all sailors and soldiers to have them swear complete loyalty to him personally, not to an unnamed commander and chief. He claimed public support by describing himself as Germany's savior from the economic depression, the Versailles Treaty, Judeo-communists, and other undesirables.

Hitler then began rebuilding Germany's economy by focusing on rearmament of the military using currency manipulation to fund his projects. He emphasized military spending ahead of unemployment relief and introduced universal military service. In 1935 and early 1936, his speeches emphasized how Germany wanted peace, and he manipulated several international agreements with this claim while he continued to build the German military. He signed nonaggression pacts with several European countries to gain time, but had no intention of adhering to them. Violence against German Jews increased, and Hitler introduced laws banning sex and marriage between Aryan and Jewish Germans and denied citizenship to Jews and other non-Aryan Germans. In 1936 his troops occupied the Rhineland, which had been a demilitarized zone since the Versailles Treaty. There was no international reaction. He spoke of the need for German "living space" and claimed that if Germany did not have the greatest military in the world then their country would be lost to communism. He signed a pact with Italian dictator

Mussolini, jointly opposing international communism, and began cooperative negotiations with Japan.

Hitler had increasingly complex ceremonies conducted in Germany to honor him as the sole hero of the German people. Parades, speeches in huge halls with thousands of swastika banners, music, and colored lights all flared as he stood in front of a large red and gold background. He stood behind a bulletproof lectern and shouted into the microphone, displaying carefully choreographed violent emotions. Films of these events show the almost hypnotic emotion aroused in his audiences whose obedience was unquestionable. He claimed that Austria and Czechoslovakia were needed by Germany for "living space" and to save the German economy. He threatened Austria with invasion, and they reluctantly agreed to be annexed by Germany. He did the same with Czechoslovakia in 1939. He then prepared for the invasion of Poland while claiming he wanted peace, manipulating the German press, and bribing foreign newspapers to applaud his actions. Hitler kept demanding more concessions from other countries, secretly wanting them to refuse and allow him to justify a war. Poland finally said "No," and he manufactured a phony attack by Poles against a German radio station and directed his armies to invade that country in September 1939. He demanded his soldiers show extreme brutality to terrorize their opponents and the German *Blitzkrieg* (lightning-fast war of movement) overran Poland in a short time. This was quickly followed by the mass murder of Polish military officers, priests, intellectuals, Jews, and aristocracy. He had negotiated a secret nonaggression pact with Stalin in the Soviet Union and gave the Soviets part of the Polish territory he had acquired in the invasion. Two days after the invasion of Poland, Britain and France declared war on Germany.

In 1939 Hitler was 50 years old, although he looked younger. He was fastidious and acted with extreme self-confidence, was widely read, and had an excellent memory. His speeches and writings were designed to excite his audience. In many small gatherings when threats were not needed, he would begin speaking in a quiet and reasonable voice that was very convincing. But he had mastered the art of lying. Hitler described himself in a speech to his generals shortly before the Polish invasion as the greatest personality in Europe, and there were no men of action who could oppose him. He believed everything depended on him. He ordered a plan of attack on France and Britain, which his generals opposed, claiming the army was not ready. They did not object to war, they merely wanted more time to prepare. At the same time, he began the systematic enslavement and murder of 10 to 15 million German Jews, communists, homosexuals, physically and mentally handicapped people, trade union members, psychiatric patients, and some religious groups. In 1941 he ordered mass exterminations by gas chambers. He stated that Jews should not simply die, they should die in agony. His ruthless hatred of these groups apparently had no limits.

Hitler had ignored the advice of his generals, whom he viewed as weak and overly cautious, and ordered his armies to invade Denmark, Norway, Netherlands, Luxemburg, and Belgium in early 1940. Mussolini joined Hitler's war in the same year, and Winston Churchill became British Prime Minister and leader in the war against Germany. Hitler respected the British and knew Churchill was formidable. British troops had been sent to help defend Western Europe but could not resist the German onslaught. France was overrun in late June, and over 300,000 British and French troops were barely evacuated from Dunkirk to England in an enormous flotilla of public and private boats. Hitler had insisted his troops stop their rapid advance, believing they were moving too fast. Overruling his generals was common for Hitler since he believed he possessed outstanding military knowledge and only he had the ruthlessness he believed he needed to continue his conquests. It was simply their duty to obey.

When France surrendered, Hitler toured occupied Paris early one morning and began planning a rebuilding of Berlin with huge avenues, fortress-style buildings, and his own office with a dome three times the size of the dome of St. Peter. He saw this as a symbol of his accomplishments. Meanwhile, Churchill vowed that England would continue fighting, and Hitler ordered bombing attacks on British air bases, radio stations, and ports. When his air force failed to neutralize the British flyers, he ordered mass bombings on British cities. His submarine fleet was directed to sink so many British ships that they could not resist a German invasion. But German submarines were suffering large losses in the Atlantic. Hitler made an overture to Churchill for a negotiated peace, but Churchill knew how Hitler dealt with international agreements and rejected the offer. Churchill emphasized his answer by nightly bombing raids on German cities that manufactured army tanks. This was soon followed by British bombing raids on Berlin, and they destroyed the German landing barges being prepared for the invasion of Britain. Hitler believed he was a great negotiator, but he lacked finesse and simply lied or threatened people into complying with his desires. He tried to convince the leaders of conquered countries to join him in an attack on England, but their leaders met him with silence or diversionary questions. After the British refused to surrender, German and Italian forces invaded Yugoslavia and Greece in early 1941. Ignoring his pact with Stalin, Hitler also began an invasion of the Soviet Union.

Soviet leaders were warned of the attack by their own Foreign Service, as well as by Britain and the United States, but they ignored the warnings and made no preparations. The Germans drove deep into Soviet territory in June 1941, and Hitler believed they would overrun Moscow by winter. He directed them to wage a war of annihilation, destroying cities and murdering the population. But he underestimated Soviet resistance, and their fighting retreat was costly on the Germans, especially when German soldiers were stopped just short of Moscow as the winter set in. The German army was not prepared for the Russian winter and suffered terribly. The same thing happened in their attack on Stalingrad. The Russians slowly drove them back from Moscow and surrounded the German force attacking Stalingrad where German soldiers were freezing, starving, and running out of ammunition. Hitler continued to overrule his generals and to make erratic and irrational decisions. He refused to allow German soldiers to retreat from Stalingrad. Over 100,000 German soldiers were killed and 180,000 were captured and marched to work camps in Siberia. About 6,000 of these survived the war. On December 7, 1941 the Japanese bombed Pearl Harbor and Hitler declared war on the United States, which was the world's largest industrial and financial power. He was also at war with Britain, which had the largest empire, and the Soviets, who had the largest army in the world. His generals had always advised against a two-front war, but Hitler ignored their input. In late 1942, Germany was also losing ground in North Africa. Hitler had spread his forces too thin and overruled his generals too often.

In 1943, Mussolini was deposed in Italy and his replacement surrendered to the Allied forces. The Russians continued to push German forces back from Moscow, and British, United States, and other Allied forces landed in France in June 1944. Hitler's aides had received warnings of the landing but ignored them. He was asleep when the landing began and his aides refused to wake him. The Allies established themselves on the beach and began to move forward. German generals then knew the war would be lost.

From the beginning of his invasion of the Soviet Union, Hitler had spent the war in various forest bunkers with his aides and summoned his generals to meet him at various times. He seldom appeared in Berlin from this point on and seemed alienated from the German people. He had been extremely generous to generals who were successful in the past—granting them houses, estates, and valuable gifts. He had also been quite considerate of his personal staff and office workers—celebrating their birthdays and keeping track of their families. But as the losses mounted, his hatred of the generals grew. He refused his greatest tank commander's advice to keep a strategic reserve of tanks, using them instead like soldiers to be sacrificed at his whim. The great German General Rommel told Hitler it was hopeless to continue fighting as the Allies pushed into France. Hitler exploded in fury, telling Rommel it was not his business to worry about the war, only his troops at the front. These outbursts became common as the losses mounted, and Rommel even decided to arrest or murder Hitler, but was prevented when Hitler left for Berlin. Rommel was later forced to commit suicide by Hitler's secret service. Toward the end when it became obvious Germany would fall, Hitler ordered the destruction of the entire German infrastructure—factories, supply depots, railways, bridges, electrical and water supplies, and communications facilities. Since the war was to be lost, he stated that Germany and its people had no right to exist. Since the remaining Germans were inferior people, they should all perish.

Several assassination attempts were made on Hitler's life by Germans during the war; most involved time bombs that did not detonate. In July

1944 one bomb did detonate at his forest bunker, Wolf's Lair. Hitler was launching into one of his long presentations that always dominated his meetings when the bomb went off, killing several German officers but inflicting only minor injuries on Hitler. He ordered the execution of the German officers who planned the attempt, as well as everyone else who might have been remotely involved. This resulted in about 2,000 executions.

As the Allies moved into Germany, Hitler retreated to his chancellery office and bunker in Berlin with his close staff, secret service officers, and his mistress, Eva Braun. He continued to insist that his troops must never retreat, resulting in enormous losses of German soldiers. He fantasized about the V-2 rockets he had used to terrorize England and his secret bomb that would change the course of the war. He screamed at people and ranted about his incompetent and traitorous generals. Some of his military advisors wondered why the German army kept fighting when they all knew they would lose. The answer was because Hitler ordered them to do so. To the end, Hitler seemed to believe that he was the only one who had maintained his honor, their losses were the result of errors by others, and his only fault was that he was not ruthless enough. In fact, he had the secret service flood the Berlin subway tunnels to hinder the Russian advance, drowning several thousand Berliners who had used them as refuge. As Soviet forces invaded Berlin and advanced on his bunker, he made a last will and testament, married Eva Braun, and said goodbye to his staff. He and his wife retired to his bedroom. The staff expected him to commit suicide and began singing, playing records, and talking in loud voices, which they had never before done in Hitler's bunker. His secret service officers entertained several young women in their quarters. Hitler and his wife actually waited until the next day to end their lives. Hitler shot himself and Eva Braun took cyanide.

Hitler's leadership is often described as that of a "Dark Charismatic." He demonstrated many of the behaviors and personal characteristics of other charismatic leaders. His ability to address German frustrations with *inspirational speeches* that appealed to national pride was most notable. His rhetoric is said to have hypnotized his audiences and he made extensive use of *symbols* and *ceremony* that added to their effects. He clearly had a high *need for power* which characterizes most charismatic leaders. His excellent memory and wide reading gave the impression of a keen *intelligence* that impressed most followers and the media. Most leadership scholars do not consider Hitler a Transformational Leader because of his destructive tendencies and the disaster he brought on the German people and all of Europe. But his policy of rearmament did transform the German nation from an underemployed depressed economy into a single focused country with high employment and considerable unity of purpose. Many of Hitler's behaviors are described in Charismatic/Transformational theories of leadership. His eventual impacts remind us that the power of charismatic leaders can be highly toxic.

Hitler was also extremely directive in his leadership. His authoritarian *dominant* directions and punitive style necessitated complete obedience and represents an extremely severe form of *toxic directive leadership*. He was very *considerate* and *supportive* of his personal staff and of the generals who were successful in military campaigns. He used *contingent reward behavior* with successful generals by granting them homes and estates and was highly *punitive* of those who were not successful. Several of these leadership behaviors are described in contingency theories of leadership including the Multiple Linkage Model, Path-Goal Theory, Situational Leadership Theory, and Fiedler's Contingency Theory. Although Hitler believed he was an excellent *negotiator*, his typical strategy was to use *threats* to *coerce* his negotiating partner into compliance or to *lie* and agree to terms that he had no intention of following. Eventually others learned of his duplicity and refused to cooperate with his threats and did not believe his lies. In the end, his external *boundary spanning* was not effective as others refused to comply with his demands in negotiations. Boundary-spanning leadership is described in the Multiple Linkage Model and Reformulated Path-Goal Theory of Leadership.

Hitler's leadership can also be viewed from the perspective of Implicit Leadership Theory because he adhered to a prototype of German military leadership that was outdated. His style of requiring absolute obedience and using draconian punishment was typical of 18th-century Prussian military leaders. It was no longer appropriate for 20th-century military campaigns with separate armies that required general directives from the top and subordinate military leaders exercising considerable freedom in troop and munitions movements. His attempt at military leadership resulted in terrible losses of German military personnel and equipment that hampered the German war effort. Hitler's *determination* and *dominance*, as well as his *self-confidence*, reflect Trait Theories of leadership. His complete *lack of integrity, poor cognitive capacity* regarding strategic military issues, his *illusions of grandeur*, and *erratic psychological/social behavior* reflected narcissistic and psychopathic elements which are described in Toxic Leadership Theory and represent major flaws in his leadership traits.

Discussion Questions

1   Why was Adolf Hitler's vision of a future Germany so attractive to German citizens?

2   What do you think were Hitler's most important capabilities that made him able to attain so much power in Germany?

3   Why do you think some charismatic leaders become cruel and destructive of their followers and others, while other charismatic leaders are constructive and supportive of their followers?

4   Is it possible that another leader could attain the power and destructiveness of Hitler in today's world? If so, how can this be avoided?

Selected References

Megargee, G. (March 3, 2011). Hitler's leadership style. *British Broadcasting Corporation-History*. Retrieved August 1, 2012 from www.bbc.co.uk/history/worldwars/wwtwo/hitler_commander_01.shtml.

Payne, R. (1973). *The life and death of Adolf Hitler*. New York: Praeger.

Roberts, A. (February 17, 2011). Secrets of leadership: Hitler and Churchill. *British Broadcasting Corporation-History*. Retrieved August 15, 2012 from www.bbc.co.uk/history/worldwars/wwtwo/hitler_churchill_01.shtml.

33 Idi Amin

President of Uganda from 1971 to 1979

Idi Amin was a Ugandan military officer who, in 1971, led a coup against the Ugandan government and had himself appointed president of that country. During his military career, Amin demonstrated brutality and cruelty towards prisoners and he continued this behavior as president. His administration became known for harassment, torture, and murder of civilians and political opponents. He was eccentric and his decisions often erratic and cruel, leading him to be feared and hated by most of the Ugandan population. He was ousted from power in 1979 by Tanzanian and Ugandan rebel forces and died in 2003.

Idi Amin was born in Koboko, a village in northwestern Uganda. He was part of the Kakwa tribe, which was not generally prosperous, and his family was poor and farmed for their food. He was raised in the Kakwa tradition that less fortunate individuals became servants of those who were successful. Little is known of his father, but Amin attended mission schools until the fifth or sixth grade where he learned to speak Swahili and English. He eventually grew to 6 feet, 3 inches tall and 230 pounds and was very athletic.

Uganda had been a British colony from the late 1800s, and the British army recruited young men in the northern provinces who had few opportunities and little education. In 1946 he joined a British military unit in Uganda named the King's African Rifles. Recruits received no political education; they were simply expected to carry out orders. Amin served in action in several neighboring colonies and became known for his obedience and respect for higher-level officers, as well as his commitment and ferocity in carrying out orders. All of this impressed British officers, and he was eventually promoted to second lieutenant. He was described as cheerful, humorous, energetic, but often brutal. He was charged with cruelty for breaking limbs and killing some cattle thieves after arresting them. Although the charges were squelched by higher-level British officers, Amin used brutal wartime methods in every confrontation and this never changed throughout his life. Although he performed his duty as a British officer, he never gained the British sense of honor or loyalty to a civilian government.

DOI: 10.4324/9781003333937-36

When Britain granted independence to Uganda in 1962, Amin was one of only two Ugandan commissioned military officers; both were promoted to captain and a year later to major. A military mutiny occurred in several African countries in 1964 including Uganda, with African soldiers and officers demanding higher pay and the ouster of British officers from their army. Their demands were granted, making soldiers very well paid. Amin was promoted to lieutenant colonel and given command of a battalion. When the southern Baganda tribe tried to oust Ugandan Prime Minister Milton Obote, Amin led an attack on the Baganda king's palace, killing several hundred Bagandas and forcing their king to flee to exile. This action solidified Amin's relationship with Obote. However, Amin had been implicated along with Obote in illegal activities, involving the gold and ivory trade with Zaire/ Congo. Once again, the charges were squelched and Amin was promoted by the prime minister to army chief of staff.

Amin liked the power of his new military position. He enjoyed giving directives and having them obeyed without question. He often drank and joked with his soldiers, which flattered them and he became popular with his men. He rewarded them to keep their loyalty—giving them extra rations, food items for their families that were hard to obtain, imported clothing, and expensive watches. Meanwhile, Obote humiliated the Baganda and allowed his secret police to harass, loot, and assault Bagandas. Amin did not object to the treatment, but disliked the conflicts this created between southern and northern tribal Ugandans in the armed forces. An unknown number of deaths occurred within the army from these conflicts and Amin spent much time traveling quickly to the points of conflict to address them and restore discipline. He spent the next five years expanding the Ugandan army by recruiting heavily in the northern provinces and in southern Sudan, among tribesmen who were loyal to him. He was gaining allies and they became a large part of the Ugandan army. Obote's control of the country came to depend on the army's backing, and Amin controlled the army.

In 1966, Obote had several of his government ministers and Amin's military rival arrested and jailed. He then gave Amin command of both the army and air force. Obote became president in 1967 under a new constitution and abolished the ancient tribal kingdoms in Uganda. Obote was badly injured by an assassin in 1969. Amin, suspected to be behind the assassination attempt, blocked the investigation. Obote imposed a national emergency, dissolving all political parties except his own. He gave a free hand to the hated secret police to arrest and imprison suspected perpetrators, cut army wages, and divided the army into two segments with one made up of his own tribesmen who reported to him alone. Amin resented this division. Obote had also started implementing a "move to the left" socialist ideology called the Common Man's Charter. Obote began nationalizing private businesses with little promise of payment to the owners. Security declined in the country, criminal gangs increased their activities, and Obote clashed with Amin over many of these changes. Obote was concerned about Amin's growing power, but he could not have Amin arrested because Amin controlled much of the army, and traveled with a heavy military convoy of loyal soldiers from his tribe. It appears that he developed a plan to have Amin replaced.

In early 1971, while Obote attended a conference in Singapore and the head of his intelligence agency was in England, army soldiers apparently intercepted a call from Obote with instructions to have Amin arrested. The soldiers notified Amin, who took charge and carried out a coup, appointing himself head of the Ugandan government. Obote fled to Tanzania and Amin released political prisoners from jail, with soldiers and many common people rejoicing. He stopped the nationalization of Ugandan industries and several Western governments were delighted that the trend toward socialism had been stopped.

At first, Amin appointed civilian and British-trained officials as his government ministers and listened to their advice. But he soon became bored because he did not understand them and felt they were wasting his time. He started to ignore them and make decisions without their input. He then required them all to join the army and take an oath to defend him as head of state and had himself promoted to the rank of general and president for five years.

President Nyerere in neighboring Tanzania refused to recognize Amin as president of Uganda, and he supported training of troops loyal to Obote to overthrow Amin. Amin promised to pardon and free guerilla troops who opposed him if they surrendered. He did not keep this promise and tribal conflicts increased in the army, resulting in hundreds of deaths. Obote was a member of the Langi tribe. At the time Amin took power, about 40% of the army was Acholi and Langi. One year later, two-thirds of these had been killed by troops loyal to Amin.

Amin asked heads of state in Israel and Britain for military aid to invade Tanzania. Israel, which had supported development in Uganda in the past, refused. Britain gave some aid but not the jet fighters and bombers requested. Amin returned to Uganda without the military support he wanted only to confront a coup, which claimed the lives of several of his loyal officers. Two American journalists investigating the coup were kidnapped and killed, apparently by army personnel. Although those responsible for the murders were identified, they were never punished and Amin paid some compensation to the journalists' families. He began courting Arab leaders for financial aid, especially Libya, which had oil money. Amin, who was a Muslim, claimed that Uganda was a Muslim nation even though Christians far outnumbered Muslims. Amin stopped all cooperation with Israel and supported the Palestinian cause, apparently to appeal to the preferences of Gaddafi, the Libyan head of state. In return, Gaddafi responded with economic and military aid to Uganda.

There were widespread robberies, arrests, kidnappings, and murders. The Ugandan treasury was empty and Amin refused to pay debts owed to Israel.

Amin could not increase taxes, fearing that peasant farmers would revolt. He decided to eliminate the middlemen in Ugandan commerce, which was dominated by Asians who had been brought to Uganda by the British colonialists to work on the Uganda Railway in the 19th century. The British had prioritized the education of Asians and used them as a buffer with native Ugandans. Many were doctors, accountants, and managers and some had developed large agricultural holdings. Asians had also worked hard as storekeepers and tradesmen, and had tried to preserve their ethnic identity. They were resented in Uganda due to their reputation for taking economic advantage of native Africans and for staying aloof. In 1972, Amin expelled all 80,000 Asians, claiming they hoarded wealth and Ugandan products and were harming the economy. Their expulsion was popular with many Ugandans who shared the belief that Asians had exploited them. Their businesses were confiscated and turned over to Ugandans who were often military officers. The new owners had little or no experience in commerce and no working capital with which to operate their business and most soon failed—leaving the Ugandan economy in worse condition than before the Asian expulsion.

Amin eliminated Obote's hated secret police and replaced them with two units of the police and army that carried out torture and murder of those suspected of threatening the government. They bore the harmless-sounding names of the Public Safety Unit and the Bureau of State Research. Amin issued a directive that allowed soldiers to hunt down and arrest or kill bands of robbers. This gave soldiers, who often wore civilian clothes, the power to make and enforce the law with little or no accountability and many became criminals themselves. Amin continued to persecute previous supporters of Obote and many were executed in groups while in prison. Others escaped to Tanzania and Kenya. When he attended a conference of the Organization for African Unity in 1972, Amin was cheered as a new African nationalist leader whose anti-colonial policies included expelling the unpopular Asians and Israelis. He often used humor in speeches to disarm listeners and to disguise his cruelty. He entertained other attendees at the conference with humor and courtesy and offered to show them how to suffocate a man with a handkerchief, explaining that he had used the technique during his military days. He returned to Uganda to confront another attempted coup and had its leaders murdered, leaving Uganda 36 hours after his return to tour other Islamic countries for more aid.

A British diplomat met with Amin to object to the expulsion of Asians, many of whom held British passports. Amin was unresponsive and later admitted he understood almost nothing of what the diplomat said. Shortly thereafter all British military trainers were expelled. The same day, Obote supporters invaded Uganda from Tanzania and were repulsed. During the battle, several British citizens including journalists were arrested, and watched as other prisoners had their heads smashed with sledgehammers. Amin eventually severed all diplomatic relations with Britain. Amin had become a tyrant who had Obote associates and tribesmen hunted down and killed. This was followed by similar treatment of intellectuals. Amin felt threatened by their education because they saw through his deception. He directed the murders of the chief justice of Uganda's highest court, the vice-chancellor of Uganda's top university, the former president of the Bank of Uganda, and many military and political officials. He became sadistic in his treatment of prisoners, humiliating them in front of others before he had them murdered.

Amin loved to watch war movies and to imitate the leaders he watched. He considered himself anti-colonial and his vision was a Uganda controlled by Black Africans, but he knew nothing of public administration or an alternative for the colonial government. He found office work difficult, giving all directives orally. He treated his government ministers like a dreaded drill sergeant treated raw recruits—slapping the face of one minister who brought him disappointing news. He was a one-man ruler whose ministers were prevented from objecting to his directives due to fear of retaliation. Consequently, he made terrible mistakes in administration and international relations. He publicly stated that Hitler was a great leader and that he and the Nazi party were correct in murdering 6 million Jews. The international community was stunned. Amin was a classic African "Big Man" who could be both charming with friends and visitors and ruthless with suspected enemies. He appealed to regular Ugandans at first because he came from a poor background and spoke their language, as well as being tough, humorous, and uneducated with the courage to stand up to superpowers such as Britain and Israel. Ironically, one of Amin's most trusted advisors, Bob Astles, was British.

Amin welcomed Palestinians and set aside 1,000 acres for their settlement. In 1976, when Palestinians hijacked an Air France passenger plane originating in Israel and brought it to Uganda, Amin welcomed them. He soon released passengers who were not Israelis, although the French crew and some others refused to leave, but he detained the Israeli passengers. Finally, a group of Israeli commandos rescued the hostages at Entebbe airport. One Israeli hostage who was in the hospital was later murdered.

In 1977, religious leaders in Uganda wrote a letter to Amin complaining of atrocities committed by the army. Amin responded by accusing the Catholic archbishop of plotting against his government. Amin had the archbishop along with two other military officers arrested and murdered in custody. By 1978, there was increased resentment by the masses towards Amin's government, only military officers had benefited economically. The economic infrastructure had collapsed due to neglect, incompetence and corruption. Mutinous Ugandan soldiers and some high-level officials fled to Tanzania to join those opposing Amin. Amin accused Nyerere of helping the dissidents and invaded Tanzania. In 1979, Nyerere's army along with Ugandan dissidents counterattacked and drove Amin's army back to the Ugandan capital of Kampala. Amin then fled the country by helicopter to Libya. One year later he received sanctuary in Saudi Arabia, which gave him a generous subsidy in return for staying out of politics. He died of apparent kidney failure in Saudi Arabia in 2003. International agencies have estimated that Amin's government was responsible for the murder of as many as 500,000 people in Uganda.

Idi Amin was clearly an autocratic tyrant who held unlimited power in Uganda and was cruel and oppressive to anyone who challenged his government. His form of *directive leadership* was *authoritarian* and demanded absolute obedience with almost no freedom of action. This obedience was enforced by the constant *threat of severe punishment* for anyone who objected to his actions. These behaviors reflect Toxic Leadership. He generously *rewarded* those who cooperated with him by giving them businesses, land, food, clothing, jewelry, and money. Although Amin's form of these leader behaviors is not recommended by leadership scholars, the basic leader behaviors of directing, rewarding, and punishing are described in the Reformulated Path-Goal Theory and Multiple Linkage Models of leadership. Amin developed an *in-group* of people who were largely military officers. He relied on this in-group and they were loyal to him and his patronage, as described in the Leader-Member Exchange Theory. He fit the prototype of the African "Big Man," patterned after the legendary Zulu warrior Chief Shaka who was brave, cruel, and built a huge empire. The importance of leader prototypes is described in the Implicit Theory of Leadership. He made efforts at *external boundary spanning* with other countries to obtain military and economic aid, with limited success. He also had little success at *internal boundary spanning* by failing to resolve conflicts among different tribal members in the army and within his own government. This leader behavior is described in the Multiple Linkage Model and Reformulated Path-Goal Theory of leadership. He demonstrated *determination* and *drive* through his energy, initiative, perseverance, and dominance. He was *self-confident* with high *self-esteem*—describing himself as a hero, prophet, and the most powerful person in the world. He loved attention and was often very *sociable* and *friendly* with visitors, other heads of state, and his army personnel. But he clearly *lacked the integrity* of a truthful and principled leader and did not possess the *cognitive capacity* to grasp the necessities of developing and leading a post-colonial government. Similar to Hitler, Amin's narcissistic and psychopathic behaviors were major defects in his leadership. This is addressed in Toxic Leadership and Trait Theories of leadership.

Discussion Questions

1   In addition to the torture and murder of Ugandan citizens, in what other ways was Idi Amin a bad leader?
2   Did Idi Amin do anything that is characteristic of a good leader? If so, what actions of his were exemplary of good leadership?

3   How do you think current African citizens can overcome the leadership prototype of the African "Big Man?"
4   Are in-groups essential for a leader's success?

Selected References

Kyemba, H. (1977). *State of blood: The inside story of Idi Amin.* London: Corgi Books.

Listowel, J. (1973). *Amin.* Dublin: Irish University Press Books.

Melady, T., & Melady, M. (1977). *Idi Amin Dada: Hitler in Africa.* Kansas City, MI: Sheed, Andrews, and McMeel.

34 David Koresh

Religious Cult Leader

David Koresh was born Vernon Howell (no relation to the author) in Houston, Texas on August 17, 1959. His mother was 14 or 15 years old at that time and unmarried, although they lived with the father, Bobby Howell, for two years. After his father left, Vernon was passed back and forth between his grandparents and his mother and stepfather until his late teens. He was hyperactive and had a learning disability, so he was difficult to handle and did not do well in school. He later stated he was mistreated by his stepfather and sexually molested by other boys. He was eventually placed in a special needs class and called "Mr. Retardo" by other kids, an experience that shocked him and that he frequently mentioned in later life. His mother belonged to the Seventh Day Adventist (SDA) Church, and David attended this church from childhood. The Christian Bible fascinated him, and by the age of 14 he had memorized a major part of the New Testament. He dropped out of school in the 11th grade and began working as a carpenter and repairman, skills he apparently learned from his stepfather. At age 18, he began seeing a 16-year-old girl and moved in with her family. When she became pregnant, her father threw Vernon out. The relationship ended, and the girl later gave birth to Vernon's first daughter.

Two years later, he was attending an SDA church in Tyler, Texas and impressed the congregation with his passion for the Bible and knowledge of scripture. When he announced that he had received a vision from God who told him he was to have the pastor's young daughter for his wife, the pastor banned him from seeing the girl. Undeterred, he continued seeing her, which resulted in two pregnancies that miscarried. Vernon also reported having other visions during this period; he believed God called on him to interpret the Bible as God's word for his people. The Book of Revelation became a focus of his attention. Revelation describes images of beasts, sinister horsemen, and natural disasters that are complex and often interpreted to represent a final confrontation between Heaven and Hell at the end of times as we know it. Many Christians believe it predicts future turmoil shortly before the return of Jesus Christ and the restoration of a new Kingdom of God on earth. The Book of Revelation is heavily emphasized in the SDA church, and Vernon claimed to have new insight to its teachings. He began

DOI: 10.4324/9781003333937-37

to disrupt services in the church by ranting and raving about his visions and interpretations and this, combined with his relationship with the pastor's daughter, resulted in him being removed from the church roles and told not to return.

At age 22, Vernon believed he had visions that showed his direct relationship with God. Soon after this, he visited Mount Carmel near Waco, Texas. This communal living facility was the home of the Branch Davidians, an offshoot of the SDA Church. Their leader, Lois Rodin, was said to be a living prophet of God. He studied their literature, began doing odd jobs for the group, and impressed them with his carpentry and mechanical skills. They were also amazed by his memory of the Bible and his speaking skills that inspired many members during the Bible studies he attended.

Vernon soon began having an affair with Lois Rodin, who was in her late 60s. Her late husband had led the Branch Davidians until his death and had emphasized preparations for establishing the new Kingdom of God in Israel. Lois had inherited his leadership position and in 1983 she supported Vernon in presenting a series of seminars at Mount Carmel describing what God had revealed to him. He titled his presentations the "Serpent's Root" studies and they established his position with Branch Davidian followers as an inspirational prophet with a true message from God. He visited Israel with Lois several times and became de facto co-leader of the Branch Davidians. This did not suit Lois's son, George, who was absent from Mount Carmel but had assumed he would become the leader after Lois's death. Hearing of the situation, George returned and eventually threatened Vernon, who wisely left the facility, taking with him a subgroup of Branch Davidians who were devoted to his teachings. They established their own primitive communal settlement about 40 miles from Mount Carmel with Vernon in charge.

Vernon wrote to George Rodin, explaining that he was the sickle-wielding angel described in the Book of Revelation and he was to gather designated believers and lead them to Israel for the restored Kingdom of God. In 1984, he married Rachel Jones who was then 14 years old and the daughter of one of the Branch Davidians. He eventually fathered three children with Rachel. Vernon and Rachel returned to Israel in 1985 where he reported having another vision. Several Russian cosmonauts had reported seeing seven angelic beings while in space. The beings were flying toward earth, and Vernon claimed to have met with them near Mount Zion. He said these beings explained to him the final mysteries of Revelation. When they returned to the United States, he began to question Lois and George Rodin's leadership at Mount Carmel.

For the next two years, Vernon concentrated on spreading his message and recruiting people inside and outside the United States to join his movement. His style was described as low key and conversational with a slow Texas drawl, and he was extremely confident in his message. In 1987, George Rodin, who had assumed leadership at Mount Carmel, challenged

Vernon to a contest to see who could raise a person from the dead. George had exhumed a body of a Branch Davidian who had died years earlier and placed the body in the Mount Carmel chapel. Vernon went to the sheriff and placed a complaint of corpse abuse against George. The sheriff said he needed proof, so Vernon and seven followers returned to Mount Carmel with fire-arms and a gun battle began between George and Vernon's group. The battle lasted some time and all were arrested with only George having minor wounds. Vernon was soon released on bail and George began pestering the court with profane accusations about the law enforcement officers and courts. He was jailed for several weeks for contempt of court, and an eventual trial resulted in all Vernon's followers being found not guilty of attempted murder and a mistrial for Vernon. His charges were eventually dropped. George was subsequently released, but shortly after this, he murdered a man and was committed to a mental institution where he died in 1998.

Lois Rodin had died, George was out of the way, and Mount Carmel was now vacant. Vernon raised money from his followers to pay off overdue taxes on the property and moved his followers in. He led his followers at Mount Carmel with authoritarian directives about their diet, work tasks, and living conditions. Only the communal kitchen had running water. He financed the group by establishing an automobile repair shop and a seams-tress business, donations from wealthy members, and eventually a gun show booth where they bought and sold firearms and military-style survival gear. Members were expelled when they refused to follow his rules. In 1989, he announced his "New Light Vision," claiming he was given the right to have sex with all unmarried Branch Davidian women, including some who were very young. In one case, he stated God had told him to have a child with his wife's 12-year-old sister. After much discussion, she and her family complied and she became pregnant at 13 and bore his child at 14. Later, he modified his New Light doctrine to allow him to have sex with married women in the Branch Davidians. He directed their husbands to have no further sexual contact with their wives and to become completely celibate. He convinced most of the members that it was part of God's plan. One member later reported Vernon had sex with at least 15 women and girls and fathered 17 children with them. He stated that his children would become the wise elders surrounding the king's throne in the new Kingdom.

While most members saw Vernon as sanctified by God and knowing God's will, almost divine, others rebelled at his sexual exploitation of young girls and women. One high-level member left the Branch Davidians after he watched a 13-year-old girl report to Vernon's room and spend the night with him. This individual reported Vernon's exploits to authorities and alerted parents outside the group to the plight of their daughters in the "House of David," as his harem was described. Several lawsuits and custody battles resulted, and some women left the group to protect their children. He directed several unmarried men in the group to marry his women, probably to conceal the fatherhood of their children and possibly to prevent deportation of those from outside the United States. A representative from Child Protective Services visited Mount Carmel to investigate reports of child abuse, but no charges were brought. Vernon's sexual exploits continued, and he began to lose followers in Australia and California. He spoke metaphorically of being put to death because of his wives and claimed that Revelation predicted he and his followers would suffer a violent death.

In 1990, he changed his legal name to David Koresh, to signify the Biblical Kingdom of David that they believed would be restored as the new Kingdom of God in Israel. Koresh was the Hebrew name for Cyrus, a Biblical leader who freed the people of Israel. Koresh believed he would be the physical ruler of this new Kingdom and Jesus Christ would be the spiritual ruler. Koresh's confidence and narcissism never wavered and his near godly status was unmatched at Mount Carmel. He told followers that Revelation provided the code to interpret all of human history as recorded in the Bible and he was chosen to unlock that code for the people.

When a delivery truck driver accidentally broke open a box addressed to Mount Carmel, he found a large number of hand grenades that had been disarmed. The driver later noticed a shipment of explosive material addressed to the Branch Davidians that could be used to rearm the grenades. He reported this to authorities who found a local gun dealer who had sold the Davidians well over 200 firearms, including semi-automatic weapons. Investigators also confirmed that Mount Carmel had received materials that could be used to convert these guns to fully automatic status. Possession of automatic firearms was legal as long as they were registered and a $200 fee was paid, but no such firearms had been registered by the Branch Davidians.

Koresh and the Branch Davidians knew they had attracted the attention of the authorities and were being observed. Military-style helicopters frequently hovered over Mount Carmel and several new residents had moved in across the road from the compound. One of these, who was an undercover agent for the federal Bureau of Alcohol, Tobacco and Firearms (ATF), began visiting Mount Carmel masquerading as a potential recruit. Most members knew he was a government agent, but Koresh treated him well and began teaching him about his message. Meanwhile, custody suits were proceeding against Koresh with much damaging testimony from previous Branch Davidians, and the media had become interested. Although in Texas it was legal for young girls to marry at 14 with their parents' permission, having sex with younger girls was statutory rape. Koresh undoubtedly knew he was guilty of child rape. He told members that "Babylon" would attack them soon and they must prepare. Babylon was a code name for what Koresh viewed as the corrupt United States society and government. He began showing graphic war movies, required the children to watch, and they debated how the attack would come and whether the government would use tanks against them.

The ATF obtained warrants to search for illegal firearms and explosives. Surviving Branch Davidian members later claimed that the ATF falsified some of their evidence to obtain the warrants. After the raid, numerous fully automatic weapons were found in the compound.

The ATF decided on a heavily armed approach to the Mount Carmel compound, a large two-story structure with multiple rooms. On February 28, 1993 armed ATF agents appeared at the front door, which was opened by David Koresh. He spoke with them briefly indicating there were children in their compound, then slammed the door and the shooting began. It is unclear who began the shooting, but the firing from both sides was intense and several agents and Branch Davidians were killed or wounded.

The shooting lasted for about two hours, then a ceasefire was called to allow the ATF to evacuate its dead and wounded. Koresh had been hit twice, in the hand and torso, but was able to continue functioning as their leader. Soon after the ceasefire, the Federal Bureau of Investigation (FBI) took charge and a 51-day siege began with the FBI having surrounded the compound. During this siege, Koresh talked extensively with government negotiators and a local radio station, explaining his scriptural message and his mission with the Branch Davidians. The FBI appeared uninterested in his theology, even though several consultants advised them that it was likely the key to achieving a peaceful end to the siege. The FBI had electricity to the compound turned off. They apparently assumed that the Davidians would eventually tire of the siege and the mothers would place their children's physical welfare as their first priority and give up. This was a mistake since it underestimated many of the Davidians' devotion to Koresh. About 35 people did surrender during the siege, several with children. Surrendering adults were apparently separated from their children and jailed. Many of the mothers remaining in the compound learned this and decided not to give up. Eventually, the FBI escalated its tactics by installing large bright lights and loudspeakers directed at the compound 24 hours a day to prevent the occupants from sleeping. A local sheriff who was friendly with Koresh tried unsuccessfully to broker a surrender.

During the siege, Koresh described himself as the lamb at the end of days and told them only a little more time would pass until his believers would be redeemed to join the new Kingdom. At one point, he told them they had arranged to surrender and many were relieved. But he changed his mind at the last moment, telling them God had told him to wait. On April 19, after 51 days, the FBI made a final assault that included injecting tear gas into the compound to pressure the Davidians to leave. A fire, whose cause was uncertain, quickly started and spread out, leading to explosions of heated propane tanks. All were killed in the compound except nine who escaped the fire. Over 80 Branch Davidians, including many women and children, died in the ATF attack, FBI siege, and fire. Four ATF agents were also killed. It seems clear that the government agencies involved made several poor decisions that contributed to the disaster. It is also apparent that David Koresh possessed much of the blame for the horrible tragedy experienced by his faithful followers.

David Koresh exhibited many of the characteristics of a *toxic charismatic* leader. He truly *inspired* his followers with his knowledge and zealous interpretation of Biblical scripture, his *grand vision* of their role in a future Kingdom of God on earth, and his *mission* to unlock the mysteries of God from the Book of Revelation. He *stimulated their thinking* about what was necessary to follow God's word and qualify for redemption from their sinful ways. His extreme *self-confidence* and apparent *personal need for power* are also consistent with Toxic Charismatic Leadership.

Although these properties are also characteristic of Transformational Leaders, Koresh was lacking in two important characteristics of Transformational Leadership by his apparent lack of true *consideration* and *selfish immoral* behavior with many of his followers. He was also an *authoritarian directive leader* who allowed no variation from his rules and regulations that governed Mount Carmel. Recall that directive leadership is not necessarily authoritarian, but Koresh's style allowed for no exceptions. He did not solicit *participation* from other Branch Davidians in making decisions, preferring to justify his directives with his own interpretations of Biblical scripture. These leader behaviors are described in Path-Goal Theory, Situational Leadership Theory, Fiedler's Contingency Theory, and the Leadership Grid models of leadership. He offered followers the *contingent reward* of salvation and a primary place in the new Kingdom of God if they were faithful to his teachings and directives. He also used *contingent punishment behavior* in expelling some followers who refused to follow certain of his rules. These leader behaviors are described in the Reformulated Path-Goal Theory and the Multiple Linkage Model of leadership. Although Koresh made an effort to represent his message, mission, and group to outsiders, he appeared to be ineffective at resolving conflicts and satisfying authorities who were investigating and besieging Mount Carmel. His *boundary-spanning* behavior was not effective and is also described in the Multiple Linkage Model and Reformulated Path-Goal Theory.

Much of Koresh's behavior and zealous preaching apparently fit a traditional Implicit Leadership Theory of evangelistic religious leaders. Although his *determination* and *self-confidence* are described in Trait Theories of leadership, his personal traits of *narcissism, visions of grandeur*, and *sexual perversion* were toxic and prevented him from being truly considerate and supportive of his followers. Koresh is an excellent example of the danger that accompanies charismatic leaders who are *self-oriented* and *narcissistic*.

Discussion Questions

1   Why do you think David Koresh had such strong influence over the Branch Davidians?
2   How can individuals protect themselves from the potential dangers of charismatic leaders like Koresh?

3   Can you think of any leadership neutralizers or substitutes that might be used to counter the influence of leaders like Koresh?
4   Can you think of other charismatic leaders like Koresh who are not affiliated with religious movements?

Selected References

Bailey, B. & Darden, B. (1993). *Mad man in Waco*. Waco, TX: WRS.

Newport, K. G. C. (2006). *The Branch Davidians of Waco: The history and beliefs of an apocalyptic sect*. New York: Oxford University Press.

Thibodeau, D. (1999). *A place called Waco: A survivor's story*. New York: Public Affairs.

Part IV

Snapshots of Great or Bad Leadership—You Decide

35 Elon Musk

CEO of Tesla and Visionary Inventor

Elon Musk is the founder of PayPal, Tesla, SpaceX, and The Boring Company. Musk is also the owner of X (formerly Twitter) and co-founder of Neuralink and OpenAI. His ventures and investments have made him the wealthiest person on the planet with an estimated net worth of more than $220 billion. Through engineering brilliance, risk-taking, and persistence, Musk has transformed human access to electric vehicles, space travel, broadband internet, and artificial intelligence. Musk is a transformational and charismatic leader and has achieved a cult status on Wall Street and among entrepreneurship, with millions of followers on social media. However, in recent years, Musk has engaged in controversial political, social, and corporate actions and statements. While Musk continues to solve complex world problems with his inventions, his actions have led some to question his moral values and status as an effective leader. The full portrait of his leadership is yet to be completed.

Elon Musk was born in 1971 in Pretoria, South Africa. He is the eldest of three siblings. He has a younger brother, Kimbal, and a sister, Tosca. His father, Errol Musk, is a South African electromechanical engineer, entrepreneur, and retired politician. His mother, Maye Musk, born in Canada, is a dietitian and former model. Musk experienced a challenging childhood. Due to his parents' divorce when he was just nine years old, his younger brother Kimbal became his closest and best company in his parents' absence. Musk also suffered serious bullying in his childhood, to the point where he had to be rushed to the hospital. Musk was a brilliant student and achieved distinctions in physical sciences and computer science. His father bought him a computer at the age of ten, and at the age of 12, he had written a software program, Blastar, which he sold for $500. Musk was opposed to the South African apartheid regime and refused to join the compulsory military service. After obtaining a Canadian passport in 1988, he moved to Canada as a pathway to pursue economic opportunities in the United States.

Musk enrolled at Queen's University, Ontario, before transferring to the University of Pennsylvania in 1992 where he graduated with two bachelor's degrees in physics and economics. Musk enrolled for a doctorate degree in

DOI: 10.4324/9781003333937-39

physics at Stanford University. However, a few weeks prior to starting classes, Netscape went public at a valuation of $3 billion. Musk saw the potential of the internet and decided to quit doctoral studies after only two days to start his own internet company, Zip2, with his brother Kimbal. Zip2 was founded in 1995 prior to the internet boom. The company developed online content publishing software that provided searchable maps and business directories. When the startup was pre-revenue, Musk and his brother had to bootstrap to keep it afloat. In early 1996, a venture capitalist firm decided to invest $3 million on condition that Musk relinquish the CEO's role, leading Musk to agree to step down. He needed the money. Due to Musk's blunt language and lack of trust for the new CEO, Musk often clashed with the new leader and with professional programmers who had been brought into the company. He moved to oust the CEO, a plan which backfired when the board decided to sell the company to Compaq in 1999. Compaq acquired Zip2 for $308 million. Despite the disappointment and humiliation of losing ownership of the company he had founded, the sale of Zip2 to Compaq made Musk a millionaire at the age of 27. He used some of the $22 million of his proceeds to purchase a home and a Maclaren F1, then the fastest car in the world.

Although ousted as Zip2's CEO, Musk's startup was a significant success at a time when dot-com bubble was about to burst. By 1999, Musk had already turned his focus to other internet ventures. As an intern at the Bank of Nova Scotia earlier in his career, he had found the banking industry lacking in innovation and had openly discussed disrupting the industry through an internet bank. Joined by his brother Kimbal, he decided to incorporate X.com, a finance startup. It was in X.com that Musk invested the rest of the $12 million from the sale of Zip2. Musk had limited knowledge of the banking industry, but was undeterred as he was inspired by supreme confidence and a matching ego. Soon X.com became a big hit with early adopters of online banking services. Musk, a self-taught programmer, had not, unfortunately, secured enough firewalls, and X.com started to lose money through fraudulent activities. Furthermore, Musk was embroiled in a bitter rivalry with Confinity, a financial startup with a similar business model founded by Max Levchin and Peter Thiel, two other brilliant entrepreneurs. Early in 2000, X.com and Confinity decided to stop their zero-sum game by agreeing on a merger, with Musk becoming the CEO of the merged companies. The merger had significant integration challenges, with Musk often disagreeing with the founders of Confinity on software preferences, fraud prevention and branding, among other things. Musk had been married to his longtime girlfriend in January 2000, but delayed their honeymoon. Later in September, while on a flight proceeding to the honeymoon in Australia, a group of X.com employees presented a letter of no-confidence in Musk's leadership to the board. Musk turned back. He tried to convince the board that he was the right person for the job, however, his fate was sealed. Musk was ousted and replaced by Peter Thiel as X.com's CEO. In 2001,

Peter Thiel rebranded X.com as PayPal. Rather than seek retribution, Musk embraced his role as advisor to Peter Thiel, and as the largest shareholder, continued to invest in the company. eBay, an online platform auction startup, was interested in acquiring PayPal, but Musk advised PayPal's leadership to be patient and accumulate more value. In 2002, PayPal issued an IPO, raising $61 million in the process. Musk's appeal for patience paid off when eBay acquired PayPal for $1.5 billion, with Musk realizing $250 million from the acquisition. Musk's reputation as a pioneering entrepreneur had been solidified.

While it was a great payday for Musk, his ego and reputation had been bruised with sections in the media portraying him as egomaniacal and a stubborn jerk while Thiel and Levchin received high praise for their wisdom. Musk's removal as CEO from Zip2 and PayPal only gave some in the media and his detractors material to portray a pattern of lack of ethics and a character of marked narcissism.

Undeterred by the sale of PayPal, Musk turned his attention to his long-standing passion for space exploration. Over the years, Musk had shown a deep interest in space science and articulated his views highlighting the limited resources on the Earth's planet and probability of an eventual extinction event which would eradicate humans. Musk was dismayed that NASA's human space program had not sent any astronaut beyond the low Earth orbit since 1972 as the space program was yet to recover from the Challenger disaster. In 2002, Musk founded SpaceX (Space Exploration Technologies Corporation) with the goal of reducing the cost of space travel and eventually colonizing Mars. Using his wealth, Musk gathered a group of brilliant space scientists and engineers to look at the viability of making humans a multidisciplinary species capable of colonizing Mars. In February 2003, NASA was hit by another disaster when the space shuttle Columbia broke up as it returned to Earth, killing the seven astronauts on board. NASA suspended space shuttle flights, spurring debate on alternative space models.

Musk felt slighted by NASA. He felt his efforts to launch a private rocket into space were being ignored by NASA and other federal agencies. To draw attention to his work and progress, Musk unleashed an audacious publicity stunt by unveiling a prototype spacecraft outside the Federal Aviation Administration headquarters in Washington, DC, along with a press conference where he explained why his rocket was cheaper and safer. The move drew the attention of legislators and bureaucrats and earned Musk publicity along with vigorous a public debate on NASA versus commercial space enterprise.

SpaceX had four failed launch attempts that almost led to bankruptcy before the first successful launch to orbit by Falcon 1 rocket. This was followed by other successful voyages to orbit, and SpaceX quickly gained prominence by developing other innovative technologies. SpaceX was subsequently contracted by NASA to resupply the International Space Center and eventually, transport astronauts to the space center. SpaceX has also launched a Starlink internet satellite constellation with more than 4,000 satellites to provide internet access to remote locations. Today, Starlink internet provides internet connectivity in Ukraine.

Simultaneously, Musk set his sights on revolutionizing the automotive industry. In 2004, he became involved with Tesla Motors (now Tesla, Inc.), an electric vehicle company. Two Silicon Valley entrepreneurs, Martin Eberhard, and Marc Tarpenning founded Tesla, in 2003. The company was named Tesla after the famous physicist and inventor Nikola Tesla. Musk had completed a project on solar energy while in college and had continued to follow the developments of renewable energy with keen interest. At the time, Musk was also keen to solve the problem of unsustainable fossil fuels by developing an electric car as an alternative. In 2004, Musk led series A funding for Tesla by investing $6.4 million. He joined Tesla's board of directors and became the chairperson.

By 2008, in the middle of the financial crisis, Tesla was at the brink of bankruptcy after spending millions of dollars developing the electric car. Musk fired the CEO Eberhard, along with 25% of Tesla's employees. He took over full control of the company as CEO and raised $40 million in series E funding. In 2009, Daimler AG bought 10% of the company for $50 million. Tesla also obtained a $465 million loan from the Department of Energy: this was critical for Tesla's working capital. In 2010, Tesla launched its initial public offering that raised $226 million. Musk announced plans to bring down costs significantly with the launch of Model S sedan that was targeted for the mainstream market.

Musk continued to develop better technologies for Tesla and raised $4.5 billion. In 2012, Tesla launched freestanding superchargers that have since become the industry standard. Tesla made its first quarterly profit in 2013. The following year, Musk announced the construction of the Gigafactory for the manufacturing of battery products in Nevada. Tesla also got into the photovoltaic industry after acquiring SolarCity, a company that was founded by Musk's cousins, for $2.6 billion. Some major Tesla's shareholders sued Musk for commandeering Tesla's negotiations for SolarCity while publicly claiming to be fully recused. The Delaware Chancery Court dismissed the case. In 2018, the Securities Exchange Commission sued Musk for speaking untruthfully and misleading Tesla investors on Twitter. As part of the settlement, Musk paid $20 million and had to step down as Chairperson of Tesla's board of directors.

Under his leadership, Musk transformed Tesla from a niche startup to a global force in electric mobility. Tesla introduced groundbreaking electric vehicle models such as the Roadster, Model S, Model 3, Model X, and Model Y. Tesla's commitment to sustainable transportation and technological advancements have reshaped the automotive industry and accelerated the adoption of electric vehicles worldwide. Tesla is the most valuable car manufacturer with a valuation of more than $800 billion, far higher than Toyota and Ford. He has created immense wealth for early investors that decided to believe in his vision.

By April 2022, Musk had accumulated 9.2% ownership stake of Twitter and more than 80 million followers. Musk was critical of Twitter's leadership and often sent tweets accusing the board and senior executives of failing to crack down on spambots and mismanagement. When the board invited him to join the company as a director, to the relief of some board members, Musk declined. Some board members were opposed to the initial offer to Musk to join the board, fearing he would dilute the company's value through his controversial public views. As a board member, Musk would have been subject to Twitter's corporate governance guidelines that he felt would impede his first amendment rights. Instead, Musk appeared to follow a suggestion by one of his followers on Twitter, and made a non-binding offer to buy the company for $54.20 per share and take the company private. Initially, Twitter's board of directors adopted a poison pill, while Musk decided to withdraw his offer. Major shareholders, however, believed the company was worth less than Musk's offer of $43 billion. Following protracted litigation, both parties agreed to the takeover and Musk became the sole owner and CEO of Twitter by announcing: "The bird is freed." Musk quickly moved to announce layoffs after dismissing the board and senior executives.

Musk conducted a Twitter poll, asking users whether he should step down as CEO. The vote passed, and Musk announced he would step down after finding a replacement. On Twitter (now renamed X) and in his public life, Musk has courted controversy by expressing controversial opinions on politics, sexual orientation, and racial issues. Musk has often used the free speech argument to justify his actions. Occasionally, he has used the platform to muzzle the voices of some X subscribers.

Musk can be described as a *transformational leader*. Transformational leaders have an enduring vision to achieve a larger purpose. The transformational approach to leadership is developed by maximizing followers' potential through idealized influence, inspirational motivation, and intellectual stimulation. Musk's leadership is exemplified by certain traits. He has consistently demonstrated high cognitive and intellectual skills. He has stated that he is naturally good at engineering because he inherited it from his father: "What's very difficult for others is easy for me." Musk has demonstrated transformational leadership by articulating a vision of the development of a commercial space program, articulating the vision to the space community, and gathering resources to achieve the goal, despite numerous setbacks. His vision to develop an electric car has disrupted the auto industry and inspired other ancillary industries. Musk is considered a rock star in Silicon Valley and among aspiring entrepreneurs due to his innovations and entrepreneurial success. He is idolized by many in capitalist systems around the world due to his immense wealth and power. Currently he is considered the richest person on the planet with an estimated wealth of US $225 billion. Others have compared Musk to Nikola Tesla, Steve Jobs, and Einstein.

Musk's charismatic leadership is shown by his *inspirational rhetoric* and a *clear vision* and *mission* for space travel and colonizing Mars. This high resonance with space scientists and enthusiasts. A second vision that has been articulated by Musk is reducing reliance on fossil fuels and developing solar and electric car alternatives. The astonishing success of Tesla has accorded Musk a cult status at Silicon Valley and on Wall Street. Charismatic leaders have exceptionally strong effects on followers by appealing to their *individual emotions, aspirations, needs,* and *values.* Many aspiring entrepreneurs and innovators around the world perceive Musk as a role model and hang to every statement he makes. It is due to this influence that Musk's opinions have generated controversies and moved markets on the stock exchange. There is a *dark side* to *charismatic* leaders. They can increase risk levels to organizations and threaten the well-being of members. The personalized need for power, negative life themes, and narcissistic tendencies of personalized charismatic leaders can lead to unethical and destructive behavior. The list of employee terminations, whistleblower lawsuits, and Security Exchange Commission complaints point to a tempestuous relationship with followers and stakeholders. Musk has publicly expressed his disdain for regulators and short-term investors in his companies. Musk's controversial public opinions often have consequences for gullible followers that idolize him.

Toxic leadership involves various forms of dominance, coercion, and the leader's focus on personal rather than collective goals. Musk's singular focus to achieve his goals at all costs has often put him at odds with employees. His official biographer has described occasions when Musk goes into "demon mode" to be highly productive, but that the alter ego can make him dark and act with a real lack of empathy. Musk's corporate leadership past in five entities that he has led is characterized by conflicts and fractured relationships with trusted employees, often leading to terminations. Musk has also had a turbulent relationship with shareholders, including regulators and the Security Exchange Commission, resulting in multiple lawsuits and settlements.

As an individual, Musk has achieved unprecedented success in technological innovations that many countries cannot achieve. His vision has led to the transformation of the car industry, photovoltaic industry, and space industry. Musk will continue to push technological boundaries to new frontiers: his full accomplishments are yet to be seen.

Discussion Questions

1   Describe and provide an assessment of Elon Musk's leadership.
2   Using relevant examples, assess Elon Musk's transformational leadership in the corporate context. Is he an effective leader?
3   Is it possible for a great entrepreneur to be an effective leader? In assessing entrepreneurial leadership, does the end justify the means?
4   What should be the role and involvement of corporate CEOs in cultural and social issues affecting their stakeholders?

Selected References

BBC. (2022, October 12). The Elon Musk Show [Video]. BBC.com. www.youtube.com/watch?v=40AWTm7r8co.

Davenport, C. (2018). *The Space Barons: Elon Musk, Jeff Bezos, and the quest to colonize the cosmos.* Public Affairs.

Paul, K. (2022, February 19). Black workers accused Tesla of racism for years. Now California is stepping in. *The Guardian.* www.theguardian.com/technology/2022/feb/18/tesla-california-racial-harassment-discrimination-lawsuit.

Koppelaar, R. (2017). *The Tesla Revolution: Why Big Oil is Losing the Energy War.* Amsterdam University Press.

Musk, E. (2017). Making humans a multi-planetary species. *New Space,* 5(2), 46–61.

SpaceX. (2022). SpaceX. www.spacex.com.

Vance, A., & Sanders, F. (2015). *Elon Musk.* HarperCollins.

Valinsky, J. (2023, February 27). Elon Musk tweets support for 'Dilbert' creator after racist tirade. *CNN.* www.cnn.com/2023/02/27/business/elon-musk-scott-adams-defense/index.html.

36 Jeff Bezos
Internet Entrepreneur, Founder and CEO of Amazon

Born in 1964 in New Mexico, Jeff Bezos is the founder of Amazon, the world's largest retailer, Blue Origin, a space exploration company, and owner of *The Washington Post*. Bezos has been recognized as an entrepreneur and innovator, often disrupting incumbents and commercializing new products such as Kindle, Alexa and space tourism. Bezos stepped down from Amazon in 2021 to focus his efforts on Blue Origin and other new ventures.

On April 5, 2017, Amazon.com CEO, founder, and Chairman Jeff Bezos announced that he would invest one billion dollars annually to commercialize space travel by 2018. Blue Origin, Bezos's space company, intends to "compete for even higher stakes" in the growing space industry and is currently in the process of developing a cargo lander destined for the Moon. Bezos always had a passion for science and had envisioned human beings in space since he was young. The commitment to invest in his dream was characteristic of his perspective on innovation, risk, and progress.

Jeffrey Preston Bezos was born in 1964 in Albuquerque, New Mexico. His mother, Jackie Bezos, saw a determination and focus in Bezos when he was still young and enrolled him in River Oaks Elementary School, a Vanguard school for gifted/talented children, which is outside Houston, Texas. Bezos has mentioned how his maternal grandparents nurtured his interest in science while living on a ranch in Cotulla, Texas. His grandfather, Lawrence Preston Gise, had worked for the U.S. Atomic Energy Commission and often worked with Bezos on science experiments and mentored him through his teenage years. Bezos graduated *summa cum laude* with a B.Sc. in Electrical Engineering and Computer Science from Princeton in 1986. The idea of starting an e-commerce business appeared to have crystallized when Bezos was working at a Wall Street hedge fund, D. E. Shaw & Co. The company had a unique approach of applying quantitative modeling and computer science to investment analyses and had computer scientists working in the firm. Although D. E. Shaw's employees were already using the internet, Bezos was interested in the internet's potential for commercial applications. He envisioned using the internet as an intermediary to sell everything to the end consumer, bypass other intermediaries, and reduce costs. He discussed the concept with his colleagues on various occasions. Bezos had also noticed

DOI: 10.4324/9781003333937-40

that web activity had grown significantly and was determined to create a business around the new technology. Bezos identified 20 products that could be sold over the internet, ultimately settling on books because consumers would know what they were purchasing. In addition, he would be able to create an unlimited online store, a capability that was not possible in a brick-and-mortar business.

Despite a promising career on Wall Street, Bezos decided to walk away and take the risk of investing in an online retail bookstore. Bezos realized that web usage was growing at an explosive rate and carried significant potential. He was determined to set up a business that would profit from this growth, and e-commerce was the immediate choice. He adopted a "regret minimization framework" that led him to start Amazon rather than experiencing regret later for not starting it. Bezos initially registered the company as Cadabra, but later changed the name to Amazon, after the largest river in the world. Bezos made an initial cash investment of $10,000. His parents also funded the startup with part of their savings for $300,000, even though he had warned them of a 70% chance of losing their money. He raised a subsequent $1 million from 20 private investors. Some potential investors saw Amazon as a big risk without potential economies of scale and declined to invest. Others invested because they were impressed by Bezos's brilliance, energy, and determination rather than the startup's viability. In later years, Bezos rationalized his decision to start the new company. He had been less concerned with risk, uncertainty, and failure than long-term regrets of missing out.

Bezos chose to establish the startup in Seattle, Washington due to the city's emergence as a technology center and as a way of minimizing state tax liabilities. Business picked up swiftly with $12,000 worth of orders during the first week. However, there was a constant cash shortage and employees had to operate by the bootstraps. Bezos was involved in the hiring process of each new employee, and looked for employees that were smart but also innovative and determined to succeed. Bezos and his team would stay up at night in a converted garage packing books for shipment. By the end of 1994, Amazon had accumulated losses amounting to $52,000. Bezos added a book review feature on the website and developed a one-click purchase feature for shoppers.

By 1997, Bezos had significantly increased the computing capacity of Amazon and hired more employees; but needed cash for further growth. With venture capitalists competing to invest in the company, Bezos opted for Kleiner, Perkins, Caufield & Byers who made an equity investment of $8 million. On March 15, 1997, Amazon's IPO raised $54 million. Early investors including Bezos's parents, his brother and sister became millionaires. Even in the early days when Amazon was incurring losses, Bezos maintained focus on his long-term value proposition of offering excellent customer service and low pricing. To this day, Amazon is less concerned with short-term projections of profitability by Wall Street analysts than long-term goals. In 1998, Amazon diversified to other retail products, beginning with the sale of CDs and DVDs.

During the mid-1990s, internet startups were being launched at a fast pace, with many venture capitalists betting on the internet as the growth vehicle for the future. In 1999, *Time* magazine named Jeff Bezos person of the year, even though Amazon was yet to make a profit. In March 2000, the dotcom bubble burst and internet stocks came crashing down. Many internet startups were wiped out from the competitive landscape. Amazon stocks took a hit, plummeting from $107 to $7 per share. Bezos's business was designed for long-term growth rather than short-term profitability and was able to endure the burst. Bezos resisted pressure from investors and executives at Amazon who did not share his long-term focus. Some employees opted to leave the company due to disillusionment from poor financial performance and the intense work pressure. During the first quarter of 2002, Amazon made its first profit of $5 million.

Over the years, Bezos built Amazon through organic development of new products as well as acquisitions. Some acquisitions successfully integrated with Amazon while others that failed to integrate were quickly forgotten. In 1999, Bezos launched Amazon's Marketplace. This service opened up Amazon's platform to other retailers who could compete directly with Amazon. Book authors and publishers tried to resist, unhappy with Bezos's decision to sell used books. Amazon's executives did not like the idea because it cannibalized existing customers. Bezos was intent on offering more choice and product variety to customers, a core part of his mission. He ignored the backlash. After experimenting with different iterations, Bezos rolled out free shipping in 2002, despite resistance from some members of his executive team. This was another way of ensuring customer satisfaction, and it is now an integrated part of Amazon Prime. Bezos launched Amazon Service in 2003. Amazon Service allowed Amazon to obtain a commission when its competitors sold their products on Amazon's platform. Amazon launched its own private label brands over the years. In 2004, it launched Pinzon (specializing in bed, bath, and kitchen items) and Strathwood that focused on patio furniture. In subsequent years, Amazon continued to launch private labels to compete with market leaders. In 2017, Amazon was awarded a unique clothing patent that allowed it to manufacture clothes on demand using a computerized system.

The introduction of the Kindle e-reader in 2007 was a significant strategic initiative for Bezos. Designed to help Amazon sell books rather than compete with other products, the Kindle sold out on the first day and remained out of stock for another five months. Bezos viewed this development as a marquee achievement. A CNN writer, Zach Ponz, described it in the following terms, "it has the curves of a Lamborghini, looks like something an astronaut might take to space and weighs only 10.3 ounces." The weight was important because an average paperback was heavier than a Kindle, which at that time could store 200 books. Later models of the Kindle were vastly more advanced than the original version. While Kindle sales have plateaued, the Kindle app allows users to read their e-books on any connected device.

Amazon eventually became unable to cope with its ever-increasing need for computing space and could not find a vendor with sufficient computing infrastructure to meet its needs. Bezos started entertaining the idea of developing a homegrown cloud computing service. As early as 2006, Amazon had launched its cloud computing service, Amazon Web Services. Bezos had not anticipated a similar need by other internet companies and Amazon became a provider of cloud computing services to other organizations. Today, Amazon is an industry leader in low-cost scalable cloud computing services, providing 30 different services in 190 countries around the world. Bezos has also developed other innovations that include video streaming, music streaming, same-day delivery services, Amazon Studios for movie production, and Amazon Echo, an audio digital assistant.

Bezos has demonstrated several personal traits that have contributed to his style of leadership. His *cognitive* and *analytical capabilities* are evident. From an early age, he achieved high standardized test scores, excelled in high school, and won numerous state awards for best student in math and science. One of the science projects was on the effects of a zero-gravity environment on a housefly. At that time, Bezos stood out because he worked hard to find solutions to problems. Those that have interacted with him since he was young have described him as *disciplined*, highly *focused on his goals*, and *resilient*. His cohorts recognized his drive, work ethic, and leadership when he led them in school projects, social activities, and sports. Even though he did not have the physique for football, he captained the high school football team due to his competitiveness and ability to memorize player positions. In its early years, Amazon made consistent annual losses for the first five years. Some Wall Street analysts, focusing on the short term, made a career out of predicting Amazon's demise. However, Bezos was resolute in sticking to his long-term plan, and was able to prove them wrong and eventually earn the respect of investors.

In 2000, when Amazon was registering heavy losses, Bezos quietly registered Blue Origin, a space company. While some may have been surprised at his decision to launch a space company, he had shared this childhood dream with his maternal grandfather. His high school valedictory speech starts with the following words: "Space, the final frontier." In 2021, Bezos stepped down as Amazon's chief executive to dedicate himself to Blue Origin, although he remains Amazon's main shareholder and its executive chairman of the board. Two years later, Bezos moved to Florida and sold 24 million shares of Amazon, temporarily becoming the wealthiest person in the U.S. He announced that he'd sell another 50 million shares within the year. Blue Origin is participating in the private company race to the Moon, competing with Astrobotic, SpaceX, and Intuitive Machines. Amazon's Blue Origin project involves the development of a reusable high-lift shuttle, New Glenn, to lift a cargo lander with a capacity for several tons of materials.

Bezos has been described as *shrewd* and *ruthless*. Since the inception of Amazon, Bezos has waged bare-knuckle battles with most major retailers, including Walmart, Target, Best Buy, Barnes and Noble, and eBay. More recently, the Federal Trait Commission and 17 states filed an antitrust lawsuit against Amazon, accusing it of monopolistic practices. The National Labor Relations Board also filed a lawsuit against Amazon, accusing the company of anti-union practices and illegal retaliation against union workers. Unionization efforts in Amazon's warehouses appear to respond to an automated mass-management process that the media has described as dehumanizing, lacking upward mobility, and chaotic. Its turnover rate was 150% even before the pandemic, almost double the industry average. Bezos has pushed back on employee claims that Amazon is a soulless, dystopian workplace. However, before stepping down as CEO, he admitted that Amazon needed a new vision to help employees succeed and make the company the best workplace on Earth.

Bezos is considered *frugal* and *demanding*. He is known to demand results especially when customers complain, showing a strong form of *directive leadership*. He has great *communication* and *persuasive skills*. Many of these personal characteristics reflect Trait Theories of leadership and his strong directiveness reflects Path-Goal and Multiple Linkage theories of leadership. Bezos is also a Charismatic/Transformational leader. These leaders focus on developing a *vision* and *initiating change* in their environments. In the early years of Amazon, Bezos developed a single-minded focus on customer satisfaction. There was pushback on subsequent initiatives such as free shipping and Amazon Marketplace, which cannibalized Amazon's gains. However, Bezos was resolute in his vision to provide an excellent customer experience. Bezos *encourages innovative behavior* by employees beginning with the hiring process. He has transformed the modern retail industry and the readership of books. Bezos is on a quest to colonize other planets. His steadfast *determination* and *drive* have been apparent during numerous periods of crisis at Amazon, and rather than take the easier path, he kept his focus on the long-term goals despite the pain. Bezos is clearly *self-confident* and *believes in the value and importance of his goals*. Employees who have stayed at Amazon have a high level of *loyalty* and consider the company to be a crucible of *innovation* where something big is always happening and they are constantly encouraged to challenge the status quo and use creative approaches to problems. Bezos has maintained the CEO's position at Amazon since inception. His leadership traits, strong directiveness (Path-Goal Theory), and Charismatic/Transformational leadership style have transformed Amazon into one of the largest companies with total revenues of $136 billion and more than 300,000 employees in 2016.

Discussion Questions

1   What leadership attributes have led to Bezos's success as the founder of Amazon?

2   How did Bezos's early life shape his later years as Amazon's CEO?

3 Why do you think Bezos was able to survive the internet bubble when most companies came crashing down?
4 How do you think Bezos, and other leaders in a similar position, manage to navigate multiple priorities on a daily basis?
5 Do you believe Jeff Bezos is a good leader? Why or why not?

Selected References

Chang, K. (July 20, 2021). Bezos launches to space, aiming to reignite his rocket company's ambitions. *The New York Times*.

Dagley, R. (December 27, 2013). eWEEK at 30: How Amazon Survived the Dot-Com Crash to Rule the Cloud. *eWEEK*. Retrieved April 21, 2017 from www.eweek.com/cloud/eweek-at-30-how-amazon-survived-the-dot-com-cra sh-to-rule-the-cloud.

Gupta, V., MacMillan, I., & Surie, G. (2004). Entrepreneurial leadership: Developing and measuring a cross-cultural construct. *Journal of Business Venturing*, 19 (2), 241–260.

Kantor, J., Weise, K., & Ashford, G. (2021). The Amazon that customers don't see. *The New York Times*, 15, 2021.

Lashinsky, A. (December 3, 2012). Amazon's Jeff Bezos: The Ultimate Disrupter. *Fortune*. Retrieved April 28, 2017 from http://fortune.com/2012/11/16/amazons-jeff-bezos-the-ultimate-disrupter.

Ponz, Z. (2008). A year later, Amazon's Kindle finds a niche. *CNN*, December 4, 2008. Retrieved April 28, 2017 from www.cnn.com/2008/TECH/12/03/kindle.elec tronic.reader.

Stone, B. (2013). *The everything store: Jeff Bezos and the age of Amazon*. New York: Little Brown.

37 Mark Zuckerberg

CEO of Meta (formerly Facebook)

Mark Zuckerberg was a Harvard sophomore who, at 19 years old, created the premier social networking Internet service that is currently used by over two billion people. He started Facebook in 2004 from his dorm suite with some help from his friends. Facebook began exclusively as a Harvard-based service, expanded to other colleges, to organizations, and eventually worldwide to everyone not less than 13 years of age. As CEO, Zuckerberg remains in control of Facebook, which continues to expand and reflect his own beliefs and philosophy about availability of information, transparency, and connectedness in the world.

Zuckerberg was born in 1984 in a small village in New York. His mother is a psychiatrist and his father a dentist, he has three sisters, and his family has been supportive of him despite his "strong willed and relentless" nature. His father taught him BASIC computer programming at an early age and hired a special tutor to continue his programming development. Mark became a precocious computer programmer and developed an early computer network for their home when he was 12. He attended an elite private high school where he was a fencing star and was able to read and write several languages by the time he entered Harvard. He is medium height with curly hair and typically wears jeans, t-shirts, and flip-flops. He looks directly at those he is speaking with, speaks quickly, and shows little body language while listening, making it difficult to read his reactions.

Harvard is filled with elite students who are ambitious, self-confident, and from well-to-do families. Unlike his portrayal in the film, *The Social Network*, Mark is very sociable and was well liked by his suite mates who often became involved in Zuckerberg's computer projects. He created Coursematch, which helped students select classes with people they liked or admired. Then he started Facemash, which sequentially compared Harvard students' faces, two at a time, and asked students to vote which one was the hottest. These programs were made available on the web to all Harvard students and were immensely popular, although he was disciplined by the Harvard administration for violating privacy restrictions. Three other Harvard students asked him to help them develop a site that would profile Harvard students to be used as a dating service. Mark agreed but did little

DOI: 10.4324/9781003333937-41

on their project while he worked on developing Facebook. Years later these students sued him, claiming he stole their idea, and a financial settlement was reached.

Zuckerberg launched Facebook on February 4, 2004, as a communication tool to help individuals keep track of their friends at Harvard. Users were invited to build their own profiles of personal information. They were required to use their real identities (verified by their Harvard email addresses) and could invite any other users to be their friends and access their profile. Profiles included a picture of the user, which could be updated at any time, and Facebook allowed users to send messages to one another. It was used for meeting people, arranging study groups and meetings, sharing preferences in movies, music, and books, and included a Coursematch connection for checking who enrolled in which classes. By May there were almost 100,000 users, including faculty and staff. Facebook appealed to the strong social needs of college students to be accepted, and a user's number of friends soon became a status symbol. It also appealed to one's vanity by letting others know about all the user's activities and accomplishments. The interest in Facebook also likely reflected an element of voyeurism.

Zuckerberg started Facebook with $1,000. As Facebook grew, Zuckerberg's roommates were inspired by his enthusiasm and success, and he hired Dustin Moskovitz to help expand the number of users and Chris Hughes to function as spokesperson. He gave his business-savvy friend, Eduardo Saverin, part ownership of Facebook to develop Facebook as a business. Zuckerberg added more features to Facebook and slowly opened it up to other colleges as they added server capacity to assure users did not experience delays. Saverin began selling ads to start generating revenue, registered Facebook as a limited liability company in Florida, and investors began calling. One group offered Zuckerberg $10 million for Facebook, but he was not interested. He was more interested in his evolving vision for Facebook to make the world a more open and transparent place. He believes strongly that the level of trust in the world has declined, that there is a trend toward decentralized power, and the amount of information has compounded so fast that people need help in dealing with these changes. He describes openness as having access to more information, and transparency as sharing things, increasing understanding, and having a voice in the world. He also describes Facebook as increasing connectedness by helping people stay in touch and empathize with one another. By promoting these processes, he believes he is making the world a better place.

During the summer of 2004, Zuckerberg rented a house in Palo Alto, near Stanford University. He and some of his roommates and friends moved there to develop Facebook and be part of the Internet industry of Silicon Valley. He encountered Sean Parker, a 24-year-old programmer and entrepreneur, who had helped start Napster (the popular music sharing program) and another Internet company. Parker described how his startups had been taken over by venture capitalists who eventually ejected him from the companies.

Mark had met Parker earlier and was impressed so he invited him to live in their house. Parker was extremely interested in Facebook, and soon Zuckerberg was describing him as president of the company. Saverin had stayed in New York, ostensibly to sell ads, and showed no interest in moving to California. Everyone at the rented house began work at midday and worked into the morning hours, increasing features, and adding more colleges to their service. All were highly intelligent and committed to Mark's vision of Facebook as the catalyst that would help change the world. Mark was always in charge. His excitement and vision were contagious, and he kept pushing them all to add "cool features" to the service. He frequently directed them to stay with him at their computers on the dining room table to finish a feature they were working on regardless of the time or whether they had not eaten for hours. He used the term "lockdown" to describe this practice, and it became part of the Facebook terminology.

Parker eventually took over Saverin's role as business manager and incorporated the company in Delaware, which has favorable tax laws. Saverin was moved out of an active role in the company although he kept an ownership interest. Costs continued to climb as they added more server capacity to manage the rapid increase in users. Local networking sites were developing at colleges they were not serving, so they used a "surround" strategy to outmaneuver these local sites. They opened Facebook to potential users at a target campus as well as all colleges in the vicinity, allowing students to communicate with their friends at nearby campuses. This strategy worked well to capture users and demonstrated Zuckerberg's competitive nature and his desire for Facebook to become the industry standard for social networking.

Zuckerberg and his family invested $85,000 in Facebook during that summer, but the operation continued to need more money. Venture capital companies were ready to invest, but Parker had made Mark wary of venture capitalists. He located an individual Internet investor, Peter Theil, who had started PayPal, and invested $500,000 for about 10% of the company. Theil became a member of the Board of Directors, along with Parker and Zuckerberg, with two empty seats controlled by Mark who was CEO and in complete control.

Zuckerberg was building an organization, and he was growing into his new job. Despite his firm directiveness when working on a Facebook project, his employees were his best friends and he socialized with them when not working. Eventually he came to support them by providing three meals per day, snacks, dry cleaning, and a housing subsidy. Zuckerberg and Moskovitz did not return to Harvard. The two were remarkably close and Dustin had an incredible work ethic, maintaining the system while adding colleges, servers, and an exploding number of users. By November, they had one million users and Facebook was ten months old. Large media companies tried to buy Facebook for around $75 million. Mark met with their CEOs to learn, but he was not interested in selling. He and most of his employees believed they were making history and did not want to stop. Eventually, he negotiated a deal with a venture capitalist Parker trusted for $13 million in exchange for 15% of Facebook. Mark was 20 years old, and he maintained complete control of the company, which was then valued at $98 million.

Parker was highly intelligent and an expert programmer, but his personal behavior became erratic. He had helped Mark raise money while maintaining control of the business, but a drug charge and long absences from work created pressure on Zuckerberg to get rid of Parker, which he eventually did. The staff was growing, and they added a photo option that allowed users to create albums on their Facebook site, comment on their own and others' photos, and identify individuals in the photos. Zuckerberg made it easy to page through a user's album, encouraging what they called the "Facebook Trance" that kept people clicking through pages on their service. The photo application became the most popular feature on Facebook and the most popular photo site on the Internet. By fall 2005, 85% of all American college students were on Facebook, their ad revenue was about $1 million per month, and they were spending $1.5 million per month.

Mark eventually held an offsite meeting with all their staff and described his long-term vision. He explained his goal was to continue pushing change that reflected his beliefs in openness and transparency, to make Facebook a major force on the Internet, and not have it taken over by outsiders. He believed that by pushing society toward more openness, people would be made more responsible and empathetic. The staff were inspired to be on the forefront of societal change. He continued to keep careful control over the type of ads on Facebook, directing that they must be helpful to users. His ad requirements limited their ad revenue and reflected his primary interest in growing and improving the service rather than making money.

Several of the features Zuckerberg added have aroused protests among users. One was Newsfeed, which periodically sent highlights of what was happening in users' lives to their Facebook friends. Another feature named Beacon broadcast buying habits of users to their friends. Huge objections and email caused Zuckerberg to increase user controls over these features. His response to feedback included apologizing on his blog, which inspired faith in Facebook by its users, but these features show Zuckerberg's bias toward sharing information. Although he maintains he is concerned about privacy, many new features urge users to reveal more about themselves. Facebook can be seductive, and some users have trouble stopping themselves from compulsively revealing personal information. Once the information is on a user's profile, Facebook has it and it is available to all the user's friends. With little privacy there is little intimacy, and interpersonal relationships can be replaced by Facebook relationships that are usually at a low emotional level. Zuckerberg has been described as "blinkered" regarding his attitude toward privacy.

In 2006 he opened the service up to organizations and non-student adults. The response by organizations was slow but other adult users grew quickly.

Zuckerberg then pushed his staff to make Facebook an Internet platform, a service where others could design and deploy their own software and deliver it to users through Facebook. Developers were not charged for using Facebook, and he allowed them to keep all the revenue they generated from their software. He saw this as another way to grow the number of Facebook users. He scheduled a launch event in May 2007 for the platform in San Francisco and invited the media. The response was immediate, and Zuckerberg and his programmers worked for the next eight hours with application developers to help make their software work with Facebook. They then retired to their hotel to turn on the platform. The next day they were overwhelmed with new applications and within six months there were 25,000 new pieces of software running on Facebook. They opened Facebook for international users in late 2007 and within a year Facebook had grown to 70 million users.

Providing service around the world was expensive and they needed to get serious about raising more money and increasing revenues. After a long negotiation, Microsoft invested $240 million for a 1.6% interest in the company. In December 2007, Zuckerberg met Sheryl Sandberg, an extremely successful ad executive with Google. Two months later he hired her as chief operating officer for Facebook. He then left for a one-month trip around the world alone with only a backpack, apparently to give Sandberg a chance to establish herself at Facebook. She held a series of meetings with the executive staff (Facebook now had about 500 employees) and they explored ways to generate revenues consistent with Mark's vision of continued growth and improvement in their users' experience. The approach they developed did not allow advertisers to see information about individual users, only aggregate data. But Facebook provided a large menu of parameters for advertisers to select a specific audience. Advertisers can thus target ads to people in specific age groups, who live in certain states and listen to music by specific entertainers. This made Facebook the most carefully targeted advertising medium in history.

Most of the key executives left Facebook over the next year. Several started their own Internet companies that work with Facebook. Zuckerberg moved the Facebook operation to a vacated manufacturing plant in 2009, shunning locations that were more elaborate. He wants to keep employees from becoming complacent. Facebook allows groups of users to form around issues and garner support. One such group formed in Columbia against FARC, the revolutionary army that kidnaps citizens for ransom. Group members organized a huge demonstration that weakened FARC and apparently led to the release of some of their prisoners. Some executives find that they receive more honest feedback from employees through Facebook than when they talk face-to-face. Zuckerberg is excited about these uses of Facebook. One Facebook biographer describes him as fearless, competitive, and very self-confident. His stockholding allows him to stay in control of his organization even after a public offering of their stock in 2012. He retains absolute authority in decision making (although he does listen to his board members) and apparently hopes to influence the evolving communication infrastructure of the world. Facebook's data set is larger and richer than the United States government, and the Federal Bureau of Investigation has shown an interest. Writers have pointed out that Zuckerberg will not control Facebook forever, and at some point, it has potential to become a huge surveillance system. For now, his vision is to empower people to communicate more efficiently, to help them manage the information that is all around them, and to help prevent institutions from overwhelming people. His coworkers say he just wants to do the right thing.

During the 2016 United States presidential election, disguised Russian groups bought Facebook ads designed to influence the outcome of the election. The ads contained language that fostered anger, outrage, and hatred among U.S. voters on controversial issues such as immigration, Muslims, and gun control. Facebook identified 3,000 of these ads by groups with fake names such as American Veterans, Secured Borders, and the Heart of Texas. Facebook removed the ads, turned them over to federal investigators and Zuckerberg pledged to devote time and money to preventing their reoccurrence. Zuckerberg continued to face public pressure to do more to ensure the integrity of ads on Facebook and that news transmitted on Facebook is from trusted sources. More news reports emerged showing how unethical actors used information on Facebook to illegally influence national events. In 2018, the Cambridge Analytica scandal came to the surface. It was discovered that Facebook had allowed Cambridge Analytica to access 50 million user profiles for psychological profiling and political microtargeting. It appeared that Zuckerberg's assumptions about openness and transparency increasing empathy, responsibility, and understanding were naïve.

In 2021, Zuckerberg announced the rebranding of Facebook into Meta, based on the concept of the metaverse. In making the announcement, Zuckerberg visualized an integration of existing social media under Meta umbrella. Meta would provide a "a virtual environment where you can present yourself with people in digital spaces. You can kind of think of this as an embodied Internet that you're inside of, rather than just looking at." In addition, Zuckerberg invested over $10 billion in the development of the metaverse platform during the first year alone. The success of Meta is yet to be determined. In the meantime, Zuckerberg has also focused on incorporating artificial intelligence (AI) on the Meta platform. He has, however, expressed the need for regulation and ethical guardrails around the use of AI.

Mark Zuckerberg may be best described as a Charismatic/Transformational leader due to his *vision* for Facebook, his ability to *inspire* employees and the media, and his *dedication* to use Facebook as an instrument of *change* in the world. He is also highly *directive* of his staff when developing new features he wants to add to Facebook. His social nature facilitates his *supportiveness* and is reflected when he helps with employees' needs for housing and food. These leader behavior patterns are described in Fiedler's

Contingency Theory, Situational Leadership Theory, Path-Goal Theory, and the Leadership Grid. Mark has shown skill at *boundary-spanning* leadership in effective negotiations with key investors and executives who seek to purchase Facebook. This leader behavior is described in the Multiple Linkage Model and Reformulated Path-Goal Theory. His behavior as CEO might also be described as Servant and/or Principle Centered Leadership through his *optimism, extreme self-confidence, competence, enthusiasm*, and his *commitment to making the world a better place*. Zuckerberg also likely fits the popular Implicit Leadership Theory of an Internet entrepreneur/CEO by being highly intelligent, intensely focused, and geekish in his demeanor. His leadership includes emphasis on rapid and efficient *sharing of core organizational knowledge* and *continuous learning*; both are elements of Complexity Leadership. His *intelligence, self-confidence*, and *determination* also reflect Trait Theories of leadership.

Discussion Questions

1   What aspects of Mark Zuckerberg's leadership do you think were most important in building Facebook into a major Internet company?

2   Do you agree with Zuckerberg's practice of directing his employees to stay at work well into the morning hours ("lockdown") until they finished the Facebook feature they were working on?

3   Do you agree with Zuckerberg's vision that the world is becoming a more open and transparent place?

4   Do you think Mark would be an effective leader in a manufacturing or retail organization? Why or why not?

5   What more should Zuckerberg do to ensure that Facebook is perceived as an ethical organization?

Selected References

Grossman, L. (2010). 2010 person of the year: Mark Zuckerberg. *Time*, January 3, 42–75.

Kirkpatrick, D. (2011). *The Facebook effect*. New York: Simon and Schuster.

38 Aung San Suu Kyi
Leader of Myanmar Democracy Movement

Aung San Suu Kyi was leader of the nonviolent revolution in Burma (Myanmar) who replaced the repressive military regime that dominated the country after a military coup in 1962. The regime's Soviet-style centralized planning, nationalized industries, and inept policies had resulted in severe economic hardships for most of the Burmese people. Citizens were denied basic rights through government corruption, intimidation, imprisonment, torture, and death. She battled the military junta emphasizing nonviolence for over 20 years to finally establish a democratic government in 2016. Suu Kyi came under heavy criticism for her failure to defend the Rohingya community against extreme violence by the military. In 2021 the military staged a coup and arrested Suu Kyi. She was charged for various crimes and given a long prison sentence. Suu Kyi suffers from poor health and was moved from prison to house arrest in 2024.

Aung San Suu Kyi was born in 1945 in the British colony of Burma. Her father, Aung San, was a nationalist leader who initially fought with the Japanese to oust the British colonial power from Burma and later sided with the British in 1945 to drive out the Japanese. In 1947 he unified the nationalist movement and negotiated with the British government to achieve independence for Burma the following year. Aung San was named head of the new Burma government. He also negotiated a power sharing agreement with ethnic minorities but he and six of his cabinet members were assassinated later that year. U Saw, a former Prime Minister, was found guilty and executed for ordering the assassinations. The plan for independence proceeded and Aung San became a hero of the Burmese people. His daughter, Suu Kyi, was two years old.

Suu Kyi's mother became a member of the Myanmar parliament, minister of social welfare, and eventually was named ambassador to India. Suu Kyi studied the writings of Mohandas Gandhi while in India with her mother, then attended Oxford University in England and met her future husband. She worked for three years for the United Nations in New York on the staff of U Thant, the Burmese Secretary General. In 1972, she returned to England and married Michael Aris, a Tibetan scholar, and they had two sons. Suu Kyi worked in Japan and Bhutan and assisted her husband in his

DOI: 10.4324/9781003333937-42

research. In 1974, under a new constitution, the Myanmar military government ostensibly handed control of the government to a single socialist party, but the military maintained power.

In 1988, her mother suffered a stroke and Suu Kyi returned to Myanmar to care for her. When she arrived, she found the country in the middle of major political turmoil. Huge crowds of students, monks, and office workers were demonstrating in the streets demanding that the government implement democratic reforms that would stop the oppression and continual drop in real income. Most of the Burmese people had little to eat (the nationalized rice market was a total failure) and were denied basic human rights and services. The government was using the military to conduct mass violence to quell the demonstrations and thousands were reported killed. Suu Kyi stated that as her father's daughter, she could not remain indifferent to what was happening. She sent a letter to the ruling socialist party calling on them to stop the violence against peaceful demonstrators, hold free multiparty elections, and release all prisoners from the demonstrations. They did not respond to her letter and in early August the military opened fire on peaceful protestors and medical personnel treating the wounded, resulting in hundreds of casualties. She was invited to give a speech in Rangoon (Yangon) on August 26, 1988, outside a Buddhist temple believed to house the guardian spirits of the nation. Her speech electrified the crowd, estimated at one million people. She spoke against the army's violence against unarmed demonstrators and violations of human rights. She emphasized the sacrifices and deaths of students during demonstrations and quoted her father that democracy was the only ideology consistent with freedom and peace. Calling for restoration of democratic institutions and human rights for all citizens, she appealed to the military (which had been organized by her father) to uphold the honor and dignity of the people. Having studied Gandhi and Martin Luther King, Jr., she strongly advocated nonviolence with discipline and unity for the demonstrators.

Suu Kyi's speech inspired the people, and she became the unofficial leader of the resistance. The ruling party changed its name to the State Law and Order Council (SLORC) and cracked down—imposing a curfew, banning public gatherings, threatening total military control of society, and promising fair elections in the future. Suu Kyi did not trust these promises and she assisted the freedom movement leaders in forming a political party named the National League for Democracy (NLD). She was made general secretary for the new party and began traveling around Myanmar setting up units of the NLD and giving speeches opposing the violations of human rights, imprisonments, and killings of peaceful demonstrators. She also appealed to the United Nations and other human rights organizations and called upon other countries to condemn the violence against peaceful and unarmed people in Myanmar.

Then in September 1988, shortly after Suu Kyi's momentous speech, the military again took full control and placed Suu Kyi under house arrest. They clearly saw her and the democracy movement as dangerous to their power. The military called for general elections in 1990 and Suu Kyi's name was not allowed on the ballot for the NLD party. Although the government continued to restrict public gatherings, her party won the elections by a large margin, but the military refused to turn over control. In 1991, the European Parliament awarded Suu Kyi the Sakharov Prize for her work advocating human rights and freedom of thought. The same year she received the Nobel Peace Prize, but she did not travel to Sweden to receive the prize, fearing she would not be allowed to return. She assigned the 1.3-million-dollar award for the prize to the Suu Foundation, dedicated to advancing the health and education of the people of Myanmar. Also in 1991, she published her book *Freedom from Fear*, describing Myanmar's oppression by its government and military since her father's death. It initiated an international reaction and demands that the oppression in Myanmar be stopped.

In her book and speeches, Suu Kyi continued to emphasize the importance of nonviolence, explaining that any movement that uses violence to gain control will merely incite more violence by those who disagree with its policies. The violence will never end. She appealed to the basic Buddhist values of kindness and compassion for all persons (Myanmar's population is 89% Buddhist) and to the necessity of having the courage to overcome one's fear of loss, pain, and suffering to achieve a valued goal for the country.

She remained under house arrest for the next six years—sometimes in solitary confinement and occasionally allowed to have visitors from the NLD or her family. She was released in 1995 but her travel was restricted. She ignored the restriction and traveled the country speaking in towns and villages for democratic governance and the NLD, before she was placed under house arrest again for violating the travel restrictions. Over the next several years Suu Kyi was released and arrested several times, survived one assassination attempt, conducted a hunger strike, and spent most of her time under house arrest. Her husband was diagnosed with cancer in 1997 but the Myanmar government refused to allow him to visit Suu Kyi. The government offered to let her visit him in England, but she again refused to leave Myanmar. He died in 1999. She was finally released from house arrest in 2010 and in 2012 her party won 43 of 45 contested seats and she was elected to parliament by a landslide. In 2015, in the first open elections in 25 years, she was elected State Counsellor, a position equivalent to Prime Minister or head of government. She was prevented by the constitution from being elected President because her sons hold British passports, but her close confidante was elected President. However, Suu Kyi was widely perceived to be the de facto leader of government in Myanmar.

The Myanmar government had faced extensive criticism because of the military's ruthless violence against several hundred thousand Muslims, known as Rohingya, who inhabited the Rakhine state on the coast of Myanmar. The Rohingya had clashed with the majority Buddhist Burmese for decades and there were deep-rooted ethnic resentments between the two groups. The Burmese viewed the Rohingya as "Bengali" and illegal residents although Rohingya had resided in Myanmar for centuries. The Rohingya had been denied citizenship, access to government services, and other human rights in Myanmar. Many had been confined to camps for displaced persons and prevented from leaving to work in their fields or to obtain food. Earlier in 2013, Suu Kyi had dismissed concerns about rising violence against Rohingya, saying Buddhists in Rakhine live in fear of "global Muslim power."

Suu Kyi did not have executive power. By 2017, the constitution of Myanmar had granted the military total control over the ministries of defense, home affairs, and border affairs. The military claimed that it was eliminating terrorists among the Rohingya who had attacked multiple police stations, killing several police officers in August 2017. Approximately one million Rohingya had fled to neighboring Bangladesh after suffering rape and murders of several hundred, including children. Satellite images showed scores of Rohingya villages burned to the ground. Bangladesh, which struggled with poverty and high population density, had created refugee camps, and attempted to save the Rohingya with international help.

Amnesty International, United Nations officials, and representatives from other countries accused Myanmar of ethnic cleansing and crimes against humanity. Suu Kyi was hesitant to blame the military and has denounced international criticism as "untruths and victim-blaming." Observers noted that she strongly condemned the military under the former government for using deadly violence against peaceful and unarmed Myanmar demonstrators and demanded the violence must stop. The predominantly Buddhist population of Myanmar clearly resented the Muslim Rohingya and Suu Kyi was anxious to keep their support for her government.

Calls were made for the Nobel committee to revoke Suu Kyi's Peace Prize. In 2018, Suu Kyi acknowledged that she had not spoken out on the Rohingya crisis because to do so would only make matters worse, sully her relations with the military, and endanger her very political existence. In 2019, Suu Kyi appeared before the International Court of Justice (ICJ) at the Hague to defend her country—and by extension herself—from accusations of genocide against Rohingya Muslims. Her personal defense of military actions at the ICJ hearing was seen as a new turning point for her international reputation. Suu Kyi and her party's government also faced criticism for prosecuting journalists and activists using colonial-era laws. A few initially argued that she was a pragmatic politician, trying to govern a multiethnic country with a complex history.

During the 2020 general elections, Suu Kyi's NLD party secured a landslide victory in both houses of parliament. A day before confirming the new parliament in February 2021, the military rejected election results and staged a coup. Suu Kyi and other senior officials of NLD were arrested on the grounds of widespread fraud in the general election. Military authorities initially charged Suu Kyi with illegally importing communication devices. Suu Kyi's trial commenced in mid-June 2021 over charges of sedition. She was found guilty of inciting dissent and breaking Covid rules in the first of a series of verdicts that could see her jailed for 33 years. The military takeover sparked nationwide protests that saw hundreds of thousands take to the streets. Peaceful demonstrations evolved into lethal clashes as the military began a brutal crackdown, arresting elected leaders, civilian officials, protest leaders, and journalists, and firing live ammunition at unarmed protestors.

In April 2024, it was reported that Suu Kyi, 78, had been moved from prison to house arrest due to a heat wave in the country. Suu Kyi's health had deteriorated in poor prison conditions without access to medical care. Her influence continued to wane following incarceration and isolation.

Aung San Suu Kyi's *inspiring speeches* and writing, her belief in the *vision and mission* of creating a democratic government in Myanmar, her *belief that with nonviolence, courage and discipline the people could be successful* in achieving their mission, and by invoking widespread *Buddhist values* of kindness and compassion, represent much of the Charismatic/Transformational Leadership approach. Her *caring* and *supportiveness* toward the Burmese people, *active listening* to the complaints of the people, firm *belief in the importance and eventual success* of her mission, and willingness to *sacrifice* her own happiness to persist in achieving a democratic government, indicate a true Servant Leader of the people. Her emphasis on *clarifying the behaviors needed to achieve their goal* and exhibiting *charismatic behaviors* represents portions of the Reformulated Path-Goal Theory. Her *determination, integrity, cognitive capacity*, and *assertiveness* are described in the Trait Theories of leadership. However, turning an apparent blind eye to the violation of human rights and murder of the Rohingya raises questions about her dedication to the constructive leader behaviors described above and to all residents of Myanmar. This brings Toxic Leadership to mind. Her cult-like followers and iconic image continue to guarantee her popularity.

Discussion Questions

1   How would you evaluate Aung San Suu Kyi's leadership prior to her election as State Counsellor in Myanmar? Why did you rate her this way?
2   How would you evaluate Suu Kyi's leadership during the Rohingya crisis? Why did you evaluate her this way?
3   Why do you think Suu Kyi is so hesitant to criticize the military's violence in handling of the Rohingya crisis, when she was highly vocal of their violence against Burmese demonstrators?
4   Do you believe Suu Kyi is a good leader? Why or why not?

Selected References

Chakraborty, B. D. (2013). Pedagogue of pacifism and human rights. In J. D. Kirylo (Ed.), *A critical pedagogy of resistance: 34 pedagogues we need to know* (pp. 121–123). Rotterdam, The Netherlands: Sense.

Kyi, A. S. S. (1991). *Freedom from fear*. New York: Penguin Books.

Kyi, A. S. S. (1997). *Voice of hope: Conversations with Alan Clements*. New York: Penguin Books.

Kyi, A. S. S. (June 16, 2014). Aung San Suu Kyi—Nobel Lecture. Retrieved February 15, 2017 from www.nobelprize.org/nobel_prizes/peace/laureates/1991/kyi-ecture_en.html.

McCarthy, S. (2004). The Buddhist political rhetoric of Aung San Suu Kyi. *Contemporary Buddhism*, 5(2), 67–81.

Safi, M. (September 7, 2017). Aung San Suu Kyi defends her handling of Myanmar violence. *The Guardian*. Retrieved September 25, 2017, from www.theguardian.com/world2017/sep/07/aung-san-suu-kyi-defends-handling-myanmar-violence-rohinga?CMP=Share_iOSApp_Other.

White, J. A. (1998). Leadership through compassion and understanding: An interview with Aung San Suu Kyi. *Journal of Management Inquiry*, 7(4), 286–293.

Wintour, P. (October 13, 2017). Aung San Suu Kyi unveils relief plans for Rohingya Muslims. *The Guardian*. Retrieved October 18, 2017 from www.theguardian.com/world/2017/oct/13/aung-san-suu-kyi-unveils-relief-plans-for-rohingya-muslims-myanmar.

39 Travis Kalanick

Cofounder and Former CEO of Uber

Born on August 6, 1976 in Los Angeles, Travis Cordell Kalanick grew up in the Northridge area of Los Angeles. His intellectual and entrepreneurial abilities were evident at an early age; by sixth grade, he knew how to code. Kalanick founded Red Swoosh, a peer-to-peer file sharing company, and Uber, a multibillion car-hailing unicorn where he became the CEO. Kalanick resigned from Uber in 2017, following public scandals and unethical practices. Kalanick continued to focus his efforts on disruptive innovations and new ventures including CloudKitchens, a ghost kitchens startup.

On Tuesday evening of February 28, 2017 Uber's CEO Travis Kalanick sent a note to Uber's employees apologizing for his leadership deficiencies and seeking help. The note had been precipitated by negative publicity for Uber, including a video that showed Kalanick making a verbal attack on an Uber driver. The note was remarkable in many ways. Few leaders of a modern tech company have demonstrated that level of *mea culpa*. Subsequently, Kalanick took a leave of absence following a family tragedy to focus on himself. On June 20, 2017 five major investors at Uber demanded a change in leadership. Kalanick announced his resignation as Uber's CEO, promising to return.

As a teenager, he went from door to door selling Cutco knives. When he was 18, he founded an SAT prep company, New Way Academy. His own score on the SAT was in the 99th percentile. After graduating from Granada Hills High School, Kalanick enrolled in a computer engineering program at UCLA. In 1998, a few months before graduation, Kalanick dropped out of college to focus on Scour, a peer-to-peer exchange service that had been founded by five engineering students from UCLA. Scour's search engine crawled users' IP addresses, indexing files and allowing other people to download the files, including music, videos, and movies. In 2000, more than 30 media companies filed a copyright infringement lawsuit against Scour. Scour declared bankruptcy and its remaining assets were auctioned for $9 million. Kalanick and the Scour engineering team started a new peer-to-peer company, Red Swoosh. Red Swoosh had developed software that helped end users access content more efficiently by delivering files from the nearest location.

DOI: 10.4324/9781003333937-43

Red Swoosh was started after the Internet (dotcom) bubble and effects of the September 11 terrorist attacks had taken their toll on the U.S. economy. Kalanick's own account of the period shows remarkable grit and entrepreneurship. For the first three years, Kalanick went without a salary. He moved in with his parents and eventually relocated to Thailand to cut costs. Kalanick's resilience paid off in 2007 when Akamai, a peer-to-peer competitor, acquired Red Swoosh for $23 million. Kalanick had become a millionaire.

In 2008, Kalanick and Garrett Camp founded Uber with $200,000 seed funding. Unable to secure a ride on a snowy evening in Paris, the two friends came up with the idea of how to "tap a button to request a ride." The company started its operations in 2009 and initially focused the app on requesting black cars in cosmopolitan markets. In 2010, Kalanick became the CEO and Uber quickly spread to cities around the world. Kalanick's salesmanship and Uber's unique model attracted the attention of Silicon Valley venture capitalists and Uber was quickly able to raise funds for expansion. Kalanick also delved into other tech ventures.

Kalanick used bold and aggressive strategies to launch Uber in the large cities with a young demographic. The process typically involved recruiting driven individuals as local managers. Cold calls would be placed to local limousine drivers who had been targeted as potential Uber drivers. Stealth social media messages would announce Uber's presence in the neighborhood. Uber would then organize exclusive VIP launch parties. Where there was opposition from regulators and lawmakers, Uber used social media to inundate lawmakers and regulators with messages of support. The overwhelming wave of change often neutralized local resistance.

By 2017, Kalanick had helped Uber to raise $11.5 billion from 95 venture capitalists and other private investors. Uber's valuation of $70 billion made it more valuable than many technological and auto companies that manufactured cars. Uber had also invested heavily in self-driving car technology. The technology had many potential advantages; however, one of the main advantages was eliminating the cost of a human driver. Uber was a main contestant in the fierce race for a breakthrough in driverless car technology. The race was to land Uber in a legal and ethical quagmire.

On February 23, 2017, Waymo (a division of Alphabet Inc.) filed a lawsuit accusing Uber of patent infringement and theft of intellectual property of its proprietary LiDAR technology. LiDAR was a laser technology that made self-driving cars possible by allowing cars to visualize and communicate with the environment. Uber had poached Anthony Levandowski, one of the key engineers working on the project at Waymo. Alphabet's lawsuit accused Levandowski of downloading and retaining 14,000 files that contained LiDAR technology. Alphabet also noted that Uber had granted Levandowski shares worth $250 million on the date he resigned without notice from Waymo. Part of the lawsuit focused on whether Kalanick knew that Levandowski had access to LiDAR technology prior to being hired by Uber.

In May 2017, Uber decided to fire Levandowski after his refusal to cooperate in the investigations and pleading the Fifth Amendment.

Uber was accumulating losses, even though its gross revenues and market share were on a growth tangent. Although not legally required, Uber decided to share its 2016 financial results with investors. Uber had $6.5 billion in net revenues in 2016 with adjusted net losses of $2.8 billion. Uber had spent a total of $8 billion since 2009; this had not deterred investors. However, Kalanick had presided over escalating ethical and leadership missteps. By 2016, some venture capitalist investors started getting nervous about his stewardship of Uber.

Kalanick's aggressive growth strategies in the U.S. and abroad involved undercutting traditional taxi services on price and convenience. Whenever Uber's business practices were challenged, Kalanick would fight back. Kalanick's aggressive stance came with related costs. In the U.S., Uber had 70 pending federal lawsuits and numerous others in state courts. There were also lawsuits in more than 400 cities around the world. The lawsuits ranged from complaints about poor employee benefits, safety, competitive practices, and passenger sexual assault. Kalanick also presided over the technologies that raised concern among local regulators, taxi companies, and customers.

By 2016, Uber created a secret software codenamed "Hell" that was used to spy on its rivals' drivers. Lyft had become a formidable competitor for Uber, and "Hell" had capabilities of spying on drivers who were double-apping (driving for both Lyft and Uber), through a unique identifier. The fake Lyft accounts created by Uber could get information about as many as eight of the nearest available Lyft drivers, those that were double-apping, and those who could accommodate a ride request. Uber used the data to create grid-like structures that could identify the behavior of all Lyft drivers. Data collected by Uber employees would be used to send more rides to Uber drivers who were not double-apping and incentivize them with bonuses. This resulted in fewer Lyft drivers and longer waiting times for Lyft passengers. A few employees at Uber, including its CEO, knew about the existence of the secret program. Early in 2017, a former Lyft driver filed a class action lawsuit against Uber.

In 2015, Apple discovered that Uber was secretly identifying users and tagging their iPhones, even after the users deleted the Uber app. Referred to as "fingerprinting," this was a common practice among app developers and carried backend benefits such as identifying returning users. Uber justified the use of "fingerprinting" as a means of minimizing fraudulent accounts where drivers would create and accept multiple fake rides. Uber denied the allegations of illegally tracking users after deleting the app. However, he seemed to contradict himself by stating that the ability to recognize known bad actors when they try to get back onto their network was an important security measure.

A consumer advocacy group filed a complaint with the Federal Trade Commission, claiming that Uber's practice of "fingerprinting" was unfair and deceptive. In an interview, John Simpson, the privacy project director of

Consumer Watchdog, stated that, "They have a track record of not paying any attention to the rules. That's why it's important, no matter what they've done with Apple, for the FTC to act." Apple's CEO, Tim Cook, reportedly told Kalanick he would remove Uber's app from the App Store if Uber did not get rid of the tracking feature.

Uber had faced backlash from incumbent taxi operators and local city administrators. Response towards the unregulated ride-hailing technology by local transport regulators ranged from embracing Uber to banning it altogether. Kalanick decided to play hardball with regulators. As early as 2014, Uber had developed Greyball technology. Using Greyball technology, Uber could use data collected from other sources to identify and evade authorities. By deploying Greyball, Uber drivers would identify law enforcement officials trying to hail a ride and the driver could cancel the ride. The program would also populate the app with non-existent cars to avoid Uber cars from being identified. Another feature of Greyball was "geofencing." When Uber moved into cities where ride hailing was illegal, the local managers would identify law enforcement officials. Uber used different methods to identify these officials including phone numbers, credit card information, social media profiles, and the type of plan on their phones. Uber would then install a digital fence around the local law enforcement to make them identifiable. Uber had used Greyball in Portland, Boston, South Korea, and Australia, among other locations. Uber stopped using Greyball in the U.S. in 2016, but continued to use the software in other countries. In March 2017, Uber announced that it would stop using Greyball to target government officials. Subsequently, Greyball became a subject of criminal investigations by the Justice Department.

In 2014, a former employee disclosed that Uber had developed "God View" software with capabilities of tracking the exact location of its customers while riding in Uber vehicles without their knowledge. During launch events hosted by Uber's senior executives, "God View" had been used to entertain guests by tracking the whereabouts of celebrities. In a related case, Uber had agreed to pay a $20,000 settlement for tracking its customers. An employee of Uber had tracked a reporter because she was 30 minutes late to a meeting. Uber subsequently agreed to settle with the Federal Trade Commission by discontinuing the practice and submitting to 20 years of third-party audits.

The constant negative publicity in the press related to Uber's business practices led to unprecedented resignations by senior executives. These included Jeff Jones, Uber's president; Brian McClendon, vice president of maps and business platform; Rachel Whetstone, head of public relations and policy; Gary Marcus, head of Uber AI Labs; Raffi Krikorian, director of engineering at Uber's Advanced Technologies Center; Charlie Miller, a key member of the self-driving car project; and Ed Baker, vice president for product and growth. Amit Singhal, a vice president for engineering, was forced to resign over sexual harassment allegations.

When Uber's 2016 financial results came out, the company showed a loss of $2.8 billion, and $700 million loss during the first quarter of 2017. Venture capital investors in the company were increasingly getting nervous about Uber's performance and negative publicity. Kalanick had developed a reputation as intensely aggressive. While this style had served him well during Uber's explosive growth, Uber seemed to be constantly in the press with negative news related to Kalanick's aggressive strategies and organizational culture. Although many at Silicon Valley considered Kalanick a tech world rock star, others thought he was a daredevil CEO. Mark Cuban, the billionaire entrepreneur had described him in more vivid terms: "Travis's biggest strength is that he will run through a wall to accomplish his goals … Travis's biggest weakness is that he will run through a wall to accomplish his goals."

Kalanick had very high expectations of employees and was known as a hard-driving leader. Early in 2017, a video showing Kalanick mistreating an Uber driver appeared to feed into the perception that Uber was a value-free environment. About the same time, Uber's board of directors hired former Attorney General Eric Holder to investigate accusations of sexual harassment and discrimination at Uber. In June 2017, Kalanick considered taking a leave of absence to grieve the sudden death of his mother in a boating accident. Around the same time, Uber's board decided to approve all recommendations regarding company culture that resulted from Holder's investigation. In a parallel recommendation on sexual harassment, Uber decided to fire 20 employees and conduct remedial training and counseling for others involved. While Kalanick was on a company visit to Chicago on June 21, 2017, two Uber directors confronted him with the information that the board wanted him to step down as Uber's CEO. Kalanick agreed to step down but made a promise that he would return to Uber.

Following Uber's public listing, Kalanick started to sell his shares in the company, netting $2.5 billion before taxes. In 2018, Kalanick established a venture capital firm; 10100 Fund, which focused on real estate and e-commerce startups. The same year, he spent $150 million to purchase a controlling stake in City Storage Systems and became the CEO. City Storage Systems is the parent company of CloudKitchens that continues to build a worldwide network of commercial food delivery kitchens. The ghost kitchen startup reported a valuation of $15 billion by 2023, with Kalanick's net worth increasing to $8.4 billion. Kalanick has also invested in MegaBite, a startup in restaurants, hotels, and the leisure industry. Kalanick sits on the advisory board of NEOM, a $500 billion Saudi Arabian futuristic city located on the Red Sea coast.

Trait leadership theory describes some of Kalanick's leadership attributes. He has superior *cognitive capacity*, proven through his academic and work career. He is *resilient, energetic, single-minded*, and has a will to succeed at all costs. He is *persuasive* with outstanding salesmanship demonstrated at an early age by successfully selling Cutco knives from door to door. He used his sales skills effectively to attract and recruit talent for Uber and most significantly, raising more than $11 billion from investors. Kalanick demonstrated great *intelligence* and *social skill*, but the element of *empathy* appeared deficient. While promoting the driverless car technology, Kalanick reportedly stated: "Once we get rid of the dude in the car, Uber will be cheaper." He *ignored the human side* such as a positive culture and working environment that are important in sustaining the organization.

Complexity Leadership Theory (CLT) describes some of Kalanick's leadership. In CLT, leadership is conceived as a complex interactive dynamic out of which adaptive outcomes such as learning, innovation, and adaptability emerge. A look at Kalanick's background illustrates that he has constantly sought out *new knowledge*. Kalanick has demonstrated complex leadership attributes by creating an *environment where knowledge is created and shared rapidly and in an efficient manner*. Some of the technology that he helped develop such as Red Swoosh and the Uber app has translated into organizational core competence with significant monetary value. Earlier on, Kalanick recognized the importance of a *decentralized structure* where cohorts and local managers were empowered to lead, based on their expertise. Kalanick realized the potential of the future of public transportation through the autonomous car technology and invested accordingly. Kalanick has led Uber to adapt and form strategic alliances with other transportation and travel companies; Uber is no longer just a ride-hailing company. Kalanick's tenure at Uber illustrates some characteristics of Charismatic/Transformational Leadership. Through his entrepreneurial skill, Kalanick was always *taking risks* and *driving change*, even when the odds were stacked against him. In a culture that values innovation and disrupting the status quo, Kalanick is *highly revered* in Silicon Valley and considered a *tech rock star*. Through sheer *grit* and *resilience*, Kalanick has *transformed public transportation* in urban areas, and disrupted the taxi industry in ways that had not been anticipated.

Discussion Questions

1   Using relevant examples, assess Kalanick's charismatic/transformational leadership style. Was he effective?
2   Despite having stepped down as CEO, why is Kalanick still revered and considered a tech rock star in some parts of Silicon Valley?
3   What were Kalanick's leadership mistakes? Is it possible for a great entrepreneur to be an effective leader?
4   What leadership lessons may Kalanick have learned from his tenure at Uber? Does he deserve a second chance?

Selected References

Carson, B. (May 30, 2017). Uber just fired the engineer at the center of its legal battle with Google because he wouldn't cooperate. *Business Insider*. Retrieved August 25, 2017 from www.businessinsider.com/anthony-levandowski-fired-from-uber-2017-5.

Christophi, H. (April 25, 2017). Class action accuses Uber of spying on Lyft drivers. Retrieved April 25, 2017 from www.courthousenews.com/class-action-accuses-uber-spying-lyft-drivers.

Conger, C. (April 23, 2017). Uber responds to report that it tracked devices after its app was deleted. *Techcrunch*. Retrieved August 25, 2017 from https://techcrunch.com/2017/04/23/uber-responds-to-report-that-it-tracked-users-who-deleted-its-app.

Fiegerman, S. & O'Brien, S. (June 13, 2017). Uber CEO takes leave of absence amid crises. *CNN Money*. Retrieved August 17, 2017 from http://money.cnn.com/2017/06/13/technology/business/uber-harassment-report/index.html.

Hill, K. (2017). 'God View': Uber Allegedly Stalked Users for Party-Goers' Viewing Pleasure. *Forbes*, October 3, 2014. Retrieved September 1, 2017 from www.forbes.com/sites/kashmirhill/2014/10/03/god-view-uber-allegedly-stalked-users-for-party-goers-viewing-pleasure/#37c1a69a3141.

Isaac, M. (April 23, 2017). Uber's C.E.O. plays with fire. *New York Times*. Retrieved August 22, 2017 from www.nytimes.com/2017/04/23/technology/travis-kalanick-pushes-uber-and-himself-to-the-precipice.html.

Welch. C. (January 6, 2016). Uber will pay $20,000 fine in settlement over 'God View' tracking. *The Verge*. Retrieved September 1, 2017 from www.theverge.com/2016/1/6/10726004/uber-god-mode-settlement-fine.

Wilber, D. & Bensinger. G. (May 7, 2017). Uber Faces Federal Criminal Probe Over 'Greyball' Software. *Wall Street Journal*. Retrieved August 18, 2017 from www.wsj.com/articles/uber-faces-federal-criminal-probe-over-greyball-software-1493948944.

Conclusion

In the 1980s, several leadership scholars began criticizing leadership theorists and researchers for "romanticizing" leadership. These writers disagreed with those who believed that leaders bore a major responsibility for an organization's performance. They typically adopted a social ecology perspective that asserted an organization's environment and individual situation were the major factors affecting organizational events—including their success or failure. They believed that most leadership scholars exaggerated the importance of leadership by inflating the leaders' influence on organizations and followers. These scholars described leadership as an internal characteristic of leaders, rather than a social influence process carried out between leaders and followers where both groups influence one another. They failed to acknowledge that the amount and type of influence exerted between leaders and followers varies with the leadership behavior exhibited by the leader—such as authoritative directive behavior versus group-oriented participative behavior. As noted in several leadership theories described in Chapter 1, a leader's behavior reflects (is influenced by) many factors including the followers' characteristics, work tasks, and culture.

Most leaders and leadership writers know that leaders are not the only factor influencing organizations. However, careful research shows that executive leadership can account for nearly 45% of an organization's performance. The remainder is influenced by market factors, competition, workforce, technological change, and a myriad of other factors. It is difficult to account for the enormous impact of leaders like Nelson Mandela, Bill Wilson, Jeff Bezos, Napoleon, or Adolf Hitler without realizing how leadership can influence people, organizations, and nations. We are all influenced by our role models, and young aspiring leaders tend to select one or more leaders to learn from. In this book, we have described leaders who have produced amazing results and we believe their stories demonstrate important leadership lessons.

Readers may have noticed that both great and bad leaders frequently use similar leadership behaviors and strategies to influence their followers. Great and bad leaders often inspire followers, reward individuals who carry out their wishes, represent their organization to outsiders, direct activities, and

DOI: 10.4324/9781003333937-44

carry out other leader behaviors common to great leaders. The difference between great and bad leaders is often found in the elements of ethical leadership addressed by Servant, Principle-Centered, or Authentic Leadership Theories. Bad leaders often fail to show concern, consideration, and support for those they lead, other than a select few. They are frequently not open and honest, empathetic, fair, altruistic, or humble. Many bad leaders demonstrate poor integrity, narcissism, little continuous learning, and their conscience seems undeveloped or ignored in their behavior. They often break promises and do not fulfill prior commitments. They may actually demonstrate the opposite of some of the ethical leader characteristics by being cruel, selfish, and uncaring instead of altruistic. They may regularly tell lies rather than being open and honest, and engage in self-promotion at others' expense, rather than being empathetic, generous, and humble. These characteristics affect how bad leaders use their directive leadership by directing followers toward unethical activities, by rewarding and supporting only those who are totally loyal in carrying out these activities, and in representing their organization by using lies and promises they do not intend to keep. These leaders seldom use participative leadership behaviors and usually support only the favored few who do not question their commands.

From the matrix at the end of Chapter 1, it appears that two leadership theories are most descriptive of the leaders described in this book—Trait Theory and Charismatic/Transformational Leadership. The most common traits for these leaders were *determination, drive*, and *self-confidence* followed by *assertiveness* and *cognitive capacity*, with *integrity* characterizing nearly all of the great leaders. The most common Charismatic/Transformational behaviors were *inspiration* shown in speeches or exemplary behavior, and describing a *group/organizational vision* and *mission* to achieve the vision. Three older behavioral theories are almost as descriptive—Path-Goal Theory, the Multiple Linkage Model, and Situational Leadership Theory. The most common leader behaviors from these models were forms of *directive* and *consideration/supportive* behavior followed by *boundary-spanning* behavior. These theories, traits, and behaviors seem to have the most widespread application, although some leaders are also well described by other leadership theories and behaviors.

The leaders described here faced unique challenges in widely different environments that are often dynamic, digital, and global. The great leaders navigated their environments with outstanding success whereas bad leaders produced incredible damage. We provided a holistic description of these leaders, identifying leadership traits and behavior patterns that were essential to their successes and failures. We also described emergent perspectives on leadership and connected theory and practice in a practical accessible manner for leadership students and aspiring leaders. We hope our readers find the leadership Snapshots described in this book to be both interesting and helpful as they prepare for leadership careers in the 21st century.

References and Source Material for this Book

We used two types of source material for this book. For the leadership theories, we made extensive use of our class notes from 40 collective years of teaching leadership. Of course, our teaching has reflected a myriad of leadership books and journal articles we have read over the years, but the actual copy for this book was written from our own understanding and teaching of these theories over the years. No copy was taken from other sources.

For the descriptions of great and bad leadership, we consulted biographies, journal articles, and web-based sources that addressed different aspects of the leaders' lives. Our strategy in researching and writing the leadership descriptions was to first consult web-based sources to obtain general information about a leader. We then consulted what appeared to be the best sources cited in those web articles and followed the reference trail to find biographies that were widely cited as outstanding sources for each leader. Once we had read and made notes on each leader, we wrote the description reflecting our own interpretation of the leader's actions and how they related to theories of leadership. These leadership descriptions and interpretations are our own and are not taken directly from any single source. No authors' quotations or written copy was taken from any of the references used for this book. The only quotations used are brief sayings or statements by the leaders themselves or their followers. The major sources used are cited in the references at the end of each chapter.

Index